TAILORING TRUTH

Studies in Contemporary European History

General Editors:

Konrad Jarausch, Lurcy Professor of European Civilization, University of North Carolina, Chapel Hill, and a Director of the Zentrum für Zeithistorische Studien, Potsdam, Germany

Henry Rousso, Senior Fellow at the Institut d'historie du temps present (Centre national de la recherché scientifique, Paris) and co-founder of the European network "EURHISTXX"

For a complete series listing, see page 263.

TAILORING TRUTH

Politicizing the Past and Negotiating Memory
in East Germany, 1945–1990

Jon Berndt Olsen

berghahn
NEW YORK • OXFORD
www.berghahnbooks.com

First published in 2015 by
Berghahn Books
www.berghahnbooks.com

© 2015, 2017 Jon Berndt Olsen
First paperback edition published in 2017

All rights reserved.
Except for the quotation of short passages
for the purposes of criticism and review, no part of this book
may be reproduced in any form or by any means, electronic or
mechanical, including photocopying, recording, or any information
storage and retrieval system now known or to be invented,
without written permission of the publisher.

Library of Congress Cataloging-in-Publication Data

Olsen, Jon Berndt.
 Tailoring truth : memory politics and historical consciousness in East Germany, 1945-1990 / Jon Berndt Olsen.
        pages cm. — (Studies in contemporary European history ; volume 15)
    Includes bibliographical references and index.
    ISBN 978-1-78238-571-4 (hardback : acid-free paper) — ISBN 978-1-78533-502-0 paperback — ISBN 978-1-78238-572-1 (ebook)
    1. Collective memory—Political aspects--Germany (East)—History.
    2. Memorialization—Political aspects—Germany (East)—History.
    3. Historiography—Political aspects—Germany (East)—History.
    4. Historical museums—Political aspects—Germany (East)—History.
    5. Sozialistische Einheitspartei Deutschlands—History. 6. Political culture—Germany (East)—History. 7. Social control—Germany (East)—History. 8. Germany (East)—Historiography. 9. Germany (East)—Politics and government. 10. Germany (East)—Social conditions. I. Title.
  DD286.2.O57 2015
  907.2'0431—dc23
                                                                            2014029576

British Library Cataloguing in Publication Data

A catalogue record for this book is available from the British Library.

ISBN 978-1-78238-571-4 hardback
ISBN 978-1-78533-502-0 paperback
ISBN 978-1-78238-572-1 ebook

To my parents, David and Audrey Olsen

Contents

List of Illustrations	viii
Acknowledgments	x
List of Abbreviations	xiii
Introduction. Tailoring Truth in East Germany	1
Chapter 1. Mobilizing Memory in the Soviet Occupation Zone	18
Chapter 2. The Politics of State Memory	51
Chapter 3. Emotional Bonds	102
Chapter 4. Broadening the Historical Roots of the State Narrative	137
Chapter 5. The Collapse of State-Imposed Memory Culture	183
Conclusion	213
Bibliography	238
Index	254

Illustrations

Tables

2.1. Fundraising effort of the Buchenwald Committee 66

2.2. Expenditures of the Buchenwald Committee 66

2.3. Visitor statistics for the Museum for German History 76

Figures

1.1. Wilhelm Pieck delivers a speech at the first postwar commemoration of Karl Liebknecht and Rosa Luxemburg at the Socialists' Cemetery in Berlin-Friedrichsfelde, 13 January 1946. 29

1.2. Renovated Socialists' Cemetery in Berlin-Friedrichsfelde, 1951. 30

1.3. Commemoration in Berlin of the 1848 March Revolt on 18 March 1948. 37

1.4. Entrance to the exhibit "The Other Germany" in Berlin, September 1948. 40

1.5. Interior view of the exhibit "The Other Germany" in Berlin, September 1948. 41

2.1. The second annual commemoration of the liberation of Buchenwald (celebrated on the Goetheplatz in Weimar), April 1947. 56

2.2. The Buchenwald Memorial featuring Fritz Cremer's sculpture after its completion in October 1958. 63

2.3. Director Alfred Meusel opening three segments of the Museum for German History covering the years 1849–1945 on 11 April 1953 with Elisabeth Zaisser, Minister of Education. 75

2.4. Walter Howard's sculpture of Marx and Engels in Karl-Marx-Stadt (Chemnitz) in 1957. 86

2.5. Ruthild Hahne working on an early version of her sculpture of Ernst Thälmann in 1951.	90
3.1. A youth group from Eisenach visiting the Buchenwald Memorial on a tour with director Klaus Trostorff, 4 April 1970.	124
3.2. A youth group from Potsdam visiting the Museum for German History examining a replica of a Spinning Jenny, 20 March 1968.	129
4.1. Reinstallation of Christian Daniel Rauch's sculpture of King Frederick II of Prussia (Frederick the Great) in November 1980.	144
4.2. Bishop Werner Leich and Erich Honecker visit the Wartburg in Eisenach with other members of the Luther Committee of the GDR after its renovation on 21 April 1983.	158
4.3. A scene from the Evangelical Church's final commemoration event honoring Martin Luther in Eisleben, the place of Luther's birth, on 10 November 1983.	162
4.4. Werner Tübke and Erich Honecker reviewing the 1:10 rendering of Tübke's panorama "Early Bourgeois Revolution in Germany" on 2 October 1982 in Dresden.	169
4.5. Werner Tübke signing his panorama "Early Bourgeois Revolution in Germany" in Bad Frankenhausen on 28 October 1987, marking the official completion of his painting.	172
5.1. Map of Berlin showing the original position for the Marx-Engels monument next to the Spree Canal on the Marx-Engels-Platz and its final position in the middle of the Marx-Engels-Forum.	190
5.2. View of the Marx-Engels-Forum with Ludwig Engelhardt's sculpture forming the focal point in the middle of the park.	193
5.3. Dedication ceremony of Lew Kerbel's sculpture of Ernst Thälmann in Berlin, 15 April 1986.	200
5.4. Dissidents preparing their banners on the eve of the Liebknecht-Luxemburg parade in January 1988.	203
6.1. Lev Kerbel's sculpture of Ernst Thälmann covered in graffiti in November 2011.	227
6.2. Ludwig Engelhardt's sculpture of Karl Marx and Friedrich Engels in Berlin, 22 July 1991. The graffiti along the bottom of the statue reads: "We are not guilty" with the word "not" covered over.	229

Acknowledgments

As with any project that spans over a decade, the work that went into this book could not have been completed without a great deal of help and support from others. I would especially like to thank my former dissertation advisor, Konrad Jarausch, whose steadfast mentoring and guidance both during and after my years at the University of North Carolina at Chapel Hill has been greatly appreciated. His firm commitment to the highest of academic standards and to the pursuit of historical investigation will serve as a model throughout my career. I would like to also thank Christopher Browning, Donald Raleigh, Jay Smith, and Lloyd Kramer, who all helped me hone my skills as an historian and cultivated my interest in cultural and intellectual history, nationalism, identity, and memory studies.

A variety of institutions and organizations have provided me with the training and opportunities necessary to pursue this project. The History Department at the University of North Carolina at Chapel Hill provided fellowship funding throughout my doctoral studies. A fellowship from the Robert Bosch Foundation made it possible for me to gain firsthand experience working with members of the German Parliament and at one of Germany's premier national history museums, the *Haus der Geschichte*. I would especially like to thank Markus Meckel, MdB, Hermann Schäfer, and Rainer Eckert for their support, guidance, and advice during that fellowship year. The United States Department of Education and the Social Science Research Council's Berlin Program sponsored further trips to Germany during graduate school, which allowed me to work with Christoph Klessmann and Martin Sabrow, both of whom challenged me to look at East German memory from new perspectives. Finally, I would like to thank Dean Julie Hayes at the University of Massachusetts at Amherst and the College of Humanities and Fine Arts for granting me a research leave in 2011, which allowed me time to return to Berlin and focus on my revisions.

The opportunity to present my work at a number of conferences and seminars has allowed me to hone various arguments and incorporate constructive feedback. I would like to thank my fellow panelists and commentators from the German Studies Association, the German Historical

Institute, the Zentrum für Zeithistorisches Forschung in Potsdam, the Public History program at the Free University of Berlin, the National Council on Public History, the Mid-Atlantic German History Seminar, and a colloquium at the University of Michigan hosted by Geoff Eley.

I have deep respect and appreciation for the knowledgeable and friendly staffs of the archives consulted for this project. In particular I would like to extend my gratitude to the staff of the Stiftung Archiv Parteien und Massenorganizationen at the Bundesarchiv in Berlin, Sabine Stein at the Buchenwald Archive, Birgit Schnabel and Jörg Rudolph at the Hausarchiv of the Deutsches Historisches Museum, as well as the staffs at the Archiv der sozialen Demokratie (Friedrich Ebert Stiftung), the Berliner Landesarchiv, the Hausarchiv of the Kulturhistorisches Museum in Merseburg, the Kreisarchiv Merseburg, the Saxen-Anhalt Landesarchiv in Merseburg, and the Weimar Stadtarchiv.

I am also grateful for the friendships and professional relationships I have made over the years, including Chris Fischer, Elana Passmann, Todd Berryman, Thomas Peglow, Brandon Hunziker, Cora Granata, Riikka Pakkala, Jennifer Kast, Christopher Barks, David Freudenwald, Elizabeth Koch, and Greg Caplan. I will forever cherish the time I was able spend with Jill Hopper. She is still missed by all of us. While researching in the archives, I was delighted to form friendships and professional ties with Bernd Altmann-Kaufhold, Molly Johnson Wilkinson, Charles Lansing, Greg Witkowski, David Tomkins, and many others.

I would especially like to thank Jennifer Heuer, Daniel Hamilton, Adam Nelson, and Benita Blessing who read through multiple drafts and offered useful and constructive critique. I also appreciate the support I have received over the years from my colleagues at *Waldsee*, where I have spent each summer since 1988 cultivating the next generation of young Americans interested in all things German. One of those colleagues, Daniel Hamilton, has been a mentor to me and broadened my perspective on the world greatly. He is a person of great moral authority and one who has devoted his life to improving German-American relations.

Since arriving at the University of Massachusetts at Amherst, I have been blessed with wonderful colleagues not only in the Department of History, but also in the German and Scandinavian Studies program, Judaic and Near East Studies, English, and Classics. I would especially like to thank Andy Donson, Jennifer Heuer, Brian Ogilivie, Brian Bunk, Anna Taylor, Marla Miller, David Glassberg, Joye Bowman, John Higginson, Audrey Altstadt, Barton Byg, and Sky Arndt-Briggs for their friendship, guidance, and mentoring over the years.

Lastly, I would like to thank my family for all of the love and support they have given me over the years. Special thanks go to my brother Todd, my sister Karin, her husband Mark, and their son Michael. I could not have accomplished this project without the moral support and guidance of my loving parents, David and Audrey Olsen, to whom *Tailoring Truth* is dedicated.

ABBREVIATIONS

AdsD	Archiv der sozialen Demokraten (Archive of the Social Democrats)
BND	Bundesnachrichtendienst (Federal Intelligence Agency)
BStU	Bundesbeauftragte für die Unterlagen des Staatssicherheitsdienstes der ehemaligen Deutschen Demokratischen Republik, Berlin (The Federal Commission for the Records of the State Security Service of the former German Democratic Republic, Berlin)
BVG	Berlin Verkehrsgetriebe (Berlin Transport Services)
BwA	Buchenwald Archiv (Buchenwald Archive)
CDU	Christliche Demokratische Union (Christian Democratic Union)
CPSU	Communist Party of the Soviet Union
CSU	Christlich-Soziale Union (Christian Social Union)
DEFA	Deutscher Film AG (German Film AG)
DGB	Deutscher Gewerkschaftsbund (German Federation of Unions)
DHM	Deutsches Historisches Museum (German Historical Museum)
FDJ	Freie Deutsche Jugend (Free German Youth)
FDP	Freie Demokratische Partei (Free Democratic Party)
FES	Friedrich Ebert Stiftung (Friedrich Ebert Foundation)
FIAPP	Fédération Internationale des Anciens Prisonniers Politiques (International Federation of Former Political Prisoners)
GDR	German Democratic Republic

KA	Kreisarchiv (county archive)
KPD	Kommunistische Partei Deutschlands (Communist Party of Germany)
LDP	Liberale-Demokratische Partei (Liberal Democratic Party)
LHASA	Landeshauptarchiv Sachsen-Anhalt
MfDG	Museum für Deutsche Geschichte (Museum for German History)
NVA	Nationale Volksarmee (National People's Army)
OdF	Opfer des Faschismus (Victims of Fascism)
PDS	Partei des Demokratischen Sozialismus (Party of Democratic Socialism)
SAPMO-BArch	Stiftung Archiv Parteien und Massenorganisationen, Bundesarchiv
SBZ	Sowjetische Besatzungszone (Soviet Occupation Zone)
SDP	Sozialdemokratische Partei (Social Democratic Party)
SED	Sozialistische Einheitspartei Deutschlands (Socialist Unity Party of Germany)
SMAD	Soviet Military Administration in Germany
SPD	Sozialdemokratische Partei Deutschlands (Social Democratic Party of Germany)
STA	Stadtarchiv (City Archive)
Stasi	Staatssicherheitsdienst (State Security Service)
USPD	Unabhängige Sozialdemokratische Partei Deutschlands (Independent Social Democratic Party of Germany)
USSR	Union of Soviet Socialist Republics
VVN	Vereinigung der Verfolgten des Naziregimes (Association of Nazi Persecutees)
ZIG	Zentralinstitut für Geschichte (Central Institute for History)

INTRODUCTION
Tailoring Truth in East Germany

The visual prominence of memorials to the heroes of communism and the German working class might strike a tourist traveling through contemporary eastern Germany as out of place so long after the collapse of the communist regime that built them. The colossal monument dedicated to the memory of former communist leader Ernst Thälmann still resides in the Berlin neighborhood of Prenzlauer Berg. Similarly, a large park and statue ensemble in the main government district in Berlin commemorate Karl Marx and Friedrich Engels. Each January, thousands gather at the Socialists' Cemetery in Berlin to honor the memory of Rosa Luxemburg and Karl Liebknecht, who were killed by radical anti-socialist forces in 1919. A large monument complex devoted to the communist struggle against fascism still greets visitors as they enter onto the grounds of the Buchenwald concentration camp. Such reminders of the past—or memory traces—are not confined to Berlin or sites of historical significance. Indeed, they can be found throughout the cities and towns in the federal states that once made up the territory of East Germany—monuments dedicated to heroes of the working class, to former leaders of the communist party, and to historical events important to the German worker's movement.

In order to interpret these memory traces, it is necessary to understand the complicated events that led to the construction of such sites of memory. Following its defeat in May 1945, Germany was divided into four occupation zones. Initially, political power in the Soviet Occupation Zone (SBZ) rested solely in the hands of the Soviet Military Administration (SMAD). Despite agreements among the four occupying powers to cooperate, the Cold War soon took its toll on keeping Germany unified. In May 1949, the three western occupation zones unified to form the Federal Republic of Germany (FRG) and in October the Soviets allowed their zone to transform itself into the German Democratic Republic (GDR). East Germany adopted many of the Soviet traits of political repression in an attempt to solidify the communist party's control over society. This included the use

---

Notes for this chapter begin on page 14.

of Soviet tanks to put down an attempted uprising in 1953, a reliance on the secret police to keep dissidents in check, and ultimately the construction of the Berlin Wall in 1961. Throughout this early period, the GDR claimed to represent Germany's sole successor state and actively sought to distance itself from its West German neighbor. Relations between the two German states improved during the 1970s and 1980s, but did not alter East Germany's claim to represent the better Germany. Despite the repressive nature of the state, there were also avenues for resistance and dissonance. These forces united during 1989 to topple the government, tear down the Berlin Wall, and bring an end to communist rule. Following a turbulent year of economic and social change, the two Germanys united on 3 October 1990.

Throughout this period, the East German state made a concerted effort to populate the memory landscape with monuments, museums, and commemoration festivals that supported its vision of the past and bolstered the regime's claim to represent the best interests of German society. Many of these socialist state-driven memory projects have seen significant changes and alterations since the fall of the Berlin Wall. Many of the spaces they once occupied have given way to places of modern, pluralistic remembrance. However, the legacy of the SED's (Socialist Unity Party) memory-work did not simply disappear in 1990—remnants of that ideological project remain visible in the debates that occurred (and to some extent continue) over what to do with the cultural heritage left behind by the GDR.

These socialist-oriented sites of memory remain a large and highly visible part of the built landscape in this portion of united Germany. They were the product of a concerted effort by the SED to cultivate a very specific form of memory culture during the forty years it was in power, 1949–1989. During the 1990s, the citizens of united Germany undertook a public discussion about which memorials constructed by the SED regime during its forty-year reign should remain, and which should be removed from public view. In short, local authorities removed those deemed out of place or superfluous, such as the colossal memorial for Vladimir Lenin or the hundreds of smaller Ernst Thälmann monuments located in towns throughout the GDR. But local governments also decided to keep many monuments that they judged as still relevant to German history and society.[1]

Calls to remove these items have not disappeared entirely. Some Germans see artifacts of an official East German memory culture as relics of the SED's repressive politics, and thus as monuments that should be destroyed, or at least quietly forgotten through a practice of benign neglect. In January 2012, Peter Ramsauer, the Federal Minister for Construction, suggested moving the Marx-Engels monument from downtown Berlin to the Socialists' Cemetery on the outskirts of the city, a place he referred to as a "socialists' dump."[2] His remarks were immediately met with arguments favoring the monument's preservation from political opponents and in the press.[3] Indeed, despite calls like Ramsauer's to remove these monuments from public view, most of the GDR's prestige memory projects remain intact.[4]

The memory landscape in eastern Germany has also seen the addition of dozens (if not hundreds) of new memory projects (memorials, museums, historical sites, etc.) that honor previously neglected aspects of Germany's past: the prisons of Bautzen and Berlin-Hohenschönhausen that held East Germany's political prisoners; the inter-German border museum at Marienborn; new interpretive exhibits at Sachsenhausen, Ravensbrück, and Buchenwald; the permanent exhibit at the *Zeitgeschichtliches Forum* (Contemporary History Forum) in Leipzig; and the Berlin Wall museums and memorials—to name just a few examples. At the same time, heated post-unification debates erupted over whether or not Germany should preserve prominent GDR-era buildings, like the East German parliament building, the *Palast der Republik* (the Palace of the Republic), or reconstruct other sites, like the Berlin City Palace (demolished in 1950) in an effort to rebuild "historic" Berlin. All of these are important debates and reveal a great deal about how a new memory culture—one that is pluralistic, open, and engaged—has emerged since 1990.[5]

Nonetheless, those markers of an East German official memory culture that remain represent the remnants of the policies pursued by the SED to saturate the public sphere with icons that it hoped would create direct, legitimizing links to it and its proclaimed mission to create a "better" Germany. The fact that many of these icons not only persist, but also have been actively preserved is telling. It indicates that, although the party's memory-work may not have won over the majority of East German society, its memory politics did indeed have a lingering effect on East German society that outlived its monopoly of power.

In his study of professional historians in the GDR, Martin Sabrow argues that, while we cannot ascertain to what extent the general population internalized the SED's historical policies, or whether they helped stabilize acceptance of the regime, the field of history functioned as an important place of conflict over the legitimacy of the party's perception of the past. Moreover, Sabrow notes that a strong divergence in historical consciousness between East and West Germany only began to converge by the middle of the 1990s.[6] A similar case can be made for the SED's memory-work, which was an extension of its policies toward academic historians. While we cannot accurately estimate how successful the SED was in manipulating popular memory, the way in which it attempted to influence perceptions of the past is still important for our understanding of East Germany as a modern state-socialist dictatorship. Indeed, Annette Leo has found that the SED's memory policies have had a lasting impact on post-1990 German society. Studying school groups visiting the Buchenwald concentration camp in 1997 and 1998, she discovered that both teachers and parents had prepared many students to view the memorial site according to the pre-1990 official interpretation and had ignored newer information about the history of the camp as a Soviet internment camp or other aspects of the memorial site that had been added since 1990.[7] Alon Confino is correct to point out that the issue of reception is the "ogre that awaits every cultural historian" and that without critically examining reception we risk "constructing the history of memory from visible signs whose significance is taken for granted."[8] However, memory-work (whether in a totalitarian state or by interest groups within a pluralist society) rarely has immediate, measurable effects on collective memory. Memory politics must be measured, when measurable at all, over a long-term period.

The period covered by *Tailoring Truth* spans from the immediate postwar period to the collapse of the East German regime in 1989 and analyzes the evolution of how the state and party sought to harness the power of memory to legitimize its own claim to rule. The GDR's attempt to present itself as the new Germany, the tragic historical shadow from which it emerged, and the presence of a West German rival all turn the state-building process in East Germany into a unique opportunity to explore the creation and eventual erosion of a new state's memory culture and its role in regime legitimation. By exploring when and how the East German state altered its course or adapted its message, we can see a culture of official memory politics emerge that differed significantly from West Germany. As Siobhan Kattago has argued, "Official memory in the GDR meant a restrictive ideological representation of the past with little public debate. Official memory in the Federal Republic, on the other hand, was a public and highly controversial topic in West German political culture."[9] Yet even within this restricted representation, we find elements of debate and negotiation—both within the party apparatus as well as between members of the party and the sculptors, museum curators, and others who were tasked to carry out the party's memory-work.

Previous studies that address East German memory politics and sites of memory in the GDR have focused on specific events or memorials.[10] The comparative approach of both James Young and Jeffrey Herf are excellent early contributions to the field, but both primarily center on memories of the Nazi period, do not engage with the many other forms of memory politics pursued by the SED, and appear to at least in part champion the West German approach toward memory.[11] In a similar fashion, Thomas Fox's

Stated Memory: East Germany and the Holocaust concentrates exclusively on the SED's treatment of Holocaust memory in East German historiography, memorials, literature, and film.[12] Konrad Jarausch and Martin Sabrow, in the many volumes that they have edited or co-edited, have both used their contributions to theorize the role of history and memory in postwar German society. The strength of Sabrow's work rests with his ability to connect the work of professional historians to broader trends of GDR society and Jarausch's contributions have stressed the societal impact of historical narratives and the political role of memory and history (*Geschichtspolitik*) in both divided and unified Germany.[13]

By focusing not only on the SED's execution of memory-work but also on the difficulties it faced in completing this task, *Tailoring Truth* bridges the gap between two different strains of historiography of the GDR. On the one hand, this study contributes to a growing body of work that examines the limitations of SED rule, while on the other hand it also acknowledges the central role of state and party institutions in establishing parameters for acceptable behavior. Historians have increasingly called attention to the limits of state power. Jeffrey Kopstein and Mark Landsman have both shown how the party failed to deliver on its stated economic goals, despite the control it wielded over the economy as a whole.[14] Alan Nothnagle and Alan McDougall have both demonstrated that the party also failed to successfully regulate the indoctrination of East German youth, so that young people did not uniformly conform to the party's vision of budding socialists.[15] Indeed, in most instances the party needed to make ideological compromises and never achieved the level of control that it desired. Esther von Richthofen addressed this limitation of party power in her work on the GDR's cultural institutions and argues that this limit was in part due to disagreement within the party apparatus itself as well as between the party and the general population.[16] Indeed, there was also a great deal of debate and negotiation present within the realm of official memory policies as well. Those charged with carrying out the party's memory policies often found it necessary to modify the party's vision of the past in order to attract an audience to a commemoration, to engage a sculptor to create a monument, or to attract visitors to a museum exhibit.

Such limits of total control stand in contrast to earlier works on the GDR that reasserted the totalitarian model during the early 1990s. Scholars like Sigrid Meuschel and Klaus Schroeder highlighted the overtly repressive nature of the East German regime where the SED was fully in control of the state and society, while other non-state actors played no real part in shaping East German society.[17] Against this resurgent totalitarian model, social and cultural historians have sought to demonstrate that life in East Germany meant more than merely accepting total party control.

This has led to new attempts to characterize the GDR as a *durchherrschte Gesellschaft* (a ruled society),[18] a *Fürsorgediktatur* (a welfare dictatorship),[19] and a "participatory dictatorship."[20] While each of these nuanced interpretations of a dictatorship take issue with the concept of totalitarianism, they do indicate a consensus that the SED desired to wield as much control over society as it could, and that it employed multiple strategies that incorporated tactics beyond simply the use of force. This same dynamic can be found in the party's memory policies. The party wanted to control the public representation of the past, yet it was never able to completely control this process and thus found itself constantly retailoring its message and launching new memory projects.

The more we study the nature of the East German state, the less we are intrigued by its collapse and instead fascinated by how it was able to appear to be so stable. Armin Mitter and Stefan Wolle attribute the apparent stability of the regime to the presence of an extensive secret police apparatus, the travel restrictions imposed by a closed border and the Berlin Wall, and to the presence of Soviet troops. Taken to its logical conclusion, they argue, once these oppressive elements were removed, the regime began to crumble and eventually collapsed entirely.[21] Against this argument, Andrew Port has argued that despite the repressive nature of the state, East German citizens were anything but silent. Indeed, the major challenges to SED rule, represented by the uprisings in August 1951 and June 1953, erupted during the height of Stalinism in East Germany. Instead, Port finds that "social fragmentation—as well as official accommodation—were nevertheless the most important keys to East German stability and the longevity of the socialist regime."[22] Alternately, Charles Maier and others disagree that the East German state was indeed stable and instead point to a long and gradual decline in the regime's political, social, and economic performance combined with decreasing tolerance by the public to accept such conditions.[23] Others, like Timothy Garton Ash, avoid the question of internal stability by emphasizing how external factors such as the growth of democratic movements in neighboring East European states, Mikhail Gorbachev's reforms, and the waning of the Cold War influenced the fall of the Berlin Wall and eventually German unification on 3 October 1990.[24]

Other historians have attempted to approach studying East German history from below, in the form of a renewed interest in *Alltagsgeschichte,* with its emphasis on how politics influenced everyday life.[25] These authors have made significant contributions to rethinking the power relationship between the party and the people, especially how the party attempted to wield its authority at the local level. Others have focused on how consumer culture and consumption operated as a means by which everyday people could and did influence party policy.[26] While the purpose of this study is not to gauge individual reception of the SED memory-work policies, it takes into consideration the voices of individuals when such sources were available, such as in the form of letters to the editor, visitor comments, and correspondence between artists and the regime.[27] The GDR only rarely engaged in the polling of public opinion and even these surveys did not ask questions geared toward the study of popular perceptions of the past. Even if they had, one cannot compare such studies with similar polls in the West, since East German respondents could not fully trust that their anonymity would be respected.[28] Instead, when assessing the "success" or "failure" of the SED's memory-work policy, this study relies primarily on the party's internal assessment. It analyzes decisions by party leaders to initiate changes in course or implement new memory policies to explore the party's willingness to continue investing state resources on certain projects or finance new initiatives instead. It also looks at the factors that led to such reconsiderations.

Thus, unearthing elements of negotiation and compromise are key elements to understanding the SED's memory-work. In order to bring its vision of the past into the public realm, the state depended on a variety of partners—the museum workers who curated exhibits, the artists who created the monuments, and the organizers and participants of commemoration activities. The formal and informal negotiations between the state and these non-state actors reveal that the state rarely pushed through its agenda without compromise. It is precisely this push and pull between the state and its citizenry over the SED's "memory-work" (*Erinnerungsarbeit*), the official party policy term, that illustrates the process of negotiation that was necessary to project a party-specific interpretation of the past into the built environment.

In democracies such as the United States or the Federal Republic of Germany, we can assume a certain amount of plurality in the way the public engages in debates about historical representation. Scholars of memory have sought to show the importance of competing voices in shaping collective memory and framing official interpretations of sites of memory in Europe. In the case of France, the contributions to Pierre Nora's *Realms of Memory* demonstrate that non-state actors played a major role commissioning monuments, building museums, or organizing commemorations independently from the state.[29] Contributors to Etienne François and Hagen Schulze's three-volume edited work have looked at similar case studies within the German national context.[30] The collection is organized into categories of memory, such as "empire," "arch enemy," or "guilt," which are explored through 121 essays focused on specific memory sites, personalities, events, or concepts throughout German history. Each essay attempts to locate the site of memory within the broader context of German history and interpret how these sites have influenced perceptions of the past: "In other words: the individual remembers, but he does not remain alone. The milieu in which he lives creates the parameters, the form, and the content that determines and defines a common memory; the historical interpretation and pattern of perception are created out of the interaction between personal recollection and the shared, collective memory."[31] Within the context of the GDR, the ultimate goal of the SED was to take control of such parameters, instill them with its own ideological interpretation, and then actively use these sites of memory as a means to shape collective memory.[32]

This goal of controlling and managing memory was common throughout the state socialist societies of Eastern Europe after the Second World War. In each case, communist governments attempted to supplant former symbols of power with new ones that rationalized their position of authority.[33] As Aleida Assmann has stated, "institutions and larger social groups, such as nations, governments, the church, or a firm do not 'have' a memory—they 'make' one for themselves with the aid of memorial signs such as symbols, texts, images, rites, ceremonies, places, and monuments."[34] Assmann argues that totalitarian states "attempt to restore the premodern state monopoly over history and under modern circumstances and with modern means."[35] In East Germany, the SED attempted to establish such a monopoly, but it was never able to achieve its goal. However, it did present a "tailored truth" about the past, which was designed to have a long-term impact on how East German society internalized the past and in turn viewed the present.[36] When opportunities arose to commemorate an historic event, construct a museum, or build a monument, the only entity with the resources to pay for such undertakings was the state. Thus, the curators, artists, and event organizers were dependent on the state, which could use its position of power to shape the public's exposure to specific strands of memory that it wanted to highlight over all other competing memories. By confining the parameters of an acceptable and usable past, the SED dictatorship hoped to control the process of state identity formation and steer it toward contributing to the party's cultural legitimacy.

In his contribution to *Verletztes Gedächtnis*, Konrad Jarausch separates memory into a hierarchy of three categories—the individual, the group, and the collective. Memories formed and represented at all three of these levels are influenced by differences in gender, race, nationality, religious affiliation, occupation, and other social experiences. Individual memories are transformed and altered as they work their way up the hierarchy from individual, to group, to collective memories. In a democratic and pluralistic society, this process often involves political actors competing to have their interpretations of events dominate in the public sphere.[37] However, in the GDR, where private memories seldom found a voice in the public sphere, the state was able to dominate public representations of the past and thus this book's analysis remains primarily at the top level of this hierarchy, but does occasional dip down into the lower two levels when the sources have allowed such insights.

The intent of this book is not to employ a top-down methodology that reifies the SED's assertion of power, but to differentiate between the party's ideological goals within the realm of memory politics and the extent to which it could implement its policies. The main assertion is that memory policies in East Germany were not static. They were not conceived in 1945 and then simply replicated throughout the entire period of the GDR. Jeffrey Herf has stated that the SED's anti-cosmopolitan campaigns of the 1950s "left a wound that never healed and an official memory of Nazism that remained intact until the collapse of the East German regime in 1989."[38] This may hold true concerning official memory of Nazism in East Germany, but not for all of the other strands of memory that fed into East Germany's official memory. Instead, the SED's approach to memory politics changed over time and adapted to changing conditions and challenges, both internal and external. The projects covered here demonstrate that the SED constantly and obsessively monitored how the state could employ memory-work to further its ideological and political goals. As a result, the state continuously attempted to resolve its shortcomings, both real and perceived, over the course of its nearly half-century of existence.

The SED hoped that memory might function as a non-material means of influence over East German society. Despite all the effort and resources committed by the state and party to this endeavor, the SED ultimately could not significantly influence how society viewed the past nor cultivate a unified historical consciousness capable of securing sufficient regime loyalty to fend off popular opposition. In fact, the state faced opposition to its public presentation of memory throughout its reign, yet it continued to invest its scarce resources in memory projects in an effort to bolster the SED's claim to power until its final collapse in the autumn of 1989. As the SED lost control over its official memory politics, ceding space in the public sphere for counter-memories, new opportunities arose that allowed opposition leaders to turn the SED's official memory culture around and use it as a means to protest against the state.

While similar examples can be found in other East European states of how the state attempted to manipulate popular perceptions of the past, East Germany's relationship with the past was unique. Unlike its East European neighbors, who often attempted to differentiate themselves from the Soviet Union, the GDR faced the extra challenge of competing for its national heritage and historical legacy with West Germany. Just as West Germany laid claim to the democratic traditions of 1848 and the Weimar Republic as the historical foundation for its collective identity, East Germany focused on a Marxist-Leninist interpretation of Germany's past on which it could also construct a collective identity. This search for historical continuity provided the basis for both West Germany's master-narrative and East Germany's antifascist-based counter-narrative.[39] While the meta-narratives in divided Germany developed in very different ways, they remained interconnected and often responded to historiographical and political developments in the other camp.[40]

The study of memory in East Germany is closely linked to the study of professional historians, an area that saw a great deal of attention even prior to German unification. Western scholars had easy access to the published scholarship of GDR historians. However, they were limited by only reading what the state approved for official publication. Nonetheless, historians such as Andreas Dorpalen and others set the standard for the intellectual history of East German historians based on the materials to which they had access.[41] Following unification, however, historians could study not only published works, but also gain slow but steady access to archival documents, directives, and other ancillary evidence. For example, Martin Sabrow's study of GDR historians and the phenomenon which he has termed the GDR's "history culture," i.e. how historians interacted with the state and party, helps us understand the politicized nature of academic history in East Germany.[42]

It is my intention to build on our understandings of the basic structures of East Germany's history culture and extend them into the public sphere. Understanding attempts by GDR historians to (re)write history and develop new interpretations that bolstered the historical continuity of the SED is a necessary first step. To take the next step, it is necessary to look beyond the writing of academics and turn our focus to forms of public historical representation. While there are many categories that might fit within the realm of official memory-work, monuments, museums, and commemorations were among the most important to the state for its instrumentalization of the new Marxist-Leninist interpretations of Germans past.

This book does not claim to provide a complete account of monuments or museums in the GDR, but rather a historical narrative that draws on a select set. These are representative examples of memory projects chosen from a wide range of possibilities, including film, literature, street signs, the names of schools and factories, and many others.[43] Some prominent memorials have been left out, such as those built by the Soviet Union or the Frauenkirche in Dresden, which was left in ruins as a monument to the victims of the "Anglo-American Terror Attack," better known as the Dresden bombing of 1945, and instrumentalized by the SED.[44] The list of other possible places of memory that could have been included here is extensive. However, the examples chosen for the case studies are intended to provide a means to trace the overall trends in East German memory policies and connect these projects to the legitimating claims of the East German regime. In each case, the state constructed or heavily influenced these memory projects in an effort to convey specific messages to the public. Monuments, such as the one at Buchenwald, or the various political monuments that dotted the memory landscape in Berlin, were constructed to visually reinforce the party's interpretation of specific events, figures, or historical sites. Many, such as the Ernst Thälmann statue in Berlin, figured directly into the state's antifascist founding myth or were meant to sustain a direct memory link between the current generation and specific, earlier heroes of the German working class. Museums in the GDR served as educational instruments for the workers and students. Factories, trade unions, and school groups organized special state-funded trips to the Museum for German History in Berlin and to local *"Heimat"* museums, such as the one in Merseburg. The most dramatic element of historical representation in the GDR were the commemoration festivals, such as the Martin Luther festival or the annual parade in honor of Karl Liebknecht and Rosa Luxemburg in Berlin. These commemorations brought a diverse group of people together to participate in the memory-work of the state and actively partake in official rituals of remembrance, yet also provided a space for alternative memories.

Using these three categories of memory culture, I identify a series of five stages in the development of a uniquely East German culture of remembrance, each of which form the focus of the five chapters that follow. Although these stages generally occur in chronological order, there are several instances where stages overlap and continue simultaneously with another phase. Chapter 1 looks at the first stage, which took place immediately following the Second World War and extended into the early 1950s. The German Communist Party (KPD)/SED faced the significant task of establishing itself as the dominant party in the SBZ. This process of legitimizing the party in the minds of the German people meant drawing on existing memories of the German working class and elevating the perceived importance of these traditions in order to claim a dominant position in the minds of the Germans. Most importantly, this stage attempted to promote the concept of antifascism as the defining element of the SED. Concretely, the party sought to shape an emerging postwar memory culture through the renovating the Socialists' Cemetery in Berlin-Friedrichsfelde, hosting an exhibit about the "Other Germany" that highlighted the role of communist resistance, and attempted to infuse the 100th anniversary of the 1848 revolution with its own concepts of how the lessons of the past should be applied to postwar Germany.

Chapter 2 focuses on the second stage of development that took root following the creation of the GDR in 1949. The SED's attention turned to grafting the party's legacy onto the new state. This process included finding and amplifying the traditions of the German labor movement. It moved beyond celebrating the communist party's antifascist traditions to incorporating broader interpretations of a struggling working class that finally achieved its goals with the founding of the East German state. The young state constructed a new Museum for German History (MfDG) that propagated its new line of Marxist-Leninist historical development that culminated in the creation of the first communist state on German soil. The state seized on opportunities to take over memorial initiatives like the one at the Buchenwald concentration camp in an effort to establish control over how this site would be remembered. This stage also saw some failed attempts at commemorating Karl Marx, Friedrich Engels, and Ernst Thälmann. Such failures highlight areas where the party was not able to impose its vision of the past on the emerging memory landscape.

The third and fourth stages involved extending the basis for this cultural legitimacy. Chapter 3 addresses the third stage, roughly from the 1950s to the 1960s, during which time the regime endeavored to transfer the memories of the antifascist struggle to the next generation and develop new interpretations of the past that spoke directly to the political concerns of the time. Additionally, the SED sought to locate the history of the East German state within the narratives of local and regional history, which it hoped would provide a more solid footing for the state's own narrative of historical development. The state transformed many smaller historical sites into politically charged interpretive memorials, revamped many of the local history museums in an effort to localize the national historical narrative, and sponsored teacher training workshops to better influence how teachers used places like the MfDG and Buchenwald to educate the youth.

Chapter 4 examines how the fourth stage of development, which covers the 1970s and 1980s, signaled a new direction in East Germany's official memory policies. The new approach allowed for the rehabilitation of historical figures and events previously determined not to belong to the GDR's "progressive" state narrative. Such "reactionary" figures as the

Prussian King Frederick II, the nineteenth-century statesman Otto von Bismarck, Martin Luther, and others were now seen in a new interpretive light. This made it possible to differentiate between acts by these figures that led to German nationalism and those that contributed to (or stunted) the growth of the German working class. By expanding the repertoire of acceptable historical figures and events that could be commemorated, the regime hoped to expand its reach beyond the party faithful and make inroads among the general public.

Chapter 5 explores how revisions to the national narrative marked the erosion of the historical narrative that the SED had so painstakingly built. This final stage is characterized by the party's resumption of memory projects it had previously abandoned. Having placed new emphasis on the "reactionary" figures during the previous stage, the party now felt it needed to return to older memory culture traditions from the founding years. The regime returned to previously abandoned efforts to construct monuments honoring Karl Marx, Friedrich Engels, and Ernst Thälmann to deflect criticism they were now being ignored. However, the difficulties that the regime faced in bringing such projects to fruition reflect not only the rigid historical conception of an aging gerontocracy, but also reveal active resistance to the party's narrow interpretation of the past. The growing distance between the memory vision of the party and the state's memory-work partners can be seen in the difficulty that the party experienced finding artists who would create the type of monuments desired by the SED leadership. The party's narrow interpretation also presented the opportunity for opposition leaders to reappropriate the memory of figures such as Rosa Luxemburg and use her legacy against the policies of the state. Thus the erosion of the memory culture that the party worked so hard to create ultimately contributed to the SED's demise.

Viewing these three categories of memory over the entire period of SED rule reveals how and why the state's memory policies changed over time. In the end, it is clear that East Germany's memory culture was dynamic. It developed in stages over the span of forty-five years. The SED drew upon pre-existing memories of the working class and tailored these memories to fit the new political realities of postwar Germany. Once in power, the party continued to construct a memory landscape intended to further bolster its authority. However, maintaining control over its own official memory policies proved difficult. Although the SED attempted to stem the tide of erosion with a new round of political monuments similar to those built during earlier stages, these new projects were unable to hold back the emerging push toward democracy and the public's rejection of a one-sided, state-imposed memory culture.

Notes

1. *Bericht der Kommission zum Umgang mit den politischen Denkmälern der Nachkriegszeit im ehemaligen Ost-Berlin* (Berlin: Abegeordnetenhaus, 1993).
2. Thomas Fülling, "Minister: Marx und Engels sollen weg," *Berliner Morgenpost*, 21 January 2012, p. 2.
3. To follow the debate that Ramsauer's remarks touched off, see: Katrin Betinna Müller, "Immer schön vergessen," *Die Tageszeitung*, 20 January 2012, p. 16; "Soll das Denkmal von Marx und Engels aus Mitte verschwinden?" *B.Z.*, 20 January, 2012, p. 8; "Leserbriefe," *Berliner Zeitung*, 21 January 2012, p. 9; and "Sakko und Jacketti," *Berliner Tagesspiegel*, 29 January 2012, p. 16.
4. While most of East Germany's prestige memory projects remain in their original form, there are a few examples where the monuments have been removed or relocated. The Lenin monument in Berlin is the most prominent example of a monument that has been completely removed from public view and the monument for Marx and Engels has been consolidated into one corner of the park rather than as its focal point. Markus Falkner, "Marx und Engels blicken sieben Jahre lang nach Westen," *Berliner Morgenpost*, 15 April 2010.
5. Martin Sabrow, Rainer Eckert, et al., *Wohin treibt die Erinnerung? Dokumentation einer Debatte* (Göttingen: Vandenhoeck & Ruprecht, 2007); Silke Arnold-de Simine, ed., *Memory Traces: 1989 and the Question of German Cultural Identity* (Bern: Peter Lang, 2005); Heidi Behrens and Andreas Wagner, eds., *Deutsche Teilung, Repression und Alltagsleben: Erinnerungsorte der DDR-Geschichte* (Leipzig: Forum Verlag Leipzig, 2004).
6. Martin Sabrow, *Das Diktat des Konsenses: Geschichtswissenschaft in der DDR 1949–1969* (Munich: Oldenbourg, 2001), p. 10.
7. Annette Leo, "Nicht Vereint: Studien zum Geschichtsbewusstsein Ost- und Westdeutscher," in Behrens and Wagner, *Deutsche Teilung*, pp. 58–68, p. 65.
8. Alon Confino, "Collective Memory and Cultural History: Problems of Method," *American Historical Review*, Vol. 102, No. 5 (December 1997), pp. 1386–1403, here p. 1395 and p. 1397. See also Alon Confino, *Germany as a Culture of Remembrance: Promises and Limits of Writing History* (Chapel Hill: University of North Carolina Press, 2006).
9. Siobhan Kattago, *Ambiguous Memory: The Nazi Past and German National Identity* (Westport, CT: Praeger, 2001), p. 3.
10. Martin Sabrow, ed., *Erinnerungsorte der DDR* (Munich: C.H. Beck, 2009); Konrad Jarausch and Martin Sabrow, eds., *Verletztes Gedächtnis: Die Erinnerungskultur und Zeitgeschichte im Konflikt* (Berlin: Campus, 2002); Carola S. Rudnick, *Die andere Hälfte der Erinnerung: Die DDR in der deutschen Geschichtspolitik nach 1989* (Bielefeld: Transcript, 2011); and Sabrow, Eckert, et al., *Wohin treibt die Erinnerung?*
11. Jeffrey Herf, *Divided Memory: The Nazi Past in the Two Germanys* (Cambridge: Harvard University Press, 1997); James Young, *Textures of Memory: Holocaust Memorials and Meaning* (New Haven, CT: Yale University Press, 1997).
12. Tomas C. Fox, *Stated Memory: East Germany and the Holocaust* (Rochester, NY: Camden House, 1999).
13. Jarausch and Sabrow, *Verletztes Gedächtnis*; Konrad Jarausch and Martin Sabrow, *Die historische Meistererzählung: Deutungslinien der deutschen Nationalgeschichte nach 1945* (Göttingen: Vandenhoeck & Ruprecht, 2002); Martin Sabrow, Ralph Jessen, and Klaus Große Kracht, eds., *Zeitgeschichte als Streitgeschichte: Grosse Kontroversen seit 1945* (Munich: C.H. Beck, 2003).
14. Jeffrey Kopstein, *The Politics of Economic Decline in East Germany, 1945–1989* (Chapel Hill: University of North Carolina Press, 1997). Mark Landsman, *Dictatorship and De-*

mand: *The Politics of Consumerism in East Germany* (Cambridge: Harvard University Press, 2005).
15. Alan L. Nothnagle, *Building the East German Myth: Historical Mythology and Youth Propaganda in the German Democratic Republic, 1945–1989* (Ann Arbor: Michigan University Press, 1999); Alan McDougall, *Youth Politics in East Germany: The Free German Youth Movement, 1946–1968* (Oxford: Clarendon Press, 2004); Uta G. Poiger, *Jazz, Rock and Rebels: Cold War Politics and American Culture in a Divided Germany* (Berkeley: University of California Press, 2000); and Mark Fenemore, *Sex, Thugs and Rock'n'Roll: Teenage Rebels in Cold-War East Germany* (New York: Berghahn Books, 2008).
16. Esther von Richthofen, *Bringing Culture to the Masses: Control, Compromise and Participation in the GDR* (New York: Berghahn Books, 2008).
17. Sigrid Meuschel, *Legitimation und Parteiherrschaft in der DDR: Zur Paradox von Stabilität und Revolution in der DDR 1945–1989* (Frankfurt am Main: Suhrkamp, 1992). Klaus Schroeder, *Der SED-Staat: Partei, Staat und Gesellschaft, 1949–1990* (Munich: Hanser, 1998). For an overview and critique of this approach, see Konrad Jarausch, "Care and Coercion: The GDR as Welfare Dictatorship," in *Dictatorship as Experience: Towards a Socio-Cultural History of the GDR* ed. Konrad Jarausch (New York: Berghahn Books, 1999), pp. 47–69.
18. Jürgen Kocka, "Eine durchherrschte Gesellschaft" in Hartmut Kaelbe, Jürgen Kocka, and Hartmut Zwar, eds., *Sozialgeschichte der DDR* (Stuttgart: Klett Cotta, 1994), pp. 547–54.
19. Jarausch, "Care and Coercion," pp. 47–69.
20. Mary Fulbrook, *The People's State: East German Society from Hitler to Honecker* (New Haven, CT: Yale University Press, 2005).
21. Armin Mitter and Stefan Wolle, *Untergang auf Raten: Unbekannte Kapitel der DDR-Geschichte* (Munich: Bertelsmann, 1993).
22. Andrew Port, *Conflict and Stability in the German Democratic Republic* (Cambridge: Cambridge University Press, 2007), p. 279.
23. Charles S. Maier, *Dissolution: The Crisis of Communism and the End of East Germany* (Princeton, NJ: Princeton University Press, 1997); Konrad Jarausch and Martin Sabrow, eds., *Weg in den Untergang: Der innere Zerfall der DDR* (Göttingen, Vandenhoeck & Ruprecht, 1999); Mary Fulbrook, *Anatomy of a Dictatorship: Inside the GDR 1949–1989* (Oxford: Oxford University Press, 1995); and Corey Ross, *The East German Dictatorship: Problems and Perspectives in the Interpretation of the GDR* (London: Arnold, 2002).
24. Timothy Garton Ash, *In Europe's Name: Germany and the Divided Continent* (New York: Vintage Books, 1993); Peter H. Merkel, *German Unification in the European Context* (University Park, PA: Penn State University Press, 1993).
25. Stefan Wolle, *Die heile Welt der Diktatur: Alltag und Herrschaft in der DDR: 1971–1989* (Berlin: Ch. Links Verlag, 1998); Hans-Hermann Hertle and Stefan Wolle, *Damals in der DDR: Der Alltag im Arbeiter und Bauernstaat* (Munich: Goldmann, 2006); Paul Steege, *Black Market, Cold War: Everyday Life in Berlin, 1946–1949* (Cambridge: Cambridge University Press, 2008); and Jan Palmowski, *Inventing a Socialist Nation: Heimat and the Politics of Everyday Life in the GDR, 1945–1990* (Cambridge: Cambridge University Press, 2009). See further, Paul Steege, Andrew Bergerson, Maureen Healy, and Pamela E. Swett, "The History of Everyday Life: A Second Chapter," *Journal of Modern History*, Vol. 80, No. 2 (2008), pp. 358–78.
26. Katherine Pence, "Schaufenster des sozialistischen Konsums: Texte der ostdeutschen 'consumer culture,'" in *Akten, Eingaben, Schaufenster: Die DDR und ihre Texte,* ed. Alf Lüdtke and Peter Becker (Berlin: Akademie Verlag, 1997), pp. 91–118. See also: Katherine Pence, "Women on the Verge: Consumers between Private Desires and Public Crisis," in *Socialist Modern: East German Everyday Culture and Politics,* ed. Katherine

Pence and Paul Betts (Ann Arbor: University of Michigan Press, 2008), pp. 287–322; and Donna Harsch, *Revenge of the Domestic: Women, the Family, and Communism in the German Democratic Republic* (Princeton, NJ: Princeton University Press, 2008).

27. I am less interested in oral history–generated memories that help explain an individual's interpretation of their pasts and more interested in how contemporaries approached these memory projects. Applying oral history methods to uncover personal memories runs into the complication of these memories being shaped by events since 1990 and would not necessarily represent how individuals interacted with the state's memory policies while they were being implemented. Such an approach would be better employed in a study of personal memories of the GDR today (that is in the present) rather than one focused on examining the role of the state's memory politics in the past. As Alessandro Portelli has demonstrated in his work on the Fosse Ardeatine massacre in Italy, oral histories are often better suited to analyze current memory debates, rather than establishing an historical record of past memory debates. Alessandro Portelli, *The Order Has Been Carried Out: History, Memory, and the Meaning of a Nazi Massacre in Rome* (New York: Palgrave Macmillan, 2003).

28. Heinz Niemann, *Hinterm Zaun: Politische Kultur und Meinungsforschung in der DDR: Die geheime Berichte an das Politbüro der SED* (Berlin: Edition Ost, 1995).

29. Pierre Nora, ed., *Realms of Memory: Rethinking the French Past* (New York: Columbia University Press, 1996). For further examples from Europe and the United States, see: Pierre Nora, "Between Memory and History: *Les Lieux de Mémoire*," *Representations* (Spring 1989), pp. 7–25; Pim den Boer and Willem Frijhoff, eds., *Lieux de mémoire et identités nationals* (Amsterdam: Amsterdam University Press, 1993); Mario Isnenghi, ed., *I luoghi della memoria*, 3 Volumes (Rome: Laterza, 1997); and William E. Leuchtenburg, ed., *American Places: Encounters with History* (Oxford: Oxford University Press, 2000). See further: George Mosse, *Fallen Soldiers: Reshaping the Memory of the World Wars* (Oxford: Oxford University Press, 1990); Michael Kammen, *Mystic Chords of Memory: The Transformation of Tradition in American Culture* (New York: Knopf, 1991); Thomas Lacquer, "Memory and Naming in the Great War," in *Commemorations*, ed. John Gillis (Princeton, NJ: Princeton University Press, 1994), pp. 150–67; Claudia Koonz, "Between Memory and Oblivion: Concentration Camps in German Memory," also in Gillis, *Commemorations*, pp. 258–80; Aleida Assmann, *Erinnerungsräume: Formen und Wandlungen des kulturellen Gedächtnisses* (Munich: C.H. Beck, 1999); and Jan Assmann, *Das kulturelle Gedächtnis: Schrift, Erinnerung und politische Identität in frühen Hochkulturen* (Munich: C.H. Beck, 1997).

30. Etienne François and Hagen Schulze, eds., *Deutsche Erinnerungsorte* (Munich: C.H. Beck, 2001), Vol. 1–3.

31. Etienne François and Hagen Schulze, "Einleitung," in François and Schulze, *Deutsche Erinnerungsorte*, Vol. 1, p. 13.

32. Jürgen Danyel, "Unwirtliche Gegenden und abgelegene Orte? Der Nationalsozialismus und die deutsche Teilung als Herausforderungen einer Geschichte der deutschen 'Erinnerungsorte,'" *Geschichte und Gesellschaft*, Vol. 24 (1998), pp. 436–75.

33. For examples from the Soviet Union, Eastern Europe, and China, where communist parties held similar control over the public presentation of memory, see: Nina Tumarkin, *Lenin Lives! The Lenin Cult in Soviet Russia* (Cambridge: Harvard University Press, 1983); Lisa Kirschenbaum, *The Legacy of the Siege of Leningrad, 1941–1995* (Cambridge: Cambridge University Press, 2009); Catherine Merridale, *Night of Stone: Death and Memory in Twentieth-Century Russia* (New York: Viking, 2000); Michael Meng, *Shattered Spaces: Encountering Jewish Ruins in Germany and Poland* (Cambridge: Harvard University Press, 2011); Michael Steinlauf, *Bondage to the Dead: Poland and the Memory of the Holocaust* (Syracuse, NY: Syracuse University Press, 1996); and the collection of essays

in Rubie Watson, ed., *Memory, History, and Opposition under State Socialism* (Santa Fe: School of American Research, 1994).
34. Aleida Assmann, "Transformations Between History and Memory," *Social Research*, Vol. 75, No. 1 (Spring 2008), pp. 49–72, here p. 55.
35. Ibid., p. 64.
36. Given the restrictive nature of East German society, it is necessary to adapt Maurice Halbwachs's concept of a "social memory" when we look at collective memory in the GDR (Maurice Halbwachs, *On Collective Memory*, trans. and ed. Lewis A. Coser [Chicago: University of Chicago Press, 1992]). Within a pluralistic society, the collective frameworks that structure Halbwachs's understanding of social memory would themselves be constructed through a social process of negotiation between interest groups with dominant and counter-veiling memories in dialogue in the public sphere. In the context of East Germany, however, the party sought to control how these frameworks functioned in the public sphere. This is not to deny the existence of other frameworks (such as personal experience or religious affiliation), but acknowledge that they were restricted by the SED from playing a significant role in determining state policy.
37. Konrad Jarausch, "Zeitgeschichte und Erinnerung. Deutungskonkurrenz oder Interdependenz?" in Jarausch and Sabrow, *Verletztes Gedächtnis*, pp. 9–37, p. 14.
38. Herf, *Divided Memory*, p. 162.
39. Konrad Jarausch and Michael Geyer, *Shattered Pasts: Reconstructing German Histories* (Princeton, NJ: Princeton University Press, 2002); Robert Moeller, *War Stories: The Search for a Usable Past in the Federal Republic of Germany* (Berkeley: University of California Press, 2003); Norbert Frei, *Adenauer's Germany and the Nazi Past: The Politics of Amnesty and Integration* (New York: Columbia University Press, 2002).
40. Martin Sabrow, "Auf der Suche nach dem materialistischen Meisterton. Bauformen einer nationalen Gegenerzählung in der DDR," in Jarausch and Sabrow, *Die historische Meistererzählung*, pp. 33–77; Chistoph Cornelißen, "Der wiederentstandene Historismus. Nationalgeschichte in der Bundesrepublik der fünfziger Jahre," in Jarausch and Sabrow, *Die historische Meistererzählung*, pp. 78–108.
41. Andreas Dorpalen: *German History in Marxist Perspective: The East German Approach* (Detroit: Wayne State University Press, 1985), Ulrich Neuhäusser-Wespy, *Die SED und die Historie: die Etablierung der marxistisch-leninistischen Geschichtswissenschaft in der DDR in der fünfziger und sechziger Jahren*. (Bonn: Bouvier, 1996), Alexander Fisher and Günther Heydemann, eds., *Geschichtswissenschaft in der DDR* (Berlin: Duncker & Humbolt, 1988).
42. Martin Sabrow, ed., *Verwaltete Vergangenheit: Geschichtskultur und Herrschaftslegitimation in der DDR* (Leipzig: Akademische Verlagsanstalt, 1997) and Martin Sabrow and Peter Th. Walther, eds., *Historische Forschung und sozialistische Diktatur: Beiträge zur Geschichtswissenschaft in der DDR* (Leipzig: Leipziger Universitätsverlag, 1995).
43. For a discussion of how textbooks perform a parallel function of reinforcing the memory politics of other objects and aid in the overall construction of a state memory culture, see: Nothnagle, *Building the East German Myth*, and Benita Blessing, *The Antifascist Classroom: Denazification in Soviet-Occupied Germany, 1945–1949* (New York: Palgrave Macmillan, 2010).
44. Cortney Glore Crimmens, "Reinterpreting the Soviet War Memorial in Berlin's Treptower Park after 1990," in *Remembering the German Democratic Republic: Divided Memory in a United Germany*, ed. David Clarke and Ute Wölfel (London: Palgrave Macmillan, 2011), pp. 54–64; Rudy Koshar, *From Monuments to Traces: Artifacts of German Memory, 1870–1990* (Berkeley: University of California Press, 2000), pp. 283–84; Anne Fuchs, *After the Dresden Bombing: Pathways of Memory, 1945 to the Present* (London: Palgrave Macmillan, 2011).

Chapter One

MOBILIZING MEMORY IN THE SOVIET OCCUPATION ZONE

Like a tailor with his scissors, needle, and thread, the political leaders of what became East German sought to shape, trim, add, and cut out pieces of a society's collective memory. Collective memory is one of many threads that weave through the metaphoric cloth that is a nation. In most democratic nations, the collective memory is the subject of great debate and contestation. The level of debate within a totalitarian state, however, is often severely restricted. Yet political leaders in East Germany still saw great value in influencing collective memory and hoped in the immediate postwar era that this would aid them in their quest for legitimacy. They sought to influence the vernacular memory culture of their citizens and thereby acquire cultural legitimacy for their policies. When the leadership of the KPD, renamed the SED in April 1946, returned to the SBZ from its exile in the Soviet Union, it set to work not only to coordinate the provision of food, shelter, and other basic necessities—it also began the process of cultivating a distinct vision of the past.

The cultural theorist Aleida Assmann has argued that memory politics in modern dictatorial regimes attempt to impose pre-modern modes of memory onto modern societies. "Whereas in premodern cultures, there were neither media nor institutions of writing independent of power and authority that could back up independent accounts of the past, the institution of censorship served the function to destroy rival media and carriers of counterhistories that threatened the stability of a uniform view and an authoritarian voice of history. Totalitarianism can therefore be described as an attempt to restore the premodern state monopoly over history under modern circumstances and with modern means."[1]

In the specific case of the Soviet Occupation Zone and the territory that would become East Germany, the SED took a leading role in attempting

---

Notes for this chapter begin on page 46.

to secure a monopoly over the political use of memory. Many of the monuments, public commemoration events, and historical museum exhibits established or staged during the immediate post-war period in the Soviet zone were specifically chosen by the party for their symbolic relevance to the party's need for support and legitimacy. The reconstruction of the Socialists' Cemetery and the resumption of the annual Liebknecht-Luxemburg parade through central Berlin allowed the party to reconnect with earlier traditions of the Berlin working class. The commemoration events surrounding the 100th anniversary of the 1848 revolts allowed the party to wage a war of propaganda against similar commemorative efforts in the western zones. Finally, the museum exhibit on the "Other Germany" curated by former concentration camp victims with assistance from the party hoped to influence popular memories of life in the Third Reich and the crucial role played by German communists in resisting Nazism. While it is difficult to suggest that any of these projects qualify as a "success" for the party, each of these initiatives reveal aspects of an overall strategy by the party to alter the visible memory landscape and use these new symbols as a means to bolster its legitimacy in the immediate postwar period.

Historians Ilko-Sascha Kowalczuk and Stefan Wolle have argued that the SMAD controlled all aspects of political life during the occupation years.[2] It is certainly true that the SMAD played a more direct role in governing and policy making in the East than did the British, French or American occupation authorities in the West. The SMAD provided a great deal of collateral support to the SED and this influenced how the SED carried out its political work—including in the realm of memory politics. However, the SED also pursued political and cultural policies independent of the Soviet authorities. An examination of these early memory-work projects reveals that the communist party leadership was intent on linking its own claim to power to Germany's past. Given the limited—and sometimes scarce—resources available to the party, the fact that it chose to invest time, energy, and financial resources in memory projects reflected its belief that such projects represented more than self-celebration; it saw memory politics as an important means to bolster party and state legitimacy.

From the capitulation of German forces in May 1945 to the founding of the East German state (the German Democratic Republic or GDR) in 1949, the KPD (after 1946 the SED) worked to establish a foothold in the memory culture of the SBZ. The strategy employed by the SED closely allied itself with similar trends to shape historical interpretation among professional historians. As Alexander Fischer has documented, leading Communist intellectuals, political activists, and historians set to work immediately following the war to employ the teachings of Marx to interpret German history. Fischer points to the pioneering work of Ernst Niekisch and Alexander Abusch as setting the tone for the party's initial interpretation of the "misery" theory of German history—tracing the roots of Nazism to a line of historical development that spanned from Frederick the Great to Bismarck, and Emperor William II to Hitler.[3] Fischer argues that both Niekisch and Abusch desired to use their Marxist interpretation of German history to combat what they felt had been a connection between "bourgeois" historians and the nationalist political establishment.[4] Within the realm of memory politics, this meant that the SED needed to reshape the memory landscape to reflect this new Marxist interpretation. Concretely, the party needed to remove symbols of memory that supported competing visions of the past and create new elements that would instead support its interpretation.

This search for a usable past was not unique to the East or to the Communist Party, but it took on a different character in the East.[5] The difference lay primarily in the KPD/SED's own ideological premise of historical materialism, the belief that history progressed according to known laws of development, the trajectory of which was predetermined and inevitable. The role of a Marxist-Leninist-Stalinist party was to speed this process along and stay in control while doing so. Moreover, this period of transition was made all the more complicated by the artificial nature of Germany's division and the party's own goal of a united (and communist) German future. Thus, during this first period following the war, the SED's priorities centered around legitimizing itself as a viable political party and consolidating its power in the cultural as well as political realm. As Martin Sabrow has argued, regardless of whether this new historical interpretation was overwhelmingly accepted as fact by the masses or not, it did begin the process of establishing politically acceptable symbols of the past.[6] Thus the party attempted during this period to populate the public sphere with its own images of the past that it felt could best help bolster its own political views.

The political situation in the SBZ remained relatively fluid during the immediate postwar period.[7] There was no overarching plan for the creation of an East German state in 1945, nor had Stalin decided how far he was going to push the Western allies on the issue of neutrality. Although the KPD/SED was the dominant voice in the public sphere, its transition to power was relatively slow. Given the uncertainty of Germany's future geographic composition, the Communists' political message was confined to the SBZ but was aimed implicitly at the entire German population. In a similar manner, Germany's general memory culture in the aftermath of the Nazi dictatorship was in a state of flux. Shame prevented public statements of remorse while guilt suppressed the open exaltation of war heroes in any of the occupation zones. Occupation forces strictly monitored the press and dictated acceptable parameters for discourse regarding the war years.

Given such restrictive parameters in the public sphere, it is not surprising that the dominant discourse in the SBZ focused on the Communist view that fascism was the climax of capitalism. Communists in the SBZ developed a rhetorical dichotomy that equated fascism with capitalism and antifascism with communism. The corollary of this dichotomy implied that only communism represented the antifascist elements of society and thus provided the struggle for communism with a strong moral argument in the effort to rally support.[8] Yet the KPD/SED still needed to convince the population in the SBZ to support this interpretation. One of the most visible methods of doing so was to occupy public spaces with new interpretations of the past and to place new emphasis on specific historical events and to remove or reinterpret sites that worked against the KPD/SED's objectives. The SED calculated that the elevation of the antifascist resistance movement as a significant and positive influence during the Nazi period could offer a liberating path out of the guilt that plagued many in postwar German society. Party officials believed that they could convince Germans who followed the antifascist corollary to its logical conclusion that they could absolve themselves of guilt by supporting the Communist (i.e. antifascist) cause. Moreover, the defeat of Nazi Germany by the Soviet Red Army reinforced the idea of the superiority and "correctness" of communism in the struggle against fascism (without reference to the other non-communist forces who also contributed to Germany's defeat).

By elevating the role of the Communist resistance movement during the years of Nazi control, the KPD and SED sought to supplant competing interpretations of the past and elevate the importance of its own history above others. Within the larger context of rethinking the German past according to the Communist perspective, the SED wanted to locate the history of Communist resistance within a longer period of struggle between workers and traditional authority figures. Instead of a national history that highlighted great figures from Luther to Bismarck, the SED now focused on the history of the German labor movement, the influence of Karl Marx, August Bebel, Rosa Luxemburg, and Karl Liebknecht or the revolts of 1848 and the attempted revolution in 1918. The most difficult hurdle facing the KPD and SED was how to project this counter-memory onto the wider German population in a way that might cultivate a new sense of historical consciousness.

Thus, the KPD/SED set out to educate the masses about these events and propagate a specific politicized interpretation in an attempt to gain loyalty and win over supporters for their cause. Early initiatives to construct places of memory in the SBZ were thus overwhelmingly "antifascist" in nature, as opposed to the more traditional Christian and "unpolitical" monuments being constructed in the West.[9] The case studies below highlight a few examples of how the KPD/SED set out to alter the memory landscape and begin the process of cultivating a new official culture of remembrance in the SBZ. These early events were also part of a learning process for the party and these lessons helped shape future memory projects. Not only do the SED's subsequent projects evolve differently due to its previous experience, but the message of this early period is also different than what we find later on. The memory projects pursued by the party during this first stage were keenly oriented toward bolstering party legitimacy and its claim to power, while later initiatives centered more generally on legitimizing the socialist state. With the establishment of an independent state in 1949, the party had more freedom to assert its vision. At the same time, aligning the party's needs with the visions of those who carried out such projects proved to be something that would plague the party's memory-work from the start.

Making Room for New Memories

As the KPD began its work in the cultural sphere it first needed to rid the public space of the visual legacies of Germany's past heroes. This process involved removing monuments erected by the Nazi regime—as well as many monuments built during Germany's Second Empire—that paid tribute to heroic soldiers and rulers. The decisions to remove such figures were neither immediate nor spontaneous. Throughout the SBZ, cities created special commissions to examine the existing memory landscape and judge each on an individual basis. For example, Berlin's department of city planning (*Abteilung für Bau- und Wohnungswesen*) produced a report for the Berlin Magistrate (the local government) in January 1946 that prioritized a list of monuments to be removed from public view. The report divided monuments into three categories: monuments to be removed and destroyed; monuments to be removed, but held for museum use; and monuments to be left in place. The first category listed monuments that were dedicated to or constructed by the Nazi regime or incorporated any of the Nazi symbols, naming the Schlageter Monument (in honor of a *Freikorps* member killed during the French occupation of the Ruhr Valley) in the palace park in Berlin-Friedrichsfelde as a prime example and one that should "be removed in coordination with an antifascist rally."[10] The report summarized that it was not "what" these monuments portrayed *per se*, but the Nazi style that determined their removal.

The second list was more complex, since it attempted to evaluate the remains of historically important monuments based on their level of destruction and artistic value. Examples included the statues that comprised the Victory Alley in the Tiergarten Park.[11] The department concluded these monuments were of minimal level of artistic worth, noting that they were constructed primarily to develop nationalist sentiment and legitimize the dynastic rule of the last emperor.[12] These monuments were eventually removed from public sight and placed into a storage facility. The last category of the report dealt with monuments constructed during the Baroque and Classical periods. Examples included Schinkel's monuments commemorating the War of Liberation as well some statues of international artistic importance, such as the Monument of the Prince Elector. One of the most interesting cases was the department's effort to preserve the famous statue of Frederick the Great. Members of the committee argued that, although one could not speak of a cult, the monument "has a place in the hearts of the Berliners, for whom it is a piece of old-Berlin life, which they experience here." Clearly, the thought was to preserve a portion of Berlin tradition (even if it might evoke a few unwanted references) in order to avoid cutting off *all* remnants of the past.[13]

Maintaining such threads of historical continuity was not only about tradition; it was also a central ideological concern for the communists. At the first Cultural Conference of the SED in May 1948, Anton Ackermann, who at the time was a member of the SED Central Secretariat and one of its leading ideologues, explained the important role of history and historical consciousness during the construction phase of socialism in Germany. Ackermann stated that all of the actions of the SED were driven by its adherence to the principles of Marxism-Leninism, including its cultural policies. Moreover, he argued: "the theory of Marxism-Leninism is the reflection of historical reality in the consciousness of the people."[14] This is to say, Marxism-Leninism was the acknowledgment that history develops according to laws, which in turn reflect a conscious awareness of the necessity and correctness of the SED's policies. Accordingly, antifascist rhetoric needed to be placed within a broader conceptualization of history's progression. The culmination of history was to be the triumph of the working class, a goal yet to be achieved on German soil in 1948.

Such ideological conceptions regarding the role of culture in postwar Germany and its instrumentalization in the struggle for communism illustrate some of the underlying themes that guided the SED's politics of memory during this period. Early commemorations included a litany of historical figures who played significant roles in the struggle of the working class: Karl Liebknecht, Rosa Luxemburg, Vladimir Lenin, Karl Marx, August Bebel, Ernst Thälmann and other leaders of the German labor movement. Events such as the hundredth anniversary of the 1848 revolution, the yearly celebration of the anniversary of the "Great October Revolution," and other great moments in communist and labor movement history formed core commemoration events of the postwar period in the SBZ. The party celebrated important "neutral" figures such as Goethe and Schiller with new emphasis on their contribution to the German humanist tradition. David Bathrick, in his study of East German culture, notes that "from its very inception as a party in the late 1940s, the struggle by the SED to appropriate and identify itself with the 'proper' cultural heritage was one means by which the ruling party elite sought to verify its claim to be the bona fide successor to all 'progressive' and 'humanistic' traditions in the German past."[15]

The KPD and SED's core message during this period intended to highlight both the correctness (the *Gesetzmässigkeit*) and the moral superiority of their policies vis-à-vis those in the Western occupation zones. The following three examples represent a sampling of the SED's early memory-work and serve as points of entry into the complex set of values and symbols employed by the party: the reconstruction of the *Gedenkstätte der Sozialisten* (the Socialists' Memorial); the 1948 commemoration of the 1848 revolution; and the 1948 traveling exhibit "The Other Germany," produced by the Association of Nazi Persecutees (VVN). These examples of KPD/SED memory-work were significant not only because of their topics but also because of their temporal scope and the amount of attention and resources they commanded. Two of these early memory projects involved reactivating and shaping recent memories in an effort to influence what Maurice Halbwachs referred to as the frameworks of memory—the parameters within which recollections are formed.[16] The third project, the 100th anniversary of the 1848 revolution, commemorated an event that was no longer a part of living memory, yet had long been sustained by popular folklore within the German labor movement. The SED intended its commemoration events to function as a link between what it saw as the working class's tradition of struggle and the SED's present struggle for a new (communist) Germany.

The Socialists' Memorial

When it came to constructing a new communist memory culture in the SBZ, details were important. For example, the pre-1945 history of the *Gedenkstätte der Sozialisten* (the Socialists' Memorial) at the Friedrichsfelde cemetery in the far eastern portion of Berlin was a central factor in determining how the site would be used in the postwar era. First of all, it was important for the later symbolic nature of the site that the first person buried at the new cemetery had been a worker—one too poor to have purchased a plot in one of the other Berlin area cemeteries. During the first part of the twentieth century, the Friedrichsfelde cemetery quickly became the preferred place of final rest for the leaders of the Berlin labor movement, including Wilhelm Liebknecht (1900), Ignaz Auer (1907), and Paul Singer (1911).[17] Following the murders of Karl Liebknecht and Rosa Luxemburg in January 1919, however, leading members of the revolutionary movement in Berlin hoped to have Liebknecht buried in a different cemetery—the Revolutionary Cemetery in Berlin-Friedrichshain, which had the graves of those killed during the 1848 revolution. The Berlin Magistrate denied the request, referring to Liebknecht as a "criminal" who belonged in the cemetery in Friedrichsfelde. Although this decision disallowed an association of Liebknecht with Germany's revolutionary tradition, his internment in Friedrichsfelde allowed his followers to trumpet a link between Liebknecht's actions and the traditions of the German labor movement.

Immediately following the funeral service for Liebknecht, Wilhelm Pieck (a founding member of the KPD and later the GDR's first president) launched a fundraising campaign to erect a worthy monument dedicated to the *Januarkämpfer*, the "January fighters" killed during the short-lived Spartacist uprising in 1919. On 15 January, the last day of fighting, both Rosa Luxemburg and Karl Liebknecht were captured and shot by the radical *Freikorps* irregular troops that the government had called in to assist against the rebellion. While Liebknecht's body was brought to the city morgue, Luxemburg's body was not recovered immediately. Her body was not found until June when it was pulled from Berlin's Landwehr Canal and then laid to rest beside that of Liebknecht.[18] Pieck and others transformed the area around both graves into a central memorial for the Socialist movement that now included thirty-two other victims of the January revolution. Bauhaus architect Mies van der Rohe designed the original monument that stood next to the two graves. The words "I was, I am, I will be"—Rosa Luxemburg's famous last written words from the day she was murdered—formed the focal point of the monument.[19]

Throughout the 1920s until the political takeover by the Nazis, the KPD and the German Federation of Unions (DGB) coordinated efforts to hold annual mass demonstrations each January at the site of the Socialists' Memorial as a way to keep the memories of Liebknecht and Luxemburg alive and politically relevant. Prior to each rally, Berlin's working class demonstrated its solidarity by organizing mass marches through the center of the city. These marches culminated at the foot of the Socialists' Memorial. Over the years the importance of the cemetery in Friedrichsfelde grew, and it not only became a site of memory for Liebknecht and Luxemburg, but also developed into the preferred place of burial for all of the "fighters" of the labor movement—those killed in the January and March uprisings in 1919, during the Kapp-Putch in 1920, the March riots in 1921, and the Hamburg uprising in 1923.[20] Thus, although its roots were found in the memory culture of the Berlin labor movement, the cemetery slowly developed into a place of memory for the German labor movement and, over time, even incorporated gravesites for members of non-German leaders of the international labor movement.

With the Nazis' rise to power in 1933, the annual protest marches were halted. The potential of the site as a symbol of resistance did not escape the Nazis, who destroyed the monument and desecrated most of the graves in this section of the cemetery during the winter of 1934/35. Upon his return to Berlin following the end of hostilities in 1945, Wilhelm Pieck began work to restore the memorial site to its original state and thereby establish a line of continuity between the traditions of the German working class and the current work of the KPD. Pieck had a personal interest in the annual Liebknecht-Luxemburg parade and memorial service, since he had been responsible for organizing the construction of the original monument and had initiated the annual memorial rallies. In December 1945, Pieck and several other leading members of the KPD surveyed what remained of the gravesites of Liebknecht, Luxemburg, and the other socialists buried in cemetery. On the same day, Pieck wrote a letter asking Karl Maron, the deputy mayor of Berlin, to request that the Magistrate of the city of Berlin restore the gravesites of these and other fighters as well as the monument. Probably sensing that his request would be perceived as overly political, Pieck suggested to Maron that the restoration project be linked to restoring the memorial for the fighters of the 1848 revolution at the cemetery in Friedrichshain so that "the restoration of the gravesites of the *Januarkämpfer* in the cemetery in Friedrichsfelde would appear more like a general restoration of all three grave sites financed by the city."[21] Pieck's priorities, however, were made clear by the qualification that he attached to this request, stating that a clear priority must be given to the restoration of the gravesites of the *Januarkämpfer* in Friedrichsfelde.

Of particular interest here is the strategy devised by Pieck in order to push through his plan to reconstruct the memorial site. Although Pieck had a personal interest in seeing the Socialists' Memorial reconstructed, for strategic reasons he suggested placing the request for help in this reconstruction project within the broader context of renovating two other cemetery sites destroyed by the Nazi regime. Moreover, he rationalized the need for the Magistrate to fund the reconstruction by emphasizing the guilt of the Nazi regime and downplaying the site's importance for the city or the nation (or the party). It is important to keep in mind that, unlike other cities in the SBZ, Berlin remained a four-power city, so decisions concerning the distribution of public funds needed to be negotiated within the city council and approved by all four occupying powers. Nonetheless, Pieck was vehement in his assertion that the most important project of the three he discussed was the reconstruction of the monument for Liebknecht and Luxemburg.

Pieck was not alone in his attempt to gather support to reconstruct the Socialist Monument. Toni Eichhorn, an old party comrade of Pieck's from the Weimar period, wrote in a personal letter in February 1946 with a similar request that the party organize an effort to reconstruct the Socialist memorial: "I first came up with the idea in January on the anniversary of Rosa and Karl's death and now on Mehring's birthday it struck me again: Wouldn't it be good to restore the grave sites of *Rosa, Karl,* and *Mehring* at the small Revolutionary-Cemetery in Berlin-Lichtenberg (the Central Cemetery in Berlin)? ... I think it would be worthwhile today to restore this place of honor; ... I know, dear comrade Pieck, that there are many more important things on the agenda at the moment, but possibly it is also now time for things like this?"[22]

Eichhorn's letter highlights two aspects of the ways in which older memory culture traditions of the working class were carried over into the process of shaping KPD and SED memory politics in the SBZ. First, Eichhorn drew on personal memories of "Karl" and "Rosa" as well as other leading members of labor movement. Yet she was also cognizant that these figures were of great importance for the party, and she implied a need to respect those killed in the struggle of the working class. Her letter suggests who had the ability to influence discussions in the SBZ regarding memory projects: gaining access to members of the KPD/SED who were in positions of taking action was extremely difficult, but party members like Toni Eichhorn, who had been an active member of the KPD during the Weimar period, were able to have their opinions heard by members of the party's inner circle.

Although it is impossible to interpret the exact role played by Eichhorn's letter, it does seem to have pushed Pieck to keep his focus centered on reconstructing the Socialists' Cemetery in Friedrichsfelde. In July 1947, the Berlin Magistrate announced a public contest for the reconstruction of the monument. The jury comprised city representatives from both halves of Berlin as well as members of the SED and SPD. In February of the following year, the jury awarded the first prize to a design team comprised of landscape architect Walter Kossow, architecture professor Eduard Ludwig, and sculptor Gustav Seitz.[23] The onset of the Cold War and the Berlin Blockade, however, quickly put a stop to intra-city cooperation and halted the initial reconstruction effort.

The project to rebuild the memorial site at Friedrichsfelde resumed in February 1949, when Pieck wrote to the new chief mayor of the Soviet sector of Berlin, Friedrich Ebert, that the previously planned site for the new monument was too small for holding large political rallies. Pieck suggested that the city reconsider the project and look for a new site for the monument and gravesites. The Berlin Magistrate, the administrative apparatus for Eastern Berlin, responded to Pieck's request and agreed to move the monument project to the opposite end of the cemetery, which provided easy access from the street and was large enough to host mass demonstrations. The original design team, however, declined to rework its proposal to accommodate the new site and abandoned the project altogether. Instead, a collective headed by the landscape architect Reinhold Lingner took over the project.

The new memorial included a large ringed-wall that displayed dozens of memorial plaques and was designed to hold the cremation urns of future socialist leaders. An inner ring held eight memorial plaques set in the ground in remembrance of Karl Liebknecht, Rosa Luxemburg, Ernst Thälmann, Rudolf Breitscheid, Franz Mehring, Wilhelm Sylt, Johnny Schehr, and Franz Künzler (later, plaques were laid for Wilhelm Pieck, Otto Grotewohl, and Walter Ulbricht). Instead of reconstructing the former monument designed by Mies van der Rohe, or even a new interpretation thereof, the party leadership chose a simple stone with the words: "The dead admonish us" (*Die Toten Mahnen Uns*).[24] Unlike the former inscription of "*Ich war, ich bin, ich werde sein*," the new inscription reflected the SED's attempt to link the struggle of the working class with the antifascist resistance movement and highlighted the symbolic idea that these victims of past struggles served as a warning to the current generation. Whereas the former memorial symbolically linked the history of the German labor movement to the revolutionary actions of 1919, the new monument extended the narrative to include the communist resistance movement and later the SED. The SED's symbolic alterations during the reconstruction of the Socialists' Memorial illustrate how the party leadership hoped to extend the threads of tradition and establish a direct connection between a working class, non-fascist legacy, and the SED's current struggle over the future shape of Germany.

The physical reconstruction of the Socialist monument, however, was only half of the story of this site of memory for the KPD/SED. The memorial grounds also saw a resumption of the working class memory rituals of the 1920s and early 1930s honoring Liebknecht and Luxemburg. In January 1946, the KPD organized the first postwar Liebknecht-Luxemburg march through Berlin, which culminated in a mass commemoration near the site of the original monument. Local party members erected a temporary monument made of wood with the original inscription painted on the side (see figure 1.1). During the ceremony, Wilhelm Pieck not only spoke of his personal memories of Karl Liebknecht and Rosa Luxemburg but also drew on his memories from the first memorial service in 1919.[25] The political goal was to reestablish this working class site of memory and the traditions with which it was associated while, at the same time, controlling its ritualized staging and messages in order to gain political support in the ideological struggle of the postwar period.[26]

The opening ceremony for the new memorial was held on 14 January 1951, and followed in the tradition of commemorating Luxemburg and Liebknecht's sacrifices for the working class struggle. Each year, the party organized a march through Berlin that culminated with a rally where orators tailored their speeches to place the memory of Karl Liebknecht and Rosa Luxemburg into the present context of the SED's political priorities. Members of the party and the state also used the site for other activities throughout the year, including the distribution of membership cards for new members of the *Freie Deutsche Jugend* (FDJ) youth organization. Candidates and full members of the SED also often received either their party membership documents at these rallies.[27] By expanding the use of this

FIGURE 1.1. Wilhelm Pieck (far right) delivers a speech at the first postwar commemoration of Karl Liebknecht and Rosa Luxemburg at the Socialists' Cemetery in Berlin-Friedrichsfelde, 13 January 1946. BArch Bild 183-H27965

Figure 1.2. Renovated Socialists' Cemetery in Berlin-Friedrichsfelde, 1951. BArch Bild 183-19000-3751.

memorial site, the SED sought to take advantage of what it saw as an important legitimizing symbol in Berlin beyond its once-a-year use during the commemoration parade.

The Socialists' Memorial at Friedrichsfelde was one of the SED's most visible early memory projects in the SBZ and GDR and retained an important place as a site where the state and party would stage events up through 1989. Each January, the party sought to use the annual parade of Berlin's workers commemorating Liebknecht and Luxemburg to reify the authority of the SED as the inheritor of the traditions of Germany's working class. The party leadership, especially Wilhelm Pieck, was cognizant of the role such memory sites could play as a legitimizing and support-gathering tool in the political process of rebuilding German society in the immediate postwar period. Ultimately, the success or failure of this effort is difficult to judge given the lack of sources about the diverse motivations behind those who participated in these rallies—ranging from coercion to blind party support or genuine enthusiasm. Nonetheless, the reconstruction of the Socialists' Memorial marked one of the first attempts by the party to establish a line of continuity between the memory traditions of the pre-1933 German labor movement and its own politics in the postwar era. It played a unique role in articulating the party's new interpretation of history and its antifascist identity.

Commemorating the Revolution of 1848 (1948)

The commemoration events honoring the 1848 revolution in the Soviet Occupation Zone provided the SED with another opportunity to articulate its vision of the past and infuse its struggle for political control with historical significance and purpose. Throughout the history of the GDR, but especially during the immediate postwar period, the SED closely coordinated its memory-work with Soviet foreign policy objectives—preventing closer cooperation between the western allies and halting any movement toward the founding of an independent West German state. The commemoration events in March 1948 need to be viewed within the larger context of the mounting tensions between the Soviet Union and its former allies in the West and as part of the SED's effort to sway public opinion and further justify its own political priorities.

Throughout the first half of 1948, the United States, Great Britain, France, and the Benelux countries met in London to discuss closer economic cooperation and ultimately a currency reform in the three western occupation zones. The Soviet Union boycotted the meetings, allowing the western allies to move forward without the USSR derailing their plans. Ultimately, the western allies voted to introduce a new currency, the *Deutsche Mark* or DM, in the western zones in April and the Soviet Union responded with the Berlin Blockade in June, which would remain in place through May 1949.[28]

Domestically, the SED focused on bolstering public support for a united Germany, albeit one that retained a chance for communist control. As Paul Steege has argued, the SED was acutely aware that the party was losing ground in the struggle to keep Germany united and stepped up its public campaign, especially in the four-power city of Berlin.[29] Throughout 1948, the SED used its party-controlled newspaper, *Neues Deutschland,* to propagate its interpretation of the revolution. It waged a publicity campaign aimed at linking its current political and ideological struggle to the legacy of those who fought during the revolution. Although *Neues Deutschland* was just one of several newspapers published in Berlin, it had a dominant position throughout the rest of the SBZ and was the newspaper of record for the party faithful. As such, we can use it to analyze how the party set out to instruct members and would-be followers how the events of 1848 remained relevant for Germany's current political climate. What follows is a case study of how the SED employed its party newspaper to propagate a new interpretation of 1848 and link the commemoration to the party's political efforts in 1948.

The first step in the process was to articulate why the history of 1848 still was important for postwar German society. On 1 January 1948, *Neues*

Deutschland ran a short article highlighting the importance of 1848 for Germany's present situation, declaring that "the remembrance of the barricade-fighters and the people's movement for national unification will make a deep impression on our citizens, especially amongst the youth."[30] According to the article, there were important lessons to be drawn directly from history: it was the historical duty of the German working class, represented by the SED, to finish the incomplete revolution of 1848. Most importantly, the paper asserted that Germans needed to learn from the mistakes of 1848, namely that the German middle class had failed to ally itself with the workers and farmers.[31] By following this strategy, the SED hoped to advance its own interpretation of the past and at the same time highlight the immediate importance of a united front against what it saw as the remnants of German conservatism.

During January and February 1948, the SED's primary rhetorical strategy was to link the catastrophe of the Nazi period with what it declared to be the "bourgeoisie's" abandonment of the working class. According to this narrative, if the two classes had united, they would have successfully steered history along a different course. Moreover, just as the revolutions of 1848 marked the awakening of the working class in Europe, they also demonstrated the willingness and ability of the working class in Germany to fight for national interests. The SED invoked this latter element, not only to allay fears that the SED was too dependent on the Soviet Union but also to demonstrate that the SED would fight for Germany's national interests. Indeed, SED leaders claimed that Germany's failed revolution of 1848 arose out of a uniquely "German" context, despite the fact that other revolutions also occurred that year throughout Europe.[32]

In the 24 January 1948 edition of *Neues Deutschland,* the SED published its official historical interpretation of the 1848 events and presented its vision for commemoration activities. Again and again, the SED told readers that the revolution of 1848 had a direct connection to the current situation in Germany, both in terms of the desire for national unification and the need to continue the "social revolution." The articulation of the SED's position came at a time when the party had abruptly abandoned its stance that there was a uniquely "German road" to Socialism and adopted the Soviet model for its party organization. Some within the party found this new internationalist (or pro-Soviet) direction dangerous in the light of Germany's still uncertain division.[33] Thus, the SED attempted—somewhat paradoxically—to frame its portrayal of the 1848 revolution in terms of national unification, yet allow room for further integration into the Soviet sphere.

This apparent paradoxical position evolved in part because the SED leadership at that time wanted to keep its options open—unification on

Soviet terms was still considered a goal and perhaps even a distant possibility. But if divisions hardened, the party leadership needed an option of deeper integration into the Soviet sphere to ensure the regime's survival. Given this ambiguity of the SED's position, it asserted, for example, that just as "the German workers' movement fought decisively and consequently for the national interests of the German people [in 1848], it [now] claims the revolutionary traditions of 1848."[34] Despite such reference to the "German" workers' movement, the article placed the German workers' struggle clearly in the Soviet camp: "In this struggle we stand on the side of the German working class, the powers of the Soviet Union, the People's Democracies, and the progressive democratic forces in the entire world."[35]

On 30 January 1948, another article attempted to fill any gaps in the public's knowledge of the events between 1848 and 1914. In an effort to compensate for censorship over schooling and the press during the Nazi years, the SED sought to "rectify" previous interpretations of the events of 1848 (with its emphasis on the Frankfurt Parliament) and highlighted instead the role of actors that it declared had been purposely suppressed (such as workers). The party also highlighted what it viewed as the negative outcomes of 1848—including "forgotten" aspects that strengthened authoritarian rule and militarism, which in turn eventually led Germany into two world wars. These elements, the SED implied, "should never be forgotten."[36] By highlighting these supposedly forgotten actors and outcomes and infusing the historical consciousness of the population with new interpretations, the SED hoped to draw a direct connection between 1848 and the current political situation. A century earlier, it implied, Germany stood at the crossroads between democracy and fascism, between socialism and capitalism. The failure of the revolution allowed the political right to lead Germany down a path that led to two world wars. Now, Germany encountered a similar fork in the road of history and the SED wanted to stress that the memory of 1848 should not only be seen as a way to glance backward, but also as a warning for the future.

This first phase of representation in *Neues Deutschland* aimed at breaking up the historical narrative of the 1848 revolution into smaller, individual event narratives. For example, in some cases, the events in 1848 during a given week were simply laid out chronologically for readers to digest without any comment on the broader historical context or meaning of these events. By the end of February 1948, readers of *Neues Deutschland* had been provided with a general outline of events that led to the 1848 March riots as well as several background articles covering the general history of the March riots themselves. Moreover, the events were retold in a way that separated them from the philosophical and ideological ideals of 1848 and, surreptitiously, separated them from values related to the creation of democracy or the overthrow of an oppressive system.

Once deconstructed, such "event narratives" provided the party with an essential reservoir of knowledge, or manufactured memories, from which it hoped it could construct a new narrative that could best sway popular opinion in its favor. The effort to now put these event narratives back together in a manner that would form a new overarching narrative began in early February with articles focusing the March riots of 1848. The articles presented a storyline that contextualized the riots' importance within a longer view of German history and emphasized the present day importance of the commemoration events themselves. One example of these miniature history lessons can be found in the 3 February 1948 edition of *Neues Deutschland*: "The approaching March-days should not be merely days of remembrance, rather the activities and public addresses should give life to the time a hundred years ago, it should be an experience, especially for the youth."[37] Such rhetoric regarding contemporary commemorative events was meant to link events of the past to the current generation.

The SED sought to bring the history of 1848 closer to the hearts and minds of the East German people by combining these events with opportunities for active participation. To this end, theaters across the Eastern Zone prepared works related to the struggle of 1848; the *Deutsche Film-AG* (DEFA) prepared several short movies dealing with themes of revolution; regional museums and libraries began preparing special exhibitions commemorating successful regional struggles; and the Ministry of Education in Thuringia sponsored an essay contest for school children dealing with the events of 1848.[38] The German Administration for People's Education took the lead coordinating these commemoration events with the intent of heightening the role of 1848 in popular historical consciousness and, most importantly, to demonstrate the revolution's relevance to Germany's present situation. Above all, the SED hoped to reach out to workers through its rhetoric that the "working class" needed to seize the reigns of history and complete the communist revolution.

Beginning in March, the first objects of this virtual museum began to appear, starting with the bust of the revolutionary hero Robert Blum. A short article and accompanying photograph introduced readers to the work of Professor Richard Scheibe and students of Berlin's *Hochschule für bildende Künste* (School of Fine Arts), who produced twelve commemorative busts of revolutionary heroes and displayed at the Berlin Palace.[39] As the highpoint of the commemoration approached, *Neues Deutschland* began detailed day-by-day accounts of the events in 1848. For example, on 10 March 1948, *Neues Deutschland* focused on the theme of demagoguery and the sense of high tension that filled the air, thus setting the scene for Berlin in March 1848. The article described a group of nineteenth-century workers who chased a "demagogue" who had supposedly betrayed the "interests of the nation" across town and finally threw him into the Spree River. Returning to the present situation in Berlin, the paper labeled West German politicians, such as "Kaiser, Neumann, Swolinzky, Schwennicke" as anti-democratic figures and traitors to Germany's national interests.[40] Moreover, it reminded readers that Berlin remained under four-power occupation, which required people of all segments of society—shopkeepers, workers, merchants, and university students—to come together in the struggle against tyranny. Thus, the rhetorical strategy of the SED employed the use of historical analogy to draw links between the present situation and the events of 1848 and hoped that such analogies could bolster the party's claim that it was now the party battling against the "anti-democratic" forces.

On 11 March 1948, the newspaper emphasized that all progressive social forces joined together at the barricades in 1848, using any and all means at their disposal to fight for the interests of the German people. Regardless of political orientation, the SED asserted, the crisis in 1848 was of such magnitude that real differences between the classes were of little concern. The bulk of the article, however, jumped ahead and asked whether things were any different in 1948. The thrust of the argument was that reactionary forces in the West continued the fascist traditions of the Nazi and pre-Nazi periods. These forces, according to the SED, used misinformation and manipulation to undermine the interests of the German people. Accordingly, it was up to the people of the SBZ to reaffirm Germany's tradition of national solidarity and collective action in the face of oppression.[41]

Neues Deutschland used historical analogy to make a direct link between events in pre-riot Berlin 1848 and contemporary events in March 1948: "reactionary" forces were dividing the working class, while the "bourgeoisie" formed new industrial interest groups. According to this rhetorical strategy, the traditions and ideals of the "revolutionaries," who represented the "progressive" forces of society at that time, were telescoped onto the "progressive, revolutionary forces" of 1948, namely the SED. As the SED's rhetoric sharpened, it became clear that its primary target was the political party just to its right, the Social Democratic Party of Germany (SPD). The SED argued that the SPD had supported the formation of industrial interest groups competing against one another instead of joining forces with the communists against the capitalists. According to the SED, the SPD was wavering on the question of unification, which was further threatened by the creation of "Bizonia" (the merging of the American and

British occupation zones) and by rumors of a possible currency reform in the Western zones. Finally, the SED's narrative sought to highlight the SED's proclaimed antifascist credentials. The article ended with a call for all people in Berlin to attend the mass demonstration at the graves of the fallen revolutionary heroes. The rally, organized by local SED leadership, hoped to capitalize on the symbolic power of the commemorative event to bolster its political message.

Again on 12 March 1948, the call went out to the people in the SBZ to follow the traditions of the 1848 revolutionaries and fight the reactionary forces of the present. Imperialism, according to the SED, remained the common enemy of the German people, now in the form of foreign, i.e. American, influence over Germany's destiny. In an attempt to mobilize popular support for a strong, independent position vis-à-vis the Western occupation forces, the SED organized a meeting of a "national" People's Congress in mid-March, harkening back to the 1848 congress in Frankfurt: "Our 'barricade' during these March days is the second German People's Congress for unity and rightful peace on the 18th of this memory-filled month in Berlin."[42]

The SED's efforts in the Soviet Sector of Berlin stood in direct opposition to and competition with a similar public campaign mounted in the three western sectors of the city. Conservative Christian Democratic Union (CDU) politician Jakob Kaiser led the campaign to hold a counter-demonstration in front of the Reichstag building next to the Brandenburg Gate, which symbolically marked the division between the Soviet Sector and the three western sectors. Together with the SPD and the LDP, Kaiser wanted to demonstrate a united "anti-front" against the SED-planned commemoration of the People's Congress.[43] While the commemoration events in eastern Berlin were planned for some months, including a dedicated youth service project to clear away remaining rubble on the Gendarmenmarkt, preparations in the West were more hurried. Yet, with the help of the American and British military governments, bulldozers and cranes managed to move away some 30,000 cubic meters of rubble in front of the Reichstag in just ten days to create a suitable place to hold the counter-demonstration.[44] The uniting slogan for the western counter-demonstration called for "freedom against totalitarian movements." In the week leading up to the two competing commemorations, each side attempted to hang posters in the other sectors, but the Soviets outlawed the hanging of posters from the western sectors and the three western occupying powers reciprocated by banning any SED posters displayed in their sectors. *Neues Deutschland* reported that American military personnel and Berlin civil servants raided SED offices in western Berlin, photographing and confiscating documents pertaining to the upcoming People's Congress.[45] Thus tensions were on the rise during the lead up to the commemorative week on both sides of the sector border and highlight the elevated importance that the party placed on the commemorative events the following week.

From 13 to 18 March 1948, *Neues Deutschland* ran day-by-day accounts of the happenings of March 1848, paired with reports on the various commemorative events in 1948. The paper devoted three or four articles a day to various accounts of the events a hundred years prior, always relating them to the "historical mission" of the working class to "complete" the unfinished revolution. Heinrich Deiters, professor of history at the Berlin University published a column during the commemorative week titled "The Lessons of 1848." Each installment drew parallels between the struggles of 1848 and 1948, reconstructing the historical context and emphasizing the timeless elements of class struggle.[46]

The commemoration week culminated with the second meeting of the German People's Congress, which called for German unity, a just peace, a democratic and antifascist Germany, and Berlin as the capital of an undivided German republic. Parades and speeches celebrated the "undying spirit of 48."[47] 2200 delegates to the People's Congress met in the Admiralspalast theater building and elected Wilhelm Pieck (SED), Wilhelm Külz (LDP), and Otto Nuschke (CDU) to the presidium of the new protoparliament of the SBZ. As a culminating event, the SED gathered the party faithful for a public act of commemoration on the Gendarmenmarkt lo-

FIGURE 1.3. Commemoration in Berlin of the 1848 March Revolt on 18 March 1948. SAPMO-BArch Bild Y1-24759 / H. Meyer.]

cated about a kilometer away from the theater and marched through Berlin to the Cemetery for the March Victims in Berlin-Friedrichshain, where Wilhelm Pieck proclaimed: "We are the culmination of the unfinished revolution."[48]

Ending the official commemoration of the March revolution at the cemetery in Berlin-Friedrichshain was a key element of the SED's overall symbolic message. The SED purposely planned and articulated a combination of past and present with the intent to transform the act of commemoration into a "site of memory," where the past, that is, the dead—were given new meaning, and symbolic life. From a strictly historical perspective, these men and women died while struggling to transform their own social order within the specific historical context of spring 1848. Yet, by investing this memory with a new timeless meaning, the SED hoped that the memory of these victims could take on a new, and powerful, significance and thus help legitimize its own rule.

Neues Deutschland concluded its three-month constant run of 1848-themed articles with an article excerpted from Franz Mehring's book on the March Revolution. The article used Mehring's legacy as a revolutionary from the 1919 Berlin uprising to summarize the party's interpretation of the March riots once again. But for the first time, it also advanced the narrative into the summer of 1848, highlighting where he (and by extension the SED) believed that the middle class delegates to the Frankfurt Parliament betrayed the working class during the summer and fall of 1848. The article ended the history lesson by arguing that the delegates in 1848 lacked the will to press for real political change and instead "threw in the towel."[49] By invoking the legacy of Franz Mehring, who fought alongside German Communism's founding figures like Rosa Luxemburg and Karl Liebknecht, the SED hoped to demonstrate that their interpretation of history and the party's continued struggle was not something new, but part of a longer German tradition.

Throughout this commemoration period in 1948, the SED used its party newspaper, *Neues Deutschland*, to present the history of 1848 to the public as individual historical events, sometimes linked to a greater line of historical continuity and at other times allowed to remain as isolated moments. Out of these "event narratives" the party sought to extrapolate elements that it felt could communicate an enduring relevance, such as the struggle for German unification and the overthrow of "reactionary" forces. These "event narratives" were then integrated into the party's public commemoration calendar. Through commemorative events such as essay contests or parades, the SED attempted to bring the experience of the events to life and make history tangible, and thus to implant these historical events into the nation's collective memory banks.

The final part of this process involved representing both the historical event and the commemorative event in such a manner as to create a link between the past and the present political process. Again and again, the SED tried to use the authoritative power of history to lend credence to its own policies, while, at the same time, emphasizing only one particular and clearly ideologically driven interpretation of Germany's past. Competing directly against the counternarrative being constructed by politicians in the western sectors of Berlin and throughout the three western occupation zones, the SED was desperate to seize hold of the commemorative moment in March 1848 and use it to propagate its own vision for the future of Germany—one that would be under its control and influence.

The VVN Exhibit "The Other Germany"

Like the resumption of the Liebknecht-Luxemburg parades and the commemoration of 1848, the museum exhibit "The Other Germany" by the VVN in 1948 provides another example of the SED's early efforts in the realm of memory-work and how the SED sought to connect the past to the present. Founded in 1947, the VVN was an outgrowth of the Victims of Fascism (*Opfern des Faschismus*—OdF) organization. While both organizations aimed to protect and lobby on behalf of those Germans who were persecuted during the Nazi regime, the VVN was more closely linked to the SED, while local OdF organizations remained non-partisan and were more focused on securing pension and disability payments for members. As such, the VVN served as a mouthpiece for the SED in educating the German public about KPD members who were imprisoned and sentenced to death for anti-Nazi political views.[50]

The original idea for a VNN museum exhibit came from Franz Dahlem, a member of the SED Central Committee, director of the SED secretariat's department of personnel, and the SED department that dealt with relations with the Western zones. His original idea for an exhibit carried the title "The Secret Germany" but changed it to "The Other Germany" in order to emphasize the differences between the experiences of those in the resistance and those of the active followers of the Nazi regime. The exhibit, put together by a four-man research team under the leadership of Heinz Zantoff, was a foretaste of future history museum exhibits in the GDR (in particular the Museum for German History).[51] The exhibit began with a history of the Peasants' War and progressed through German history, highlighting failed attempts and missed opportunities in Germany's revolutionary tradition, including March 1848, November 1919, and throughout the Third Reich. In other rooms the VVN sought to portray how "false" beliefs in autocratic or "bourgeois" power relations led to political catastrophes—in the Weimar Republic, under the Hitler dictatorship, and other examples from across Europe. Thus, the pedagogical aim of the exhibit was to vilify most of the previous forms of German government and demonstrate how each form had prevented the working class from achieving political power.

For the exhibition objects, the VVN relied primarily on memory pieces of former concentration camp prisoners, works of art either by these former inmates or depictions of life in a concentration camp, newspaper articles, and textual explanation. In order to gather the necessary documents and objects, the VVN sent out a call to its local chapters in March 1947 asking that each chapter form a working group to research the history of the resistance movement in their area. In a similar vein, VVN members who were imprisoned together were called upon to also form working groups to document the history of their internment.[52]

The VVN exhibit organizers displayed the objects and accompanying texts in a simplified form. They consistently portrayed the politically persecuted (i.e. the communists) as the heroes of the resistance movement. The exhibit brochure set the tone with an introductory greeting from Ottomar Geschke, the leader of the VVN in the SBZ. Geschke made it clear in his greeting that the exhibit was first and foremost about the political aspects of Nazi aggression: "The KZs [concentration camps] were built for

FIGURE 1.4. Entrance to the exhibit "The Other Germany" in Berlin, September 1948. SAPMO-BArch Bild Y1-22336.

them, the political opponents of the Nazis in their own land."⁵³ The exhibit organizers split the narrative into eight sections. The exhibit began with a room that served as an introduction to the exhibit and focused on pre-1918 events that included the Peasants' War of 1525, the March Revolts of 1848, the November Revolution of 1918 and ended with the underground resistance movements during the Nazi years. From here, visitors were led into a room dedicated to the "pre-history" of the Nazi years—from 1918 to 1933. Here, the exhibit organizers focused on the political history of the Weimar Republic with special attention placed on what they called "the constant military conspiracies and attacks against life and the progressive development of the Republic."⁵⁴

The third room of the exhibit was a room of honor—displaying portraits of sixty-four victims with various political affiliations who died as a result of Nazi aggression. The exhibit brochure alerted the visitor that the room was meant as a place of honor and reflection—preparing the visitor for the rooms that followed. In the fourth room of the exhibit, visitors learned about life under Nazi rule. The primary message of the exhibit was to proclaim that preparations for war were at the heart of the Nazi political process and that the underground resistance stood alone it its attempt to warn the German people of the dangers that lay ahead.

The fifth and sixth rooms of the exhibit covered the period of the war, which it labeled the "enslavement of the European peoples," and the col-

FIGURE 1.5. Interior view of the exhibit "The Other Germany" in Berlin, September 1948. SAPMO-BArch Bild Y1-22361.

lapse of the Nazi regime. In both rooms, the exhibit attempted to illustrate that the underground resistance was not able to gain enough strength to topple the Nazi regime on its own. In the end, outside military forces were needed to free the German people from the Nazi yolk. By emphasizing the lack of support for resistance among the majority of Germans, the exhibit hoped to link the failure of political resistance during the Nazi period back to those earlier "failures" from the introductory room—the "failed" revolts of 1525, 1848, and 1918. The "lesson" that the exhibit desired to teach was that contemporary Germany must learn from these failures when rebuilding postwar Germany. Indeed, this message formed the core of the last two rooms of the exhibit, which covered the "liberation" and Germany's rebuilding. In both sections, the exhibit emphasized that there were Germans who had always resisted Nazi aggression and that these same Germans were now ready to lead Germany into a better future.[55]

Important places such as Buchenwald and other concentration camps were not covered in the exhibit (probably due to the fact that the SED had not yet secured a dominant position within the Buchenwald victims group and thus could not control any of the contributions that would have been made—see chapter 2). Resistance groups or actions by non-communists, such as the attempted assassination of Hitler on 20 July 1944 by German conservatives (one of the most important examples of resistance in the West German narrative) were not addressed in the exhibit.[56] All in all, the portrayal of the German resistance movement in this exhibit was one-sided, self-serving, and did not represent the broad range of experiences shared by other members of the German population.

Through descriptions of the exhibit and reports published in the local newspapers in East Berlin, the SED hoped to convey its intended meaning and purpose. The newspaper reports emphasized (or overemphasized) the role played by the German communist resistance movement in the struggle against Hitler and fascism: "In the eight exhibition rooms one sees the entire tragic path of German people through artistic images accompanied by text, statistics, and documentation. Every phase in German history is accompanied by the struggle of progressive people for democracy."[57] Other articles were more specific: "When one has wandered through rooms 1 through 7, one is exhausted. It is, however, not a physical exhaustion, but the emotional shock from the horrors. ... But when one enters room 8 one receives an answer to the question of the purpose of this suffering without measure or limits. [This is] an authentic answer, found in the artistic works of antifascist artists, who suffered and at times even lost their lives."[58]

The newspaper reports portrayed the communists as martyrs and victims who died for a greater cause and whose memories told the story of the "other Germany." The intent was to align the struggle against fascism with the SED's contemporary struggle with the West over the future of Germany and to demonstrate the correctness of this position to the general public.[59]

At the Berlin exhibit there was a box placed near the exit into which visitors could place notes with their thoughts and reactions to the exhibit. Many of the comments were positive, such as one by Vera R., a student at the economics school in Prenzlauer Berg: "I enjoyed the exhibit. ... It is good that school children are being shown this proof, since up until now, most people have not fully understood what happened."[60] Others pointed to the necessity for all Germans to be exposed to this interpretation of the recent past, like Friede S. of Johanisthal who proclaimed: "A people (*ein Volk*) must be forced to see this exhibit, *in order to understand and be reminded!*"

Many negative responses also accompanied the positive ones and highlight some of the problems and challenges that the SED faced during these early attempts at reshaping the postwar memory culture. Many respondents linked the current internment of Germans by the Soviet occupation forces with the Nazi concentration camps: "The exhibit appears incomplete. Where are the millions who have been murdered since 1917 in Russia? Where are those who are now imprisoned in the concentration camps run by the Russians and the SED? Has anything changed? My boys report that many antifascists, who spent time in concentration camps under Hitler, are there once again. Your 'exhibit' is communist rubbish!"

Here, the visitor drew a parallel between the harsh treatment of prisoners portrayed in the exhibit to question the tactics of the communists and of the Soviet occupation forces who had taken control of many of the concentration camps and used them as detention camps (as was the case with Buchenwald, which was used by the Soviets until 1950).

> Where is the room for how things are now?
> NSDAP   SS
>   SED   NKVD
>   The same[61]

In this example, the visitor used the comment slip to draw a parallel between the SED and the NSDAP and between the SS and the Soviet NKVD, implying that the new dominant party and its secret police (here making reference to the Soviet secret police) had much more in common with each other than the exhibit portrayed.

> I am deeply impressed by the exhibit and as a Christian I am against every form of terror and inhumanity. But when will humanity ever learn??? My uncle and

two friends as old as myself were killed in today's concentration camps!! When will we humans finally stop all this??? How can I support the current political orientation given such incidents? — A friend of humanity, 20 years old.

This last example drew not only on the images of the exhibit, but also on the visitor's own personal and familial experience. He saw no difference between the terror felt under the Nazis and the current feelings of terror experienced by people in the SBZ. Other comments aimed their hostility directly at the organizers of the exhibit: "With the exception of the exhibit, everything was great. Otherwise a pile of rubbish!!!"; "This exhibit is proof of your *stupidity*"; and "This is all nonsense. You all are stupid." Still others focused on a desire to forget the Nazi past rather than be reminded of what had happened in Germany, such as this visitor comment: "One should not show such things to children. Wouldn't it be better to just forget everything?" These examples indicate that many Germans disagreed with the VVN's portrayal of Nazi persecution and antifascist resistance during the war. Moreover, given the open nature of the city of Berlin in 1948, it is difficult to isolate whether these comments come from those in the East or from Germans living in other sectors of Berlin.

Most impressive from a memory culture perspective, however, were responses that drew a connection between the main topic in the exhibit—life in the concentration camp—and the plight of current victims of communist and Soviet terror. In such cases, the respondent looked past the correctness or legitimacy of the VVN's portrayal of life in the Nazi concentration camps and linked memories of the camps to the current political situation, a side effect that the SED certainly did not intend to generate with this exhibit.

The exhibit in Berlin was also a learning experience for the SED and the VVN. After its initial stint in Berlin, the exhibit toured throughout the SBZ. The box into which one could place such anonymous opinions (anonymous here being the key problem with the system in Berlin) was replaced by a guest book near the exit into which visors could write down their impressions in public and most probably in the immediate vicinity of a museum staff member. The effect of this new system was reflected in the types of responses that visitors wrote (at least those which were carried over into the party reports). They were strictly positive.[62]

This VVN exhibit illustrates some of the limits the SED encountered in its early efforts to occupy certain symbols and sites of memory as it attempted to forge a particular "socialist" memory culture that could help legitimize its rule. Personal memories from the Nazi period and earlier sometimes conflicted with the information being portrayed in the exhibit. Such contradictions were interpreted (as seen in the visitor responses) as blatant communist propaganda and thus lost its effectiveness to build loyalty to the SED's current political agenda. The SED learned through its efforts in this exhibit that future attempts to control interpretations of the past would need to be more sophisticated and nuanced. Above all, the SED learned from this first attempt at propagating a new national narrative that the process of reshaping a society's memory culture and influencing its historical consciousness was going to take a sustained effort and was not something that the party could simply create out of sheer will.

Conclusion

Together, these three examples show how the KPD and SED attempted to reshape the memory culture and historical consciousness in what was to become East Germany. Each example highlights several of the challenges and reveals some of the motivations behind the SED's memory politics. Unlike in western Germany, open public discussions regarding the selection of new political symbols were not part of the memory culture formation process in the East. The memory projects that the party chose to focus on during this first stage of reconstruction included a mixture of older traditions drawn from the history of Germany's working class and new attempts to embed the concept of antifascism into the new narrative of German history. The party sought to appropriate select elements of German history and interpret them in ways that it believed could help legitimize its own rule. The process of changing an entire memory culture was a complex and drawn-out affair. Results were not immediate and the impact on the public was hard to gauge. The goals set forth by such memory projects depended on the long-term secondary effects of association, and their ultimate usefulness as symbolic representation of the party's authority was equally dependent on the ability of the manipulators, in this case the SED, to provide future events or programs that drew on the core values and ideals portrayed in these works of memory.

The key element to the SED's attempts to style and shape a postwar memory culture that could help support and legitimate a new political system was the party's effort to draw upon a set of values and traditions embedded in the past and link these to the current situation. The reconstruction project at the cemetery in Berlin-Friedrichsfelde was a primary example of the SED's attempt to mobilize a previous memory ritual and appropriate this memory to serve the legitimating needs of the party. With the construction of a new monument in 1951, the SED both altered and expanded its meaning as a memory site. The legacy and memories of the labor movement were combined with those of the antifascist communists in an attempt to strengthen the roots of the new narrative. The commemoration of the 1848 revolution and the VVN's "The Other Germany" exhibit are both examples of how the SED projected its new historical narrative to the public, and attempted to connect past struggles of the working class to overcome what the party viewed as unjust power relationships with more recent and more present memories of resisting fascism. The competing commemorations in eastern and western sectors of Berlin in March 1948 also demonstrate that the SED was not completely in control of crafting its vision of the past and had to respond to countervailing voices from the west. The VVN exhibit also illustrates some of the differences and tensions between the SED's "official memory" and the vernacular memory of the German population. Mobilizing memory through the exhibit meant, first and foremost, educating the population about specific memories from a subset of those who had survived the concentration camps (and all but ignoring other camp narratives, most notably those of the Jews).[63]

These three examples do not address all the components of the vast spectrum of memory-work engaged in by the SED or the multiple experiences of the German people during this period. Nonetheless, they illustrate some of the basic tenants of the SED's memory-work. During the immediate postwar period, the future of Germany was still very uncertain. There were no concrete plans for its permanent division. With the reality of open borders, the SED viewed the mobilization of memories as an important tool in its search for non-material means of cultivating a loyal group of supporters. As mentioned, the overall success of these efforts is difficult, if not impossible, to gauge. Yet thousands of people attended the annual Liebknecht-Luxemburg parades, participated in the 1848 commemorations, and visited the VVN exhibit, demonstrating that the SED's memory-work was reaching some subsets of the East German population. More importantly, the SED laid the groundwork for future memory-work projects in the GDR and learned valuable lessons regarding how to engage in memory politics and how the party might need to adapt and change its approach in the future.

Notes

1. Aleida Assmann, "Transformations Between History and Memory," *Social Research*, Vol. 75. No. 1 (Spring 2008), pp. 49–72, p. 64.
2. Ilko-Sascha Kowalczuk and Stefan Wolle, *Roter Stern über Deutschland* (Berlin: Ch. Links, 2001), p. 63.

3. Alexander Fischer, "Der Weg zur Gleichschaltung der Geschichtswissenschaft in der SBZ 1945–1949," in *Geschichtswissenschaft in der DDR: Band I: Historische Entwicklung, Theoriediskussion und Geschichtsdidaktik*, ed. Alexander Fischer and Günther Heydemann (Berlin: Duncker & Humblot, 1988), pp. 45–75, here p. 67; Ernst Niekisch, *Deutsche Daseinsverfehlung* (Berlin: Aufbau Verlag, 1946); and Alexander Abusch, *Der Irrweg einer Nation: Ein Beitrag zum Verständnis deutscher Geschichte* (Berlin: Aufbau Verlag, 1946).
4. Martin Sabrow, *Das Diktat des Konsenses: Geschichtswissenschaft in der DDR, 1949–1969* (Munich: Oldenbourg, 2001), pp. 8–10.
5. For work on West German memory: Robert G. Moeller, *War Stories: The Search for a Usable Past in the Federal Republic of Germany* (Berkeley: University of California Press, 2001); Ian Buruma, *Wages of Guilt: Memories of War in Germany and Japan* (New York: Farrar Straus Giroux, 1994); and Charles Maier, *The Unmasterable Past: History, Holocaust, and German National Identity* (Cambridge, MA: Harvard University Press, 1988). For comparative work on East and West German attempts to come to terms with the past: Jeffrey Herf, *Divided Memory: The Nazi Past in the Two Germanys* (Cambridge, MA: Harvard University Press, 1997); Ulrich Herbert and Olaf Groehler, *Zweierlei Bewältigung: Vier Beiträge über den Umgang mit der NS-Vergangenheit in den beiden deutschen Staaten* (Hamburg: Ergebnisse, 1992); and Peter Reichel, *Politik mit der Erinnerung: Gedächnisorte im Streit um die nationalzozialistische Vergangenheit* (Munich: Hanser, 1999).
6. Martin Sabrow, *Das Diktat des Konsenses,* pp. 33–34.
7. Jürgen Kocka and Martin Sabrow, eds., *Die DDR als Geschichte: Fragen, Hypothesen, Perspektiven* (Berlin: Akademie Verlag, 1994).
8. This concept of a rhetorical dichotomy is discussed at length in Herf, *Divided Memory.* See also: Sigrid Meuschel, *Legitimation und Parteiherrschaft: Zum Paradox von Stabilität und Revolution in der DDR 1945–1989* (Frankfurt am Main: Suhrkamp, 1992); Josie McLellan, *Antifaschism and Memory in East Germany: Remembering the International Brigades, 1945–1989* (Oxford: Clarendon Press: 2004); and Dan Diner, "On the Ideology of Antifascism," *New German Critique,* No. 67 (Winter 1996), pp. 123–32.
9. Rudy Koshar, *Germany's Transient Pasts: Preservation and National Memory in the Twentieth Century* (Chapel Hill: University of North Carolina Press, 1998), p. 209.
10. Berliner Landesarchiv, C Rep 110/188 (Stadtverornetenversammlung und Magistrat der Hauptstadt der DDR, Berlin: Bauwesen: Abt. H.A. Hochbau), unpaginated.
11. The Victory Alley (*Siegesallee*) was first constructed in 1873, but expanded under the rule of Emperor William II to include almost 100 white marble statues of Prussian royalty and other notables. The surviving statues can still be viewed at the Spandau Citadel in Berlin.
12. Berliner Landesarchiv, C Rep 110/188, unpaginated.
13. Ibid.
14. SAPMO-BArch, NY 4090/286, pp. 49–50.
15. David Bathrick, *The Powers of Speech: The Politics of Culture in the GDR* (Lincoln: University of Nebraska Press, 1995), p. 42.
16. Maurice Halbwachs, *On Collective Memory,* trans. and ed. Lewis A. Coser (Chicago: Chicago University Press, 1992), p. 39.
17. SAPMO-BArch, NY 4036/611, p. 430.
18. In July 2009, the website *Spiegel Online* published an article indicating that the corpse buried at the Friedrichsfelde Cemetery may not indeed be that of Rosa Luxemburg. A preserved corpse was found at Berlin's Charité hospital that researchers believe might be that of Luxemburg. "DNA-Test: Haarprobe soll Luxemburg-Geheimnis lüften," *Spiegel Online,* accessed 28 April 2013, http://www.spiegel.de/wissenschaft/mensch/dna-test-haarprobe-soll-luxemburg-geheimnis-lueften-a-636960.html.

19. SAPMO-BArch, NY 4036/611, p. 432. "Ich war, Ich bin, Ich werde sein."
20. *Neues Deutschland*, 13 January 1952.
21. SAPMO-BArch, NY 4036/611, p. 16.
22. Ibid., pp. 31–32 (Abschrift pp. 33–34). The emphasized text appears as underlining in the original.
23. Heinz Voßke, *Geschichte der Gedenkstätte der Sozialisten in Berlin-Friedrichsfelde* (Berlin, Dietz, 1982), p. 70.
24. Eva-Maria Klother, *Denkmalplastik nach 1945 bis 1989 in Ost- und West-Berlin* (Münster: Lit, 1996), pp. 35–40.
25. "Im Zeichen der Einheit der Arbeiterschaft: Wilhelm Pieck sprach an der Grabstätte Karl Liebknechts und Rosa Luxemburg," *Tägliche Rundschau*, 15 January 1946, p. 2.
26. Walter Bartel, Pieck's personal secretary at the time, recalled in an article published in *Neues Deutschland* that: "neither the prohibition during the Weimar era, nor rain, nor snow, nor fierce cold has kept the Berliners away from marching to Friedrichsfelde and honoring the dead of the revolution each January. … It was always a day of 'in spite of all odds'—the words written by our very daring and strong Karl Liebknecht in his last article." (Walter Bartel, "Gedenkstätte der Sozialisten," *Neues Deutschland*, 13 January 1952.) Such direct associations with the former traditions of the working class were essential to the new memory culture in the SBZ/DDR and demonstrate the active role by leading Party members in publicly cultivating the "correct" meaning of the past through speeches and the press. Whether Bartel's recollections here were true or part of a propaganda effort cannot be fully established. However, this example further demonstrates how the party used multiple modes of communication to articulate its vision and "teach" the public about how it wished to represent the past.
27. Voßke, *Geschichte der Gedenkstätte*, p. 86.
28. Henry Ashby Turner, Jr., *Germany from Partition to Reunification* (New Haven: Yale University Press, 1992), pp. 22–24.
29. Paul Steege, *Black Market, Cold War: Everyday Life in Berlin 1946–1949* (Cambridge: Cambridge University Press, 2008), pp. 167–78.
30. "Das Jahr 1848," *Neues Deutschland*, 1 January 1948, p. 5.
31. Following this article we see a chronological listing of all the major events of 1848, so as to prepare the reading public for future articles and commemorative events.
32. "Von der Paulskirche bis zum Volkskongreß: Politische Richtlinie zur Durchführung der Veranstaltungen 1848–1948," *Neues Deutschland*, 24 January 1948, p. 3.
33. Martin McCauley, *Marxism-Leninism and the German Democratic Republic: The Socialist Unity Party (SED)*, (London: Macmillan, 1979), pp. 52–53.
34. "Das Jahr 1848," *Neues Deutschland*, 1 January 1948, p. 5.
35. "Von der Paulskirche bis zum Volkskongreß: Politische Richtlinie zur Durchführung der Veranstaltungen 1848–1948: Beschluß des Parteivorstandes der SED vom 15. 1. 1948," *Neues Deutschland*, 24 January 1948, p. 3.
36. "Lehren der Geschichte: 1848 Warnung und Mahnung," *Neues Deutschland*, 31 January 1948, p. 3.
37. "Die Jahrhundertfeier 1848/1948: Die Pläne der Deutschen Verwaltung für Volksbildung," *Neues Deutschland*, 3 February 1948, p. 3.
38. Ibid.
39. *Neues Deutschland*, 2 March 1948, p. 6. It should be noted that the *Hochschule für bildende Künste* was located in the western half of Berlin and Scheibe was not a member of the SED. The Berlin Palace, on the other hand, was located in the Soviet Sector of Berlin—all of this highlights the fact that Berlin was still relatively open and the SED was not constraining its activities just to the Soviet Sector.

40. "Vor 100 Jahren und heute," *Neues Deutschland*, 10 March 1948, p. 4. Reference here is to the West-Berlin politicians Jakob Kaiser (CDU), Franz Neumann (SPD), Carl-Hubert Schwennicke (LDP), and Curt Swolinzky (SPD).
41. "Vor diesem 18. März," *Neues Deutschland*, 11 March 1948.
42. "1848/1948," *Neues Deutschland*, 12 March 1948, p. 1. The SED stressed the concept of a "national" assembly, since it hoped to be able to draw delegations from across all four occupation zones and the four sectors of Berlin.
43. "Märztreiben," *Der Spiegel*, 13 March 1948, p. 3.
44. "Zwei Puffer," *Der Spiegel*, 20 March 1948, p. 3.
45. "Polizeiaktionen gegen Volkskongreß im US-Sektor Berlins," *Neues Deutschland*, 12 March 1948, p. 1.
46. Heinrich Deiters, "Die Lehren von 1848," *Neues Deutschland*, 13 March 1948, p. 3; 14 March 1948, p. 3, 16 March 1948, p. 3; 17 March 1948, p. 5.
47. "Unsterblicher Geist des 18 März," *Neues Deutschland*, 18 March 1948, p. 1.
48. *Neues Deutschland* reported crowds of some 100,000, which was most likely greatly exaggerated. *Der Spiegel* estimated a crowd of only 30,000 marched through the streets to the cemetery in Berlin-Friedrichshain. "Zwei Puffer" *Der Spiegel*, 20 March 1948, p. 3.
49. Franz Mehring, "Die Märzrevolution von 1848," *Neues Deutschland*, 18 March 1948, p. 2.
50. For more on the VVN see: Elke Reuter and Detlef Hansel, *Das kurze Leben der VVN von 1947 bis 1953* (Berlin: Edition Ost, 1997).
51. Sven Wierskalla, *Vereinigung der Verfolgten des Naziregimes (VVN) in der Sowjetischen Zone und in Berlin, 1945–1948* (Norderstedt: Grin Verlag, 1994), p. 78.
52. Wierskalla, *Vereinigung der Verfolgten*, p. 79.
53. SAPMO-BArch, DY 55/V 278/2/8, brochure for the exhibit "Das andere Deutschland."
54. Ibid.
55. Ibid.
56. Manfred Overesch, *Buchenwald und die DDR oder Die Suche nach Selbstlegitimation* (Göttingen: Vandehoeck & Ruprecht, 1995), pp. 255–57; Wierskalla, *Vereinigung der Verfolgten*, pp. 195–201; and the exhibit brochures found in SAPMO-BArch, DY/55/V 278/2/8.
57. "Das andere Deutschland," *Neues Deutschland*, 1 September 1948, p. 5.
58. "Die Kunst des anderen Deutschland," *Neues Deutschland*, 9 September 1948, p. 3.
59. The level of success that this early exhibit enjoyed is questionable. Given the controlling nature of the SED and how it often coerced groups to visit such exhibits, it is difficult to know exactly who these people were, what motivated them to see the exhibit, or why they decided to leave a comment. The official statistics indicate 269,072 visitors for the entire tour through the SBZ from September 1948 through February 1949. Even if this is an inflated number, it does not point to an overly strong urge among the public to either support this depiction of the past or even attempt to engage the topic. Berlin saw the highest number of visitors, officially nearly 50,000, with the exhibit in Dresden coming in just behind with about 200 fewer visitors. The lowest turnout was in Schwerin, which only managed to attract around 21,500 visitors. However, the motivations behind those who did attend the exhibit and those who chose not to remain unclear; certainly there were plenty of practical issues (like reconstructing bombed-out homes) that took priority over visiting a museum exhibit.
60. This excerpt and all of the following ones from the visitor responses are found in SAPMO-BArch, DY 55/V 278/2/9, unpaginated.
61. In the original, this handwritten note includes arrows connecting both "SED" and "NKVD" to "The same," thus leaving no room for interpretation of what message the visitor intended to convey.

62. Summaries for each of the exhibits outside of Berlin, including excerpts from the visitor comment log, can be found in: SAPMO-BArch, DY 55/IV 278/2/9 and DY 55/IV 278/2/10.
63. Jeffrey Herf has convincingly documented the absence of Jewish memory within the GDR state memory policies. See: Herf, *Divided Memory*.

Chapter Two

THE POLITICS OF STATE MEMORY

The division of Germany into two states in 1949 resulted in a stepped-up effort by the SED to expand and deepen its political and cultural legitimacy. Political legitimacy continued to focus on material concerns of the postwar period—maintaining a safe and steady food supply, housing, employment, and the like. The cultural legitimacy and historical continuity in which the SED had previously invested now needed to be directed toward the legitimacy of the new East German state. The rationale for the division of the German nation into two states needed bolstering and the SED wanted to continue the process of rationalizing its place as the dominant, controlling force in the East. Naturally, the presence of the Red Army was also a central factor in sustaining the SED's monopoly of power in the GDR, as the response to June uprisings in 1953 demonstrated dramatically. Nonetheless, the SED continued to invest resources and energy to its memory-work efforts.

As during the immediate postwar era, the SED leadership primarily sought to use memory-work to create a sense of inevitability, a feeling that the current situation was meant to be. The leadership needed to create a delicate balance between acknowledging the assistance of the Soviet Union and the Red Army in establishing the SED as the dominant power, and a desire to demonstrate a real indigenous following in Germany. Indeed, the SED's coordinated effort to create and sustain a new sense of historical consciousness seems to be directly linked to its craving for public signs of legitimacy. A related, and at times equally important, impetus for this stepped-up effort to shape memory culture in the new GDR was party ideology. Although Stalinist tactics for controlling society heavily influenced the party leadership's approach, it also acknowledged the need to provide an ideological explanation for its political and cultural endeavors. The answer, according to the party, centered around Marx's laws of

---

Notes for this chapter begin on page 96.

historical materialism, which dictated the inevitability of progress and the triumph of the working class. Together, these two motivations dominated the vision that guided the SED leadership's memory policies in the years following the establishment of the East German state.

Like its East European neighbors, the German Democratic Republic was formally a "people's republic" representing the interests of German workers and peasants. It purported to be the true government for all of Germany. Just as the SED needed a convincing interpretation of the past to support its ideology based on historical materialism, the GDR state required an equally credible line of historical continuity to legitimize its existence vis-à-vis the new West German state. While chapter 1 examined how memory-work in the immediate postwar era aimed to cultivate party loyalty and legitimacy, this chapter explores how that emphasis shifted to the state. The establishment of an East German state in 1949 necessitated popularizing new links between the past and the institutions of the new state-socialist regime.

Throughout the 1950s the SED undertook several major memory projects, including the establishment of three "national" memorials on the grounds of the Buchenwald, Ravensbrück, and Sachsenhausen concentration camps, lesser monuments in cities like Dresden, Leipzig, and Rostock, as well as local monuments to the victims of fascism throughout the GDR. The opening of the *Museum für Deutsche Geschichte* (Museum for German History) in 1952 provided the party with a means to publicly display an official historical narrative for the new state centered on the history of the German working class. The new Berlin museum was just one of several new museums across the GDR that highlighted the triumphs of the working class, yet this museum played a significant role as the standard bearer for all history museums in the country and used its central role to set guidelines on official museum policies throughout the land. Lastly, the 1950s also marked a period of honoring not only the fallen victims of fascism, but also the heroes of the German labor movement such as Karl Marx and Friedrich Engels as well as Ernst Thälmann. However, due to issues relating to both the overall reconstruction of the city of Berlin and a move away from monumental sculptures within the artistic community, both of these projects were suspended until their ultimate unveiling in 1986. All three of these examples during the 1950s shed light onto the overall trends in state-sponsored memory-work and help identify some of the frustrations that the state experienced in the process.

With the exception of the initial efforts by local survivor groups in Weimar to construct a memorial for the victims at Buchenwald, the memory projects covered in this chapter were driven by the central government in Berlin. They reflect the desire of the SED both to control popular memory and steer it in a direction that would directly link public displays of memory to the legitimacy of the GDR state. This apparent top-down structure for the creation of these particular monuments does not, however, imply that the state had an entirely free hand in shaping its memory policies. The initial impetus for the Buchenwald monument was local and the state would need to commandeer or suppress competing memories before it could successfully occupy that memory space. The Museum for German History was also a tourist attraction that needed to draw in visitors and thus could not present a historical narrative that was as straightforward as party ideologues may have wanted without alienating significant sectors of society. Likewise, the state failed to push through its plan to construct monuments in Berlin honoring Marx, Engels, and Thälmann against the wave of resistance from the artist community as it began to move away from the aesthetics of monumentalism in a post-Stalinist society.

Compared to its East European neighbors, the SED faced several unique hurdles in its attempts to legitimize its rule and the new East German state. Unlike its East European neighbors, the GDR had to compete with West Germany for its claims to the national past. Another complicating factor for the GDR was the large contingent of Soviet troops stationed on its soil. Despite the presence of these troops, the GDR desired to portray itself as possessing political legitimacy independent of the Soviet Union. Such political myth-making is common to most modern societies and East Germany was no exception. As Raina Zimmering has argued, political myth-making is a tricky endeavor and one cannot diverge too strongly from popular memory or it will lose its legitimating power. However, Zimmering also notes that the core narrative of a myth is malleable and can be reshaped over time and adjusted to account for new political challenges.[1] Zimmering's assertions hold true in the realm of memory politics as well. The three examples below point to areas where the state struggled to stabilize and control elements of its historical narrative without attempting to construct it out of whole cloth. Had the state diverged too greatly from the accepted historical record, it would have sacrificed its ability to employ the past as a legitimating element.

Thus, when the government leaders noticed local attempts to construct a monument at the site of the Buchenwald concentration camp, they organized an effort to take it over and ensure that the final product fit with the state's desired historical narrative. Yet, because many survivors were active in the campaign to build a monument, there were limits to how far the state could shape its message without alienating this important constituency. In a similar fashion, the historical narrative developed by the Museum for German History attempted to transfer the new line of historical interpretation developed by Marxist historians to a prominent museum venue, but was limited by its form—museums depend on material objects to narrate its display. Finally, although Marx and Engels had been heroes of the German labor movement for generations, the East German state was the first German entity that attempted to place a national monument in their honor in the capital. Similarly, the state desired to erect a monument honoring Ernst Thälmann in Berlin to draw a symbolic link between his resistance to fascism under the Nazis and East German's identity as an antifascist state. Despite its best efforts and the resources the state allocated to both of these projects, the young GDR was unable to complete these memory projects, which would ultimately drag into the 1980s before finally being built.[2]

The Buchenwald Monument and the GDR's "Founding Myth"

On 14 September 1958, more than 80,000 people gathered for the dedication of the new Buchenwald monument just beyond the gates of the camp located atop the Ettersberg Mountain outside of Weimar. Otto Grotewohl, minister president of the GDR and the president of the Buchenwald Board of Trustees, gave the dedication speech. He referred to the monument as symbol of the East German state's greatest heroes, proclaiming: "September 14, 1958, should not just be a day of memory for the time of the horrible Nazi dictatorship, a day of remembrance for the deaths of our great fighters, but this day should also provide us with a renewed warning and bind us not to surrender our fight against every form of inhumanity too soon, until we have removed every form of fascism in every country and for all time."[3] The tone set by Grotewohl's speech, the press coverage it received, and the vast resources invested by the regime to construct this site of memory all reveal the central role that the Buchenwald memorial played in grafting party history onto the new state.

It is precisely this linkage that has led many historians to refer to Buchenwald as the East German state's "founding myth."[4] Yet as a place of memory, the Buchenwald monument and the museum built by the state were more than just mythical creations by a manipulative regime. The Buchenwald monument took over ten years to build and did not begin as a state-sponsored memory-project. Indeed, this long period of preparation reveals an interesting road toward consolidating state control over memory projects at the site and constructing a monument that the state felt was in its best interest. The party was not alone in its desire to commemorate those who had died at the Buchenwald site. There were several independent attempts by competing groups and organizations to construct monuments. The state allowed some to proceed, while it intervened to stop others. The initial attempts to commemorate Buchenwald's liberation and the SED's efforts to popularize and democratize the process of constructing the Buchenwald Monument reveal how the state slowly took over control of the site in a way that it hoped would allow it to shape the meaning of the past.

The first act of memorialization occurred just over a week after the liberation of the camp on 19 April 1945, when 21,000 former prisoners gathered on the roll call grounds for a memorial service and erected a four-sided wooden obelisk. Werner A. Becker, a former Jewish inmate at Buchenwald, voiced the first call for a permanent monument in a pamphlet he self-published titled "The Truth about the KZ Buchenwald."[5] Beckert, who claimed to speak in the name of all of the former prisoners, argued against flattening the buildings in the camp and for maintaining the site as a place of memory. Beckert's plan, as well as any that might have been held by other former prisoners, was put on hold by the establishment of the Soviet internment camp (*Speziallager No. 2*) in August 1945. This was one of ten "special" camps in East Germany that imprisoned thousands of Germans who were accused of Nazi crimes, acts of collaboration, or non-compliance with the Soviet authorities, but also included some imprisoned due to mistaken identity or arbitrary arrests.[6] While the camp would ultimately be transferred over to the East German state in 1950, its use by Soviet forces prevented the camp's immediate transformation into a site of memory.

Soviet control of the Buchenwald site did not, however, stave off the desire by former inmates and members of the KPD/SED to organize commemoration services and monuments in nearby Weimar. A temporary memorial was erected for the occasion of the second anniversary of the liberation of the Buchenwald camp on 11 April 1947. Because the Soviets were using the camp as an internment site, the festivities were held in downtown Weimar on the Goethe Platz, thus displacing memory from its actual site to one of associated memory. The monument constructed for this occasion was designed by Hermann Henselmann, Director of the State University for Architecture and Visual Arts (*Staatliche Hochschule für Baukunst und Bildende Kunst*) in Weimar. It consisted of a wooden triangular structure covered with tightly stretched red cloth (see figure 2.1). The monument's form and color reflected a new direction in the definition of victimhood and elevation of the political (i.e. communist) prisoners over all others, since the red triangle was the symbol that political prisoners had been forced to wear as an identifying mark on the outside of their prison uniforms.

To understand the politicization of the Henselmann memorial we need to look at the events that preceded the 1947 commemoration. About a

FIGURE 2.1. The second annual commemoration of the liberation of Buchenwald (celebrated on the Goetheplatz in Weimar), April 1947.
BArch Bild 183-2005-0901-524 / Erich Dumm.

year prior to the second anniversary festivities, Werner Beckert launched a second effort to construct a monument in honor of those killed in Buchenwald. Beckert called for the construction of a "noble and traditional monument" (such as the obelisk from 1945 or an urn filled with ashes) to be placed near the *Fürstengruft* (the Prince's Crypt) in Weimar's old cemetery. By locating the monument in the direct vicinity of the burial sites of both Goethe and Schiller, Beckert hoped to create a symbolic link between the traditions of German classicism and those killed by the Nazis at Buchenwald. Although he received preliminary authorization from the local Soviet Military Administration, his political opponents were quick to respond. Among his critics were Ernst Busse, a former Buchenwald prisoner, long-time member of the KPD, and at this point the Deputy Minister President of the state of Thuringia, and Stefan Heymann, another former Buchenwald prisoner and later founder of the GDR's Antifascist Committee, both of whom argued that Beckert's motivation was personal glory and greed, rather than a true desire to remember the victims of fascism.[7]

Beckert's initiative for a monument in the Weimar cemetery spurred local communists to create a counter-proposal. Communist activists turned to Hermann Henselmann, architect and fellow KPD member, to offer both an artistic critique of Beckert's proposal and to develop a counter-proposal that would reflect the party's desire for a politicized representation of the crimes in Buchenwald. Henselmann's artistic critique centered on the banality of Beckert's proposed traditional memorial form, accusing Beckert of confusing the symbolic representation of gravestones with those found in memorials intended to honor the dead:

> When fulfilling such a responsibility, one must differentiate between ideas of burial [*Bestattungsgedanken*] and ideas of memory [*Erinnerungsgedanken*]. Mr. Beckert's suggested solution mixes together these two entirely different spheres of ideas. Since the ashes are to be placed in an urn, this speaks to the natural human desire to have the remains of the deceased to be dealt with in an appropriate manner, such as being placed in an urn, and be buried. With such a memorial [*Totenmal*] one then places this urn in a special room designed for this purpose and not, as the proposal calls for, as some sort of button placed on top of a stone box. This vault could be constructed in an entirely simple manner. A demarcation through stone or metal fence or something along these lines would even be acceptable. The urn itself must be created in a natural form. The suggested form is unsatisfactory and does not meet today's sense of style.[8]

Henselmann also attacked Beckert's proposal at a political level, arguing that the placement of a Buchenwald memorial in such close vicinity to the graves of Goethe and Schiller would confuse the gravity of the crimes committed, by association with symbols of the humanist tradition. Moreover, Henselmann argued that the monument needed not only to mourn those lost, but also to warn future generations of the terror inflicted by fascism. As such, the memorial needed to be placed not in a far off corner of the city, but rather in a central place. He suggested that it be constructed on the Karl-Marx-Platz in the city's center.[9]

Henselmann's first proposal called for the transformation of the entire complex of Weimar's former *Gauforum*, the former Nazi district headquarters, into a permanent Buchenwald memorial. According to the protocol of a meeting from 16 January 1946, Henselmann argued, "Just as the name of Goethe is tied to Weimar, so too must be the name of Buchenwald, and this in a positive manner: Prisoners from 36 nations welded together the solidarity of the new Europe under the burden of terror."[10] Henselmann's plan called for the southern wall of the central hall to be covered in black (either out of glass or slate) and incorporated a water fountain consisting of 36 different streams of water (the symbol of life) that flowed into a single stream by the time it hit the standing pool of water. This visualization of common experience and a unifying element for the new Europe was compounded by incorporating soil from these 36 nations to be buried on the grounds surrounding the memorial. The hall itself was not to be used for mass demonstrations, but rather dedicated to cultural purposes and thus be transformed into Germany's new cultural center.[11]

These plans, however, were quickly quashed by the local Soviet Military Administration's decision to take over the former *Gauforum* for its own purposes, enclosing the Karl-Marx-Platz with a fence and using it as a parking lot. The city celebrated the first anniversary of Buchenwald's liberation instead at the *Weimarhalle* (Weimar Hall) and included a re-dedication of Walter Gropius's monument to the *Märzgefallenen* (those killed in the March 1919 uprising) in Weimar's central cemetery. The communists would have to wait another year before they could move forward with Henselmann's 1947 provisional monument. The popularity of Hanselmann's three-dimensional red triangle, however, resonated with the Victims of Fascism organization, which adopted this symbol as its preferred memorial marker when it erected dozens of smaller memorials throughout the SBZ. The construction of Henselmann's second provisional monument in 1947 also marked the end of the first stage in the communists' effort to seize control over the public representation of Buchenwald's memory. Although the struggle during this phase was primarily local, members of the party leadership understood Buchenwald's symbolic potential and soon began taking a much keener interest in imposing its vision of the past on any future memorials.

The second wave of memory politics at Buchenwald can be traced primarily to the efforts of the VVN beginning in February 1947, when the

VVN formed the Buchenwald Committee. The VVN was an inter-zonal confederation of survivors groups founded in 1947. Its membership drew from a wide social base, including Jews, communists, and democrats alike. While inter-zonal in name, the SED quickly assumed a dominant position in the VVN chapters located in the SBZ.[12] The VVN's Buchenwald Committee was led by former political prisoner Walter Bartel, who began to push for the construction of a permanent Buchenwald monument atop the Ettersberg Mountain outside of Weimar. Real progress on the memorial project only started in April 1949, shortly before the establishment of the East German state, when SED Party Secretary Walter Ulbricht gave Bartel permission to destroy the Bismarck Tower located just outside the camp on the southern slope of the Ettersberg and prepare the site for the construction of the new Buchenwald monument.

In June 1949, the government of Thuringia passed a resolution that designated the two mass gravesites on the southern slope of the Ettersberg as a place of remembrance and called for the construction of a monument as well as the creation of a permanent exhibit about the Buchenwald camp.[13] To assist these projects, Thuringia's Minister President Eggerath wrote to GDR Minister President Otto Grotewohl on 14 December 1949, asking that the GDR state include 1.5 million Marks in its next budget for the construction of a monument at Buchenwald, since this project was of national and international importance and extended beyond the competencies of the state of Thuringia.[14] Eggerath's proposal, however, did not find much support from Grotewohl, whose personal assistant Hans Tschorn, writing to Walter Bartel and referring to Eggereth's letter, mentioned that Grotewohl would rather see such a sum of money used for the construction of new apartments for the victims of fascism than for a monument.[15] Bartel did manage to solicit support among some ministers, including Minister for Finance Hans Loch, but in the end Minister of Planning Heinrich Rau notified Grotewohl on 11 March 1950, that "due to the shortage of material in 1950 we will be unable to fund the proposed memorial and monument in this year."[16] Thus ended, temporarily, the attempt to construct a state-funded monument at Buchenwald.

This setback, however, did not kill the idea of constructing a monument at Buchenwald. Shortly following the government's decision not to back the memorial project, the SMAD decided to shut down its internment camp at Buchenwald. In its directive to Berlin the Soviets called on the SED to restore the camp to place of respectful memory and thus blew new wind into the sails of the Buchenwald project. With the Soviets vacating the *Speziallager* on 1 March 1950, it was now possible to conceive of a memorial plan that would encompass both the remnants of the concentration camp and the mass gravesites on the perimeter. In most cases the Soviets handed over such internment camps to local or regional authorities. However, in the case of Buchenwald, the newly formed East German government prevented local control by passing a resolution that placed the entire complex under its protection instead. This act had the effect of elevating the importance of the Buchenwald site to the state level. What had begun as a relatively grassroots effort by former inmates was slowly being taken over by centralized state authorities. There would be one more hurdle (seizing control of the VVN), but ultimately the state was now in a position to dictate the construction of any future memorial at the site.

Initially the SED *Politbüro* seemed uninterested in a memorial to those buried in the mass graves. Instead, the party leadership concentrated on preserving the camp itself. Ulbricht and other party leaders also wanted to focus specifically on popularizing the memory of Ernst Thälmann, who was killed by the Nazis while imprisoned at Buchenwald in 1944, by constructing a memorial for him. In an internal SED memo dated 7 July 1951, Walter Ulbricht passed along the task of constructing a monument in Buchenwald for Thälmann to Franz Dahlem and Walter Bartel: "It is now possible to construct a memorial for Ernst Thälmann with a sort of museum as well to be built in Buchenwald. I ask you to draft a proposal with sketches for the design of this memorial for the [SED] secretariat."[17] Although memorializing the thousands of (communist) victims who suffered at the Buchenwald camp, the primary impetus for the state to take over control was at first more closely related to the fact that high-ranking members of the party leadership, like Ulbricht, were mainly concerned with cultivating a perception of Thälmann as the party's founding martyr and symbol of the antifascist struggle. Over time, however, this singular focus on Thälmann would give way to a more inclusive memory that others in the party felt could connect with a wider segment of society.

It took several more years for the East German state to gain full control over the Buchenwald memorial. Ideology was not the only driving factor behind its interest in the Buchenwald site. Beyond its desire to emphasize the Communist Party's involvement in resisting Hitler, the state wanted, and indeed needed, to deemphasize competing memories of Buchenwald's more recent role in the persecution of Germans by the occupying Soviet forces. The problematic history of this dual-usage of this camp also contributed to the party's sudden interest to take a more leading role in shaping popular memory of the site, hoping to establish a direct link between the history of the camp during the Nazi period and the founding principles of the new state, while obscuring memories of its use between 1945 and 1951.

On 14 January 1951, the presidium of the Council of Ministers of the GDR passed a resolution for the construction of the "National Buchenwald Memorial" as the "central memorial for the victims of fascism."[18] The resolution called not only for Buchenwald to be the primary place of memory for the victims of fascism, but also authorized the construction of a monument dedicated to Ernst Thälmann, scheduled to be dedicated on his seventieth birthday on 16 April 1956. By adding a separate monument to the "national" memory site at Buchenwald, the party signaled its intention to elevate Thälmann's legacy to one of national importance. Whereas the larger Buchenwald monument would draw on a diverse set of images of men struggling against the Nazi regime and ultimately freeing themselves from its bondage, the Thälmann monument could establish him as the key martyr of the communist resistance. Although the Thälmann "cult" had not yet gained a strong following in the GDR at this time, he would soon become one of the most important icons linked with the memorialization of the Buchenwald site.[19]

At this point the VVN took over the day-to-day planning efforts for the monuments (Thälmann and the Buchenwald *Ehrenhain*), while the Berlin-based Museum for German History (*Museum für Deutsche Geschichte* or MfDG) assumed the project of developing a museum exhibit inside the camp. Progress toward transforming the Buchenwald site into a national memorial was extremely slow, largely because there were few resources available for nonessential building projects.

An official competition for the monument opened on 14 December 1951, and solicited proposals from a small group of "acceptable" architects and sculptors resident in the GDR for the "architectural, sculptural, and landscape gardening design for the memorial [*Ehrenhain*] in remembrance of the victims of fascist terror in Buchenwald."[20] Among the GDR artists invited to participate were architects Richard Paulick and Otto Engelberger; sculptors Gustav Seitz and Fritz Cremer; landscape architect Reinhold Lingner; as well as the artists collective "Marenko," comprised of architects Ludwig Deiters, Hans Grotewohl, and Kurt Tausendschön, landscape architect Hubert Matthes, and sculptors Robert Riehl and Peter Götsche. The limitation of the competition to these specific artists further emphasizes the party's vision of Buchenwald as a GDR-national monument (i.e. only GDR-based artists were invited) and the necessity of conveying the "correct" political interpretation of Buchenwald (all of these artists were politically acceptable to the SED). The decision to limit the competition to GDR artists also marked a departure from Walter Bartel's original proposal for a more open international competition that would include entries from all of the "Buchenwald nations."[21]

The prize committee released its awards to the public on 28 March 1952. Fritz Cremer, Reinhold Lingner, and the writer Bertolt Brecht formed the team behind one of the entries, which included an amphitheater dug into the ground atop the Ettersberg Mountain with two of the mass graves on either side encircled with a cement ring. At the head of the grouping stood a small memorial hall with a sculpture mounted on top of it. The critique from the prize committee centered on the amphitheater, stating: "Rallies held at this memorial are not sitting events. The honorable memorializing of the victims of fascism is bound together with standing people."[22] The prize committee did, however, like the basic elements of Cremer's sculpture as well as the idea of a memorial hall. The prize committee also found several elements in the proposal from the Marenko collective to their liking. The committee found the Marenko model had presented the best overall conceptualization of the memorial complex, offered the best political interpretation, and integrated well with the remnants of the camp itself. The Marenko proposal called for a directed pathway lined with nine large reliefs (one for each year that the camp was used as a Nazi concentration camp). Each relief would depict the history of the underground struggle against the Nazi regime. This pathway was meant to represent the "blood street" at the camp that was built by the inmates. The downward slope of the pathway leading to the first of two (later three) mass gravesites was to symbolize the decline of Nazi power. The pathway then continued to the second mass grave and then led the visitor up a long stairway to the top of the complex with a tower and sculpture group, symbolizing the long and hard struggle of the prisoners for freedom.[23] The prize committee awarded both proposals prizes and they became the working basis for the future monument (the architectural layout of the Marenko model combined with the sculptures of Fritz Cremer).

The memorial project hit a roadblock yet again on 21 February 1953, when the SED disbanded the VVN. Although the leading members of the VVN had been closely associated with the SED, the disbanding of the organization allowed the party to take direct control over the Buchenwald project and more directly steer public interpretations of victimhood and resistance during the Nazi period.[24] Additionally, Walter Bartel, who as the chairman of the Buchenwald Committee of the VVN had championed the monument project at the national level ever since its inception, was stripped of all party positions.[25] The Committee of Antifascist Resistance Fighters, a committee comprised of about twenty SED-friendly members, formally replaced the VVN and thus marked the transformation to complete party domination over the memory-work projects of the VVN. Moreover, the symbolic shift from the victimhood inherent in the VVN's membership to that of active resistance against the Nazi regime embodied by the new organization also played a significant role in the party's public representation of the Nazi past.

The Politics of State Memory | 63

FIGURE 2.2. The Buchenwald Memorial featuring Fritz Cremer's sculpture after its completion in October 1958. BArch Bild 183-58959-0002 / Wittig.

The final step in the state's takeover of the Buchenwald memorial project came on 1 April 1955, ten years after the first makeshift memorial ceremony in Buchenwald when Minister President of the GDR Otto Grotewohl, chaired the first meeting of the Board of Trustees for the Construction of the National Memorials in Buchenwald, Sachsenhausen, and Ravensbrück.[26] The board was comprised of leading political and cultural figures and representatives from all of the major mass organizations. With the creation of the new board of trustees, the state was able to subsume the Buchenwald memorial project into a larger effort to establish three "national" sites of memory. All three of the sites chosen by the state were places where political prisoners (primarily communists and social democrats) comprised the majority of inmates. Of the three, however, Buchenwald remained the most important, garnished the most attention by leading political figures, and received the greatest infusion of money to support construction efforts.

Although the state had now taken control of the Buchenwald monument project, it did not have sufficient funds to pay for its construction along with all the other rebuilding efforts. This shortfall forced the state to turn to the general public to raise the necessary funds though a large-scale fundraising effort led by the board of trustees.[27] Overall, the fundraising campaign achieved its financial goals. Although there appeared to be broad support and high levels of participation at all levels of society, members of the board also exerted political and social pressure on individuals, groups, and organizations in order to increase participation levels. In addition to the monetary contributions that went into the campaign, volunteers flocked to the Buchenwald site to help physically construct the new monument. Both the fundraising and the volunteer elements of the construction point to interesting devices of memory-work employed by the state during this project. By allowing and encouraging direct participation by the wider public in the construction process, the state was able to increase the overall impact of the project and give some agency (albeit limited and specifically directed) back to the public.[28]

The day-to-day work of the fundraising campaign fell to Ernst Saemerow, the secretary of the working committee of the board of trustees. Otto Grotewohl remained the titular head of the working committee and added the necessary political and social prestige to Saemerow's campaign efforts. The committee employed a wide variety of fundraising methods, including partnering with the postal service for several series of special edition stamps with a 20 Pfennig differential going to the fund, a special lottery run by the Ministry of Finance, as well as the sale of photos and postcards. The most prevalent and effective fundraising method employed was the sale of *Bausteine* and *Spendemarken*, which were simply a special form of receipt for donations collected. Yet these *Bausteine* and *Spendemarken* themselves became collector items and symbolic markers of an individual's personal engagement in support of the memorial projects.

Publicity for the fundraising campaign was primarily done through the press. For example, *Neues Deutschland* ran a lengthy promotional article on 28 July 1955, in which it played not only on feelings of respect and sorrow for those who suffered, but also on national pride and the necessity to teach future generations: "The construction of the National Monuments for the Fighters against Fascism, who gave their lives for a better future, is an issue of national honor for the German people. To help must be a duty of honor for all German patriots."[29] *Bausteine* and *Spendemarken* were also available for purchase at each of the memorial sites and through numerous societal organizations such as the FDJ youth organization or the FDGB workers' union.

Maintaining the high level of participation by such organizations was not an easy task. At times members of the committee were called upon to apply pressure to groups with whom they were associated in order to press upon the organization leadership the necessity for fulfilling its participation goals. For example, in a letter from 8 June 1955 sent to all directors of large industrial factories, Minister for Heavy Industry Fritz Selbmann stated: "My request to you today is win your support in the collection of funds for the construction of these memorials and given our close association with the development and leadership of the socialist industry I ask you to make my request a priority for yourself and make a considerable contribution to the fulfillment of this great national task that the board of trustees has set."[30] Such pressure by the minister of heavy industry to these factory directors indicates that participation was not always entirely voluntary nor did it happen without the exertion of a certain level of coercion (at times rather subtle) on behalf of state officials.

Another example of such political pressure is evident in a letter dated 11 April 1956, in which Minister President Grotewohl himself addressed the low participation rate of the FDJ in the overall fundraising effort. In an attempt to spur more direct engagement by the organization's leadership, Grotewohl pointed to the importance of youth participation in this project for the party's larger goals of socialist education: "It is not enough to simply encourage the sale of the *Bausteine*; the participation in the construction of national monuments is a great obligation for youth… Especially in the *Freie Deutsche Jugend*, the recruitment for the sale of the *Bausteine* must, therefore, be carried out within the context of political education."[31] Karl Nomokel, First Secretary of the FDJ, responded to Grotewohl in a detailed letter a week later. In this letter, Nomokel admitted that the FDJ had not taken the type of aggressive promotion of the project that it warranted.

Moreover, he pointed to problems stemming from two other competing fundraising projects that the FDJ had been engaged in, but assured the minister president that the FDJ would follow through with its commitment and do more to link the sale of the *Bausteine* to the political education of the youth.

TABLE 2.1. Fundraising effort of the Buchenwald Committee

Fundraising Sources (as of 1961)	
Bausteine and *Spendemarken*	11,136,069.64 Marks
Photographs, Books, and Pamphlets	1,133,177.03 Marks
Memorabilia and Postcards	1,196,934.80 Marks
State Contributions (Lotto and Bank Interest)	10,365,974.80 Marks
Postage Stamps	6,275,062.07 Marks
Other	2,043,431.01 Marks
Total	32,150,649.35 Marks

Source: SAPMO-BArch, NY 4090/550, pp. 359–62. "Bericht der Tätigkeit des Kuratoriums" dated 3 January 1962. The original documents use the designation "DM" to denote the "Deutsche Mark der Deutschen Notenbank" which was the official currency of the SBZ and GDR from 24 July 1948 to 31 July 1964. On 1 August 1964, the GDR switched over to the designation "MDN" to denote the "Mark der Deutschen Notenbank" and on 1 January 1968 it again changed the designation of its currency to "M" to denote the "Mark der Deutschen Demokratischen Republik." Officially, the East German Mark was traded at parity with the West German Mark, although its true market value was much lower. As a point of reference, however, 32 million West German Marks would have traded in 1961 for approximately $7.7 million.

TABLE 2.2. Expenditures of the Buchenwald Committee

Expenditures (as of 1961)	
Buchenwald	14,335,626.06 Marks
Ravensbrück	3,251,923.50 Marks
Sachsenhausen	7,183,851.31 Marks
Other Expenses	229,487.42 Marks
Production Costs for Fundraising Materials	2,211,060.11 Marks
Advertising	10,368.45 Marks
Administrative Costs	41,479.56 Marks
Salaries	129,370.94 Marks
Premiums for Employees	8,302.71 Marks
Total	27,401,470.06 Marks

Source: SAPMO-BArch, NY 4090/550, pp. 359–62. "Bericht der Tätigkeit des Kuratoriums" dated 3 January 1962.

Overall, however, it is difficult not to view the fundraising efforts by the committee as successful. Looking at the final tally as of 1961, the board of trustees had raised over thirty-two million Marks, of which only about ten million could be considered as state contributions (or rather forgone state income). The other twenty million came from donations (ranging from ten

Pfennig to one thousand Marks) and from the sale of collectible memorabilia such as porcelain medallions with a portrait of Ernst Thälmann from the famed Meissen studio, limited edition postcards, and special edition postage stamps. While it is uncertain what level of participation was truly voluntary and how much coercion was involved, the state did achieve its goal of involving a wide swath of society and project the impression that people from all levels of society were actively involved in constructing the national monuments. Moreover, the dependence of the state on raising substantial outside funds for its memorial projects forced it to engage the public on a more personal level than would have been the case had it been in the position to simply fund these projects on its own. There were now millions of people who had directly contributed to the construction of the memorials. Although the project began as a memorial ceremony by small group of former Buchenwald inmates, it had now become a memorial project by and for the entire GDR.

The dedication ceremony of the Buchenwald monument illustrates the ambiguous mixture of somber remembrance and festive commemoration that characterized many of the memorial services during this period in the GDR. The plans called for beginning the ceremony by launching rockets that carried flags from the countries that had inmates imprisoned at Buchenwald. This was to be followed by the ringing of the bell for one and a half minutes in complete silence and then another one and a half minutes during which the dead would be honored with the lighting of the victim's bowl (*Opferschale*). Following these opening rituals, Otto Grotewohl, Minister President of the GDR, was scheduled to hold a thirty-minute speech followed by one sentence from each national delegation. Georg Spielmann, who was in charge of the logistics of the dedication, stressed the international importance of the event by highlighting plans by radio stations across Eastern Europe to broadcast the opening ceremony and urged those in the West to press for similar coverage in their countries. Spielmann summarized his vision for the ceremony as an event like no other: "The dedication of Buchenwald will be an event that will overshadow everything that has come before. I want to emphasize once again that this festive manifestation is not to be interpreted as an affair solely for the former Buchenwald inmates, but is something for all former political prisoners, all deportees, resistance fighters, partisans, etc. Therefore we intend to center this event on everyone who is true to the ideals of resistance against the return of German militarism and fascism, who fights against war and champions peace and international friendship."[32] The conclusion of the ceremony called for the release of twenty-five to thirty thousand doves while those present read aloud the "Oath of Buchenwald," the legendary oath that was sworn by the surviving prisoners upon their liberation during the first memorial service.

The Buchenwald dedication, however, encompassed much more than the ceremony atop the Ettersberg Mountain. The entire city of Weimar was called on to participate—the SED instructed theaters, movie houses, and folk art ensembles to relate their work to the theme of resistance. The local party leadership made special arrangements for hosting delegations from around East Germany and from throughout the world. Local theaters and cafés hosted special literary readings in honor of Buchenwald. All of these ancillary events created a festive atmosphere for the dedication, which had now become one of the most extravagant public events in the early history of the GDR.

The inclusive nature of the event was evident from the very beginning of the day's preparations. At the first meeting of the Buchenwald Dedication Committee on 3 June 1957, Otto Grotewohl asserted that the place of memory was to be dedicated not only to those killed at Buchenwald, but to all of the fighters killed by the "fascist murderers" and would "continuously warn [us] to protect the principles of humanism, to keep the peace, and deepen our friendship between people."[33] The purpose of the event was to connect as many people as possible to the memorial project.

The planning committee invited over 3,000 people from abroad and an additional 2,000 from West Germany and West Berlin. They expected a turnout of between 70,000 and 80,000 people from within the territory of the GDR. This meant rerouting traffic, trains, busses, and even using cargo trains to transport people to the event.[34] Erich Honecker, the future leader of East Germany, was placed in charge of organizing a tent encampment for between 7,000 and 10,000 members of the FDJ youth organization.[35]

The 14 September 1958 dedication ceremony came at the end of a rapid succession of anniversaries and related dedication events: the 18 August 1958 dedication of the Thälmann monument in Weimar, the "Day of Freedom" on 1 September, and the "Memorial Day for the Victims of Fascism" on 7 September.[36] The ceremony went as planned, although the actual turnout was slightly less than predicted. Grotewohl held his speech calling on everyone present not only to honor the deeds of those who suffered under the Nazi regime, but also to be inspired by their actions and take up the fight for world peace. The speech was carried live over the radio, broadcast both nationally and internationally. Newspaper coverage was extensive throughout the GDR. Thus even those who were not physically present had the opportunity to participate in this ritual of blessing the holy ground on which the future GDR was symbolically built.

Grotewohl also made sure that the division between East and West was placed within the "correct" historical context. In his speech he declared:

"Today there are two German states in the world. One has learned from the lessons of history. It has found good and rightful lessons. It is the GDR, a state of freedom and socialism. The West German state is, however, a depository of reaction, in which militarists and fascists have managed to regain power and whose aggressive character is demonstrated by their reactionary acts."[37] Thus, the culmination of the ceremony and its elaborately staged dedication established the final element of control by the state over the popular memory of Buchenwald and by extension of the entire communist resistance movement during the Nazi period.

The Buchenwald memorial was the most important of the three official national memorials in the GDR for remembering the victims of fascism and the Holocaust. Whereas West German monuments and concentration camp memorials focused primarily on the experience of the European Jews, this story and these memories remained secondary to the overarching desire and need by the East German state to claim this experience as its own. The state needed the public to view the communists as the greatest victims so that their triumph (the creation of the GDR) would be even more heroic. The SED hoped that all of these efforts would contribute to a moral underpinning for the party and ultimately to a certain level of cultural legitimacy for the East German state as the better alternative to its West German counterpart. Throughout its forty-year existence, the GDR state would rely heavily on the memories of Buchenwald in its effort to sustain its cultural legitimacy as the better Germany, the protectors of the "other" Germany that resisted fascism and broke away from the traditions of German militarism and reactionary politics.

Beyond the symbolic importance of Buchenwald as a central site of postwar memory, the enormous amount of effort asserted by the party leadership to seize control over what had begun as a non-party memory project and to essentially "nationalize" it and claim it in the name of the state was an important step in establishing a coherent memory policy for East Germany. Other national memory projects, like those at the Sachsenhausen and Ravensbrück, would replicate Buchenwald's message of communist suffering and antifascist resistance. As a crucial element in the state's foundational narrative, these sites of antifascist memory were extremely important to the party's fundamental claims to power. Future sculptors also looked to the work of Fritz Cremer for inspiration and for guidance regarding how best to capture the essence of East German socialist memorial art. Over time Buchenwald became an important destination for school groups, workers, soldiers, and tourists and was what James Young has termed a "place in the mind" of East Germans—"where character, courage, and communist identity were forged."[38] As a site of memory, Buchenwald promoted a sense of self-assurance that the East German state was born out of a struggle against fascism and reinforced the regime's overall memory-work aimed at ratifying its own claim to legitimacy as representing fascism's staunchest opponents and primary victims.

The Museum for German History

The Museum for German History also played an integral role in the SED's efforts to entrench within the East German population a separate memory culture—but with only limited success. The SED sought to create the first museum to portray Germany's national history from a Marxist historical-materialist perspective and the first to focus primarily on the history of the working class at a national level. Although state and party functionaries wielded a heavy hand in the museum's inception and ideological message, the process of how the museum was developed and the apparent lackluster reception it received reveal how the SED intended the museum to function and some of the limits of how such a museum could support the party's larger memory-work agenda. The narrative of the museum's permanent exhibit allowed the party to present the public with a new interpretation of German history based on the scholarly writings of the party's professional historians. This new narrative was meant to place the young East German state within a longer line of historical development that was more complex and reached much further back in time than had been the case with the traveling exhibit "The Other Germany" from 1948 discussed in chapter 1.

Fred Oelßner, who headed the propaganda division of the Secretariat of the SED Central Committee, made a trip to the Soviet Union during which he had visited several Soviet history museums, including the Lenin Museum and the Revolution Museum. The high number of visitors that such museums were able to attract especially impressed him. He immediately set to work on creating a similar museum in the GDR, which led the SED to call for the creation of a "Museum of the Revolutionary Movement" in May 1950.[39] Indeed, an informant for the West German SPD claimed that direct involvement by the Soviet Union was much stronger and that the idea for the museum actually stemmed from officials in Moscow.[40]

Several weeks following the Third Party Congress, the state named Eduard Ullmann, at the time a young staff member at the Marx-Engels-Lenin-Institute in Berlin, as the provisional director of the new history museum. The former *Zeughaus* on Unter den Linden, located in the center of Berlin's government district, became the home for the new museum.[41] The history of the *Zeughaus* building is itself symbolically interesting. Originally built as Prussia's armory, the imperial government converted the building in 1877 into a weapons and military history museum following German unification. The museum played an active role during the imperial period as a place for the state to promote nationalist sentiments. The *Zeughaus* building, unlike most of Berlin, had not sustained considerable damage during the war and the Berlin Magistrate decided to make it the repository for less fortunate city museums. Thus the building presented itself as the logical place for the new museum, since it already held many of the historical artifacts needed to launch the museum.

Planning for the museum was already under way before the state made its official announcement to the public. On 8 December 1951, Ullmann met with Kurt Hager and a few others at the Ministry of Higher Education (*Ministerium für Hoch und Fachhochschulen*) to discuss the drafting of the document "Duties, Structure and Construction of the Museum for German History." The initial draft pointed to four key areas of competence for the museum. First, the museum was intended to collect and display historical documents and items of material culture that represent important historical events in German history. Second, the museum should "vividly" display the historical development of the German people, its material culture and the role of the revolutionary class struggle, especially the German working class. Third, the museum's leadership would carry out a broad political "enlightenment" and educational program for the general public. Finally, the museum was charged with identifying and maintaining all of the historic sites that had to do with the founders of socialism as well as others associated with the historical development of the German working class.[42] This initial conceptualization of how the MfDG would function within the SED's larger plans for memory-work illustrates how the museum as a public institution would need to be adapted in order to serve such a function.

Unlike a local museum or an interpretive display at an historic site, this new museum was supposed to tell the story of the German people through displays comprised of items representing its material culture. Moreover, the museum was charged not only with displaying a Marxist narrative of historical development but also with propagating and actively "enlightening" the masses about the "proper" interpretation of historical events and personalities. The SED intended that the museum would take on an important role that extended far beyond the walls of the *Zeughaus*. Indeed, the SED expected that the museum identify and maintain all of the major sites that related to the history of the German working class and oversee preservation efforts, thereby coordinating the message of the state's memory-work throughout the GDR.

The initial conceptualization for the museum's exhibit, however, found strong criticism within the ranks of the SED elite. On 5 January 1952, Minister of Education Paul Wandel hosted a meeting to discuss the plan for the museum. Also present at the meeting were his State Secretary Gerhard Harig, Kurt Hager, who coordinated education policy for the SED Central Committee, Prof. Alfred Meusel, who a day earlier had been selected as the new director of the museum, Director of the Marx-Engels-Lenin Institute Bernhard Dohm, and several other noted personalities representing universities and party institutions.

Kurt Hager, who would later rise to be the SED's chief ideologue and Minister of Culture, began the conversation by emphasizing that the museum's primary function must be to educate a wide public. He also emphasized the central role that the museum would play in training future historians, that it should be the central institute for historical research, and that it spread its reach throughout the GDR through traveling exhibits and subsidiary institutions. Others criticized the need for the museum to function simultaneously as both an exhibition hall and center of historical research, "why then do we need the university and party institutes?"[43] Another key criticism of the plan focused on the initial conceptualization of the periodization, claiming that the initial draft was a confusing mixture of "bourgeois" and Marxist historical interpretations that incorporated traditional historical turning points like the formation of the German Empire in 1871 instead of basing the periodization entirely on economic markers fundamental to a Marxists interpretation.

The famous economic historian and intellectual Jürgen Kuczynski laid out a lengthy argument against an institute that was too large and charged with too many duties to function as anticipated. He argued for a clear delineation between the museum and the research institutes of the universities and the SED. There were undoubtedly practical motivations behind the efforts of Kuczynski and others representing research institutes and universities, who did not want to see another institute take control over directing all historical research and training in the country. Yet for Hager, Wandel, and Harig, the museum played a key role in presenting the SED's vision of the past to the general public in a way that freed it from the constraints of academic historical writing. Moreover, Harig cautioned the professors present at the meeting that the museum might be a blow to the universities, but a necessary one if they hoped to consolidate research efforts and overcome the splintering of historical interpretations found in university departments. He mentioned one such department by name, at the University of Rostock, suggesting that it might need to be liquidated, and further cautioned that it might not be the only one.[44]

The tone of this meeting delivers a clear picture of just how important the museum was not only for the SED's desire to create new national museum, but also for its overall plans to revamp the structure of historical research and propaganda for the GDR. Certainly, there were competing visions of the museum's message and structure, yet all were convinced of its importance in the overall goal of strengthening the historical consciousness of a wide public. The initial plan also indicates that the museum planners wanted their museum to appeal to a wider cross-section of society and not merely those who were already sympathetic to the SED. At the same time, however, the document reflects a keen awareness that the museum's focus needed to be the Marxist-Leninist interpretation of German historical development, which the planners argued would strengthen the legitimacy of the young East German state.[45]

On 18 January 1952, State Secretary for Higher Education Gerhard Harig convened the first official meeting of the museum's leadership, including its new director Alfred Meusel and assistant director Eduard Ullmann.[46] The following day, Minister President Otto Grotewohl formally announced the creation of the museum to the public during the first meeting of the museum's academic advisory board. The official press statement from the museum highlighted the goals and the general framework from the perspective of director Meusel. According to the press statement, the museum's primary goal was to provide a new interpretation of Germany's national history and "demonstrate that not the emperors, the kings, military leaders, and diplomats, but the working people in the city and countryside are the real creators and shapers of German history."[47] The museum leadership intended this Marxist interpretation of Germany's historical development to mark a clear break from previously dominant historical interpretations of history that focused primarily on the acts of a few key events and figures.[48]

The SED wanted the Museum for German History to be viewed not as an institution constructed solely by the state, but as a *Volksmuseum* (people's museum). To this end, the museum issued a call for people in East and West Germany to donate historically significant artifacts—documents, certificates, diaries of famous personalities, photographs, posters, newspapers, flyers, records, as well as items of everyday life such as furniture, clothing, and tools.[49] The call was aimed especially toward those living in West Germany, noting that participation by Germans living in the western part of the "fatherland" would demonstrate their "solidarity" with the efforts to preserve the concept of the nation through the establishment of a German national history museum in Berlin.[50]

Alfred Meusel and the museum staff had only a very short timespan to complete their plan for the new museum, as it was scheduled to open in the summer of 1952. Although historians like Meusel had already made strides in theorizing how German history could be interpreted according to Marx's theory of historical materialism and the progression of changing power relationships (i.e. the class struggle), there had been relatively little published research using such methodology and thus the museum staff could draw on only a limited amount of material. While the staff had little difficulty adapting the periodization of German history into distinct epochs of historical and economic development using Marx's interpretation, further differentiations within each epoch proved to be more challenging.

The framework for the periodization called for dividing German history into seven distinct epochs, each of which highlighted different dominant economic relationships. Accordingly, curatorial departments were formed to cover the areas of early history, the Middle Ages up through 1517, 1517–1848, 1848–1895, 1895–1918, 1918–1945, and a final department that focused on the present day. Accordingly, the periodization would guide the visitor starting with the history of the Germanic tribes and feudalism into the Renaissance and the age of absolutism, from the birth of democracy to the heights of imperialism and the horrors of fascism, finally concluding with the "glorious" culmination of German history in the creation of the first worker's state on German soil.

During these six months, the museum's curators set to work interpreting each epoch of German history according to Marxist theory. They sought to piece together a new socialist master-narrative that would form the over-arching interpretation for the museum. Given its function as the central "national" history museum, high-ranking officials played an active role throughout this process to ensure that the state's interests were represented. Ernst Diehl from the Ministry of Propaganda and another representative from the State Secretariat for Higher Education took part in all of the discussions and oversaw the political aspects of the museum's interpretive framework.

Museum curators set to work drafting exhibit scripts that outlined the goals of each section of the museum and proposed which objects or artifacts could be incorporated to meet such goals. They completed the first drafts of scripts by the end of February and submitted them to the academic advisory board for discussion. Meeting on 1 March 1952, the board presented its initial feedback and offered changes it felt would better present the party's desired interpretation of historical events. By June the curators completed their revisions and work on setting up the displays commenced.

The museum opened to the public on 5 July 1952 with a narrative that strung together major events in German history in a manner that was quite different from how most Germans had learned about their history prior to 1945. As visitors moved through the exhibit they were confronted with displays that highlighted the constant struggle between the "progressive" and "reactionary" forces that had dictated the historical development of the German nation. The tension between these two forces mounted from room to room until it culminated in the defeat of fascism in 1945. Within each period, the exhibit attempted to juxtapose militarist and reactionary policies of the German national elite with the everyday life and resistance efforts by members of the lower classes.[51]

Overall, the visitor statistics and visitor responses reflect a relatively ambiguous relationship between the visitor and the museum's exhibits. Typically, according to the museum's own studies, visitors did not tend to visit the entire museum during a visit. Rather, visitors usually restricted themselves one or more of the individual departments of the museum. The nature of how visitors experienced the museum thus broke up the overall continuity within the museum's narrative and did not have the overall effect that its planners may have hoped. Indeed, throughout the first decade, the piecemeal manner in which the museum slowly moved into its permanent building on Unter den Linden further prevented visitors from experiencing the museum narrative as it had been originally conceived.

The motivations for those who visited the museum ran the gamut from organized school or factory visits to independent tourists who were simply looking for something to see while visiting Berlin. Despite its efforts to draw in new visitors to special exhibits and commemorative events, the

FIGURE 2.3. Director Alfred Meusel (middle) opening three segments of the Museum for German History covering the years 1849–1945 on 11 April 1953 with Elisabeth Zaisser (right), Minister of Education. BArch Bild 183-19151-0002 / Günter Weiß.

museum never saw the high level of success that Fred Oelßner observed at Soviet museums during his 1950 visit. Concern for raising the museum's profile continued throughout its history.

Trends in the visitor statistics do demonstrate a steady growth in museum attendance and its traveling exhibits. This growth, however, appears to taper off after reaching a highpoint in 1959, coinciding with the tenth anniversary of the GDR, and suffering its most dramatic drop in visitors in 1961, presumably a direct result of the construction of the Berlin Wall and the new impediment that this barrier now became to attracting visitors from the West.

TABLE 2.3. Visitor statistics for the Museum for German History

Year	Main Exhibit in the *Clara Zetkin Strasse* and *Unter den Linden*	Traveling Exhibits	Total Visitors
1952	49,320	–	49,320
1953	185,195	–	185,195
1954	144,256	–	144,256
1955	134,736	–	134,736
1956	147,916	6,765	154,681
1957	207,704	60,845	268,549
1958	367,861	233,412	601,273
1959	514,952	307,840	822,792
1960	180,420	259,320	439,740
1961	88,311	211,425	299,736

Source: DHM, Hausarchiv: MfDG/1185. "Besucherzahlen—Museum für Deutsche Geschichte."

In January 1953, a young history student named Ulrich B. wrote a letter to the party newspaper *Neues Deutschland* in which he strongly criticized the work of the museum and its representation of German history from a Marxist-Leninist perspective. The newspaper in turn forwarded the letter to Director Meusel for comment. Most of the student's critique centered on instances where he felt the museum had not stated clearly enough how the history of a class society was the history of class struggle. Ulrich B. named many examples in which the museum's interpretation of an event did not sufficiently convince the visitor of the transition from one form of oppression to another and how this transition was achieved through class warfare. For instance, he took issue with the lack of attention paid to the social conflicts in medieval cities and complained that the exhibit's handling of feudalization underplayed the role of the peasant in fighting for better living conditions. Ulrich B. argued that the primary problem was that the museum curators had merely presented the historical facts without providing sufficient political interpretive information. He also pointed out that since the majority of the German population had been schooled in the "bourgeois" interpretation of history, it needed to be retaught how to interpret the past. Ulrich B.'s proposed solution included increasing the number of quotations by Marx, Engels, Lenin, and Stalin in order for the visitor to "correctly" interpret the meaning of the past.

Director Meusel took this criticism quite seriously and instructed his staff to respond to the individual areas of critique within each of their departments. The resulting memos provide a picture of a museum that was struggling with its dual role as traditional history museum as well as a propaganda instrument of the new state. Each of the department heads admitted that there were definite shortcomings within their departments, yet they also defended their work as correct from a museum pedagogical perspective.[52] Meusel drafted a response to the editor of *Neues Deutschland* based on the internal memos in which he laid out his argument against publishing Ulrich B.'s letter. Meusel admitted that there were still improvements to be made in the museum, yet did not feel that the paper should support an attack on the integrity of the museum. Meusel argued that the museum must be seen as the "*museum* for German history and not the *textbook* of German history."[53]

Indeed such critique from the left was probably more dangerous than critiques from the right, which one could simply fend off with the use of class rhetoric. Ulrich B.'s critique was so potentially damaging to the integrity of the museum because it called for a more aggressive political role for the museum and attacked the overall interpretation of German history as not socialist enough. Meusel and his team were well aware of such shortcomings, but also understood that they needed to balance their Marxist interpretation with a reasonable degree of museum professionalism if they were to uphold the academic integrity of the institution. This integrity was important for the state's overall claim to legitimacy, since the museum's academic integrity provided the underpinnings for its historical interpretation and thus cultural legitimacy of the entire political system in East Germany.

The culmination of the first stage in the development and societal function of the Museum for German History came in 1960 with the special exhibit "15 Years of Liberation." Between 1953 and 1960 there had been fourteen different special exhibits ranging from ones that honored individuals such as Karl Marx and Wilhelm Pieck to broader topics like the German Peasants' War, Red October, and Germany from 1917 to 1919. Curators designed each of these exhibits to impart the visitor with a sense of historical continuity between the present political situation and the past, yet the special exhibit in 1960 took on a particular importance in differentiating the GDR state from its West German neighbor.

According to the working documents, the exhibit primarily aimed to display the historical legality—and thus legitimacy—of socialism's victory over imperialism. The entire exhibit was designed to contrast life in the SBZ/GDR over the previous fifteen years with the developments in neighboring West Germany. The contrasting elements hinged on the assertion that unlike West Germany, the GDR had indeed broken the thread of imperialist dictatorial states, referring to imperialism as the "most aggressive, most robbing, regardless if [in the form of the] Prussian-German *Kaiserreich* under Wilhelm II, the openly terrorist Nazi dictatorship under Hitler, or as the clerical-militarist authoritarian regime disguised as democracy under Adenauer."[54] The disposition for the exhibit argued that the founding of the GDR was the strongest blow against the resurgence of German imperialism in West Germany. The GDR was to be portrayed as the rightful successor to the German nation, since it alone fulfilled the principles of the anti-Hitler coalition and because it was the product of the "peace-loving democratic and progressive forces of the German people who fell victim in the struggle against Hitler-fascism."[55]

These concepts of historical correctness and continuity of struggle were the main tenets that governed the entire exhibit, whose ultimate goal was to demonstrate the heroism and legitimacy of the "progressive" forces in Germany that fought to establish a better German state in the form of the GDR. Yet, the memories invoked by the exhibit were greater than simply the struggling against Nazism and delved deeper into the entire history of struggles against imperialism. This connection was particularly important for the state's desire to justify the necessity for a continued division between East and West Germany.

The special exhibit glorifying the fifteen years since the collapse of the Third Reich actually dedicated over half of its physical space to dealing with events prior to 1945. Curators divided the exhibit into three sections covering the periods 1933–1945, 1945–1949, and 1949–1960 in an area of approximately 1500 square meters (ca. 16,000 square feet). The goal of the first section of the exhibit was to illustrate that imperialism had been Germany's historical archenemy, which had only led to "suppression, enslavement and war."[56] The second portion of the exhibit focused on the reconstruction following the Second World War and the division of Germany into two competing visions for Germany's future—one in which the principles of the anti-Hitler coalition were being realized (in the East) and one in which imperialism had been restored (in the West). The final section of the exhibit linked the two previous segments to the present-day struggle between East and West Germany. The planners hoped that the visitor would see that the politics of the GDR represented the interests of all Germans who were interested in maintaining peace. Finally, the exhibit hoped to promote the idea that the combined powers of "peace, democracy, and social progressiveness were strong enough to thwart the war policies of the German imperialists."[57]

The timing of the exhibit, just one year prior to the construction of the Berlin Wall, cannot be overlooked when analyzing the political importance of the commemorative exhibit and the state's attempt to manipulate memory in order to justify its politics. The steady flow of refugees fleeing East Germany for a new life in the West began to take its toll on the East German economy and society. Within this political context, the museum exhibit sought to emphasize the moral superiority of the GDR at a time when political, material, and social forms of legitimacy were clearly failing.[58]

The need to reassess the function and effectiveness of the museum was not lost on its second director, Eduard Ullmann, who wrote a report outlining both the successes and shortcomings of the Museum for German History during its first eight years. Above all else, Ullmann stressed the unique character of the museum as a groundbreaking approach toward visualizing and presenting history to the public. Never before, he argued, had history been presented using new aesthetic principles that allowed the visitor to absorb the deeper meanings of history and internalize its lessons.[59] Yet Ullmann also noted many areas where he felt that the museum needed to expand its work and increase its effectiveness. The biggest frustration still facing the museum was the lack of general exposure among the public to the over-arching narrative of German history from a materialist perspective. He claimed that the opportunity to relate this interpretation has only been recently possible on a large scale and that the museum was more effective with younger students educated in the GDR than with the older generations.

Ullmann also pointed out that the museum remained too reliant on two-dimensional forms of presentation, primarily written documents and photographs. He called for greater integration of three-dimensional exhibit objects in order to increase the aesthetic representation of the past.[60] Indeed, Ullmann portrayed the need to bridge the gap between what he described as the two dominant "bourgeois" forms of museum exhibits— the "show" museum and the "academic" museum. Ullmann believed that the Museum for German History fell in between these two and formed what he called a "designed academic museum"[61] in which the visitor could have both an aesthetically rich experience, while also viewing the material in a manner that served a pedagogical goal.

Like many of the other state-sponsored memory-work projects during the 1950s, the SED intended the Museum for German History to document specific lines of historical continuity, while simultaneously delimitating the state from other possible interpretations of Germany's past. Both of these functions were seen as a vital component of the state's overall attempt to promote itself vis-à-vis West Germany. However, even according to the museum's own assessments, it was never able to achieve these goals. Throughout its entire existence, but especially during the 1960s and 1970s, the museum's pedagogical department continued to study how visitors reacted to the exhibits and experimented with new ways to improve its educational impact, especially among the youth (see chapter 3).

Honoring Marx and Engels

The physical reconstruction of Berlin was a slow and much politicized project that involved many competing visions both of how the city center should look and the symbolic role Berlin's architecture would play in the future. Moreover, the political-ideological division of Berlin into four sectors, the separation of the Berlin Magistrate into two bodies in 1948, and the founding of the German Democratic Republic in 1949, further complicated the efforts of city planners, architects, and preservationists. Until 1948, leading SED officials, such as the Chairman of the Berlin SED Hermann Matern, characterized Berlin as an insignificant city on the fringe of the Western Zone and spoke of Frankfurt am Main as the probable site of a new German national capital.[62] With Germany's division into two states in 1949, the SED quickly took on a more controlling role over city planning efforts in East Berlin.[63]

In late August 1950, the GDR government published its first official construction plan for the center of the "New Berlin." The ruins of the Berlin palace were to be replaced by a "Central Square" and a high-rise "Central Building" intended to be the primary seat of government and modeled after the Stalinist high-rise wedding cake-style buildings in Moscow. The plan also called for nationally significant monuments to be placed in the heart of the old city center. These included a monument for the FIAPP (International Federation of Former Political Prisoners) on the site where the Wilhelminian national monument once stood across from the main entrance of the Berlin palace and as a statue honoring Ernst Thälmann in front of the former Reich Chancellery. This constellation of memory projects, together with new government buildings, would mark the beginning of an effort to establish the young East Germany as one of the "victors of history." Moreover, the addition in late 1950 of plans to rename the Central Square to Marx-Engels-Platz and to construct a monument in their honor completed the overall concept for the government quarter, which although never fully realized in its original form remained the dominant model throughout the entire history of the GDR.

The way in which the SED sought to transform the government district during the first decade following the establishment of East Germany is an important component of its overall memory politics during this period. Once the division of Berlin was official, the new government in the East had a greater ability to impress its vision into the built environment of this historically important part of the city. In theory, given the dictatorial aspirations of the party, the SED leadership should have been able to simply impose its will on the city planners and preservationists. However, this was not entirely true. In fact, the party leadership found it quite difficult to rebuild Berlin the way it desired. Instead, it faced resistance from both city planners and artists who were commissioned to complete new monuments for the city center. This resistance stemmed from both practical limitations of what sort of rebuilding was actually feasible and shifting cultural trends, especially after the death of Stalin in 1953.

The SED leadership looked to Moscow as its primary model of inspiration for rebuilding the new city center. Like other East European capitals at the time, Berlin planers contemplated constructing buildings based on the seven wedding-cake style high-rise structures in Moscow that form a ring around the inner city. Warsaw's "Palace of Science and Culture" paved the way for similar projects throughout the Eastern Bloc, but ultimately it remained the only project that saw completion. Unlike their Polish neighbors, the GDR city planners decided to place symbolic importance on the power of the state instead of on science and culture. Since East Germany competed for legitimacy against the Bonn government and the West German model, East Berlin's city planners wanted to emphasize the power of the socialist state in the center of the city and create the impression of socialist victory over Germany's fascist and imperialist past. Thus the GDR planners intended the new central building, its accompanying square, and historical monuments to become the central icons of the new Berlin cityscape and the GDR.

Given the symbolic importance of the city rebuilding project and the new monuments, the party did not want to leave to the work to the local Berlin Magistrate or other interest groups. Instead, the SED *Politbüro* inserted itself directly into the city planning process and commanded oversight of the project. With the dissolving of the FIAPP as an international organization of the victims of fascism in December 1950, the *Politbüro* decided at its 30 December meeting to replace the planned FIAPP monument with statues in honor of Karl Marx and Friedrich Engels.[64] The *Politbüro* also created a Marx-Engels Monument Committee comprised of Wilhelm Pieck (chairman), Otto Grotewohl, Walter Ulbricht, Friedrich Ebert, Fred

Oelßner, and Kurt Liebknecht. All of the members of the committee were high-ranking members of the SED and only Kurt Liebknecht (president of the German Academy of Architecture) had a background in city planning. The composition of the committee is a clear sign that SED leadership saw the rebuilding of Berlin first and foremost as a political act.

The Central Committee followed up the *Politbüro* decision with its own resolution on 21 January 1951, directing the Berlin Magistrate to construct a monument on the west side of the new Central Square, which was to be renamed Marx-Engels-Platz on 1 May of that year. At its meeting on 2 February 1951, the Marx-Engels Monument Committee specified the parameters of the project. The monument was now to be built on the East side of the Marx-Engels-Platz atop a large reviewing stand (a *Tribüne*) capable of holding between 1,500 and 3,000 people. The committee called for a bronze statue, placed atop a pedestal, positioned in the middle of the reviewing stand with a height of 3.6 meters (slightly less than 12 feet).[65]

The Marx-Engels Monument Committee published a call for an international competition for the design of the monument on 18 April 1951. The call envisioned a monument in honor of the "greatest geniuses of mankind" that would demonstrate that the German people were "willing to break from a past in which it thrust itself and others into such misfortune."[66] Furthermore, the monument was intended to show that the GDR had created the basis on which the free and peaceful society that Marx and Engels first imagined would now become a reality. The committee also called on the artists to emphasize the strong, lifelong friendship that bound the two great men together in their struggle for a better future. Beyond reiterating the need for the monument to be bronze and positioned atop a reviewing stand, Marx was to be positioned on the left and Engels on the right with both of them jointly holding a volume of *The Communist Manifesto*.[67] These specifications extremely limited the scope of the project and left little room for personal artistic interpretation.

Yet the Marx-Engels monument project quickly ran into problems with the city planning objectives for this section of Berlin and the project stalled. The problem was rooted in differences between the artistic community and the political leaders in the SED, who were set on having a colossal monumental sculpture as the dominating figure on the Marx-Engels Square. Although the exact differences are difficult to trace from the sources, it is clear that the artists were not interested in overly large sculptures and felt that life-size figures were a more accurate portrayal with greater artistic legitimacy. The evidence also suggests that there was a difference in opinion whether such a monument could even be completed in time for the 135th anniversary of Marx's birth in 1953 as desired by the party leadership.[68]

Some members of the committee met with East Germany's leading sculptors to discuss the challenges presented by the project. They decided that an international competition for the construction of the monument would take too long and that it would be better to limit the competition to five, later three, invited artists. Among those invited were Fritz Cremer, Gustav Seitz, and Walter Howard.[69] Kurt Liebknecht recommended that the artists use the Ernst Reitschel monument of Goethe and Schiller in Weimar as an example of how to best portray the greatness of Marx and Engels. The choice of this particular sculpture is interesting, since it also indicates an attempt to draw a direct link between the humanist traditions of Goethe and Schiller and the teachings of Marx and Engels, and thereby between Germany's cultural heritage and the current Marxist political system in the GDR. Moreover, the choice of this famous monument to serve as the primary model indicated the desire to create a monument that the masses could readily relate to and interpret the "correct" meaning.

On 12 May 1951, President Pieck convened a meeting with some of East Germany's most recognized sculptors to discuss how the project should move forward.[70] During the discussion, Gustav Seitz informed Pieck that the party's vision for the Marx-Engels monument was architecturally out of place given the proximity to the Berlin Cathedral next to the square. He suggested that it was time to tear it down. Pieck responded that this would be impossible given the delicate relationship that the young state had with the church. Pieck then suggested that a Soviet sculptor should possibly be brought in to lead a group of German sculptors who could work on the monument collectively. This suggestion met a stern rebuttal from Fritz Cremer, who insisted that "it must be a German sculptor who receives such an important commission."[71] Gustav Seitz added that Germany had a strong tradition in sculptures and it would be a blow to their self-confidence to prevent German artists from winning the commission. Cremer went so far as to say he would not even tolerate a Soviet sculptor assisting him, were he to receive a commission to which Walter Howard agreed.

Gustav Seitz also took it upon himself to voice additional criticism about the planned monument in a letter addressed to the director of the East German Academy of Arts, Rudolf Engel. Seitz complained that the desired proportionality of the sculpture would be entirely out of place within the architectural landscape of the Marx-Engels-Platz. Instead, he pointed to three sculptures that he felt were models of correct proportionality and in turn should be the models for the Marx-Engels monument—the sculpture of Goethe and Schiller by Reitschel in Weimar, the equestrian statue of Elector Frederick William by Schlüter in Berlin, and the equestrian statue of Frederick the Great by Rauch in Berlin. In each of these examples, Seitz related how these sculptors had captured the correct proportionality for the portrayal of heroic figures. Above all, he noted that the planned Marx-Engels monument needed to be closer to life size so that the observer could better relate to them as figures of history. Seitz ended his letter by asking that he be removed from the Marx-Engels jury, stating, "under these conditions ... I can hardly take responsibility."[72]

Given Seitz's assessment of the planned monument and in opposition to the resistance of Cremer and Howard to involve a Soviet sculptor, Walter Ulbricht sent a telegram to the Central Committee of the Communist Party of the Soviet Union (CPSU) requesting that a Soviet sculptor be commissioned for the monument.[73] Ulbricht's request as well as a follow up request from Pieck at the end of November did not succeed in enlisting help from the Soviet Union.[74] The committee decided to move forward with a competition limited to five invited East German sculptors, who were asked to have sketches of their work ready by the end of January.[75] Wilhelm Pieck invited two Soviet artists to come to East Germany and review the progress of the sculptors participating in the Marx-Engels monument competition, meet with other artists, and visit the four leading schools of art to assess the artistic ability of East Germany's sculptors. The Soviet visitors, Sergei Aljoschin and Sergei Orlow, met with Pieck at the end of their trip on 8 February 1952. In his personal notes, Pieck wrote that Aljoschin and Orlow expressed a very negative impression of German sculptors.[76] The written report they delivered to Pieck pointed out that none of the sculptures were conceived within the broader context of the Marx-Engels-Platz nor did the artists' portrayals of Marx and Engels reflect existing portraiture, which they stated was vitally important in order to connect with the wider public.[77]

The following day, Wilhelm Pieck wrote to Mikhail Suslov at the Central Committee of the CPSU explaining the negative assessment by Aljoschin and Orlow requesting that the CPSU commission a Soviet sculptor for the Marx-Engels monument.[78] As with Ulbricht's request during the summer of the previous year, the Soviet government did not act on Pieck's request. Instead, the SED *Politbüro* passed a resolution on 12 February 1952 calling for a new competition. The resolution stipulated that the Marx-Engels-Institute needed to provide appropriate biographical information to the artists and that Minister President Grotewohl would work closely with the artists throughout the competition phase. Finally, the *Politbüro* called for the selected artist to travel to the Soviet Union for consultations with Soviet artists.[79]

The prize committee was reformulated to include Wilhelm Pieck, Otto Grotewohl, Walter Ulbricht, Friedrich Ebert, Fred Oelßner, Herbert Warnke, Helmut Holzhauer, and Kurt Liebknecht from the SED leadership together with the artists Fritz Dähn, Ruthild Hahne, and Edmund

Collein. The new competition was confined to Walter Arnold, Fritz Cremer, Waldemar Grzimek, Walter Howard, Fritz Koelle, Will Lammert, Rudolf Oelzner, and Gustav Seitz. The composition of the prize committee and the limited number of participants illustrates that the SED leadership desired to retain tight control over the construction of the Marx-Engels monument. Moreover, the committee went to far greater lengths than previously to articulate its vision that the Marx-Engels monument must be large enough to dominate the square and that "only a realistic representation can reflect the importance of this monumental memorial."[80]

Ultimately, the prize committee selected Walter Howard's sculpture as the best representation of its vision. It featured an image of Marx and Engels walking together with Marx holding a copy of *The Communist Manifesto* and was indeed very similar in its presentation to the Goethe-Schiller monument suggested by Kurt Liebknecht in 1951. Yet, once again, the project ran into difficulty, when the SED representatives on the committee continued to press for a colossal monument that would be proportionate to the large parade square and the height of the planned government high-rise building. During 1953 and 1954, Grotewohl made several visits to Howard's studio to offer advice and make sure that he continued to develop his sculpture along the lines desired by the SED leadership. Howard, a student of Gustav Seitz, remained reluctant to enlarge his monument to the size desired by Grotewohl and others in the party leadership. In November 1956, Howard and Minister of Culture Johannes Becher wrote to East Berlin Mayor Friedrich Ebert in an attempt to find a new place for monument next to the Palace Bridge opposite the *Zeughaus* building.[81] In the end, a special commission was set up to look into the possibility of moving the monument elsewhere in East Berlin, but instead came to the conclusion that it should be offered to the city of Karl-Marx-Stadt (now Chemnitz) instead.[82] Given that Howard styled his monument after the Goethe-Schiller monument in Weimar, it is fitting that the local government in Karl-Marx-Stadt decided to place the monument in its Schiller Park.[83]

The SED did not completely abandon its efforts to construct a fitting monument for Marx and Engels in the GDR capital. The memorial project continued to move forwards in spurts throughout the 1950s. Each time the artists believed the project would move forward, the state postponed it—either because party members continued to disagree with the artists' conceptions of the project or Berlin city planners kept changing the overall layout for the government district. With each alteration in the overall concept for Berlin, the nature and composition of the Marx-Engels monument was also adjusted and expanded as more ideas began to be incorporated into the ever-growing monumental structure. A 1958 plan by architect Gerhard Kosel called for a Marx-Engels-Forum to incorporate not only the

Figure 2.4. Walter Howard's sculpture of Marx and Engels in Karl-Marx-Stadt (Chemnitz) in 1957. BArch Bild 183-46722-0008 / Schlegel.

monument and reviewing stand, but also a museum of the history of the German worker's movement. A hall of honor was to be added into the forum to house the manuscript of *The Communist Manifesto* and a first edition copy of *Das Kapital*. The "holy books" of the communist movement would thus take on pseudo-religious meaning and the monument of Marx and Engels would be transformed into a shrine for the followers of Marxism.[84]

Yet none of these ambitious plans were ever realized in their original form. The decision by city planners in the late 1950s to move away from the idea of a high-rise government building in central Berlin meant that a colossal monument of Marx and Engels no longer fit the scaled down plans for the government district. Although the desire to honor Marx and Engels in the capital of the GDR would remain, the party and the Berlin city planners turned their attention to other priorities. Ultimately, Erich Honecker would be the one to resurrect the Marx-Engels monument project and its Thälmann monument counterpart in an effort to complete the tasks of legitimizing the state through these heroic figures in the 1980s (see chapter 5). Despite the fact that the party had almost complete control over the reconstruction process in East Berlin, the SED leadership clearly failed to impose its desire to populate the cityscape with its symbols of its own power. Although it was able to wrestle control of other memory projects like we saw at the Buchenwald memorial, there were clearly limits to just how much control the party could wield over the memory landscape. Some of these limitations were practical, but others also demonstrate divisions between the party leadership and those who were charged with carrying out the party's memory-work. We also see the emergence of a mutually dependent relationship between the party and its memory-workers (in this case the artists). The state and party held a monopoly over the commissioning of large-scale works of public art, thus making East German artists who desired to remain active dependent on commissions from the state. At the same time, these same artists possessed unique skills that the state needed if it wanted to have East Germans (as opposed to foreigners) create its national monuments. This relationship of mutual dependence continued throughout the history of the GDR and ultimately became the focus of even greater tension between the artistic community and the state during the 1980s (see chapter 5).

Ernst Thälmann in Berlin

Just as the SED sought to cultivate the images of Marx and Engels as the preeminent symbols of the new Germany, the party also attempted to instrumentalize the figure of Ernst Thälmann. We have already seen how the party used Thälmann's image as a martyr at the Buchenwald site, but now the party wanted to relocate his memory to the capital, to further nationalize his image, and to expand the number of public symbols that reified the party's claim to power. Thälmann, who was the last leader of the German Communist Party during the Weimar Republic through the Nazi seizure of power, turned out to be an ideal choice as a permanent symbol for the SED's proclaimed antifascist heritage. Before the party could capitalize on Thälmann's legacy it needed to streamline and stylize his image in order for him to be presented as both an ardent leader of the communist struggle and the consummate martyr in the fight against fascism. Although Thälmann led the KPD until the Nazi seizure of power in 1933, he spent most of the Nazi period in various prisons and concentration camps and was ultimately executed by the Nazis in Buchenwald in 1944. While Thälmann was in prison, Wilhelm Pieck and Walter Ulbricht controlled the vast majority of the party apparatus that remained faithful. Pieck and Ulbricht were not in Germany, but in exile in the Soviet Union and thus did not personally possess the antifascist credentials that they were now hoping to place in the hands of their fallen comrade. At the same time, Ulbricht, who was beginning to assert his own personal control over the party (even more so following the death of Stalin in 1953) saw the figure of Ernst Thälmann as a safe way to promote the memory of a hero without promoting any personal competition. Gradually throughout the 1950s, Ernst Thälmann emerged as the dominant mythical figure in the GDR and became the central icon for the popular portrayal of the German communists as antifascist resistance fighters.[85]

Similar to the proposed construction of the Marx-Engels monument, the proposal for a national monument in honor of Ernst Thälmann in central Berlin was part of a larger effort by the party to rebuild the government district in a manner that would visually underscore the triumph of socialism. The first step toward the monument's construction began in February 1950 when the *Politbüro*, followed by a similar proclamation by the Central Committee, authorized a national competition for the construction of the "Ernst Thälmann National Monument of the German People."[86] The national importance of the monument, like that of the Marx-Engels monument, is reflected in the composition of the competition's prize committee. Minister President Otto Grotewohl and First Secretary Walter Ulbricht headed the committee, which also included Minister of Public Education Paul Wandel, sculptor Gustav Seitz, and the landscape architect Reinhold Lingner.[87] The monument was to be placed directly across from the former Reich Chancellery in the square formerly named the Wilhelmplatz and recently renamed the Thälmannplatz.[88] Together the placement of the

Marx-Engels and the Thälmann monuments were intended to demonstrate the victory of the working class over the two most recent forms of oppression—imperialism and fascism—which the new East German state, and by extension the SED, had conquered. By occupying and altering the historical interpretation of each of these sites of memory, the SED intended to send a clear message to the public regarding the permanence of its victory.

Following a public exhibition of the proposals in May 1950 at the new Academy of Arts building in East Berlin, the prize committee decided not to single out one particular proposal, noting that many were inspiring. Instead, the committee awarded prizes to the sculptors Fritz Cremer and Richard Horn as well as to a joint proposal from sculptor Ruthild Hahne and architect Waldemar Heinrichs.[89] Overall, the committee praised the artistic interpretation of each of the sculptors, but leveled heavy criticism at the architectural components. The critique, however, was only indirect, since the committee cited a lack of information from city planners, which limited the ability of the artists to integrate their work correctly into the city surroundings. Cremer's proposal showed a lone statue of Thälmann standing between two tall rectangular blocks of stone, symbolizing his individual struggle against the forces of Nazism that surrounded him. Horn's work depicted a large square pedestal with a relief of Thälmann on the front and a group of freedom fighters with waving flags on top. The proposal submitted by Hahne and Heinrichs was one of the more elaborate proposals, featuring a double semi-circular concave relief. The two semicircles faced one another with a small entranceway to the right and left. From inside the circular environment the visitor would be surrounded by two opposing relief sculptures. On the one side was a relief depicting Ernst Thälmann leading a parade of marching working class figures. On the opposite side stood a street that was lined with onlookers welcoming and honoring the marchers.[90]

Although the prize committee had not singled out one proposal, Walter Ulbricht convened a meeting on 7 August 1950 that resulted in commissioning Ruthild Hahne, René Graetz, and Kurt Liebknecht to create a new design based on Hahne's original submission, to be completed by mid-October of the same year. The committee seemed drawn to the immersive aspects of Hahne's proposal, but favored Graetz's sculptural skills. The result should have been a hybrid of the two proposals, but weighted more to the side of Hahne's vision of Thälmann as the undisputed leader of the German labor movement.

The sculpture created by the newly formed artists collective, however, featured a central sculpture of Thälmann set off from a long wall of relief sculptures featuring different archetypal depictions of the working class.

In the end, the new design more resembled Graetz's original proposal of a large relief, which had been rejected by the prize committee, than Hahne's proposal. Wilhelm Pieck and Walter Grotewohl visited the studio at the end of October and remarked that the sculpture did not conform to the original request by the party. Although the committee did not completely halt Hahne's project, it did stipulate that the next version be based more directly on Hahne's work than Graetz's. Following Pieck and Grotewohl's visit, the committee transferred responsibility for the project to the Ministry of People's Education (*Volksbildungsministerium*), which allotted Hahne a budget of 400,000 Marks for the project.[91] This was a substantial amount of money allocated to the construction of a monument and reflects just how important the Thälmann project was for the party's political agenda. Moreover, it is telling that this project was transferred to the Ministry of People's Education rather than the Ministry of Culture, as was the case with most of the other memorial projects. As such, it is clear that the state intended the Thälmann monument to function as a significant propaganda tool for the state.

Hahne and Graetz worked on the new project for the rest of 1950 and through the winter of 1951. They produced a basic conceptual model that Hahne would continue to refine until the project's cancellation in 1965. They retained from Hahne's original proposal the image of Thälmann leading the marching crowd, but modified the symbolism inherent in the

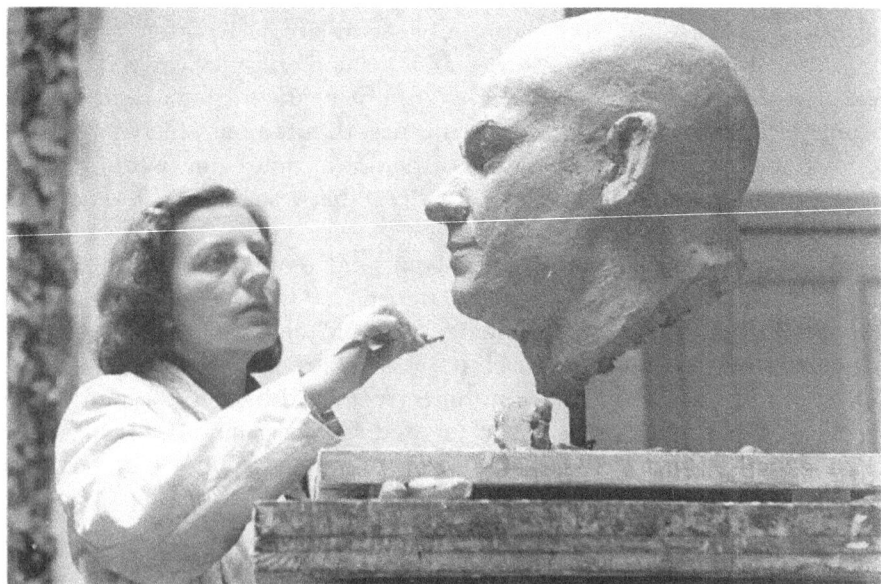

FIGURE 2.5. Ruthild Hahne working on an early version of her sculpture of Ernst Thälmann in 1951. BArch Bild 183-09958-0433.

depiction to illustrate Thälmann's role in unifying the divergent working class movements into one party, i.e. the SED.[92] The new monumental sculpture formed a large horizontal V-shaped structure with Thälmann marching at the tip of the "V" with a raised right fist. The figures that formed the relief images along each side of the "V" numbered 65 in all and were to measure 5–6 meters in height. Hahne and Graetz intended to place this enormous relief atop a circular base with a diameter of 60 meters. The inside portion of the "V" was designed to portray several scenes from Thälmann's life. The overall effect of transforming the monument from a two-dimensional walled relief to a three-dimensional "V" generated the perception that the crowd marching behind Thälmann grew larger and larger as one moved from the front of the sculpture to the rear.[93]

Sculptor Hans Kies replaced René Graetz in 1952 as Hahne's chief collaborator after the *Politbüro* chose to adopt Hahne's realistic portrayal of Thälmann over Graetz's more aesthetic interpretation.[94] The SED leadership's insistence on adhering to the standards of socialist realism and monumental structures began a process of distancing most of the best-known East German sculptors from the Thälmann project. Over the next decade, East Germany's leading sculptors were drawn more toward historical monuments that were more easily justified with their placement at real sites of memory—Fritz Cremer would concentrate on his sculptures for the Buchenwald and Ravensbrück memorials, while Walter Arnold turned his attention to the statue of Ernst Thälmann in Weimar.[95]

Yet the loss of support for Hahne's project from within the artistic community did not hinder the political desire on behalf of the SED leadership to see the project through to an acceptable end. Hahne's close personal friendship with the leading figures of the SED leadership such as Ulbricht and Grotewohl was probably the only thing that kept her project alive as long as it did. Indeed, the political and historical importance of the site now centered on the placement of the monument instead of the monument representing the historical significance of the site. Whereas the original idea behind renaming the Wilhelmplatz to Thälmannplatz had been to link the Reich Chancellery as a symbol of Nazi power to the plight of Thälmann as the nation's greatest martyr in the struggle against fascism, the political symbolism inherent in the Hahne project no longer had any connection with the historical site.

Political support for the project went through a series of crises and reassessments over the following decade. During the summer of 1953, a delegation of artists from the Soviet Union came to visit and critique the project. Fyodor Davidov, a leading Soviet artist, reported to Grotewohl that although he was impressed with the concept behind the statue and the portrayal of Thälmann leading the masses, he did not believe that

Hahne possessed enough artistic ability to execute the project as planned. In 1954, Fritz Dähn, who was in charge of fine arts at the Ministry of Culture, proposed that the *Politbüro* authorize an immediate solution to the problems facing the project and suggested placing a simple, stand-alone statue of Thälmann on top of a pedestal.[96] The *Politbüro*, however, decided to stay the course and again endorsed Hahne's project and transferred responsibility of the project over to the Ministry of Culture, probably in hopes of finding more resonance and support from the artistic community.

The critique by the Soviet artists and greater GDR artistic community also prompted the SED leadership to try and bolster Hahne's artistic credibility. In 1958, Ruthild Hahne, Gruson,[97] and Karl Schönherr traveled to the Soviet Union at the request of Walter Ulbricht with the aim to foster personal contacts between the East German artists and their Soviet counterparts. The intention of the trip was also for the artists to visit large-scale monuments in Moscow and gather information on the techniques employed by Soviet sculptors in creating such works. Upon their return, the sculptors were asked to apply this new knowledge to their work of the Thälmann monument in Berlin.[98]

The group toured many monuments in Moscow, including the Pushkin monument on Gorki Street and visited an exhibit of a competition for a new Lenin monument. Yet upon returning to Berlin, Hahne's work on the Thälmann monument continued along similar lines as before. By 1961, Hahne had completed a 1:3 model of the project. The figures had improved in their development and realistic representation; however, the number of figures remained above fifty, which had been seen as too many by the visiting Soviet artists and many in the GDR artistic community.

Indeed, the latest plan for Berlin, published in March 1961, called for the destruction of the former Reich Chancellery due to the straightening of the Otto-Grotewohl-Strasse (formerly the Wilhelmstrasse). This meant that any historical relevance that the Thälmannplatz once had would now evaporate with the removal of the very site to which it was supposed to stand in opposition. Further complications arose during the summer with the construction of the Berlin Wall in August 1961. The division of Berlin meant that the Thälmannplatz now lay within a few hundred meters of the border between East and West Berlin and would no longer hold a central place within the grand concept for rebuilding Berlin. In a final attempt to further rationalize her project and save the Thälmann monument in its existing form, Hahne suggested turning the museum section of the monument (i.e. the inside portion of the "V") into a lounge for the border guards, thus attempting to place her project within the new context of protecting the state's borders.[99]

Beyond the political, artistic, and city planning problems confronting Hahne's Thälmann project, there were also mounting practical limitations that began to signal the end for the planned monument. One such limitation came to light after an assessment by the foundry that was preparing to increase the size of the original sculpture. In 1962, Hahne had a foundry in Lauchhammer use plaster to enlarge mechanically the original sculpture to a size of 2:1. The new plaster model was supposed to be again doubled in size to a final perspective of 4:1. Once completed, stonemasons would use the new model to create the finished monument. Two problems arose from this enlargement process. First, the task of moving from the 2:1 perspective to the 4:1 enlargement was not possible at the foundry, since the finished product would have been too large. Moreover, it was doubtful whether there were sufficient trained stonemasons in the GDR to finish the project in the ten years that had been estimated for its completion.[100]

An official end to Hahne's project came on 13 July 1965, when the *Politbüro* passed a resolution calling for the cessation of current efforts to construct a monument for Ernst Thälmann.[101] Moreover, the *Politbüro* called on the President of the Academy of Arts and the Ministry of Culture to initiate steps to cultivate skills among GDR sculptors for working on large-scale monumental projects in the future. Thus, the political will to continue a project long opposed and abandoned by many within society finally evaporated. Yet the political necessity to have a Thälmann monument in Berlin persisted and was taken up again in the 1970s and 1980s under Honecker, albeit by the Soviet sculptor Lev Kerbel (see chapter 5).

The project failed on several fronts, but like the Marx-Engels monument, such national memorial projects need to be seen as part of a larger attempt by the state to occupy key places within Berlin's memory landscape. Whereas the placement of the Marx-Engels monument on the grounds of the former imperial palace was meant to demonstrate the triumph of Marxism over the power of the Emperor, the placement of the Thälmann monument in the square opposite the former Reich Chancellery was meant to represent the triumph of communism over the political control of the Nazis. With the SED now occupying the government district in central Berlin, the seat of power for both the Second Empire as well as the Nazi dictatorship, the party hoped it could use such monuments to influence popular memory and legitimize the SED's rule.

Yet neither historic site ultimately captured the desired political message espoused by the SED leadership. The Marx-Engels monument had little connection with a triumph over German imperialism once the City Palace had been torn down. The inability of Berlin's city planners to move ahead with a plan that made room for either of these monuments further frustrated efforts to connect the monuments with their architectural surroundings. Moreover, many in the GDR artistic community opposed large-scale monumental works and offered little support for Soviet-style memorials that were so cherished by the party leadership. This splintering between the vision of the party and the self-perception of the GDRs artists further distanced the regime from those who could fulfill its political goals. Nonetheless, both of these projects were resurrected in the late 1970s during a time when the GDR government again desired to use these political figures as legitimizing symbols of its own correctness.

Conclusion

The first decade of SED rule in East Germany was marked by attempts by the party to use its memory-work projects to legitimate the authority of the new East German state. It sought to appropriate the memory of resistance and antifascism through its takeover of the memorial project at Buchenwald. With the opening of the new Museum for German History, the party saw a chance to popularize a Marxist interpretation of German history that went beyond traditional historical scholarship and focused on the use of material culture to convey its message that the East German state was the culmination of the German working class's struggle to gain power. Yet, the party did not have the power to complete all of its memory-work projects in the manner that it desired, as we saw with its failure to construct monuments for Marx, Engels, and Thälmann.

Building on the momentum generated by its initial attempts to shape German memory culture in the SBZ, the SED in the 1950s and 1960s attempted to appropriate an even wider array of pre-existing threads of history. During the initial phase of the postwar era the aim was to legitimize the SED and its vision of a new Germany. During this second phase the goal was to create new forms of cultural legitimization of the new state. The resulting historical narrative needed to facilitate a new mindset aimed at interpreting the past in a manner that spoke directly to the correctness and inevitability of the current state structure in the GDR (and counter West Germany's claims as Germany's rightful successor).

The transformation of the Buchenwald monument from a local initiative to one that established a direct link between the antifascist resistance movement and the new state was essential in creating a legitimizing founding myth for the GDR. The SED wanted to portray the GDR as the inheritor of an heroic struggle against the evils of fascism. The use of the burial sites outside the Buchenwald camp allowed the state to create a myth of martyrdom out of those who died in the struggle against fascism.

According to the party's narrative, the survivors of this struggle were now those leading the state and were thus continuing the struggle.

Compelling stories such as those about the Buchenwald prisoners and about the communist resistance during the war, however, were themselves not enough to articulate fully the SED's message about the historical importance and inevitability of communism's triumph over fascism and all forms of capitalism. Inherent in the SED's own claim to power was a belief in a Marxist progression of history in stages of economic and social development. This conceptualization of history, however, was not shared by the majority of people, who had been schooled in what the party claimed was a "bourgeois" conception of the past. One solution to overcoming this "misperception" of history was the creation of the Museum for German History as a way both to educate the populace about the party's interpretation of the past and at the same time anchor the new East German state in this progression of events and provide an extended range of historical legitimacy to the existing situation. The museum played an important role in the party's agenda to politically educate the East German people through its permanent exhibit and its politically timed series of temporary exhibits.

The SED's plans to press forward with all of its plans for memory-work projects in East Germany did not always go smoothly. The party's failure to construct monuments in honor of Marx, Engels, and Thälmann, all of whom it had elevated to a quasi saintly level demonstrates that there were limits to its ability to saturate its vision of the past in East Germany's memory landscape. Both of these failed projects also reveal a striking split between the desire of the party leadership to replicate the Soviet Union's colossal monument style and the East German artistic community's aspiration to develop its own memorial style that was both "socialist" and "German." Even when the party could find an artist willing to take on a commission for a colossal monument, like with Ruthild Hahne, the artist often lacked the necessary artistic training or skill to complete the project. The party also found it difficult to coordinate its city planning goals with its dreams of re-appropriating specific sites of memory it felt could demonstrate its victory over pre-1945 institutions of authority. Once a building was demolished or significantly altered, the monuments commissioned by the SED no longer projected the same sort of legitimizing message that they might have previously had.

Despite the shortcomings of these two memory projects and the considerable political and economic resources that the state placed in them, they, together with the Buchenwald memorial and the Museum for German History, demonstrate a clear attempt by the SED leadership and the ranking members of the GDR government to manipulate popular memory of the past to link it to the history of the existing state structure. Just as the SED had sought to root itself in the history of the German working class, it attempted during the 1950s and 1960s to establish a lineage for the young East German state by anchoring it in a Marxist conception of German history and by elevating the memory of resistance (in particular communist resistance) to the national level.

These initial steps during the formative years of the East German state set the stage for future memory-work projects in the following decades. The party's memory-work priorities and modes of operation, however, were not set in stone. Over time, the party continued to adapt and alter its approach to its memory-work policies as new challenges emerged or its own ideological priorities changed. Party and state officials continually sought to assess the memory landscape of the GDR, finding new sites of memory they wanted to cultivate or returning to existing sites that they felt needed revision or reinterpretation.

Notes

1. Raina Zimmering, *Mythen in der Politik der DDR: Ein Beitrag zur Erforschung politischer Mythen* (Opladen: Leske + Budrich, 2000), pp. 28–29.
2. See chapter 5.
3. As quoted in: Deutsche Akademie der Künste (DDR), *Das Buchenwald Denkmal* (Dresden: Verlag der Kunst, 1960), p. 5.
4. Manfred Overesch, *Buchenwald und die DDR, oder Die Suche nach Selbstlegitimation* (Göttingen: Vandehoeck und Ruprecht, 1995), Peter Reichel, *Politik mit der Erinnerung* (Munich: Hanser, 1995); Alan Nothnagle, *Building the East German Myth: Historical Mythology and Youth Propaganda in the German Democratic Republic, 1945–1989* (Ann Arbor: University of Michigan Press, 1999); and Mary Fulbrook, *German National Identity after the Holocaust* (Cambridge: Polity Press, 1999).
5. Werner A. Beckert, *Die Wahrheit über das Konzentrationslager Buchenwald* (Weimar: 1945), unpaginated.
6. Petra Weber, *Justiz und Diktatur: Justizverwaltung und politische Strafjustiz in Thüringen 1945–1961* (Munich: Oldenbourg, 2000), p. 100.
7. Volkhard Knigge, *Versteinertes Gedenken: das Buchenwalder Mahnmal von 1958* (Spröda: Edition Schwarz Weiss, 1997), pp. 14–15.
8. STA-Weimar, HfA nach 1945, 008/2/6. Letter from Henselmann to Faust, Mayor of Weimar, dated 25 March 1946.
9. Ibid. See also: Knigge, *Versteinertes Gedenken*, p. 16, and Hasko Zimmer, *Der Buchenwald-Konflikt: Zum Streit um Geschichte und Erinnerung im Kontext der deutschen Vereinigung* (Münster: Agenda Verlag, 1999), pp. 70–71. The difference in opinion over the public placement also represents a difference between the concept of a *Denkmal* (monument) and a *Mahnmal* (also a monument, but one intended to warn future generations about some horrific event). Another concept that is often heard in the Buchenwald conversa-

tions is *Ehrenmal* and *Ehrenhain*—both relate to memorials that place emphasis on honoring (either victims or heroes as the case may be). The semantic importance of these terms is that the tradition of the *Denkmal* is a concept historically linked to nineteenth-century middle class society and its tradition of memorialization and glorification with an additional element of sentimentalism for a time gone by.
10. BwA, 06 2/28, as quoted in: Knigge, *Versteinertes Gedenken*, p. 17.
11. STA-Weimar, HfA nach 1945, 008/2/6. Protocol of a city planning meeting, 16 January 1946.
12. Elke Reuter and Detlef Hansel, *Das kurze Leben der VVN von 1947 bis 1953: die Geschichte der Vereinigung der Verfolgten des Naziregimes in der sowjetischen Besatzungszone und in der DDR* (Berlin: Edition Ost, 1997).
13. Zimmer, *Der Buchenwald-Konflikt*, pp. 71–72.
14. SAPMO-BArch, NY 4090/551, p. 1.
15. Knigge, *Versteinertes Gedenken*, p. 31.
16. BwA, 06 2/13.
17. SAPMO-BArch, NY 4182/931, p. 243.
18. SAPMO-BArch, DR 1/7515.
19. For more on the cult of Ernst Thälmann, see Nothnagle, *Building the East German Myth*.
20. BwA, 06 2/14. Letter from the General Secretary of the VVN Fritz Beyling to Walter Bartel dated 14 December 1951.
21. Knigge, *Versteinertes Gedenken*, pp. 52–53.
22. BwA, 06 2/24, as quoted in Knigge, ibid., p. 59.
23. Knigge, ibid., pp. 59–60.
24. The contributing factors that led to the eventual disbanding of the VVN are numerous and are not all related directly to the Buchenwald project. For the best coverage of the VVN organization see: Reuter and Hansel, *Das kurze Leben der VVN von 1947 bis 1953*. In 1956, the SED rehabilitated Bartel, who took up a new position as a professor of history in Leipzig and later in Berlin and also held the position as the director of the German Institute for Contemporary History (DIZ) in East Berlin.
25. Bartel's fall from favor came as part of a larger purge of former Buchenwald inmates, including Ernst Busse, Erich Reschke, and Robert Siewiert, all of whom had played large roles in the early attempts at constructing a monument at Buchenwald. For more detailed information regarding the Bartel case see: Hermann Matern, "Ergebnis der Untersuchung Walter Bartel: 24.5.1953" in *Der gesäuberte Antifaschismus*, ed. Lutz Niethammer (Berlin: Akademie Verlag, 1994), pp. 403–13.
26. *Das Kuratorium für den Aufbau Nationaler Mahn- und Gedenkstätten in Buchenwald, Sachsenhausen und Ravensbrück.*
27. The board of trustees was in charge of coordinating the efforts to build all three of the new "national" monuments.
28. One of the most direct ways in which larger public participation was achieved was by means of the *Freiwillige Arbeitseinsätze*, the volunteer workers who traveled to Buchenwald to take part in the construction process. From the perspective of many of the engineers, the presence of these volunteers often slowed down their progress, but from the perspective of the SED, volunteers were a vital part of democratizing the memory project and mobilizing mass participation in its construction.
29. "Bausteine für Nationale Gedenkstätten: Sache der nationalen Ehre unseres Volkes" *Neues Deutschland*, 28 July 1955.
30. SAPMO-BArch, NY 4090/550, p. 33.
31. Ibid., p. 83. Letter from Grotewohl to the First Secretary of the FDJ Karl Nomokel dated 11 April 1956.

32. BwA, VA/109/1. Protocol of a meeting with the secretaries of the international fraternal organizations of former Buchenwald inmates with Georg Spielmann, the administrative secretary of the Committee of Antifascist Resistance Fighters on 14 January 1958.
33. SAPMO-BArch, NY 4090/552, p. 92.
34. The irony of the use of cargo trains (*Güterzüge*) was apparently not recognized by the planners and demonstrates a level of insensitivity to the experience of the Jews and other victims of the Holocaust who were transported to the concentration camps in similar train cars. SAPMO-BArch 4090/552 p. 169. "Notiz: 2. Dezember 1957 Besprechung mit den Genossen Spielmann, Otto und Saemerow."
35. Overesch, *Buchenwald und die DDR*, p. 320.
36. Ibid., p. 325. Overesch also correctly points out the irony that the GDR would focus its own founding myth around the same time of year when the German Empire celebrated its national holiday—Sedan Day.
37. As quoted in Overesch, *Buchenwald und die DDR*, pp. 326–27.
38. James Young, *Textures of Memory: Holocaust, Memorials, and Meaning* (New Haven, CT: Yale University Press, 1999), p. 73.
39. Karen Pfundt, "Die Gründung des Museums für Deutsche Geschichte in der DDR," *Aus Politik und Zeitgeschichte*, No. 23 (1994), pp. 23–30, here pp. 23–24.
40. FES/AdsD, SPD/PV/Ostbüro/0285. "Ein Informationsbericht über die Bildung des Museums für Deutsche Geschichte in der DDR." The same informant also raised the issue that the museum was supposed to appear to be an entirely academic endeavor, yet the high level of SED and state resources devoted to its construction was a clear indication of the importance to the state that the museum succeed in its political education goals.
41. SAPMO-BArch, DY 30/J IV 2/3/131, pp. 4–5.
42. SAPMO-BArch, DR 3/1481, p. 5. "Ministerium f. Hoch- und Fachhochschulwesen, Sekretariat des Staatssekretärs: Aktennotiz vom 8. 12. 1951."
43. SAPMO-BArch, DR 3/1481 pp. 37–38. "Besprechung: Abt. Propaganda" dated 5 January 1952.
44. SAPMO-BArch, DR 3/1481, p. 38.
45. For further information on the conceptual discussions that framed each of the museum's departments see: Helmut Heinz, "Die Konzeption der ersten Ausstellung im Museum für Deutsche Geschichte 1952," *Zeitschrift für Geschichtswissenschaft*, Vol. 28, No. 4 (1980), pp. 340–56.
46. The other members of the museum leadership (the departmental heads) included: Karl-Heinz Otto (ancient history), Heinrich Sproemberg (Middle Ages), Leo Stern (1815–1895), Albert Schreiner (1918–1945), and Kurt Dünov (Lenin-Stalin).
47. DHM, Hausarchiv: MfDG/40, p. 25. "Aufruf des Museums für Deutsche Geschichte an alle Deutschen in Ost und West."
48. See Martin Sabrow, *Das Diktat des Konsenses: Geschichtswissenschaft in der DDR 1949–1969* (München: Oldenbourg, 2001), especially pp. 35–71. See further: Martin Sabrow, ed., *Verwaltete Vergangenheit: Geschichtskultur und Herrschaftslegitimation in der DDR* (Berlin: Akademische Verlagsanstalt, 1997).
49. DHM, Hausarchiv: MfDG/40, p. 26. "Aufruf des Museums für Deutsche Geschichte an alle Deutschen in Ost und West."
50. Ibid.
51. For an extensive look at the museum's narrative see: H. Glen Penny III, "The Museum für Deutsche Geschichte and German National Identity," *Central European History*, Vol. 28, No. 3 (September 1995), pp. 343–72.

52. DHM, Hausarchiv: MfDG/79. The name Ulrich B. has been substituted for the student's full name.
53. DHM, Hausarchiv: MfDG/79, p.16. Letter to *Neues Deutschland* regarding Herrn B. dated 23 April 1953. The italicized portions appear as underlined in the original.
54. DHM, Hausarchiv: MfDG/87, p. 43. "Entwurf einer Gesamtdisposition für die Ausstellung '15 Jahre Befreiung.'"
55. Ibid., p. 44.
56. Ibid., p. 45.
57. Ibid., p. 47.
58. The visitor statistics also speak to this point. Whereas a reported 453,804 people visited the special exhibit celebrating the tenth anniversary of the GDR state in 1959, only 143,652 people visited the special exhibit honoring fifteen years of liberation. See: DHM, Hausarchiv: MfDG/Päd. Abteilung/Besucherstatistik. "Sonderausstellungen."
59. DHM, Hausarchiv: MfDG/103, pp. 1–2. Eduard Ullmann, "Probleme der weiteren Entwicklung des Museums für deutsche Geschichte," 1 August 1960.
60. Ibid., pp. 3–6.
61. A direct translation is difficult here, in the original a *"gestaltete Studiensammlung."*
62. Simone Hain, "Berlin Ost: 'Im Westen wird man sich wundern'" in Klaus von Beyme, Werner Durth, Niels Gutschow, Winfried Nerdinger, and Thomas Topfstedt, eds., *Neue Städte aus Ruinen: Deutscher Städtebau der Nachkriegszeit* (Munich: Prestel, 1992), pp. 32–37, here p. 41.
63. In official East German usage after 7 October 1949 "Berlin" referred to what is commonly called "East Berlin," while "West Berlin" referred to the three Western sectors of Berlin.
64. SAPMO-BArch, NY 4036/624, p. 16.
65. SAPMO-BArch, NY 4036/624, p. 22. Protocol from the first meeting of the Marx-Engels Monument Committee, 2 February 1951.
66. SAPMO-BArch, NY 4036/624, p. 31. "Wettbewerb zur Erlangung von Entwürfen für das Marx-Engels-Denkmal auf dem Marx-Engels-Platz in Berlin."
67. SAPMO-BArch, NY 4036/624, p. 33. Protokoll No. 24 of the Politbüro of the Central Committee of the SED from 30 December 1950.
68. See Bruno Flierl, *Gebaute DDR: Über Stadtplaner, Architekten und die Macht* (Berlin: Verlag für Bauwesen, 1998), p. 132.
69. SAPMO-BArch, NY 4036/624, p. 42.
70. The notes from this meeting only list the sculptors Gustav Seitz, Fritz Cremer, and Walter Howard along with several representatives from the SED. Wilhelm Pieck's personal notes from the meeting, however, note that the sculptors Walter Arnold, Waldemar Grzimek, Ruthild Hahne, and Rudolph Oelzner were also present. SAPMO-BArch, NY 4036/624, p. 41. "Aktennotiz über die Besprechung am 5.12.51 beim Präsident der Deutschen Demokratischen Republik Wilhelm Pieck um 10 Uhr im Parteihaus;" SAPMO-BArch, NY 4036/624, p. 42. "Handschriftliche Notizen von Wilhelm Pieck" dated 12 May 1951.
71. SAPMO-BArch, NY 4036/624, p. 41. "Aktennotiz über die Besprechung am 5.12.51 beim Präsidenten der Deutschen Demokratischen Republik Wilhelm Pieck um 10 Uhr im Parteihaus."
72. SAPMO-BArch, NY 4090/556, pp. 16–17. Letter from Gustav Seitz to Rudolph Engel dated 27 June 1951.
73. SAPMO-BArch, NY 4182/931, p. 244. "Telegramm an das ZK der KP, Moskau" dated 28 July 1951.

74. SAPMO-BArch, NY 4036/624, p. 50. Letter from Wilhelm Pieck to Mikhail Suzlov dated 22 November 1951.
75. SAPMO-BArch, NY 4036/624, p. 52. Letter from Helmut Holzhauer, director of the State Arts Commission, to Max Opitz, head of the Presidential Chancellery of the GDR, dated 17 January 1952.
76. SAPMO-BArch, NY 4036/624, p. 58. "Handschriftliche Notizen von Wilhelm Pieck," from 8 February 1952.
77. SAPMO-BArch, NY 4036/624, pp. 61–62. Translation of the report filed by Aljoschin and Orlow dated 8 February 1952.
78. SAPMO-BArch, NY 4036/624, p. 65. Letter from Wilhelm Pieck to Mikhail Suzlov dated 9 February 1952.
79. SAPMO-BArch, NY 4036/556, p. 19. "Protokoll der 92. Sitzung des Politbüros des ZK" from 12 February 1952.
80. SAPMO-BArch, NY 4070/556, pp. 22–27, here p. 24. Draft of the "Wettbewerb zur Erlangung von Entwürfen für das Marx-Engels-Denkmal auf dem Marx-Engels-Platz in Berlin" dated 5 March 1952.
81. Bruno Flierl, *Gebaute DDR*, p. 135.
82. SAPMO-BArch, DR 1/1800, p. 5. "Aktennotiz" from 18 February 1957. The debate over the correct socialist-realist presentation of the human form in GDR art continued into the 1980s with the result that no GDR sculptor ever created what one might refer to as "colossal" art. The only four sculptures that might fit this category are the Soviet War Memorial in Treptow Park, the Lenin and Thälmann monuments in Berlin, as well as the Lenin monument in Dresden—all created by Soviet artists. For an interesting rationale for the East German approach to monuments, see Fritz Cremer's interview with Sybille Pawel in the 14 January 1969 edition of the *Berliner Zeitung*. Here Cremer argues that socialist-realist monumental art should not be equated with "monstrosity." See also: Simone Simpson, *Zwischen Kulturauftrag und künstlerischer Autonomie: Dresdner Plastik der 1950er und 1960er Jahre* (Cologne: Böhlau, 2008), p. 103, and Helmut Netzker, *Formen-werten-wirken: Zum bildhauerischen Schaffen in der DDR 1965 bis 1982* (Berlin: Dietz, 1985), pp. 35–60.
83. In 1965 the monument was moved to the Karl-Marx-Platz, which was later renamed the Platz der Opfer des Fascismus.
84. Gerhard Kosel, "Aufbau des Zentrums der Hauptstadt des demokratischen Deutschlands Berlin," *Deutsche Architektur*, No. 4 (1958), pp. 177–83, here p. 178.
85. See Maoz Azaryahu, *Von Wilhelmplatz zu Thälmannplatz: Politische Symbole im öffentlichen Leben der DDR* (Gerlingen: Bliecher, 1991) and Nothnagle, *Building the East German Myth*.
86. SAPMO-BArch, DR 1/1799, p. 60.
87. Ibid. Prof. Seitz and Prof. Lingner were also instrumental in the construction of the Friedrichsfelde Socialist Monument as well as the Buchenwald monument. Other members of the prize committee included Deputy Minister President Hermann Kastner, Berlin City Council Director Brockschmidt, architect Peter Friedrich, Prof. Scharoun (Director of the Institute of Construction at the Academy of Sciences), and author Willy Bredel.
88. There had been several attempts to name a street after Ernst Thälmann in the eastern sector of Berlin, but none were implemented due to differences of opinion regarding the best place to honor his name. Interestingly, there were several successful attempts to rename streets in the western sectors, although these were short-lived once the division of the city became permanent after 1949.
89. SAPMO-BArch, NY 4090/55, pp. 64–70. "Sitzungsbericht des Preisgerichts im Thälmann-Wettbewerb."

90. The semicircle containing the Thälmann figure was apparently supposed to be coming from the West into the East and the welcoming crowds were to be on the eastern side of the memorial, which might have been an additional symbolic element designed to illustrate the jubilant reception of Communism by the East Germans. Fritz Cremer would later remark sarcastically that one could not tell if Hahne's sculpture featured a group marching in from the West or one exiting to the West. See Thomas Flierl, "'Thälmann und Thälmann vor allen': Ein Nationaldenkmal für die Hauptstadt der DDR, Berlin" in *Kunstdokumentation 1945–1990: Aufsätze-Berichte-Materialien*, ed. Gunter Feist, Eckhart Gillen, and Beatrice Vierneisel (Köln: DuMont Buchverlag, 1996), pp. 358–85, here p. 373.
91. Thomas Flierl, "'Thälmann und Thälmann vor allen,'" p. 370.
92. Strictly speaking, Ernst Thälmann had no role in the unification of the SPD and KPD into the SED, but the symbolism worked for the masses, since the SED had popularized the image of Thälmann as the vanguard of the working class. The fact that the political parties representing the interests of the working class united after he had died was interpreted simply as the continuation of what Thälmann would have done had he still been alive.
93. Ironically, the fact that it was indeed an open "V" rather than a triangle would have ruined this perception as soon as one entered the interior section of the "V." In a similar vein, the open "V" shape hinted at the hollowness of the claims being made by the front facade.
94. SAPMO-BArch, DY 30/IV 2/2/240.
95. Thomas Flierl, pp. 371–73.
96. SAPMO-BArch, DY 30/IV 2/906/91, p. 207.
97. In the report, only "Gruson" is mentioned. This might refer to Otto Gruson of the "Gruson Eisengießerei und Maschinen-Fabrik" of Bruckau.
98. SAPMO-BArch, DR 1/1799, pp. 16–18.
99. See Thomas Flierl, p. 347.
100. SAPMO-BArch, DR 1/7695, "Aktennotiz" dated 17 February 1962.
101. SAPMO-BArch, DY 30/J IV/2/2/994.

Chapter Three

EMOTIONAL BONDS

The SED memory-work projects during the formative years of the immediate postwar era and the period immediately following the founding of East Germany set the stage for projects it would tackle in the 1960s and 1970s. The process of shaping the memory landscape was not finished. The East German government continued to invest considerable resources into expanding the number of memorial sites as well as reshaping existing institutions of cultural memory. Beginning in the 1960s, the GDR also faced a new generation of youth who had lived entirely under SED rule and were now coming of political age. Unlike previous generations, these young men and women did not share pre-1945 memories on which the party could draw when formulating its memory-work. This meant that the SED needed to revise or expand important memory sites in order to speak to this new generation in the hopes of fostering emotional bonds with the East German state.

Despite just over a decade of division, the "German question" remained a hot topic in political discourse in the 1960s and 1970s. Political leaders, professional East German historians, and others continued to work on how best to conceptualize a new "socialist" German nation. Additionally, a growing economic gulf between East and West Germany led the state to pursue several campaigns aimed at bolstering regime loyalty. As Mark Allinson has argued, the SED's ability to develop this sort of voluntary regime loyalty remained weak in 1960, despite its active and seemingly perpetual anti-western propaganda. The construction of the Berlin Wall in 1961 created a more stabilized social and political social order in East Germany, albeit one that remained somewhat superficial and fragile.[1] This new sense of stability did not, however, mean that the government abandoned memory-work aimed at building regime loyalty and instilling a "proper" historical consciousness amongst its citizens. On the contrary,

---

Notes for this chapter begin on page 133.

it reinvigorated these efforts. Many within the party leadership felt that the ideals of socialism could be successfully transmitted to a new generation. After the closing the last breach in the inter-German border, the state launched several new programs aimed at intensifying its educational approach toward winning over the postwar generation.[2]

The East German government had not ignored memory-work projects outside of Berlin, but the state now began to assert increased centralized control over such projects in an attempt to better coordinate its message throughout the country.[3] The state's public memory-work during this period also reflected new trends of historical interpretation developed by the GDR's professional historians. Beginning in the late 1950s and continuing through the 1960s, GDR historians attempted to delineate East Germany's historical development from that of West Germany. As Ulrich Neuhäußer-Wespy has argued, East German historians "not only continued to claim the traditions of the German working class, but intensified such claims."[4] In a similar vein, Martin Sabrow has argued that the SED strengthened its efforts to consolidate control over professional historians, especially following the construction of the Berlin Wall in 1961.[5] Indeed, acting on directives stemming from the SED's XXIV Party Plenary in 1962, the Central Institute for History (ZIG) issued a document calling for increased collaboration between factory historians, lay historians (especially local historians) and functionaries of the non-SED political parties. The party's intent was to homogenize the historical narratives of professional historians.[6] These new initiatives and policies within the historical profession quickly found their way into the work of public historians and memory-workers.

During this period, the state prioritized memory-work initiatives that celebrated the history of the German working class, but allowed the state to assert its narrative beyond the large central museum of Berlin. The SED sought to project its Marxist national historical narrative into local histories by emphasizing that local events both contributed to and reflected national trends. We see these trends in two main areas. The first was an attempt to regularize and streamline the museums and historical sites located in the GDR that were important for retelling the history of the German working class. The state built new hybrid house museums for figures like Karl Marx, Clara Zetkin, and Ernst Thälmann as well as new historical sites that documented important milestones in the history of the German working class. Each of these memory projects aimed to enhance the historical consciousness of the East German public, and the younger generation in particular, while at the same time producing a concept of historical progression that was more tangible to the average citizen than what could be found in professional scholarship.

The second major area where we see this attempt to localize the GDR's national narrative are through exhibit renovations at local history or *Heimat* museums, like the one in Merseburg outside of Halle, which underwent significant revisions in the 1960s in an attempt to highlight the local history of workers. Many local history museums reopened during the immediate postwar period. While the party had already attempted to assert some control over these reopened museums, it now sought to streamline the historical narrative of these local museums and align their message more closely with the master narrative developed by Berlin's Museum for German History during the 1950s. In each case, the key change to the local narratives involved localizing the national narrative—incorporating local events and narratives to retell Germany's past through a Marxists perspective.

The SED's other priority in memory-work during the 1960s was to find ways of revising past projects in order to appeal to a new generation. From the state's perspective, this new generation had the advantage of only attending East German schools, but it lacked personal memories of the pre-1945 period. Instead, the party focused particularly on cultivating a sense of duty among East German youth, not only by tailoring the flow of information and content of school materials in order to influence the "correct" interpretation of history, but also through promoting interaction between the youth and older generations of communists and through routinized observances at places of memory such as Buchenwald or during trips to the Museum for German History.

Several commonalities tie these projects together during this third stage in the developmental arc of memory politics in East Germany. The most significant was the state's goal to evoke an emotional response, either through facilitating a more a personalized experience at a site of memory or by emphasizing specific connections between individuals and historical events. This connection might be based on living in the same town as an historical event, sharing a common profession with an important figure of history, or meeting with older generations who shared their pre-1945 stories of fighting in the name of Communism. The regime hoped that such links could create a bridge between past and present and influence the historical consciousness of the individual.

Beyond Berlin—Controlling Memory Outside the Capital

With the construction of the Berlin Wall in 1961, the division of Germany into two competing states became more concrete. The SED had pursued various memory-work projects outside Berlin since 1945, but beginning in the 1960s, the state began a new effort to sponsor memory projects that would allow it to anchor its historical narrative more firmly in events and historical sites that were physically located on East German soil and thus reinforce East Germany's independent historical development vis-à-vis West Germany. State and party cultural operatives set to work documenting the lives of historical personalities, such as Karl Marx and Vladimir Lenin, and relating them to sites within the GDR's borders. Unlike what we might refer to as sites of displaced memory (museums or monuments that have no apparent connection to the physical space they occupy), these new historical sites aimed to provide the East German historical narrative with an additional sense of authenticity.

Although the SED continued to populate the Berlin cityscape with additional monuments supporting its ideological goals, the party also wanted to take advantage of the powerful numinous effect that genuine historical sites can have on visitors. While it is not clear whether the party was fully aware of such connections, it is useful to employ such a theoretical framing in order to better understand the strategies that lay behind the party's shift toward incorporating more and more "real" historical sites into its official memory landscape. The religious philosopher Rudolph Otto first used the concept of numen to articulate the emotional connection a believer experiences when confronted with an object or site that is deemed holy. As Catherine M. Cameron and John B. Gatewood have argued, visitors to historic sites can also experience a numinous emotional response when objects or sites are directly connected to a nation's history.[7] It is precisely this emotional connection that the SED sought to establish when it made a concerted effort during the 1960s to increase the number of memorials and museums located on historical sites where significant events took place or important personalities lived. The hope was that by developing these new historic sites on GDR territory, the party could claim a greater level of authenticity for its legitimizing historical narrative.

Many of the new monument projects continued the SED's emphasis on promoting the role of the KPD in the antifascist struggle. In this light, the government completed national monuments at the former concentration camps of Ravensbrück and Sachsenhausen, the Karl Liebknecht memorial in Leipzig, and renovated the Ernst Thälmann memorial at Ziegenhals outside of Berlin. Other memory projects during this period concentrated on commemorating historical events or personalities more generally linked with the history of the German working class or the development of communism in general. SED cultural functionaries paid increasing attention to historical places where important events in the development of socialism and struggle of the German working class had taken place, as well as to figures like Karl Marx and his family, Clara Zetkin, and August Bebel. In each case, however, they continued the established practice of not commemorating an isolated event, but rather using the commemoration to establish a clear line of continuity between the event or personality and the existing situation in divided Germany.

The state had already designated many of these places as memorial sites or listed them as buildings under historical protection. Local governments, party members, or hobby historians had initially developed the historical narratives at most of these sites. In several cases, however, the SED decided that it needed to take on a more active role and reinterpret the place of memory so that it could maximize its functionality within its larger conception of a "proper" socialist historical consciousness. In the examples covered below, the party acted to transform these local sites of memory into sites of GDR-national importance. The MfDG in Berlin took the lead in coordinating the state's message. Its position as the leading historical museum in the GDR gave it the authority to direct the work of local curators and party members as they constructed and modified these sites of memory. The MfDG's function was similar to the one played by the Central Institute of History among professional historians; instead of shaping the publishing agenda for historians, it served as a clearinghouse for museums and monuments. Throughout the 1960s and 1970s, the MfDG worked to standardize the country's public portrayal of history, drawing on its knowledge of similar projects across East Germany. The SED felt that this level of coordination was necessary to ensure that it was communicating a coherent message as the number of GDR-nationally important memory sites grew. As a result, the museum concentrated on the creation of hybrid institutions of memory that were part history museum, part memorial, and part academic institution, usually incorporating a library or a lecture hall to facilitate ongoing research and sustain interest in the event or person being commemorated.

A prime example of this new wave of memory projects was the transformation between 1966 and 1970 of the Jenny Marx Memorial in Salzwedel into a museum designed to portray the social milieu of the Karl Marx family. The GDR did not control any of the houses that Karl Marx had owned—these were all in West Germany or further abroad. However, the state did possess the childhood home of Jenny Marx and decided to transform it into a place of memory for Karl Marx as well. The new museum attempted to bring the visitor closer to the teachings of Karl Marx through a more personal association with the way in which Marx lived and worked while living in this house: "The works of Karl Marx, from the 'Communist Manifesto' to the 'Capital' should stand at the center, but also the family itself should be portrayed—the influence of Jenny, the raising of the children, and friends (especially Engels)."[8] By first exploring the local social conditions, the exhibit could then compare that situation with the social conditions in other places where Marx lived and worked—in Paris, Brussels, and especially in London. Simultaneously, the exhibit sought to educate the visitor about the party's interpretation regarding the situation of the working class, its concerns, and the injustices it suffered. It highlighted personal relationships between the members of the Marx family and the very special friendship between Marx and Friedrich Engels in order to render these historical figures more human and less abstract. The museum's narrative did not end with the death of Karl or Jenny Marx; rather, it continued on by portraying the roles played by Marx's daughters and stepsons in the organizing of the German working class, such as his daughter Eleanor's role in the 1890 SPD Party Congress in Halle or Lenin's visit with another daughter, Laura, in 1910.

The culmination of the museum's new narrative traced the legacy of Marxist ideology through Lenin to the present East German state-socialist regime. The planners hoped to develop the memorial and museum into an eventual research center for the history of the Marx family. Like many other of the new memory projects of national importance around the GDR, the intention behind the Jenny Marx house museum was to transform it from a static place of representation to one that could more directly link the past to the present (and the future). The museum now took on a more active agenda of public events and lectures. It contained a library for specialists and hosted special events in its meeting rooms. Moreover, the location of the house on the territory of the GDR allowed the curators to connect it symbolically with other Marx residences not accessible to the GDR citizens and thereby extend the scope of the exhibit and incorporate a much broader interpretation of Marx and his work beyond the time spent at this single location.[9]

A similar transformation project was undertaken at the former home of Clara Zetkin in Birkenwerder in 1970 and 1971. Zetkin had been a leading Marxist theorist of the early twentieth century, an activist for women's rights, and a loyal member of the pre-1933 German Communist Party. The state designated her house as a memorial in 1957, but by the end of the 1960s the exhibit contained within no longer reflected the desired pedagogical aims of the party. The revamped exhibit emphasized Zetkin's role as one of the leading figures of the German and international workers' and women's movements. Depicted as the ideal revolutionary figure, Zetkin's historical persona told the story of a woman who spent over seventy years fighting for societal change. The museum portrayed Zetkin as the driving force behind the fight for women's equality, an educator of the working class, a friend of the Soviet Union, and an ardent opponent of imperialism, militarism, and fascism. According to the curators, the intended function of this new exhibit was to "contribute to an increase in the class-consciousness of the working class and to the solidification of the workers' socialist consciousness, especially that of women."[10]

The SED viewed the Zetkin project as an important element in its overall memory-work campaign, especially as a means of speaking directly to the role of women in a socialist society as well as providing a role model for young women. In particular, the museum emphasized Zetkin's efforts to combat the rise of fascism in 1929 up through her death in 1933. The Zetkin project clearly marks an attempt to reach out to the GDR's female population with its emphasis on her role as a female activist, but also by linking her legacy to women's rights in the GDR. Out of all the state-sponsored memory projects, the Zetkin memorial remained one of the few to single out the role of women in constructing socialism. Like the Jenny Marx Memorial, the resulting Zetkin museum was a hybrid memorial merging together the formats of a house museum, a museum of working class history, a library, and a conference center. The multiple uses of the site created a dynamic place where the state could interact with society more frequently and propagate a message of sustained relevance of Zetkin for contemporary society.[11]

After completing the renovations at the Jenny Marx and Clara Zetkin Memorials, the MfDG turned its attention to the memorial for the 1875 Gotha Conference of the SPD. The state wanted to take advantage of the 100th anniversary of the conference in 1975 and decided to renovate the existing exhibit so that its message aligned better with the party's dominant historical narrative. The city of Gotha had hosted the historic meeting where Ferdinand Lassalle's General German Workers' Union (*Allgemeiner deutscher Arbeiterverein*) and the League of Workers' Clubs (*Verband deutscher Arbeitervereine*), headed by Wilhelm Liebknecht and August Bebel, merged to form the Socialist Workers Party of Germany (which became the Social Democratic Party of Germany in 1890). The revamped memorial now sought to communicate that this historic union of the workers' parties into a single party marked the beginning of a concerted effort by organized workers to strive for a common future. The centennial anniversary presented the SED with an opportunity to draw on the history of the Gotha Conference and use it to highlight how the SED continued to work in the name of German workers. It expanded this narrative to show how the GDR also cooperated with the Soviet Union and other international workers' movements toward a common goal. Above all, the curators hoped that the new exhibit would portray "the desire for revolutionary unity within the labor movement based on the foundation of Marxism, and later on Marxism-Leninism."[12]

The original site of the Gotha Conference already housed a small museum that opened in 1953. However, in advance of the centennial, the SED decided to renovate the permanent exhibit in order to place the conference within a longer line of historical development and strengthen the link to the existing political situation in East Germany. Whereas the original exhibit was predominantly a display of text and graphic illustrations confined only to the events directly related to the meeting, the new exhibit attempted to capture the atmosphere of the meeting and highlight some of the key ideological questions debated during it. The SED wanted the museum experience to elicit an emotional response by the visitor. To this end the exhibit was split into two parts, the first functioning primarily as a memorial and the second as a museum. The first part restored the conference hall to its original state in 1875 and enhanced it with artifacts from the conference as well as a copy of Marx's critique of the new party's platform. A separate room housed the museum exhibit, which provided an overview of events leading up to the Gotha Conference and examined its legacy, highlighting the unification between the KPD and the Independent Social Democratic Party of Germany (USPD) following the Kapp Putsch in 1920, the cooperation of the KPD and SPD in the "People's Front" during the Nazi period, and the unification of the KPD and SPD to form the SED in 1946. Finally, the exhibit highlighted the cooperation of the SED with other communist parties, especially the CPSU, as well as communist liberation movements throughout the world.[13]

The three memory projects above highlight only a small fraction of the new role played by the MfDG. Between 1959 and 1977 the MfDG worked either as a direct partner or as a consultant on over twenty different memorials and museums in the GDR. While one of the projects was in Berlin and several others were located on its outskirts, the vast majority of the memory projects involving the museum were spread out across the territory of the GDR. This clearinghouse function led to a coordination of historical interpretation and enabled the individual sites of memory to fit better into the state's overarching narrative of German and working class history. The renovations of these sites of memory transformed them from static places of remembrance into active sites of historical learning. Unlike the central history museum in Berlin, these new sites could draw on the numinous effect of authenticity—visitors were at Jenny Marx or Clara Zetkin's house or at the site of the historic Gotha Conference. In each case, the state attempted to extend the importance of the site into the present day through drawing connections between these sites and the present political and social policies of the SED.

The Localization of History and the Merseburg County Museum

History museums are typically housed in buildings with little or no connection to the subject matter that they contain. Unlike authentic historic sites, history museums represent the past through the use of artifacts and explanatory devices such as text or visual aids. Yet certain types of history museums claim greater levels of authenticity based on the geographic proximity to their subject matter. A prime example of this is the *Heimatmuseum,* a history museum dedicated to the history of a locality.[14] While many local museums reopened after the Second World War and were subject to oversight by local SED functionaries, the central party leadership made a concerted effort in the 1960s and 1970s to revamp these museums and coordinate their historical narratives.[15] The party's attempt to appropriate these local institutions coincided with an initiative to cultivate a socialist sense of *Heimat* that not only allowed the party to gain access to the inherent patriotic elements of this sentiment but also provided a bridge between local history and the party's socialist national narrative.

Interest in *Heimatgeschichte* increased steadily throughout the 1950s and there was an upsurge in new publications, ranging from the *"Thüringer Heimat"* and *"Berliner Heimat"* to *"Unser Ostseebezirk"* and *"Aus der Vergangenheit der Stadt Erfurt"*—all of which focused on local and regional history.[16] The organization *Natur- und Heimatfreunde* (Nature and *Heimat*-Friends), which had existed since 1950, increased its membership and began working in earnest to reopen more *Heimat*-museums across the country. Despite the active participation by organizations like the *Natur- und Heimatfreunde,* the quality of these local museums varied widely and the party leadership felt the need to better coordinate the historical narratives on display at these local history museums.

To address such inconsistencies, the Ministry of Culture organized a conference in Bitterfeld in 1959 that set the tone for state's appropriation of the country's local history museums. The conference produced a set of principles, which in turn were used to form general guidelines for the institutions that dealt with the public portrayal of national culture throughout the GDR and included the "Principles for a socialist reorganization of the *Heimatmuseen* in the GDR."[17] Despite the new set of guiding principles, many theoretical and practical obstacles remained in the way of the party's attempt to revamp the regional history museums.

A turning point for research into and the public display of regional and local history came in 1961 following the Görlitz Conference on *Heimat-* and Regional History. One of its participants, Karl Czok, produced a conference report in which he argued that historians of regional history needed to create and propagate a socialist concept of *Heimat* that could be differentiated from what he called the "bourgeois" version. The answer, he argued, was to define *Heimat* from a class perspective. Accordingly, socialist *Heimat* referred to the natural and social surroundings of people who were bound together politically, economically, culturally, intellectually, and emotionally and need not be identical with the place of one's birth; that is, the factory could become one's *Heimat*. Moreover, the socialist interpretation of *Heimat* was to be understood as being in a constant state of evolution toward a more humanistic form—as opposed to the static nature attributed to the "bourgeois" interpretation of *Heimat*. Lastly, love for one's *Heimat* was intended to be active rather than passive and be demonstrated through participating in the construction and maintenance of the East German socialist state.[18]

Despite a series of national conferences, concrete efforts to reform local museums around the country were slow and relatively uncoordinated. In 1964, in an attempt to assume greater control over the country's diverse landscape of museums, the Ministry of Culture formed a new institution—the Council for Museums. The primary task of the council was to reform and coordinate the cultural content of all museums throughout the country—from the largest institutions to the smallest *Heimat*-museum.[19] The party hoped that the council would allow the GDR's cultural institutions to take a more active role in forming people's socialist consciousness.

The reconstruction of the *Kreismuseum* (county museum) in the city of Merseburg (near Halle) provides a prime example of how the SED attempted to transform local *Heimat*-museums in the GDR into clear ideological and pedagogical tools to appropriate local history. Like many local museums in the GDR, the Merseburg museum suffered damage during the war. The history of its postwar reconstruction and its interpretive overhaul during the 1960s typifies the transformation of such museums throughout the GDR. The Merseburg museum was among the first to undergo a party-initiated renovation, and its location near two of the GDR's largest industrial plants, Leuna and Buna, allowed the party to make a strong connection between local working class history and the state historical narrative. Already by 1952, the Merseburg museum was singled out by the Expert Commission for Museums of the "Nature and *Heimat* Friends" organization as a "model museum."[20] Its evolution highlights the conceptual transition of a local museum into a museum of state history from the local perspective and demonstrates how the state sought to treat local history as a component element in its overall appropriation of German history.

The *Kulturgeschichtliches Museum* (Cultural Historical Museum) in Merseburg originally opened in 1950 after a year and a half of planning. The initial exhibit concentrated on local cultural history from the prehistoric period up through the present day, and relied almost entirely on what remained from the previous inventory of the pre-1945 *Heimatmuseum*. Although the museum building had been destroyed during the war, much of its inventory had been saved.[21] The museum's new name was the first departure from the former model of the *Heimatmuseum*, which had also displayed artifacts related to the natural history of Merseburg and its surroundings. The new building was divided up into seven separate exhibition rooms: 1) Pre-History; 2) the Leuna Room; 3) Merseburg city history during the early historical period; 4) The Guild Room—Merseburg in the late Middle Ages; 5) The Modern Room—Merseburg 1848 to 1950; 6) the Brown Coal Room; and 7) the Salt Room. This layout of the museum was simple in its design and was thus likely not very contentious. Although elements of the former *Heimatmuseum* were replicated, the new emphasis on Leuna, the brown coal industry and the salt industry certainly would have been welcomed by the local SED leaders as well as the general community, who were dependent on the Leuna chemical works for much of their livelihood. The connection between the city and these industries was logical and easily accepted.

The potential effectiveness of the *Kulturhistorisches Museum* was restricted by its own limited hours of operation—in the 1950s the museum was only open between 11 A.M. and 1 P.M., indicative of the limited resources devoted to such museums in the early years of East Germany. The first director of the museum, Gustav Pretzien, was also the chairman of the local *Heimatkundeverein* (*Heimat* club) and was also the honorary custodian of cultural history for the county of Merseburg. Walter Zwarg, who had volunteered in the museum, and its predecessor, since 1947, succeeded Pretzien in 1954. It was not until 1956 that the *Kulturhistorisches Museum* and the *Museum Natur und Mensch* (Museum for Nature and Mankind) were merged into one institution now called the *Städtische Museen Merseburg* (the City Museums of Merseburg). The new leadership of Alfred John in 1962, however, marked the first real cooperation of the two museums beyond an administrative level. John took it upon himself to merge the two museums into a new unit that would be more in line with existing trends in the GDR with regard *Heimatgeschichte* and its relationship to the overall narrative of the German nation and the East German state.

During the late 1950s the city administration discussed moving both the *Kulturhistorisches Museum* and the *Museum Natur und Mensch* into the Merseburg Castle following its reconstruction (it had been badly damaged in the war). The move allowed the museum directors to develop several different plans for the space and a complete reorganization of the museum's layout and overall message. In 1962 Walter Zwarg and Alfred John developed a plan for a "Merseburg County Museum for Nature and Society, Chemistry and Brown Coal." The shift away from a cultural museum to a local museum that focused on nature, society, chemistry, and brown coal marked a significant change in the presentation of local history and the place of the museum within the greater realm of local historical education. Due to construction delays, the actual move into the renovated Merseburg Castle did not begin until 1966 and was finally completed in 1968. Coinciding with the move, the museum's governance structure was altered and it now came under the jurisdiction of Merseburg's city administration and no longer functioned as an independent institution. This meant that local SED cultural functionaries and bureaucrats from the District Ministry of Culture now played a more direct role in overseeing the content and function of the museum.

The new concept for the museum departed radically from *Heimat* museums of the past and thus provides us with a clear example of how SED attempted to adapt the GDR's national narrative to the local level. The pedagogical and museological goals contained in the new concept were firmly rooted in the ideas of historical materialism and Marxist museum studies. The new museum now aimed far beyond the simple idea of displaying the history of a city and instead sought to "illustrate the development of human society in our county and the interrelation between man and environment in its dialectical unity."[22] The museum's primary goal was to demonstrate the economic and socioeconomic conditions that led to important political, cultural, and scientific events in the county of Merseburg with special emphasis given to the relationships between people, the role of the classes, and class warfare in the area. The newly defined mission of the museum called for reconfiguring the exhibit's major segments and reorienting each section's pedagogical objectives.

The revamped museum, like its predecessor, was divided into several smaller, self-contained units, each of which conveyed drastically different messages. The museum's first segment centered on the geomorphologic development of the area in and around Merseburg. This area dealt primarily with the Ice Age and the post-Ice Age period (the Pleistocene Era), ending with references to the first traces of human life. The second section of the museum covered the prehistoric era and focused on the emergence of human society and the organization of humans into communities (hordes and clans). Here, the curators placed a special emphasis on early man as pure and uncorrupted—stressing the absence of private property, the products of communal labor, and the equal distribution of wealth. They also highlighted the presence of Slavic settlements in the region beginning in the sixth century, "proving that Slavic and Germanic peoples lived side-by-side."[23] By including the history of Slavic settlements, the curators hoped to position the history of Merseburg within a longer history of German-Slavic coexistence, and by extension Germans-Soviet friendship through tangible examples of cooperation that could be located in the Merseburg area.

The third section of the museum focused on the feudal period, which the museum defined as the period between the tenth century, with the consolidation of feudal power, and the French Revolution of 1789. In this section of the museum, curators placed special attention on the role of Christianity and on the Church as a center of power and the impetus for the expansion of German power to the east. Within this context, the city of Merseburg quickly grew as a center of both military and church power. Merseburg Castle (also the place of the new museum) became the official residence of the bishop, its land was integrated into the Saxon-Otto (*sächsische-ottonischen*) Palatinate, and on occasion the castle served as the residence for the German Emperor. Adding to the city's dual role as a military and church power center, its geographic location also allowed for considerable economic growth until the larger markets in nearby Leipzig surpassed Merseburg as an economic center. Nonetheless, the curators argued, the socio-economic remnants of these economic interests remained a powerful force in the city, despite the relative loss of influence within the region. The Peasants' War of 1525 formed the internal focal point for this section. The museum depicted Merseburg citizens and peasants not only as artifacts of history, but also as real people who lived and worked in the same town as those viewing the exhibit. Although the city of Merseburg itself was not the site of a major battle, the exhibit included battles that took place in areas surrounding the city. Thus, the exhibit attempted to make a personal connection between the visitor's own experience in the region and the historical events that influenced the historical development of the city (and the German nation).

Within the context of the Peasants' War, the museum also dealt with the broader issues of the Reformation and its impact on the city's transformation from a bishopric into a secular seat of power. The areas that retold the history of the Thirty Years War (1618–1648) and the Seven Years War (1756–1763) focused on the pain and suffering brought upon the people of Merseburg and its surroundings, thus emphasizing the Marxist interpretation of the social conflicts inherent to feudalism. This part of the museum concluded by depicting peasant unrest during the second half of the eighteenth century in and around Merseburg, characterizing—and exaggerating—the unrest as attempted resistance against the feudal system and increased exploitation.

The fourth section covered the "era of capitalism," beginning with the French Revolution and continuing through the defeat of Nazi Germany in 1945. The definition of this period, according to the curators, rested on the transition from feudal power to a system of cooperation between the former feudalist powers and the new middle class. Highlights in this section were the Napoleonic battles of Merseburg in 1806 and 1813, the latter of which was placed in the context of the 1813 Battle of Nations in Leipzig, and thus allowed a direct link between this "national" event and Merseburg's local history. The Battle of Nations also provided another opportunity for the museum to stress the relationship between the region and the Russians, who were vital to the victory in Leipzig. With the connection of Merseburg to the Thuringian rail system in 1846, Merseburg's transition to an industrial center began in earnest. The first area of growth came in the brown coal industry, which along with the local sugar factory provided the basis for the region's first labor movement. The revolutionary events of 1848 were prominently displayed, both those of national importance as well as the corresponding local uprisings—all of which were designed to demonstrate the continued cooperation between the upper and middle classes. As industrialization grew in the area, so too did the power of organized labor. The rise of unions, especially within the metal and tobacco industries, led to the establishment of a local Social Democratic Workers Party and illegal resistance during the years of the Socialist Laws.

The museum characterized the First World War as the consequence of monopolistic capitalists pursuing imperialist aims. With the construction of Merseburg's first ammonia plant during the war in 1916, the city entered into the chemical industry, which from this point on would define its industrial development. The role of the ammonia factory in supporting the war effort stood in sharp contrast to the portrayal of local workers at the Leuna factory, who struck in the spring of 1917 in protest of the war. The "Great Socialist October Revolution," the museum argued, inspired further worker uprisings during the short-lived November Revolution of 1918. It placed special attention on the role of local Worker and Soldiers' Councils. The section covering the early years of the Weimar Republic focused on the local history of the KPD, its union with the left wing of the USPD in 1920, and workers' uprisings in 1920 and 1921.

The unit on years leading to the Nazi seizure of power dealt primarily with the continued industrial development in the chemical industry and those areas of production that would become essential to the impending war effort—such as Indian rubber and synthetic fuel. Attention quickly turned to the efforts by the local KPD to organize resistance against the Nazis, highlighting resistance groups active in the Leuna, Buna, and Lützkendorf factories. The focal point of this section emphasized the misery and destruction brought to the region by the fascist powers, documenting memories from many of the region's residents and displaying them in a way that sent a clear political message about the causes of this destruction. The section ended with Germany's military defeat and a rationalization for the seizure of property from large landowners and industrialists.[24]

The final section in the museum's exhibit dealt with the period of socialism—from the end of the Second World War to the present. This section began with the founding of the "antifascist" political parties, including the KPD, the SPD, and their union in 1946, always focusing on the relationship between the national political trends and their impact on local political developments. As with the previous period, the exhibit singled out the chemical and coal industries for special attention. While museum organizers stressed the misuse of these industries during earlier periods, they now placed the development of Merseburg as a highly industrial region within the positive tradition of state-socialist economic development. Other social changes accompanied the new wave of economic growth in the region—the transition to a socialist agricultural system, educational reform, new directions in culture and science, as well as city administration. The curators intended these (in their view positive) social changes to form the culmination of the region's historical development in the eyes of the visitor.

As its creators noted, the ultimate goal of the museum was to use the first four stages of historical development in the Merseburg region to draw the visitor into the correct interpretation of more recent events. The overview provided background information covering significant historical events and placed a special emphasis on the development of industry and class warfare. The culminating section on local history since the founding of East Germany could then be interpreted by the visitor as the logical conclusion to a millennium of social, economic, and political development. Through this new conception of local Merseburg history, the curators hoped to make East Germany's national historical narrative more personal and accessible.[25]

Once the museum opened its permanent exhibit to the public, it continued to fine-tune various elements of its display and build new components. The overall narrative, however, remained in place. By 1974, the museum attracted over 39,000 visitors annually, which ranked it among the most visited local history museums in the GDR. While such visitor statistics might be viewed as a measure of success, it needs to be noted that around sixty percent of the visitors were school children and youth groups. While the museum administration attributed its success to the strength of its narrative, especially its emphasis on the history of the working class and on regional history, it also noted that its rich collection of medieval weaponry was its most popular attraction.[26]

As the museum continued to grow and revamp its permanent exhibit, it made what would be its last major addition in 1986 by transforming the final section of the museum, formerly focused on socialism, into a section dedicated to the "history of the GDR as seen in Merseburg."[27] The groundwork for the exhibit's reworking was completed as part of an M.A. thesis by one of the curators, Petra Koch, under the direction of the museum's new director Dieter Kleinbauer.[28] The new exhibit continued the previous narrative and focused to an even greater extent on the political and economic development of Merseburg County. Again, the thrust of the post-1945 narrative focused on the growth and importance of the chemical and coal industries, but also made an effort to highlight the everyday life of workers in these industries.

Koch's additions to the museum's narrative expanded the exhibit space devoted to the post-1949 era, which coincided with a straightforward emphasis on the duty of the museum to "correctly" educate young people about socialist society in East Germany. Overall, the changes are best described as growth or expansion rather than revision. Spatially, this meant a reallocation of rooms so that the first four sections of the museum, covering the pre-historic era to the defeat of fascism, were contained in 700 square meters, while the extended post-1949 section was now given 150 square meters.

The expanded exhibit walked the visitor through nine segments, beginning with the situation in Merseburg in 1949 and ending with contemporary life.[29] It placed additional emphasis on the impact of the planned economy on the growth of the chemical factories in Leuna and Buna and their role in the strengthening the foundations of the socialist economy. It portrayed workers from the two factories not only in the context of their work, but also their participation in the factory-based armed fighting units, eventually as part of the National People's Army (NVA). Symbolically, the inclusion of such images was meant to strengthen the state's proclaimed need to protect and defend the GDR's socialist achievements and instill a sense of socialist patriotism in the visitors, especially among the young.

Other areas included the growth of technology in the agricultural sector, technological developments in the chemical industry, and cultural events in Merseburg (such as the Workers Festival in 1959). The museum incorporated quotations from local citizens reflecting on their experiences under state socialism, such as in the section that dealt with the collectivization of agriculture beginning in 1952. Here, Koch employed text to explain the general context of collectivization in the GDR, based on the "Leninist principles of the cooperative."[30] This general contextual information about the GDR was followed by a photograph of the first collective farm in

Merseburg, known as the "Progress"-Mücheln collective, and a reference to its establishment on 17 June 1952. The key component, however, was a picture of one of the first workers on the collective farm, Alfred Koerth, and a quotation from him explaining his experience: "We are proud to have been part of the pioneers of agriculture, who were among the first to pave the way to a better way of life in our village. We are certain that the implementation of agricultural technology will make our work easier, increase our production, and thereby increase the living standard for all working people."[31] By featuring a local citizen relating his experience during the period of collectivization, the exhibit sought to create a much more personalized experience for the visitor and to establish a stronger emotional link to the general historical development of socialism in the GDR.

Another addition attempted to address the problems of environmental degradation in the brown coal region of nearby Geiseltal. The curators sought to demonstrate that the SED was addressing the environmental problems in Geiseltal, cleaning up the area and restoring parts of its natural habitat in ways that would return a sense of *Heimatliebe* (love of one's *Heimat*) to the area residents and reduce the tension between the socialist economic policies and their impact on the environment. This portion of the exhibit began with a reproduced copy of an order for the "reclamation of land used for mining purposes" in the region around Merseburg accompanied by photographs of new forests and nature trails in Geiseltal.[32] The accompanying text attempted to link the state's environmental policies to the locality by making these policies relevant to the lives of those living in and around Merseburg: "In the center of the socialist conservation and environmental protection measures stands the meaningful shaping of relations between humans and their environment."[33] By connecting the regime's environmental policies to tangible local initiatives, the museum sought to instill additional emotional bonds between the citizens and the state.

The exhibit ended by leading the visitor into the present day—Merseburg's role in current events, the GDR's role in the world, and the workers' role in shaping socialism. For instance, the section began with a large photograph of the Seventh Party Congress in 1971, when the SED placed renewed emphasis on the GDR's economic difficulties and proclaimed the party's dedication to raise the social and cultural living standards. The exhibit traced the accomplishments in Merseburg between the Seventh Party Congress and 1976 and cited Erich Honecker's 1975 ten-point plan for the intensification of production, which included categories such as scientific and technological advancement, the extraction of raw materials, and the further development of creative talents. Above all, the exhibit drew attention to increased production levels in the region. In an effort to demonstrate Merseburg's contribution to the GDR's desire to solve the housing shortage by 1990 (a key element of Honecker's political agenda), the exhibit cited the construction of 2,694 new apartments between 1971 and 1975, and referred to the construction of another 100,000 apartments in neighboring city of Halle-Neustadt for the workers at the Buna factories. In the cultural realm, the exhibit drew attention to the cultural festivals held at the Leuna and Buna factories, the regular events and lectures held at the Leuna club house, and Leuna's 1974 national award for artistic achievement (*künstlerisches Volkschaffen*).[34] This manner of concluding an exhibit with direct references to contemporary political and social issues provided the museum with an additional avenue of connection between what visitors viewed in the exhibit and the world they would reenter upon leaving the building.

The localization of the GDR's national narrative in *Heimatmuseen*, such as the one in Merseburg, was a key component in personalizing East Germany's historical narrative. Its primary purpose was to transform the emotional pull embodied in the German idea of *Heimat* from one that longed for a simpler time into a concept that could help support the state's social and political initiatives. Merseburg, like many other cities around the country, contained segments of the GDR's national narrative. By isolating those segments of local history that could be directly linked to the state's overall self-legitimizing historical narrative, museums such as this one were meant to function as a bridging mechanism connecting not only the past to the present, but also the local to the national.

The Dissemination of Historical Consciousness to a New Generation

By the 1960s, East Germany possessed a generation of youth who had lived their entire lives under communism and had no personal memories of life under Nazism or the "antifascist struggle" that had been key components to the state's memory policies of the 1950s. In order to address these changing demographics, state institutions like the Buchenwald Memorial and the Museum for German History revamped their educational offerings to make their political message more accessible to a new generation and also impose greater control over how their exhibits were presented to visitors (especially to the youth). The party's problem of connecting with East German youth was not confined to the area of memory-work. In her research on East German youth education, Dorothee Wierling came to the conclusion that by the end of the 1960s, "the socialist project had lost hold of all the youth."35 The efforts outlined below were thus part of a larger effort by the party to reconnect with its youth population and cultivate a sense of loyalty to the East German state.

The following examples reveal that the SED and its cultural functionaries recognized that the general populace was not absorbing the party's intended political message. This recognition prompted the party to make practical and operational changes at both the Buchenwald Memorial and at the Museum for German History aimed at amplifying certain aspects of their memory-work and reworking the didactical aspects of a visitor's experience. Despite the SED's monopoly of power, the party continued to face difficulties in transferring memories and historical consciousness to a new generation. Internal reviews suggested that both institutions struggled to connect with the country's youth, an aspect that had been taken more for granted during the 1950s, but now needed to be addressed through changes in the exhibit and how museum educators interacted with the visitors.

The Buchenwald site had been a popular place of interest since the end of the war. Pilgrims came to the site, survivors paid their respects, and tourists took a side trip while vacationing in the cultural city of Weimar. Yet the SED understood the importance not only for people to visit the site, but also to take away specific lessons. For the average tourist, a visit to Buchenwald in the 1960s entailed an introductory film, a guided tour around the grounds of the camp, a visit to the museum exhibit, and probably a walk around the Buchenwald Memorial just outside of the main camp.

School groups and youth organizations, however, took part in a much more detailed educational program, which was often longer in duration and structured around specific pedagogical goals. When possible, students met with survivors of the camp to hear firsthand about the stories of the great heroes of the antifascist struggle. The Buchenwald Memorial administration entered into several cooperation contracts with schools, universities, and youth organizations to provide educational opportunities outside of classroom instruction.

The party also sought to engage young people with the Buchenwald site in other ways. The memorial hosted an annual Buchenwald Orientation Run,36 it managed a large youth hostel (in the former SS barracks), its staff pursued research projects that included working with classes and youth groups on certain aspects of the camp's history, and it organized cleanup and restoration projects for which groups could volunteer.37 One of the most common ritualistic uses of Buchenwald for GDR youth was the *Jugendweihe*, a secular coming-of-age ceremony, during which the youth took an oath to support the aims of the state.38 SED also used the Buchenwald site to induct members into the FDJ youth organization. By 1968, Buchenwald was hosting over 10,000 such ceremonies annually.[39]

Despite the wide variety of activities hosted by the memorial site, the memorial's leadership was not satisfied with the museum's ability to project its desired political and education message. Complaints from private citizens, union leaders, and party members had been steady since the museum's opening—typically pointing to the unorganized nature of groups wandering around the camp or to incorrect statements made by the museum's tour guides. Rudolf Agsten, a member of the party leadership of the Liberal Democratic Party, wrote in 1956 complaining that his tour guide spoke more about resistance actions within the *Wehrmacht* than at Buchenwald and feared that this could leave a false impression, especially among foreign tourists.[40] This complaint and others like it—from both East German and foreign visitors, prompted the museum leadership to formalize how visitors toured the site and to increase training for its tour guides. In 1959, the memorial staff rewrote its tour-guide script in an attempt to streamline its message and avoid off-script supplements of their own. The new script called on the tour guides to provide a detailed history of the camp from its construction in 1936 through its liberation in 1945 within the historical context of Nazi Germany and to emphasize the role of active communist resistance both inside and outside the camp. Following the introductory lecture, visitors were taken through the camp and ended with a tour of the Buchenwald Memorial grounds. At each point along the tour, visitors were told about the acts of injustice endured by the prisoners and how they attempted to stand up against Nazi oppression.

Despite such revisions, the memorial leadership continued to discuss problems that they identified, or that were brought to their attention by outside visitors. In a report to the Ministry of Culture in 1962, Buchenwald's director Edwin Bergner alluded to concerns that students (and teachers) were not properly prepared for their visit and indicated that the Buchenwald administration felt the need to intervene and better coordinate educational visits. Bergner noted that over 80,000 youth had visited the Buchenwald site in 1961 alone and expected that this number would grow in the future. Given the large number of youth visiting the memorial site, Bergner argued that the memorial needed to have a more direct role in overseeing the content of instruction. He feared that the teachers had not adequately prepared the youth for their visit and could leave the site with only a superficial understanding of its historical importance. In order to correct this inadequacy, the Buchenwald staff designed a special course intended not only to instruct the teachers on the best methods of instruction, but also to inspire them and make them more effective multipliers for the SED's cause. Bergner argued that by correctly training teachers who would bring students to Buchenwald, the memorial could more effectively instill a sense of socialist historical consciousness among the East German youth and bolster the ideological aims of the party.[41]

The teacher training workshops launched by the memorial in 1962 became one of the more important aspects of Buchenwald's role as a place of youth education. The seminar organizers borrowed a slogan from Lenin—"Only the schools can solidify the victories of the revolution"—as the title for the seminar, which they hoped would inspire teachers to internalize their role as the link between the students and the future of East Germany.[42] The primary aim of the five-day courses was to train teachers how to prepare their students, especially those participating in the *Jugendweihe* ceremony, prior to their visit. The museum staff also designed the course to broaden the teacher's own knowledge about the period of fascism in Germany, particularly in regard to what it characterized as the "dangerous politics" of German imperialism and militarism. Most importantly, the course drew attention to acts of resistance by communist prisoners at Buchenwald and spelled out the links between the KPD, antifascism, and the GDR's contemporary social and political system.[43] These seminars were aimed specifically at educators in history, social studies, and within the party itself, who were the main points of contact for the state in its political education of East German youth. By first training teachers how to teach about both the subject matter and how to integrate a visit to Buchenwald into their lesson plans, the memorial staff hoped to solidify the East German state's image as being firmly rooted in antifascism.

During the seminar, teachers met with Walter Bartel, a former member of the prisoners' committee at the end of the war, former aide to President Wilhelm Pieck, a key organizer behind the creation of the Buchenwald Monument, and professor of history at the Humboldt University in Berlin. In their discussions with Bartel, the teachers tended to raise questions that centered around two key points—how much did the average German citizen know about the atrocities happening in camps such as Buchenwald and what group should be blamed for allowing this to happen. For instance, when one teacher asked to what extent the German people knew about such camps, Bartel's response was: "Absolutely yes. I myself am a witness; already in the prison, albeit behind bars, we knew that there were concentration camps. And immediately before that, in the spring of 1933, when I was arrested, we already knew of Dachau and of the concentration camp Orianienburg, as it was called at the time and which later became Sachsenhausen."[44] More generally, Bartel's answers focused on the guilt of the Nazi party and its ability to influence people's perception of reality through instilling them with such a sense of fear that they did not attempt to resist. When asked specifically about the situation in the city of Weimar, Bartel responded, "First, people knew about it [Buchenwald], ... but everyone was terrified when they heard the word concentration camp."[45] On the other hand, those who had been "morally strong", i.e. the communists, had resisted Nazis, yet they were outnumbered and rendered mute either through incarceration or death. Bartel retold stories at great length regarding specific personalities in the camp, about the 903 children they were able to save by convincing the guards that they were very learned tradesmen, about his personal relationship with Ernst Thälmann, and the de-Nazification process as it concerned those involved with the Buchenwald camp.[46] Bartel was uniquely qualified to function as a moral and historical guide for these teachers, since his qualifications as a survivor and a professor provided him with a double dose of authenticity and authority. Indeed, this mixture of training and active participation was a key element of the teachers' seminar.[47] Whether all of the teachers internalized Bartel's lesson equally is difficult to gauge, however, one teacher remarked "I think, my fellow colleagues, that we are all now very well aware that when we return from this short seminar, in light of what Professor Bartel has shared, that we will go home with the realization that things can never go so far as they did under the SS and fascism."[48]

The highpoint of the seminar, according to Otto Jakob, one of the first participants in the seminars, came on the fourth day. Together with Buchenwald inmates, the class toured the former concentration camp. A documentary film first set the mood for the visit. The group then proceeded to the camp entrance, where they held a short ceremony honoring the memory of Ernst Thälmann and other resistance fighters who lost their lives. The group then closed its short memorial service by singing the "Internationale," which gave the entire ritual a quasi-religious effect. Once the tone was set, the participants toured the site alongside the survivors and listened to their stories as they went. The tour closed with the viewing of another film, *"Mahnung für alle Zeiten"* and a visit to the memorial site just outside the grounds of the former concentration camp.[49] The ritualistic and well-orchestrated tour was designed to demonstrate the manner in which the state believed these teachers should view this site of memory when they returned with their own classes. A visit to Buchenwald was far more than merely a sightseeing tour—it was educational and it was designed to impart a sense of duty to the memory of those who suffered there at the hands of the Nazis. Reflecting on his experience in the course, Otto described it as being more like a "passionate retelling of personal memories with impressive films and sight-seeing" rather than attending a series of lectures.[50]

In his report to the Ministry of Culture, Director Bergner emphasized that the seminar had met its goals and characterized it as a "complete

FIGURE 3.1. A youth group from Eisenach visiting the Buchenwald Memorial on a tour with director Klaus Trostorff, 4 April 1970.
BArch Bild 183-J0404-0005-001 / Dieter Demme.

success." The teachers, he stated, left the seminar full of enthusiasm and asking for more seminars to be organized in the future. The teacher seminars continued at Buchenwald and were expanded to include youth leaders from the FDJ and the Young Pioneers. During the early 1970s the seminars and the educational materials were further expanded to address an ever-growing spectrum of visitors. Special attention, however, continued to be placed on training and developing appropriate curricula for the leaders of school groups, youth organizations, factory workers, and units from the NVA.[51] With each new cohort of students, as well as an emerging generation of teachers, who had no personal memory of events prior to the founding of the GDR, the state's need to connect the present with an ever increasingly distant past became more and more pertinent. During the 1970s, Buchenwald expanded its direct contacts with schools and universities and began sponsoring and mentoring scholarly work at nearby universities and offering practical internships to local Weimar schools.[52]

The Buchenwald monument was not the only national institution concerned with the pedagogical aspects of its social function. The leadership of the Museum for German History in Berlin also called for a series of internal reviews meant to adapt the museum's permanent exhibit and educational programs to the changing needs of the state during the 1960s and 1970s, especially in the area of youth education. Similar to the situation at the Buchenwald Memorial, the museum's primary educational goal was to instill the "correct type" of historical consciousness among East German youth. To this end, the museum staff developed extensive pedagogical materials—special visitor guides for school groups of various ages, thematic guides for *Jugendweihe* ceremonies, FDJ-school groups, Young Pioneers, and first-year party members. The museum also organized special after-school activities for local youth, including its own youth club— "Junge Historiker."[53]

In 1962 the pedagogical department of the museum undertook a major study of its own function within the museum's broader role as a place of public education. The department saw itself first and foremost as the primary conduit for propagating the "correct" interpretation of historical events and relating them to specific contemporary political events or situations. It also viewed itself as the intermediary between the academic and creative departments of the museum and the public who would see the final product. According to the operational structure of the museum, the pedagogical department needed to clear all changes to the exhibits before being released for public display, thus it held a key role in defining how the museum presented its narrative to the public.

The other primary task of the pedagogical department concerned the training and coordination of the museum's tour guides. According to the report, this was the area in which the department felt the greatest need for improvements and expansion. Without the correct interpretation of the historical artifacts, the department feared that individuals could come away from a visit with an interpretation entirely different from its intent. To develop the correct strain of historical consciousness in the public, the tour guide needed to act as an interpreter in a dialogue between visitors and the objects of history.[54] Here the report cites the greatest need for improvement, both quantitatively and qualitatively. In the first half of 1962, the museum had 39,765 visitors, of which only 12,919 were given tours by the museum's own tour guides. Another 2,040 were a part of groups without a tour guide, 24,806 were individual visitors, and 975 were given tours by guides not associated with the museum. Because less than one-third of all visitors were being given tours by its own employees, the department felt that it could not maintain adequate control over the dissemination of information.

Another internal report from 1962 specifically addressed the museum's ability to reach out to students—especially university-age students, but also youth in general. Although the report claims that the museum had contributed to the cultivation of a socialist historical consciousness among the East German population as a whole, it acknowledged that its work with students was a particular weak point. University-age students ranked among the museums smallest segment of visitors; only seventy-seven visitor groups came from the Humboldt University (just down the road) during the past three years.[55] Above all, the report discussed frustration that the university professors did not view the museum as a vital partner for training the next generation of historians (especially the next generation of teachers). To this end, the report emphasized that the museum should function as an extension of the lecture halls—offering concrete material evidence of what is taught at the university.[56]

The museum was not only concerned with its exposure to university-age students. Subsequent reports were full of new ideas and methods with which the museum could make itself more attractive to younger audiences and improve its educational outreach programs with school groups. Pointing to what it could offer those attending the polytechnic high schools, the museum's pedagogical unit highlighted its ability to let students touch objects of history, like an axe made of stone, to demonstrate how early man wielded control over nature, or the regalia from bishops and princes, to illustrate the vast difference in wealth between the aristocracy and the peasants in 1848.[57] The pedagogical department also sought to craft its message toward the fifth and six-grade curriculum, noting: "the ten and eleven year olds are among the most attentive and open visitors."[58] Rather humorously, however, the report continues with the observation that such "tours" were rarely of the traditional kind—the children's questions quickly derailed any attempts to offer a structured tour. Nonetheless, the report concludes that teachers often returned for a second, much more successful, tour once they had completed their studies on a topic.

Beyond the museum's work with school groups, it also offered a variety of other activities aimed at reaching a wider population of East German youth. In 1961, it offered, for example, eighty so-called youth hour events on the topic "How Man Learned to Rule Over Nature." Like the entire museum, these youth hours also contained an embedded political and ideological message. While the content focused on the history of early mankind, the museum pedagogues stressed the idea that work (with the aid of tools) was the key element that allowed early man to separate himself from the animals and conquer nature, thus relaying to the youth how important work and labor was for today's society.[59] The museum also constructed a series of "teaching cabinets" for use by school groups on the topics such as the German Peasants' War of 1525, society on the eve of the 1848 revolutions, and the 1918 November revolution in Germany. These teaching cabinets housed additional objects, which students could come in much closer contact with than in the permanent exhibit.

Only a small number of classes, however, from high schools, trade schools, the military, university classes, and West German groups took advantage of the three teaching cabinets. The pedagogical department placed the blame for the low numbers not on its content or method of instruction, but rather on the museum's lack of publicity. Nonetheless, the staff did undertake a few changes the following year. The museum left the 1848 cabinet mainly intact, since it had attracted the most groups (40), and decided to expand the cabinet about the Peasants' War, which had attracted twenty groups. The pedagogical department, however, suggested that the 1918 November revolution cabinet be discontinued, since it only managed to attract fifteen groups.[60] The larger lessons learned by the pedagogical department through its experiment with the teaching cabinets was that the museum as a whole should make its objects, when possible, more accessible to the visitor. They suggested photocopying texts, newspapers, and other documents from the exhibit for users to hold in their hands and read. Another suggestion that came from this experiment was to keep as many of the machines (like looms and spinning wheels) functioning and either offer active demonstrations or allow visitors a hand at operating the machines.

The educators at the Museum for German History faced similar difficulties to those their counterparts encountered at the Buchenwald Memorial. They found it frustrating that the students were ill prepared for their trip prior to visits. In an effort to correct for this and to better influence how teachers used the museum, they began offering a series of teacher training courses during the winter and summer holidays in February and July 1965. The museum hoped that its rich holdings of original documents and artifacts could be used to inspire teachers (and by extension the youth) to become more engaged with history and experience the museum in a manner that would contribute to building a socialist historical consciousness. Over the course of five days, the museum offered the teachers a series of lectures by members of its curatorial staff, including one by Walter Nimtz, the director of the museum, which covered each of the main sections of the permanent exhibit. Following the lectures that referred to the museum's periodization, the museum offered additional lectures and workshops dealing with how to use artifacts and documents as historical sources and how to structure a successful class museum visit.[61] The courses were considered a new key component of the museum's pedagogical outreach and continued to develop these courses and other continuing education courses as a result.[62]

While the museum staff concentrated on its efforts to reach out to youth and influence how they visited the museum, the pedagogical staff also began looking into how they might employ new technology to shape the visitor experience more generally. In October 1965, the museum's pedagogical department prepared a report for the director outlining how a sampling of other museums from the GDR, West Germany, Czechoslovakia, England, and Italy had used new technologies to improve their guided tours. According to the report, the pedagogical department favored personalized audio tours using portable tape recorders, but also saw potential benefits through the use of localized radio signals, and controlled lighting that could better direct the pace of a tour (lights that would automatically turn off when a group was supposed to move on to the next section of the exhibit). Yet, the personalized audio tours offered a distinct advantage of being able to develop tours highlighting different themes or tailoring tours for different constituencies.[63]

Despite the efforts of the pedagogical department at the museum, its report for the year 1965 again pointed to similar deficiencies and regretted its inability to increase the overall numbers of visitors, although it had been able to greatly increase the number of guided tours. It identified additional shortcomings of the museum, like its inability to modernize its displays in order to make them more life-like, aesthetically pleasing, and convincing.[64] Visible in each of the yearly reports throughout the 1960s is a continued attempt by the pedagogical department to improve the ability of the museum to connect with visitors in a manner that contributed to what the museum leadership saw as its institutional mission, namely the historical education of the masses and the cultivation of a socialist consciousness. To this end, it created a new visitor's council, comprised of SED party functionaries, trade union leaders, teachers, and representatives from the military and the youth organizations. The museum's leadership now began meeting regularly with this advisory council in an effort to better connect with those it identified as its key constituencies.[65]

While the museum's prime objective remained shaping its pedagogical message to the citizens of the GDR (and especially to its youth), the museum leadership was also interested in understanding what non-GDR visitors thought about their experience. In the spring of 1967, the museum carried out a survey of West German visitors in an effort to gauge the reception of its permanent exhibit. The survey asked questions ranging from statistical queries about how long visitors stayed or whether they had visited before to substantive questions about their overall impression of the exhibit or what they thought about the quality of the presentation.

Overall, the museum could claim some positive results—like the fact that 109 out of 176 respondents found the exhibit "clear" and another 60 found it "impressive," but there were still 45 visitors who did not hesitate to state that they found the exhibit "unconvincing." For most of the respondents, this was their first trip to the museum, only 23 had said they had been there before and the majority of the visitors were school children, 115. Beyond these statistics gathered by the museum, visitors were encouraged to leave comments on their survey as well, which reveal much

Emotional Bonds | 129

FIGURE 3.2. A youth group from Potsdam visiting the Museum for German History examining a replica of a Spinning Jenny, 20 March 1968.
BArch Bild 183-G0320-0028-001 / Rainer Mittelstädt.

more about the impressions of the West German visitors. The most repeated comment was that the museum lacked "objectivity," citing that it was too "one-sided" and wished it reflected "not only a Marxist interpretation." Others asked that the museum include other resistance groups, like the 20 July 1944 assassination attempt or the White Rose resistance group in Munich. Such comments reflect not only the impressions of the West German visitors, but also the divergent historical narratives taught in both Germanys. In his summary report regarding these visitor comments, Joachim Ave, director of the pedagogical department, attempted to downplay these criticisms, stating, "one should not overestimate these individual statements, they are often full of contradiction."[66]

An internal report prepared by the pedagogical department in 1969 attempted to assess the museum's contributions to the creation of a socialist consciousness in East Germany. The report primarily sang the perceived accomplishments of the museum in making significant contributions to the overall historical education of the public. It noted that museum had had over six million visitors since opening its doors and that the museum functioned as both a center for research and education. But it also showed a conscious reflection that the museum's role, and the role of history more generally, had reached a significant turning point. The report noted that by 1975, the "political, social, and cultural basis" for a majority of workers in East Germany would have occurred under socialist rule and that "overcoming fascist German imperialism" would no longer need to be the state's primary historical message.[67]

Looking at the year-end reports going into the 1970s, it is clear that the museum continued to retool its offerings for a new generation and a new type of constituency. These yearly reports also reveal that the museum staff never felt it had entirely accomplished its goal of reaching the majority of visitors. Its increased emphasis on designing its programs and exhibits primarily for youth indicate that it believed its best chances for connecting with visitors came by focusing on a constituency who was already cultivated in the state's interpretation of the past and for whom pre-existing conceptions of history might not conflict with the museum's historical narrative. The resistance by the West German visitors to the polemical interpretation of Germany's past highlights to what extent the museum had already tailored its narrative to the needs of the East German state.

Conclusion

As the GDR began to see the emergence of a new generation of citizens whose personal memory no longer reached beyond the collapse of the

Nazi regime, memory-workers in East Germany became more actively involved in trying to shape society's historical consciousness. While during the first two stages we saw attempts to first legitimize the SED and then the new East German state, memory-workers during this third phase attempted to find new ways to expand how the state connected to its citizens and create new emotional bonds. In some instances, the state memory-workers attempted to take advantage of the numinous emotions that can be activated by visiting historical sites and through genuine historical artifacts as we saw with the prominent renovation of sites associated with important figures or events in the history of German socialism. The state also attempted to expand its reach through establishing better historical links between the narratives of local histories and that of the new socialist East German "nation" as with the new narrative of local history museums like the one in Merseburg. Finally, state and party functionaries stepped up their efforts to connect with a new generation of youth—both directly and through new teacher training programs at sites like Buchenwald and the Museum for German History.

This turn also marks the beginning point in the transformation of East German memory culture into a routinized and staged culture of historical commemoration rather than one of celebrating figures who were probably still vividly remembered among many Germans during the 1940s and 1950s. This transition from memory to history was aided by the party's attempts to link each important aspect of Germany's historical development to the existing social and political reality and thereby to link history directly to the personal experiences of those visiting a site of memory or participating in a commemoration celebration. While cultivating the "correct" historical consciousness among the East German population had always been important for the SED, it now began to take on even more importance in the GDR's overall memory-work agenda.

The geographic extension of the SED's control over the memory landscape across the country served a similar purpose. Each new monument and museum that the party was able to construct or control meant an increase in the reach of its socialist historical narrative. Moreover, by renovating such sites as the Jenny Marx house, the Clara Zetkin house, and the Gotha Conference, the party transformed these places into hybrid sites of memory—allowing the state to add interpretive exhibits to existing historical sites and thereby increasing its control over how such sites were viewed by the public. By 1983, there were ninety-three museum-monuments dedicated to the history of the working class and the number continued to grow throughout the 1980s.[68] The multifunctional aspects of these renovated institutions brought the visitor into contact not only with artifacts of history but walked the visitor through a narrative that sought to relate these artifacts and subject matter directly to the visitor's own experience and thus to create an emotional link between past and present.

While the state had invested a great deal in cultivating its official historical narrative at places like the Museum for German History in Berlin, it was also conscious that this narrative did not always speak to the ways in which different regions saw their own history. In an effort to cultivate similar regional narratives that could feed into a larger national narrative, the state set out to reform regional and local history museums throughout the GDR's territory so that the narrative of each locality could be viewed as an integral part of its national historical narrative. Local events were no longer static historic moments in time, but rather waypoints on the path toward the GDR's existing social and political situation. By emphasizing the evolution of socioeconomic development at the local level, within the greater context of national trends, the SED sought to create a strong link between local history and the national experience. Moreover, by localizing the national narrative, the state sought to supplement its top-down interpretation of history in Berlin by giving the impression that each locality contributed to the new national narrative.

This geographic expansion of the national narrative was accompanied by increased awareness that new generations would need greater support in processing this information. The state's goal of cultivating a socialist historical consciousness among youth and workers meant that it needed to become a more active intermediary and interpreter for the masses. Teachers and tour guides needed to become better conduits for the transference of history into historical consciousness. GDR youth needed to be taught not only history but also an "appropriate" and "acceptable" way in which to process and understand it.

In the state's overall memory-work agenda, it is clear that museums in particular continued to take on an increasingly central role. By 1969, there were more than 600 museums in East Germany, which employed nearly 5,000 workers. According to official statistics, these museums attracted roughly 17.9 million visitors in 1968.[69] Given the importance that the party placed on cultivating and sustaining "correct" perceptions of the past, it is not surprising that the East German state invested such large amounts of resources. However, these institutions did not remain static places of memory—historians, party functionaries, and museum pedagogues continually worked to increase their effectiveness and adapt these institutions to shifts in GDR historiography and the ideological needs of the party.

Thus, this process of cultivating a socialist historical consciousness became an integral component of the memory culture landscape in the GDR. The lack of opinion polls, the absence of national testing, and the repressive nature of the regime, with its control over information and limits on freedom of expression, do not allow for an accurate assessment of the success or failure of this process. Yet from party documents and other evidence we can glean that, at least from the perspective of the SED, such efforts were at best a mixed success. The state's continued investment in monuments, museums, and commemoration ceremonies suggests that these institutions of memory contained enough perceived value to the party to justify continued investment. At the same time, party functionaries, like those at the Museum for German History and at the Buchenwald Memorial site, were also cognizant of the state's shortcomings, which forced them to continually reassess the effectiveness of its policies and seek to reform and improve its memory-work.

Notes

1. Mark Allinson, *Politics and Popular Opinion in East Germany 1945–1968* (Manchester: Manchester University Press, 2000), pp. 119–38.
2. Dorothee Wierling, "Youth as Internal Enemy: Conflicts in the Education Dictatorship," in *The Socialist Modern: East German Everyday Culture and Politics*, ed. Katherine Pence and Paul Betts (Ann Arbor: Michigan University Press, 2008), pp. 157–82, here p. 157.
3. For an excellent look at earlier party initiatives at the local and regional level aimed at constructing a sense of socialist national identity and the concept of *Heimat* in the GDR see: Jan Palmowski, *Inventing a Socialist Nation: Heimat and the Politics of Everyday Life in the GDR, 1945–1990* (New York: Cambridge University Press, 2009).
4. Ulrich Neuhäußer-Wespy, *Die SED und die Historie: Die Etablierung der mazistisch-leninistischen Geschichtswissenschaft der DDR in den fünfziger und sechziger Jahren* (Bonn: Bouvier, 1996), p. 21.
5. Martin Sabrow, *Das Diktat des Konsenses: Geschichtswissenschaft in der DDR 1949–1969* (Munich: Oldenbourg, 2001), p. 137.
6. Sabrow, ibid., pp. 139–41.
7. The original concept of numen and the numinous come from Rudolf Otto, *The Idea of the Holy* (London: Oxford University Press, 1958). The concept was further developed in Rachel Maines and James Glynn, "Numinous Objects," *The Public Historian*, Vol. 15, No. 1 (Winter 1993), pp. 9–25. See also: Catherine M. Cameron and John B. Gatewood, "Excursions into the Un-Remembered Past: What People Want from Visits to Historical Sites," *The Public Historian*, Vol. 22, No. 3 (Summer 2000), pp. 107–27.
8. DHM, Hausarchiv: MfDG/97.
9. DHM, Hausarchiv: MfDG/1043.
10. DHM, Hausarchiv: MfDG/1174.
11. Ibid.
12. DHM, Hausarchiv: MfDG/1200.
13. Ibid.
14. The concept of *Heimat* can mean a variety of feelings associated with one's place of birth, or homeland. While it can be used to simply evoke a sense of nostalgia or benign patriotism, it can also be used to connote a blind allegiance to one's homeland. On the

emergence of the concept of *Heimat* and its complicated history see: Celia Applegate, *A Nation of Provincials: The German Idea of Heimat* (Berkeley: University of California Press, 1990).

15. Jan Palmowski points to the folklore museum (*Volksmuseum*) in Schwerin, which opened in 1946, as the model for how *Heimat* museums during the earlier postwar period. See Palmowski, *Inventing a Socialist Nation*, p. 39.
16. Dieter Riesenberger, "Heimatgedanke und Heimatgeschichte in der DDR" in *Antimodernismus und Reform: Beiträge zur Geschichte der deutschen Heimatbewegung*, ed. Edeltraud Klueting (Darmstadt: Wissenschaftliche Buchgesellschaft, 1991), pp. 320–43, here pp. 323–24.
17. Rolf Kiau, "Zur Entwicklung der Museen der DDR," *Neue Museumskunde*, Vol. 12, No. 4 (1969), pp. 415–59, here p. 436. See also Dieter Riesenberger, "Entwicklung und Bedeutung der Geschichtsmuseen in der DDR," in *Geschichtswissenschaft in der DDR: Band I: Historische Entwicklung, Theoriediskussion und Geschichtsdidaktik*, ed. Alexander Fischer and Günther Heydemann (Berlin: Duncker & Humblot, 1988), pp. 479–510, here pp. 492–93.
18. Karl Czok, "Die Gründungstagung der Arbeitsgemeinschaft Heimat- und Landesgeschichte der Deutschen Historiker-Gesellschaft in Görlitz," *Zeitschrift für Geschichtswissenschaft*, Vol. 9, No. 8 (1961), pp. 1876–81.
19. Kiau, "Zur Entwicklung der Museen der DDR," p. 445.
20. SAPMO-BArch, DY 27/719, "Arbeitsbericht: über dei Museumsrundfahrt des Fachausschusses Museen der Zentral-Kommission 'Natur und Heimatfreunde' am 13. bis 15. Juni 1952," p. 1.
21. SAPMO-BArch, DY 27/719, p. 3.
22. LHASA-Merseburg, Bezirksleitung der SED Halle, IV/A2/902-40, p. 134. "Inhaltliche Konzeption für die Einrichtung des Kreismuseums Merseburg," April 1967.
23. Ibid., p. 135.
24. Ibid., pp. 133–34; also KA-Merseburg, Archiv Nr. 10489. "Themenkonzeption zum Aufbau der II. Etage des Kreismuseums Merseburg, Abteilung I, 1815–1945."
25. LHASA-Merseburg, Bezirksleitung der SED Halle, IV/A2/902-40, p. 134–39.
26. KA-Merseburg, Archiv Nr. 10489.
27. KA-Merseburg, Archiv Nr. 10489. Letter dated 9 April 1986.
28. Petra Koch, "Die politische und ökonomische Entwicklung des Kreises Merseburg von 1949 bis zum IX. Parteitag der SED 1976, dargestellt an der Entwicklung der chemischen Grossindustrie, des Braunkohlenbergbaus und der Arbeits- und Lebensweise der Werktätigen," Fachschulabschlußarbeit an der Fachschule für Museologen Leipzig, 20 May 1977 (non-inventoried document in the house archive of the *Kulturhistorisches Museum* in Merseburg).
29. KA-Merseburg, Archiv Nr. 10489. In Koch's version up through the Ninth Party Congress in 1977, and updated again when it was finally completed in 1986 to cover the time up until the Eleventh Party Congress in April of that year.
30. Koch, "Die politische," p. 118.
31. Ibid., p. 119.
32. Ibid., p. 135.
33. Ibid., p. 135.
34. Ibid., pp. 142–44.
35. Dorothee Wierling, "Youth as Internal Enemy," p. 176.
36. The Erfurt regional arm of the East German Hikers and Mountain Climbers Association organized the first annual Buchenwald Memorial Orientation Run on 23 and 24 April 1960 to commemorate the fifteenth anniversary of the camp's liberation. BwA, VA/123,

letter from Knopf and Kaiser, Deutscher Wanderer- und Bergsteiger-Verband, Bezirksfachausschuss Erfurt, dated 21 December 1959 and BwA, VA/123, letter from Kaiser dated 26 February 1960.
37. Klaus Trostorff, "Die Nationale Mahn- und Gedenkstätte Buchenwald," *Neue Museumskunde*, Vol. 18, No. 2 (1975), pp. 85–92, here p. 91.
38. Marina Chauliac, "Die Jugendweihe," in *Erinnerungsorte der DDR*, ed. Martin Sabrow (Munich: Beck Verlag, 2009), pp. 161–68.
39. BwA, VA/80, letter from Edwin Bergner, director of the Buchenwald Memorial, to Joachim Ave, head of Working Group for Schools and Museums at the Ministry for People's Education, dated 21 March 1968.
40. BwA, VA/111, p. 44, letter from Rudolf Agsten to the Komitee der Antifaschisten Widerkämpfer in der DDR dated 12 April 1956.
41. BwA, VA/45, letter from Edwin Bergner, Director of the Buchenwald Memorial to the Ministry of Culture, dated 22 March 1962.
42. BwA, VA/45, "Die Siege der Revolution kann nur die Schule festigen."
43. "20 Jahre Lehrerkurs an der NMG Buchenwald" in *Buchenwald-Information*, No. 1 (1982), p. 3 as quoted in Hasko Zimmer, *Der Buchenwald-Konflikt: zum Streit um Geschichte und Erinnerung im Kontext der deutschen Vereinigung* (Münster: Agenda, 1999), p. 77.
44. BwA, VA/45. "Tonbandprotokoll: Gespräch mit Walter Bartel."
45. BwA, VA/45. Bartel went on to relay a story of a transport vehicle carrying bodies from Buchenwald to a nearby crematorium. The vehicle had an accident and some of the coffins were thrown off. During the collision, several of the coffins broke open to reveal multiple bodies in one coffin and thus amplified the fears of the townspeople in Weimar. According to Bartel, as a result of this and several similar incidents the SS decided to build its own crematorium at Buchenwald in order to shield the average citizen from what was really happening.
46. BwA, VA/45.
47. BwA, VA/45. "Auswertung des Ferienkursus für Geschichts- und Staatsbürgerkundelehrer an der Nationalen Mahn- und Gedenkstätte Buchenwald," 22 March 1962, a report filed by Director Bergner to the Ministry of Culture, Department of Art and Museums.
48. BwA, VA/45. "Tonbandprotokoll: Gespräch mit Walter Bartel."
49. BwA, VA/45.
50. BwA, VA/45. Otto Jacob, Halle, "Abschrift: Erster Geschichtslehrer-Kursus in Buchenwald." A shorter version of his experience appeared as a letter to the editor in the "*Deutsche Lehrerzeitung*" from 13 April 1962.
51. BwA, VA/54. "Entwurf zum Perspektivplan der Nationalen Mahn- und Gedenkstätte Buchenwald für die Jahre 1970–75."
52. Ewald Deyda, "Zur Zusammenarbeit der Nationalen Mahn- und Gedenkstätte Buchenwald mit Studenten und Schülern," *Zeitschrift für Geschichtswissenschaft*, Vol. 27, No. 6 (1979), pp. 529–34.
53. DHM, Hausarchiv: MfDG/139.
54. DHM, Hausarchiv: MfDG/161. "Vorlage über "Aufgaben und Perspektiven der Pädagogischen Abteilung, 6. July 1962."
55. DHM, Hausarchiv: MfDG/152, p. 62. The number of visitor groups for the three previous years were: 1,228 (1959), 1,434 (1960), and 1,217 (1961) according to the year-end report from 1963.
56. DHM, Hausarchiv: MfDG/152, pp. 69–71. Draft report titled "Studenten im Museum."
57. DHM, Hausarchiv: MfDG/152, pp. 91–92. "Einige Gedanken zu den Beziehungen zwischen Sonderschulen und Geschichtmuseum."
58. DHM, Hausarchiv: MfDG/152, pp. 93–94. "Geschichtsmuseum für Zehnjährige?"

59. DHM, Hausarchiv: MfDG /152, pp. 98–100. "Zur Durchführung der Jugendstunde 'Wie die Mensch die Natur beherrschen lernte' im Museum für deusche Geschichte."
60. DHM, Hausarchiv: MfDG/161, pp. 49–51. "Erste Analyse über die Kabinettsarbeit" dated 25 April 1961.
61. DHM, Hausarchiv: MfDG/161, p. 69. Brochure "Ferienkurse."
62. DHM, Hausarchiv: MfDG/323, unpaginated. "Jahresbericht 1966" dated 5 January 1967.
63. DHM, Hausarchiv: MfDG/161, pp. 57–58. "Auswertung der bisherigen Erfahrungen anderer Museen bzw. Ausstellungen bei der Verwendung von technischen Mitteln für Führungen (UKW-Funk, Tonbandführungen, Lichteffekte u.a.)."
64. DHM, Hausarchiv: MfDG/120 "Bemerkungen zur Jahresstatistik 1965."
65. DHM, Hausarchiv: MfDG/139, pp. 22–23. "Besucherrat des Museum für Deutsche Geschichte."
66. DHM, Hausarchiv: MfDG/185 (unpaginated). "Besuchertest—März, April, Juni 1967."
67. DHM, Hausarchiv: MfDG/Pädagogische Abteilung, "Perspektive und Aufgaben des Museums für Deutsche Geschichte in der Periode der Gestaltung des entwickelten gesellschaftlichen Systems des Sozialismus in der DDR (Memorandum)" dated 1 April 1969, p. 7.
68. Hans Maur, "Heimatgeschichtliche Forschungen erhöhen Bildungsniveau musealer Gedenkstätten der Arbeiterbewegung," *Heimatgeschichte,* No. 15 (1983), p. 20.
69. Rolf Kiau, "Zur Entwicklung der Museen der DDR," p. 415.

Chapter Four

BROADENING THE HISTORICAL ROOTS OF THE STATE NARRATIVE

East Germany's relationship with the past entered a period of expansion and change during the late 1970s and early 1980s. West German Chancellor Willy Brandt's 1969 declaration of two German states in one nation prompted the GDR to switch from the stated goal of unifying Germany to embracing a separate East German nation. This had an important influence on the selection of figures from the broader German past that the state now decided to celebrate. This sense of national independence was bolstered by the signing of the Basic Treaty with West Germany in 1971, the formal acceptance of both Germanys as separate states at the United Nations in 1973, and western acknowledgement that postwar borders could not be changed by force as part of the Helsinki Accords in 1975. Beyond these formal steps toward normalizing relations between East and West Germany, the willingness of the Soviet Union, the GDR, and others to engage in greater people-to-people exchanges indicates that Brandt's approach became accepted policy in the west, also among his successors—Chancellors Helmut Schmidt and Helmut Kohl.[1]

Yet, Brandt's *Neue Ostpolitik*[2] also brought new challenges to East Germany's claims of legitimacy and forced the East German regime to reassess its categorization of many historical events and figures as either exclusively "progressive" or "reactionary." Until then, the GDR had continually professed a so-called dual-line theory of history in which East Germany had inherited all the "progressive" elements of Germany's national history, while West Germany had inherited all of the "reactionary" elements. During this period of reassessment the state sought to broaden its own legitimizing national narrative by moving into the "progressive category" a growing number of historical subjects that had previously been deemed "reactionary" and cleanse them of their previous negative connotations.

Notes for this chapter begin on page 176.

This reassessment was rooted in the GDR's well-established tradition of honoring Germany's greatest cultural figures such as Johann Wolfgang von Goethe, Friedrich Schiller, Johann Sebastian Bach, and many others, especially those whose activities could be located within the territory of the contemporary GDR. In this way the regime sought to localize certain historical figures on East German soil. It was easier for the state to single out these cultural giants for their contributions to humanistic culture than to address their political counterparts. The fact that many of them had served some of the most powerful kings and emperors of German history was considered necessary in order for them to have the freedom to create their cultural masterpieces. In many ways, the new trend of rehabilitating many of Germany's great political figures followed this same logic. According to the new line, their cooperation or association with reactionary elements was necessary in order for them to make contributions to social and political progress.

The debate in East Germany over reassessing the place of certain figures in German history first entered the political mainstream during the Ninth Party Congress in 1976. The SED openly called for expanding the conceptual framework governing what aspects of German national history were acceptable to allow the state to differentiate itself from and wage class warfare against its West German counterpart.[3] Despite its intent to expand the heritage of the GDR to include figures and events that had been previously deemed "reactionary," the party continued to proclaim that its legacy formed the "source of patriotic pride toward our socialist fatherland."[4] As East German historians and other memory-workers rehabilitated new segments of the German past and deemed them to be at least in part "progressive," the East German state could now call upon a seemingly endless range of historical events and figures.

Heritage and Tradition from the Historian's Perspective

Among East Germany's professional historians, such reassessment was the center point of a theoretical debate that ran throughout the 1970s and 1980s concerning the difference between "heritage" and "tradition" (*Erbe und Tradition*). This theoretical shift in defining the appropriate historical lineage of national history sought to further develop the sense of a uniquely socialist national identity in the GDR, one that was not only based upon different historical traditions than West Germany, but was also able to draw upon a much wider and deeper conception of heritage. As such, acceptable historical subjects departed from the more tailored and party-centric approach of previous decades. This departure reflected both the party's confidence that it had made inroads into influencing popular memory and historical consciousness and the party's desire to place a claim over an even wider array of historical figures and events in an attempt to widen its appeal to the GDR population.

According to the prominent GDR historian Walter Schmidt, the national history of the GDR was no longer based solely on the progressive traditions of the German working class, but rather on the entire history of the German people.[5] Fellow historian Horst Bartel took the theory one step further in his article *"Erbe und Tradition in Geschichtsbild und Geschichtsforschung in der DDR"* in which he laid out the theoretical argument for separating the concepts of heritage and tradition.[6] According to Bartel, traditions were those elements of a society that were timeless and consciously sustained in order to maintain continuity and a sense of purpose. Heritage, on the other hand, contained the positive elements of history that provided the foundation for historical progress, according to the scientific interpretation of historical materialism. Bartel's interpretation thus allowed for the inclusion of positive currents stemming from not only the working class, but also from the "exploiting classes" as long as they aided the progress of historical development. As an inheritor of "everything that exists in history, the entire history in its full contradictoriness," it was the duty of the Marxist historian to sort out which parts of the German past, however reactionary, also contributed to the general progress of societal development.[7]

This new conception of history allowed the GDR to venture into areas of commemoration that had previously been outside its political parameters. The reemergence of Frederick the Great in 1980, the "Prussian Renaissance" in 1981, the commemoration of Goethe in 1982, Luther in 1983, Schiller in 1984, Bach, Händel and Schütz in 1985, the 750th anniversary of Berlin in 1987, and Thomas Müntzer in 1989 were all part of this new interest in broadening the historical and cultural heritage of the GDR's national history. The concrete aim of this conscious effort to reinterpret the GDR's historical heritage was bound together with an attempt by the regime, as Martin Sabrow has argued, to free itself from "the corset of the dual-line-concept by employing a vision that better suited the socialist dictatorship's changing needs for legitimization."[8]

Indeed, as the decade of the 1980s marched on, the SED faced many new challenges to its assertion of a distinctly "east" German society. The party sought to cultivate new perceptions of the past during a period of increased challenges in delineating itself from the west. The treaties of the 1970s began to open up more and more avenues for cultural exchange and greater permeability of the division; West German television, for example, ceased to be jammed. The SED hoped that placing greater claims over this shared history might allow it to better control how the general population absorbed it. New challenges, like the popular protests against the deployment of Pershing and SS20 missiles, spawned peace movements in both German states, which in turn allowed some, especially the youth, to continue to see a common bond between East and West Germany that transcended Germany's physical division. It is precisely these sorts of challenges to the SED's notion of GDR nationhood that it hoped a new sense of historical identity might be able to thwart or at least minimize.

Despite the enthusiasm for developing new ideas of heritage and tradition among academics and the party leadership, some within the SED had difficulty understanding the party's sudden interest in historical figures who had previously been categorized as reactionary and who were now being heralded as important as the heroes of the German working class. Ursula Ragwitz, head of the SED's cultural department, struggled to write an informational pamphlet for local party leaders regarding the role of cultural heritage in the GDR. She found two questions particularly difficult to explain to the party masses, which she then addressed to Kurt Hager, the SED's chief ideologue and member of the *Politbüro*:

> What are the reasons behind why the GDR recently turned two bourgeois and noble Germans, the religious leader Luther and the General Clausewitz, into national heroes? The handling which both of these great men of German and European history have recently received in the GDR, including their personal involvement, has up until now been solely reserved for the heroes of the communist movement. As you know, General Clausewitz was an enthusiastic supporter of the monarchy, while Martin Luther has been vilified for years in the GDR as a traitor to the rebellious peasants. And even you personally recently chaired a meeting that dealt with the preparations for the 500th anniversary of Martin Luther's birthday in 1983.[9]

To this, Hager wrote a lengthy reply articulating the SED's position on this subject. He refuted the idea that this signaled any change in the party's approach toward the past or its heritage. Hager stated that the current approach toward the past was "fully in keeping with the traditions of Marx, Engels, and Lenin, in the traditions of the German labor movement and our own history since 1945." Moreover, he declared that:

> We are in no way ignoring the historical and class boundaries of these or other personalities from German history, their negative traits, their contradictory behavior or sometimes historical tragedy in which they find themselves trapped. It corresponds with our worldview to study history in its objective and factual progression and in its entire dialectic … Thus, we judge such personalities through the way in which their influence extends beyond their time, what they have contributed to societal progress and to the development of humanist culture. At the same time we raise the question of how we can make this heritage productive for our time and our society. Martin Luther is without a doubt one

of the greatest sons of the German people and a man of worldwide progressive influence.[10]

Hager clearly aligned the new understanding of political figures such as Luther and Clausewitz within the more established interpretation of the cultural heritage that had existed in the GDR since the 1950s. By extending the definition of culture beyond creative figures such as Goethe, Schiller, Beethoven, and other "high culture" personalities, Hager was able to extend the concept of cultural legacy to a broader grouping and rationalize the inclusion of figures who had been previously judged out of bounds.

Ragwitz's second question to Hager raised the issue of competing for control with West Germany over common historical figures: "Is it right, when I say that the breakthrough in this respect came from the results of Mrs. Ingrid Mittenzwei's book, namely the biography of Frederick the Great? Are you not risking the fact that the GDR and the FRG are partially celebrating the same national heroes of the past?"[11] Previously, the GDR had an easier time claiming a direct and singular linkage between the heroes of the German labor movement and the East German state without much competition from the West German state.[12] Now, it appeared that the GDR would have to either share or fight over these newly rehabilitated historical figures.

In his response, Kurt Hager disagreed with the idea that there had been any "breakthrough" regarding a new interpretation of the past. Rather, Hager argued, the new assessment was part of the sustained development of Marxist-Leninist historical interpretation aimed at providing the masses with access to history's treasures. In response to her specific reference to West Germany, Hager wrote: "As experience has shown, heritage preservation in our socialist society has nothing in common with the official heritage preservation policies practiced in the FRG. This is true even when the same figures, objects, or events from our historical or cultural legacy enter the public sphere in both German states." Moreover, he maintained: "This is to say nothing of the fact that many unholy traditions have come to light again in the FRG, which we would never view as heritage worth preserving." Thus, delineation between East and West Germany was not only a political matter, but also a matter of cultivating a cultural heritage that was remembered and utilized in a distinctly different manner from that in the West. It no longer mattered to the party that the same figures could be incorporated into both German state's narratives as long as the GDR maintained a unique interpretation, based on its Marxist-Leninist interpretation of history.

A close look at three examples of rehabilitation and commemoration reveals some of the nuances involved in the SED's efforts to alter popular perception of the past in the GDR. The first example centers on the general emergence of the image of Prussia during the first few years of the 1980s. The theoretical underpinnings developed by the historians and SED leadership now found a broader audience as Prussia's history took on a more prominent role in Berlin's public spaces. The second example deals with the 1983 commemoration of Martin Luther, a figure who had previously stood a distant second to his more radical contemporary Thomas Müntzer. The Luther celebrations illustrate a case where the state attempted to appropriate a memory and tradition that had been kept alive by the Evangelical Church and tried to subsume his image into the heritage and traditions of the GDR state. Third, the construction of the panorama memorial in Bad Frankenhausen provides a glimpse into how the process of altered historical interpretation influenced a memory project that spanned across the entire decade up until the months just prior to the regime's collapse. The panorama, which began as a memorial to Thomas Müntzer and a specific battle at Bad Frankenhausen, morphed to include a broader interpretation of the Peasants' War and eventually the entire era surrounding the period officially referred to in the GDR as the "Early Bourgeois Revolution."

These new interpretations of the past brought new forms of remembrance and commemoration into the public sphere during this fourth phase of the GDR's memory culture development. They also suggest that that the GDR's strict hold over official memory was beginning to erode. While the state always had to negotiate with its memory-work partners and compromise on the ultimate form that its memory projects took, the coarser filter that previously divided the "progressive" from the "reactionary" was much simpler for the average citizen to apply and interpret—as long as he or she also subscribed to the overall concept that the GDR was trying to be a morally correct version of its West German sibling. By applying a finer filter that rehabilitated elements of the German past formerly deemed as "reactionary," the theoretical and moral differences between East and West Germany became less and less obvious to the casual observer—or the average citizen. Expanding East Germany's memory landscape to include topics like Prussian history, the Reformation, or Martin Luther expanded the segment of its population who were now willing to engage with its memory-work. Yet at the same time, this expansion allowed for a wider array of interpretations and thus made it increasingly difficult for the state to assert its control.

Rediscovering Prussia

A large portion of the GDR's territory fell within the borders of the former Prussian state. In part, new interest in Prussia's past during the late 1970s and early 1980s arose from the GDR's attempt to localize the historical development of the German working class within its own borders. Yet, the figures of Bismarck and Frederick the Great had very little to do with the actions of the working class, and GDR historians had long characterized the state of Prussia as the most militant and chauvinistic in German history. The emergence of a Prussian Renaissance points to the efforts by the GDR state to expand the quantity of historical sites of memory within its territory in a way that could further differentiate it from West Germany.

The first publication signaling a shift in the GDR's interpretation of Prussia was Ingrid Mittenzwei's *Friedrich II von Preussen* in 1979.[13] The author, at the time, headed the Department of History 1648–1789 at the GDR Academy of Sciences and set the tone for interpreting Frederick the Great and the Prussian state throughout the GDR. Mittenzwei contended that while Prussia was a reactionary and militaristic state, its leaders made great contributions to social development, including technological and scientific advancements and early industrialization. The elite ruling class, she argued, were clearly acting to serve the interest of the land-owning *"Junker"* nobility and created a social atmosphere that would eventually enable the German working class to develop its social and political consciousness.[14]

Although Mittenzwei rejected the idea that her work was apologetic toward Prussia, she did argue that the GDR needed a more differentiated view of Prussia's contributions to the German nation and the impact of this legacy on the contemporary situation in the GDR. In the closing paragraphs of her biography of Frederick II, she wrote:

> Prussia is a part of our past. When one travels through cities in the GDR, through Berlin and Potsdam in particular, one can come into contact with the stone witnesses of Prussian history at every turn. They are just one sign that we are bound by an invisible thread with the past. Certainly, one will always have to approach this period of our past critically. The German revolutionary working class came of age and took up its unmistakable procession of struggles against the reactionary *Junker*-bourgeois forces of the Prussian-German military state. However, one should not forget that Prussia was not identical to the dominant class.[15]

Mittenzwei went on to argue that even with great figures of history such as Frederick II one must differentiate between those actions that aided the progressive forces of historical development and those actions that prevented such progress. Thus, even by suppressing workers, such figures created a social context in which the working class became conscious of its plight and furthered the cause of the German workers' movement.[16]

One of the most striking indications that the SED leadership had officially rehabilitated Prussia came with the return of the equestrian statue of Frederick II to its former site on Unter den Linden Street in the heart of Berlin in 1980. In 1950, the state removed the monument from Berlin, placed in storage, and made a public promise to place it on display in Potsdam's Sanssouci Park on the grounds of the historic summer palace of Germany's emperors. It wasn't until May 1962 that the state finally took his statue out of storage, restored it, and put it on public display. Although the GDR kept its promise to place the monument in Sanssouci Park, it chose to place it in one of the most remote corners, in the *Hippodrom* section located at the extreme south end of the park, where few visitors ventured.[17] The first news that the statue would return to Berlin came during an interview Erich Honecker gave to the English language publisher of his autobiography on 4 August 1980.[18] With its return to the Unter den Linden Street on 28 November 1980, it was clear that the GDR was serious about rehabilitating and reclaiming Prussia's history for its own purposes. The popularization of Frederick II's image did not stop with the return of the monument. Tourist shops in Potsdam now sold busts of Frederick II, East German orchestras performed his orchestral compositions, and bookstores began selling copies of his political writings.[19]

The GDR's renewed interest in Prussian history was also partially a response to the parallel wave of popular interest in the Federal Republic. East German Historians wanted to redefine Prussia's historical legacy so

FIGURE 4.1. Reinstallation of Christian Daniel Rauch's sculpture of King Frederick II of Prussia (Frederick the Great) in November 1980.
BArch Bild 183-W1127-030 / Karl-Heinz Schindler.

that the GDR could claim some of the progressive legitimating elements of Prussian history and not leave it entirely to the "imperialist" historians of the neighboring state to define Prussia's legacy. The approach involved separating the reactionary from the progressive elements within Prussia's history and integrating these positive elements into the traditions of the GDR. In particular, the GDR pointed to the museum exhibit in West Berlin "Prussia—An Attempt at Balance" as a sign that even "flexible" Western historians, those engaged in a social or cultural approaches critical of the Prussian state, were only providing an historical account that justified the "imperialist" aims of the Federal Republic and its allies.[20] East German political leaders had good reasons to be concerned about the temporary exhibit in West Berlin's *Kunstgewerbemuseum* in 1981—it drew more than a million visitors between August and the middle of October.[21]

However, the resurgence of interest in Prussian history cannot be entirely attributed to the mounting wave of interest in the Federal Republic. East German political leaders continued to feel that the state's legitimacy rested in the ability of the average citizen to find a link of continuity between the past and the present. SED Chairman Erich Honecker began publicly referring to Frederick II as "Frederick the Great" and at the same time observed that a "deep relationship with history strengthens the citizens' attachment to their socialist fatherland and increases their pride in the achievements of the socialist revolution."[22] Honecker and other politicians who invoked the image of Prussia were clearly attempting to bolster their own legitimacy by strengthening its argument that East Germany was the true inheritor of Prussian history.

The figures of Frederick II and the state of Prussia played a different role than that of Prussian historical figures such as Scharnhorst, Gneisenau, Yorck, or Blücher, whom the GDR had used during earlier periods to legitimize specific political objectives such as German-Russian cooperation or the defense of the German nation. This role was much more broadly defined, much more complex, and much more deeply rooted in the East German regime's desire to lay claim to entirety of German history rather than only that of the German working class or specific elements that had direct ties to specific political goals.

The public rehabilitation of the figure of Bismarck was more complicated than the other Prussian figures. West Germans had long claimed him as the principal founder of the German Empire. The Federal Republic had attempted to integrate Bismarck's legacy into its own national narrative as early as 1965, when the West German parliament held a special session in honor of Bismarck's 150th birthday.[23] Until the mid-1980s, East Germany officially saw Bismarck as the embodiment of the negative aspects of German nationalism and military expansionism. Above all, many party loyalists believed that because Bismarck had repressed socialists, he could not be rehabilitated alongside Frederick the Great and other Prussian figures. Yet, by the mid-1980s Bismarck's image in the GDR also began to change.

As with the more general changes in the GDR's approach toward the history of the Prussian state and Frederick II, the first signs of Bismarck's rehabilitation came through attempts by GDR historians to differentiate between his "reactionary" policies and his "progressive" accomplishments. In a 1983 interview with the Free German Youth newspaper *Junge Welt*, historian Heinz Wolter broached the idea that although Bismarck was "not the infallible master of the art of statesmanship, showing the German people the path to glory and greatness, as he is often made out to be," he was also not "the great villain who is to be personally saddled with the responsibility for the fatal course of Prusso-German history."[24] Some of Bismarck's accomplishments that GDR historians now found "progressive" included his work toward unifying the German nation, which created a single national market and allowed capitalism to blossom. Bismarck's economic and currency reforms, historians argued, provided the basis for the development of a capitalist market, which produced conditions in Germany that allowed for the creation of a modern industrial proletariat and efforts by the German labor movement to organize on a national level. Chief ideologue Kurt Hager, during a speech in 1983, singled out Bismarck's "realist" approach to foreign affairs, especially in Germany's dealings with Russia, as an example to be followed.[25] In 1984 Walter Schmidt, Director of the Institute for the History of the German Labor Movement, noted: "In 1871 Bismarck brought about social progress by creating a bourgeois German national state through 'revolution from above.' Although it was not the ideal variant of progress, it was progress nevertheless."[26]

Ernst Engelberg's 1985 biography *Bismarck: Urpreuße und Reichsgründer* signaled Bismarck's entrance into the official pantheon of GDR historical figures. Engelberg continued Mittenzwei's differentiation between the positive "progressive" achievements and "reactionary" traits when critiquing Bismarck's contributions to Germany's historical development. He singled out Bismarck's role in Germany's unification as the single most progressive act, despite the fact that it was done through war: "Thereafter [after 1848/49 and 1866], historical progress could only happen in the form of a revolution from above. The royal-Prussian revolutionary that Bismarck was, as even Karl Marx admitted, the executor of the 1848 revolution, while at the same time the protector of the counterrevolution in so far as he defended resolutely the prerogatives of the crown."[27] In his concluding remarks, Engelberg offered a summation of Bismarck's contribution to Germany's political and social development: "Germany was no longer a plaything of the Great Powers. ... The German workers' movement was also able to better gather its forces on the basis of a united Germany and lead the struggle for its own political and social goals; the very fact of having a platform in the Reichstag, the elections, their own press even during the period of the Socialist Law, provided them with new possibilities for independence and organization."[28]

This upsurge in regional or territorial history was not unique to the area of Prussia, although it did reflect the main thrust of the state's memory politics at the time. Popular interest in the regions of Saxony, Thuringia, Mecklenburg, and Brandenburg also grew. Although East German dissolved its five federal states in 1952 and replaced them with fifteen districts, the state was never able to erase popular memories connected with these former territorial boundaries and the rich history that they symbolized. The GDR's approach toward these regional histories paralleled how it approached Prussian history—the GDR was the inheritor of all of the region's history, yet filtered out those elements that were merely remnants of the past from those that were considered part of the traditions that comprised the GDR's "national" identity.

In a report on "Territorial History in Historical Propaganda," Manfred Unger articulated how new interest in regional and territorial history had an impact on the historical consciousness of citizens in the former region of Saxony.[29] Part of the state's propaganda effort included a lecture series by leading historians over eight Saturdays, each lasting approximately five hours in length. Each session included four lecture presentations and a discussion with the audience. While the lectures drew audiences of between 100 and 200 each, Unger was struck that only a small fraction of them were professional historians. Indeed, he found that the great majority had come merely out of a keen interest in Saxony's history and Unger rationalized from this observation that people had a natural link with the history of places that they see each day. Most of all, Unger argued that the *Land*[30] level was more approachable for these "friends of history, whose special interest in *Heimat*-history and the locality is at play. This level had a central position in between national history and local events, and offered the possibility to observe national and world historical conditions of local processes."[31]

Yet, Unger also acknowledged that this renewed interest in regional history sparked an increased demand in bookstores for biographies and memoirs, without any recognition of the inherent contradiction such an interest posed to the development of a Marxist historical consciousness.[32] Owing to the progression of history as a result of historical materialism, the formation of a Marxist historical consciousness should be independent from the acts of individuals, since all human beings are a product of their time. Unger acknowledged that the public expected to see history through portrayals of certain historical personalities and that the role of territorial history was to "demonstrate the problems [of these personalities] at the time, their progress, and their reaction." However, such an assertion only describes the rationale for the GDR's memory policies, but does not examine the motivating factors behind the increased interest for "great" historical figures such as Frederick II, Bismarck, or August "the Strong."

The specific reasons for this resurgent interest in regional histories are multiple, and difficult to identify definitively. It could have been a way for the average citizen of the GDR to escape into a time that they did not associate either with the current political situation in the GDR or with the darker aspects of Germany's past, such as the Nazi period. Such increased interest in regional history might also signal an inherent interest in all humans to want to learn about the histories of where they live, similar to what Manfred Unger observed. Finally, it could also indicate that the East German population had grown tired of the constant emphasis on antifascism and labor history. The new emphasis on regional history simply presented something new. It also suggests, however, that the GDR had been unsuccessful in suppressing memories and interest in regional history. For example, Saxony was not simply a region within Germany, but had also been an independent state for much of German history. Germans from this area had held a strong regional identity even during the Weimar and Nazi periods. Since 1952, the state had attempted to downplay such regional identities in lieu of cultivating a GDR-based identity.[33] As the state relaxed its restrictive hold over regional histories, these regional identities began to reemerge.

Whatever the reasons for the revival of popular interest, it is clear that the state attempted to capitalize on it. The state also facilitated certain aspects of such interest, in an attempt to better link these regions to the GDR in a way that would allow it to depart from its stringent dual-line concept of German historical development centered on the traditions of the working class.

Commemorating Luther in the GDR[34]

The commemoration of the 500th anniversary of Martin Luther's birth in 1983 by the GDR marked a significant departure from previous official interpretations of his contributions to the state, to its socialist traditions, and to German history. As it did with the "Prussian Renaissance," the SED rehabilitated the image of Luther in an attempt to expand the historical basis for its legitimacy. It sought to create popular support by appropriating aspects of Luther's teachings and actions into its own set of traditions. As a shared memory of a united German state began to fade, the state also began to emphasize that most of the important Luther-related sites were located on the territory of the GDR. Luther was now less important as a figure of German history than as a key component of the heritage of the East German state. After three decades of sole rule, the SED now felt confident enough to offer a differentiated vision of Luther that could potentially bolster the cultural legitimacy of the SED regime. The Luther Year commemorations also marked a substantial change in the SED's relations with the Evangelical Church of the GDR, which allowed for considerable cooperation as well as new avenues for the church to demonstrate its institutional independence. Most importantly, the GDR hoped to solidify its claim of being the sole inheritor of Germany's humanist historical legacy and bolster its policy of cultural delimitation vis-à-vis West Germany. The Luther commemoration was also part of the regime's effort to create new avenues to vent popular frustration without allowing for direct challenges to its primacy of power.

The Cold War context of the early 1980s also played a significant role in motivating the party to ensure that the Luther celebrations were a success. Throughout the 1970s and 1980s, the SED leaders strived to increase the GDR's international stature, especially among West European countries. The crisis over the stationing of Pershing II missiles in West Germany spawned peace movements in both states. East Germany's economy was worsening, forcing it into negotiations with West Germany over a new line of credit—negotiations that were hampered in turn by the Cold War interests of the superpowers. All the while, East Germany struggled to maintain an independent sense of identity, one that was simultaneously "German" and still "socialist."

Until the 1970s, official interpretations of Luther were based on works published by Marxist historians during the early 1950s. In 1952, Alfred Meusel, the first director of the Museum for German History and later the director of the Institute for Historical Science, published a monograph, *Thomas Müntzer und seiner Zeit*, in which Müntzer, not Luther, was portrayed as the embodiment of the progressive, revolutionary tradition that formed the core identity of the German nation (and by direct association the East German state). Although Meusel portrayed Luther in a relatively good light during his early years when he began to resist the controlling elements of the "establishment," i.e. the church, Luther lost favor when he decided to side with the land-owning class. Luther's stay at the Wartburg under the disguise as the nobleman "Junker Jörg," according to Meusel, only solidified the theologian's abandonment of the popular reformation movement he had helped begin.[35] Leo Stern, who had led the team drafting the Museum for German History's concept for an exhibition on the period, also published an early work that defined the official GDR historical interpretation of Luther. In his analysis, Stern relied primarily on Friedrich Engels's observation that the turning point in the Peasants' War came with the publication of Luther's pamphlet against the peasants and indicated Luther's decision to serve the interests of the "oppressors" instead of the "people."[36]

In 1983, Erich Honecker, speaking with a West German journalist for the magazine *Lutherische Monatshefte,* discussed his understanding of how the GDR could celebrate both Martin Luther and Thomas Müntzer.[37] Honecker stated: "To think that we honor Luther at the expense of Müntzer would be wrong. For the historical and traditional consciousness of our people in Socialism, it is important that Luther and Müntzer not be placed in irreconcilable opposition with one another. In fact, one must view them dialectically as the two great figures of the first German Revolution. Luther released a movement, which needed a Müntzer to make it possible. In this sense both figures, Luther as well as Münzter, belong irreplaceably to our heritage and our tradition."[38] Against criticism that the GDR historians were moving away from previous state-sanctioned interpretations of Luther and his importance for the GDR, Honecker claimed that such corrections were a positive sign and demonstrated the intellectual freedom found in the GDR. Moreover, Honecker highlighted that this correction came about as a result of GDR historians reexamining the entire epoch surrounding the "early-bourgeois revolution" which corresponded with a re-interpretation of its meaning for the GDR state.

Before focusing on the commemoration activities in East Germany, it is necessary to note that parallel Luther celebrations were taking place in West Germany. In stark contrast to the elaborate plan of events in the East, the commemoration activities in the Federal Republic were much less centrally coordinated, yet played just as significant a role in the public sphere. The West German media dedicated more coverage to the celebrations than to any previous Luther celebration and arguably, to any other event in 1983. Johannes Rau, the minister president of North Rhine-Westphalia, noted that, in contrast to the well-coordinated, centralized planning undertaken by East Berlin, the volume of information regarding the figure of Martin Luther circulating in the West could give rise to confusion, since the various pieces of literature, films and articles all presented different points of view.[39] However, within the pluralistic society of West Germany, this was admired as a sign of diversity and openness. The Luther celebrations in the West included many special events organized by the West German Evangelical Church as well as local events, such as those in Worms and Nuremberg. There were official state acts commemorating aspects of Luther's life and teachings, lecture series, radio broadcasts, academic conferences, television programs, and even a street festival in West Berlin. Despite the diversity of the activities in the West some common themes emerged, such as the idea that Luther and his teachings had the ability to unify the German people. In the West, Luther appeared as a symbol of unity in a divided Germany. At the opening of an exhibit in Nuremburg, Federal President Karl Carstens gave a speech titled "*Vom Symbol der Spaltung zum Symbol der Einheit*" (From a Symbol of Division to a Symbol of Unity) in praise of Luther as a figure whom Protestants and Catholics in both German states could celebrate.[40] West German Chancellor Helmut Kohl spoke in Worms of Luther's theological teachings and his contribution to Germany's humanist traditions, especially his teachings about the freedom of beliefs. Kohl was reserved when discussing national unity; however, he did venture to mention that Luther was an important figure "for both parts of our fatherland."[41] Likewise, former Chancellor Willy Brandt emphasized that Luther belonged to all Germans and that his legacy could not be divided into Western and Eastern portions. Such examples from West German politicians emphasize a concerted effort not to politicize the Luther commemoration, in stark contrast to the events in neighboring East Germany. Ironically, though, by collectively asserting Luther's nonpolitical nature, they were indeed politicizing him within the context of the Cold War.

Preparations for the East German commemoration officially began in June 1980, with the first meeting of the Martin Luther Committee of the German Democratic Republic. In his opening speech, Erich Honecker lauded Luther as one of the greatest sons of the German people.[42] Honecker began his speech by articulating the role of commemoration within the political context of the GDR, stating: "Days of remembrance for us are not mere formalities; instead they are an opportunity to understand an historical event, the deeds of great persons and to apply them to the present."[43] He specifically referred to Luther's "historic deed" of initiating the Reformation, which was an integral part of the "bourgeois revolution," and his role in creating an atmosphere for social progress. He praised Luther's contribution to standardizing the German language through his translation of the Bible into German and the fact that this translation allowed his progressive ideas to spread throughout the land. Luther's ideas found mass appeal among the peasant population, who rose up in battle under the leadership of Thomas Müntzer. Yet, at the very point where traditional GDR acceptance of Luther's contributions stopped, Honecker continued to praise Luther's later influence as well. Although Luther had not supported the peasants during the Peasants' War, he nonetheless continued pushing an agenda of reform in sermons, schools, and universities.

Moreover, Luther's desire to help the poor and redistribute church land was seen as forming the root for social consciousness in contemporary Germany. Overall, Honecker's speech avoided any controversial criticism of Martin Luther and attempted only to highlight the positive, progressive aspects of Luther and his legacy, which the GDR state could now claim as a part of its tradition.[44]

On 19 June 1980, just days after the Luther Committee's first official meeting, an academic colloquium was held at the Karl Marx University in Leipzig on "Luther's image in contemporary historical writing." The colloquium brought together leading academics in the field to discuss the current status of research and prepare a research plan that would enable them to prepare for the upcoming 500th anniversary. Max Steinmetz of Leipzig began the discussion by presenting the works published in the GDR on Luther since 1952. The participants agreed that the focus of new research would need to be on the "later Luther" as well as Luther's philosophical and theological (i.e. ideological) contributions. They also concluded that it was necessary to locate revolutionary elements within Luther's teachings as well as changes in the ways the working class had perceived Luther over time. Like Honecker, the historians treated Luther's relationship with Müntzer in dialectical terms and argued that both great figures needed each other to perform their historic functions, but agreed in the end that much more research was necessary in order to place Luther properly within the greater context of his time.[45]

In September 1981, official "theses" for the Martin Luther Year further articulated basic premises concerning Luther's new place within the GDR's conception of the past. The theses were written by a commission of social scientists and historians drawn from the GDR Academy of Sciences and universities under the leadership of Horst Bartel, the director of the Central Institute of History at the GDR Academy of Sciences. The theses, which numbered fifteen in all, conveyed the SED's new interpretation of Luther and his importance for the present political system of the GDR. Most notably, they claimed that "the Reformation became an essential element of the start of the revolution, became the ideological support for the highly different class forces behind it and provided the framework for its rapid differentiation over the future course of the revolutionary process."[46] The text consistently portrayed Luther's struggle with the Pope as one of theology, which within the social circumstances of the time led to a revolutionary attempt to alter the dominant political system. Even Luther's role after the Peasants' War, from 1526 to 1546, was now viewed in a relatively positive manner. Luther, it was argued, continued the reformation from above with the help of the princes.[47] In all, the theses represented a major shift in the interpretation of Luther and signaled his integration into the revolutionary line of tradition of the GDR.[48]

The primary differentiation between the state's and the church's representation of Luther as an historical figure rested on his political, or ideological, implications versus his Christian, or theological, teachings. Bishop Leich, attending the opening session of the state committee's meeting as a guest, spoke of Martin Luther "not as a great person, but rather we want to bring his message of the almighty God in the form of the joyous tidings of Jesus Christ close to the people and put it at the center of all church activities."[49] This differentiation was important for the church in order to stress its institutional independence and the different orientation of its own commemorative activities. For the church, Luther was to be celebrated for his religious and theological interpretation of the Bible and the implications of these teachings for the members of the Evangelical Church. Whereas the state sought to emphasize only those elements that would increase Luther's political role, the church believed that the figure of the reformer needed to be grounded in the current work of the church and not isolated as a historical actor.

The publication of the official state theses, however, only covered the theoretical side of preparing for the year-long commemoration activities. Attention now turned toward coordinating and planning these events, while maintaining state control over the process. Unlike the celebration in 1967 of the 450th anniversary of the Reformation, when the state all but ignored the Evangelical Church in the GDR, it now made a much more concerted effort to coordinate its official celebration with that of the church. The most significant and symbolic form of official cooperation was Erich Honecker's personal participation as chairman of the state's Luther Committee. In 1967, by contrast, Gerald Götting, the leader of the East German Christian Democratic Party, headed up the state's commemoration efforts. One probable explanation for the lack of state support in 1967 can be traced to the GDR's efforts at the time to break the ties between the East and West German church institutions, which until 1971 remained a single entity.[50] In 1983, the state no longer needed to fear the direct intervention from Western interests through the church and was in turn much more supportive, both financially and logistically, in its efforts to make sure that the Martin Luther celebrations were a success.[51]

In order to coordinate this new level of cooperation, leading church officials were invited to attend the state Luther Committee meetings as guests and members from both committees took a tour in 1982 of Luther-related historical sites in the GDR to assess the progress of the various restoration projects.[52] Of all the restoration projects targeted by the two committees, particular care was given to the complete restoration of Luther's birthplace in Eisleben, including the so-called *schöner Saal* (beautiful hall), which also included restoring portraits of Luther, Melanchthon, and several Electors of Saxony.[53] Other projects included the fourteenth-century monastery in Erfurt where Luther joined the Augustinian Order in 1505, the Erfurt Cathedral where Luther was ordained, the Wartburg Castle in Eisenach, as well as several buildings in Wittenberg, including the Parish Church of St. Mary, the Collegium Augustinum (part of the former University of Wittenberg), and Augustinian monastery that became Luther's residence in 1532.

Although the Evangelical Church of the GDR solicited international funds for some of the renovation and restoration projects, the state's contributions were estimated to have cost roughly nine million Marks. The SED was confident the GDR could recoup this investment through the increase in tourism that would follow during the Luther Year and beyond. Over a million visitors from abroad, most spending hard currency, were expected to visit the Luther historic sites during 1983 alone. Indeed, in order to accommodate the expected increase in foreign tourism, the national tourist board in the GDR prepared seven different tourist packages for "following in the steps of Martin Luther."[54]

Official preparations were not, however, limited to such restoration projects nor completely inspired by hopes of improving East Germany's image abroad. GDR publishing houses produced over a hundred books, sound recordings, and picture books related to Luther and the Reformation. GDR universities, museums, and the educational society "Urania" conducted numerous exhibits, lectures, concerts and other public events. DEFA, the GDR's official film production company, produced a television series on Luther's life in preparation for the Luther Year celebrations.[55]

The work involved in preparing for the 500th anniversary celebrations extended beyond coordinating commemoration festivities with church officials, producing new history texts, and the restoration of Luther related historical sites. As early as 1980, the organizing office of the celebration activities circulated an "Order for the Coordination of Measures for the Cultural-Political Propaganda, Agitation and Public Relations Work on the Occasion of the Martin-Luther-Celebration of the German Democratic Republic" to all of the district government offices.[56] In general, the guidelines outlined the overall conception of the state-sponsored celebration and the steps necessary to accomplish the celebration with the greatest political impact.

The specific directives of the order were designed to provide a clear line of continuity between Martin Luther's theological and social contributions and the present situation in the GDR. With explicit reference to the domestic audience, the order called for the "integration of Martin Luther's life work and his importance for the upheaval in which the German states and Europe entered the bourgeois revolution from the decline of feudalism into the national cultural heritage of the German Democratic Republic."[57] Such integration corresponded with an increased effort to popularize the Marxist-Leninist interpretation of history and link Luther's works to current events and social issues in the GDR.

The order also contained specific goals for external relations with non-socialist as well as socialist countries. Accordingly, the Martin Luther celebration was intended to win over support from Christian groups and individuals who had formerly dismissed association with East Germany. The GDR aimed to portray "how Luther's humanistic ideals and his aspiration for a just society are preserved and realized through the politics of the party of the working class and for the welfare of the people in peace."[58] The order portrayed the preservation of memory sites, monuments, and works of architecture associated with Luther and his life as an integral part of the socialist cultural heritage policy followed in the GDR, despite the fact that the government had neglected most of these sites up until this celebration. This emphasis highlights the GDR's belief that to gain outside recognition it needed it show that it was capable of preserving such important historical sites such as those associated with Martin Luther. In stark contrast, the directives aimed at relations with socialist states referred only to the ideological aspects of the celebration, such as Luther's progressive social politics, his place within the German tradition of revolution and democracy, as well as how the Luther celebration is an example of a progressive cultural heritage policy in the GDR.

In order to guarantee a cohesive interpretation of information regarding Luther, his work, and his importance for the current situation in the GDR, the organizing office included a detailed list of examples and interpretations that members working in an official capacity could use when preparing for local events, speeches, and publications. The profile was based on the official interpretation developed in Berlin, although it expanded some aspects to include contextual information and generally simplified material to make the theses more accessible to a wider public. For example, whereas the official "Theses" went into considerable detail about the impact of Luther's translation of the New Testament during his stay at the Wartburg, the simplified version in the information profile focused on Luther's translation as Germany's most-read book in the period and its use of the Thuringian-Upper Saxony dialect, which signified Luther's close connection to the common people.[59]

Following the guidelines set down by the organizing office of the Luther celebration, each political district formulated its own plan of action and interpreted the directives and information profile for implementation in its own region. Of all the political districts in East Germany, Halle had the greatest role in translating the state celebration into action at the local level, since a number of key Luther-related memory sites fell within its borders, including both Lutherstadt Wittenberg and Lutherstadt Eisleben. Accordingly, the Halle district council prepared a local plan of action for popularizing Luther in the region and for specific preparations that would fulfill the state's goals. Beyond the large restoration projects in Wittenburg and Eisleben, the action plan also incorporated cultural and political programs aimed at spreading the word about the new official interpretation of Luther and his legacy: "All available possibilities are to be utilized to promote the deepening of the socialist historical consciousness and the feelings of a socialist *Heimat* in the district of Halle." Concretely, the district council called for the coordination of such efforts by groups working in public relations, cultural, artistic, and educational institutions. On the cultural front, the district called for the literature to be distributed and popularized through local libraries and book stores as well as the production of theatrical plays and orchestra concerts aimed at highlighting Luther's cultural legacy in the GDR.[60] All of these elements combined to form a cohesive program for translating the SED's new interpretation of Luther as an historical figure into tangible acts of commemoration.

The SED's renewed emphasis on rehabilitating Luther at the expense of commemorating more traditional heroes of the German working class was not readily accepted by some within the party. In an attempt to strike a balance and reverse the popular perception that the SED had departed completely from its previous interpretation, the state suddenly proclaimed in November 1982 that the year 1983 would now also be an official "Karl Marx Year." In the official "theses" published in preparation for this new commemoration, the state now referred to Karl Marx as "*the* greatest son of the German nation," differentiating Marx from its previous proclamation that Martin Luther was "*a* great son of the German nation" and thereby reminding the GDR citizenry that the state's overall hierarchy within the pantheon of its socialist heroes had not been completely altered.[61] Such celebrations are difficult to quantify; however, when one combines all of the various smaller celebrations, commemorations, renovations, publications and other special events, the Martin Luther Year of 1983 was by far the most extensive state-coordinated celebration in the history of the GDR. Any attempts to balance it with a Karl Marx commemoration most likely went unnoticed by the average citizen.

The SED was concerned about the potential for political unrest during the various church celebrations. SED *Politbüro* member Paul Verner headed a special working group within the Central Committee charged with coordinating and controlling political activities during the Martin Luther celebrations. In an address he made to the working group in April 1983, Verner emphasized the need to maintain the strictest adherence to the laws governing public events, gatherings, and the distribution of printed material. At a press conference in January, he reprimanded church officials who had distributed a printed press packet to western journalists that had not been approved.[62] He also called for continued vigilance and surveillance of potential political resistance. He noted that some within the church believed that the presence of international guests at the celebrations would "provide 'free spaces' which would reveals gaps in the state security operations where anti-socialist actions could take place."[63]

Although 10 November 1983 marked the official day of commemoration for the quincentenary anniversary, minor commemorative events took place throughout the year. The GDR hosted a series of political, academic, and cultural events aimed at examining Luther's life and works. The Evangelical Church of the GDR also held conferences and hosted several smaller celebrations at historic places where Luther lived, such as in Eisleben, Wittenberg, and Eisenach. Almost a million tourists from around the world flocked to the historic sites during the spring and summer months. The events that spanned February through November 1983 marked one of the most extensive commemorative projects ever undertaken in the GDR and highlighted many of the difficulties that the state faced in clearly articulating its interpretation to the general public.

The first event on the commemorative calendar during the GDR's Luther Year was the opening of the newly restored house in Eisleben where Luther was born and died. The date chosen for the opening celebration fell on the anniversary of Luther's death, on 18 February. The symbolism of this choice set the tone for all future state commemorative events—the most important aspect of Luther was his legacy for contemporary GDR society. Visitors to Eisleben were also confronted with the competing memories brought about by the state's decision to commemorate both Marx and Luther during the same year. In a city with statues dedicated to both Luther and Lenin located just meters away from one another, shop windows devoted equal space to displays featuring Luther and Marx memorabilia—"left a corner for Marx, right a corner for Luther" as one newspaper reporter described the situation.[64] These shop windows were just one example of the confusing message sent by the state. Although its preparations for the Luther commemoration had been extensive, it could not seem to control completely popular interest in Luther.

The reopening of the Wartburg Castle on 21 April 1983 provided Erich Honecker with another prominent opportunity to articulate the GDR's official interpretation of Martin Luther. In his toast to the invited guests, he stated "the reconstruction of the Wartburg and the renewal of its exhibits make clear that a primary duty of our socialist state of workers and peasants is to preserve and promote the humanistic and progressive heritage of our people."[65] Honecker also attempted to link the experience of visiting the Wartburg to the desire among many citizens of the GDR to "strengthen their feeling of *Heimat*" and direct these feelings to inspiring progressive contributions to life in the GDR.[66] Honecker also praised the cooperation between the church and the state in preparing for the Luther year commemorations, noting that maintaining an open dialogue between the church and the state was the best means for overcoming differences. This last reference could also be seen as an assertion of state power and that any differences in opinion should be addressed to representatives of the state and not aired publicly. Over time, the ability of church leaders

FIGURE 4.2. Bishop Werner Leich (right) and Erich Honecker (second from right) visit the Wartburg in Eisenach with other members of the Luther Committee of the GDR after its renovation on 21 April 1983. BArch Bild 183-1983-0421-428 / Karl-Heinz Schindler.

and clergy to use church services and other events to voice opposition became a major contributing factor to the eventual popular uprising in 1989.

The first church-sponsored event of the Luther Year took place a few months later on 4 May at the Wartburg in Eisenach, where Luther had translated the New Testament into German under the protection of Frederick the Wise of Saxony from 1521–1522. Representatives from seventeen Protestant churches, as well as from the Russian Orthodox, Roman Catholic, Baptist and Anglican faiths attended the church celebration. Horst Sindermann, chairman of the East German *Volkskammer*, and Gerald Götting, deputy chairman of both the State Council and the state Luther Committee as well as leader of the East German Christian Democratic Party, attended on behalf of the state. The message and tone of this initial church celebration was clear. The church intended to honor Luther's religious and theological contributions, instead of his historical or national importance, and stressed the significance of Luther's teachings for individual Christians.[67]

Some members of the church leadership had feared that the state would usurp its own theological interpretations of Luther. They worried particularly about the state's emphasis on Luther's deference to political leaders in making political decisions. Others were concerned that the state's official "theses" were too anti-Catholic, which could lead to decreased cooperation between the two churches. Another concern revolved around the perception that the church's involvement in the celebration might come at the cost of not fighting other, more important, social issues in the GDR, such as the discrimination of Christians in education and in the military or issues of censorship over church publications.[68] Thus the church used its commemorative events to maintain its own steady interpretation of Luther as a religious reformer and interpreter of the Bible and thereby distance itself from the state's desire to appropriate Luther's theological reforms as political ideology.

The church's commemoration festivities continued two weeks later on 15 May with the first of seven regional congresses, each dedicated to a different social cause, such as peace and disarmament, environmental issues, education and other social issues. The first commemorative congress, held on the square in front of the cathedral in Erfurt, was dedicated to the GDR's youth and sent a message of nonviolence aimed at the emerging peace movement.[69] Overall, such commemorative events by the GDR Evangelical Church attracted over 200,000 participants and significantly aided in the church's efforts to reinforce its institutional independence and ownership over its interpretation of Martin Luther's legacy. Official tourist reports registered the 44,621 western foreigners and 25,910 West Germans had participated in "Luther trips" ranging from three to six days on average.

Paul Verner's fears about potential disruption at the church-sponsored events were not without warrant. While internal reports from the opening festivities at the Wartburg characterized the event as a success and a demonstration of stabilizing church-state relations, reports from later events indicate that some within the church attempted to use the commemoration to express their opposition to the state. In a memo to Erich Honecker in July 1983, Heinz Mirtschin, director of the *Parteiorgane* office within the Central Committee, reported that certain members of the local church leadership in Dresden had used the church commemoration festivities to spread their own views on the topics of peace and the environment, which did not fully mesh with those of the state. He also pointed to the growth of so-called peace circles in the Dresden area headed by members of the church who had previously been disruptive. He noted that in an effort to prevent further disruptions, the party canceled several of the church's planned cultural events and refused to extend an independent art exhibit that had been on display in Dresden.[70] In a joint report to the Central Committee in October 1983, State Secretary for Church Questions Klaus Gysi and Rudi Bellman, head of the Central Committee's Working Group for Church Questions, noted that some church leaders used their public addresses to press issues related to the GDR's educational, security, and censorship policies and openly called the people's trust in the government into question.[71]

The state, however, did not leave the commemorative events entirely in the hands of the church. As part of the official celebratory events during the summer of 1983, the Museum for German History in Berlin curated a special exhibit dedicated to Luther, his work, and the role of the Reformation as the ideology behind the Peasants' War. The museum exhibit portrayed Luther within the greater social and economic context of the time before and after the Peasants' War. In keeping with the GDR's historiographical representation of Luther, any mention of Luther in the museum prior to 1983 had been limited primarily to his life prior to the Peasants' War and was generally negative. The new depiction of Luther reflected the recent changes in Luther's image and a great deal of the exhibit was dedicated to Luther's later years following the Peasants' War. The general layout of the exhibit paralleled the chronology and main points addressed in the official state "theses" about Luther and placed a great deal of emphasis on Luther's theology as the ideology of a social movement. What might be more significant than the content of the museum's exhibit was its enormous attraction to the general public. Within the first few days over 30,000 visitors had viewed the exhibit. Whether or not each visitor understood and accepted the state's interpretation of Luther cannot be ascertained, yet the sheer volume of visitors reflects the interest that the Luther year celebration had generated.⁷² While some may have internalized the party's message, it is likely that others came away with new feelings of a shared heritage with West Germany—something that the state surely did not intend.

The culmination of the GDR's official state celebration of Martin Luther came on 8 November in the form of a special ceremony held at the *Staatsoper*, the main opera house, in East Berlin. Present were the members of the state Luther Committee, the SED, the *Volkskammer*, representatives from the Evangelical Church, and other invited foreign dignitaries. However, several highly visible international guests who had been invited, such as West German Federal President Karl Carstens, Queen Margarete of Denmark, and the kings of Norway and Sweden, decided not to attend and thus thwarted Honecker's hopes of increasing the international prestige of the event and of the GDR. Although Honecker was present at the ceremony he elected to allow the State Committee's Deputy Chairman Gerald Götting to hold the main commemorative speech. In keeping with previous official statements, Götting referred to Luther as a great reformer and social activist and differentiated between the GDR's celebration of Luther from previous commemorations by pointing out in his speech that, "Luther anniversaries in the old Germany were primarily something for the Protestant Church and the ruling class of the time. Here, in our country based on the new social foundation of Socialism, we see how the workers and the entire population are in a position to justly appreciate the reformer—free from reactionary misuse of the past—in his societal position and with all his deeds."⁷³

Although Honecker did not speak during the official celebration, he did take a moment during the reception that followed the event to reiterate the official stance that "the socialist historical and national consciousness of the citizens of the German Democratic Republic receives great impulse through the creative appropriation and continuation of the progressive and humanist heritage of the history of the German peoples."⁷⁴ Clearly, the importance of this event for the GDR regime was to not simply to honor the figure of Luther, but to reiterate the importance of those elements of Germany's past were beneficial for building support for the current political and social aspirations of the SED.

A day later, on 10 November—the actual anniversary of Luther's birth—the Evangelical Church of the GDR held its final official commemorative celebration in Eisleben, Luther's birthplace. The events in Eisleben were the culmination of five years of preparation by the church. The event ran all day, beginning with a special church service held at the city's central church and continued throughout the day with special festivities on the city's market square.⁷⁵ The church service was broadcast live throughout

FIGURE 4.3. A scene from the Evangelical Church's final commemoration event honoring Martin Luther in Eisleben, the place of Luther's birth, on 10 November 1983. BArch Bild 183-1983-1212-306 / Thomas Lehmann.

the GDR as well as in West Germany and other European countries with high percentages of Protestants. Indeed, the GDR's Evangelical Church was much more successful in gaining international support for its celebrations than the GDR state had been. Church dignitaries came from around the world to participate in the church's commemoration—including archbishops and bishops from over twenty countries, representing most of the West European states, several Eastern European states, and such faraway places as Brazil and Tanzania.[76] Although the state attempted to alter the popular perception of the great reformer, its efforts were continually confronted with the alternative view of Luther put forward by the church. And even though the state now offered a more positive image of Luther, it was unable to completely take control of his legacy and attach its own interpretation to his popular image.

The 500th anniversary of Luther's birth occurred at a crucial moment in German-German relations. The effects of Willy Brandt's *Ostpolitik* had begun to take form. Brandt's concept of "two states, one nation" was being challenged by East Germany's attempt to delineate itself from West Germany and propagate its version of "two states, two nations." Although Luther was a great "German son," an attempt was made to present the image of Luther as one of the GDR's greatest sons, denying ownership over his image to West Germany. It was primarily the new context of détente that made it possible for the East German state to extend and alter its interpretation of Luther. With the division of German now accepted as stable (at least from the perspective of 1983), the East German state allowed and encouraged its historians to rethink the position of Luther and how he and his teachings related to current East German society. The views that emerged seem to comprise two main elements. First, Luther was interpreted as a necessary precondition of the "early bourgeois revolution." And whilst the Peasants' War, second, had been led by Thomas Müntzer, it had been made possible through the absorption by the people of Luther's teachings of self-governance.

It was now acceptable to look at the whole of Luther's life and teachings and to relate them to the current situation in East Germany. Luther was no longer divided into progressive and reactionary parts; instead East Germany inherited his legacy in its entirety. However, the Evangelical Church challenged such efforts, seeking to differentiate itself from the state's interpretation and resist attempts to usurp its own interpretation of Luther's legacy. Ultimately, the message presented to the East German public was a confusing one—a state image of Luther as a critical figure on the long path of German history that led directly to the founding of the East German state and the current "triumph" of communism, and on the other hand the East German Evangelical Church's image of Luther, which was free of political meaning. For the church, the most important things were to ensure that Luther's teachings of peace and community were understood as timeless and to make these teachings relevant to the current population.

In vivid contrast to the massive coordination effort in the East, the celebrations in West Germany were purposefully uncoordinated. This was an effort on the part of West Germany to distance itself from the official celebrations in the East while subtly asserting that Luther's legacy was inherited by all Germans. In the end, we see a very complex web of memories that drew on distinctly different elements in order to cultivate different aspects of historical consciousness. The massive information campaign and the high numbers of visitors to the year's commemoration events demonstrate that there was indeed large-scale interest in the figure of Luther that probably would not have been sparked without the active participation of the East German state. Yet instead of further bolstering the cultural legitimacy of the state, the long-term effect was more likely the establishment of the East German Evangelical Church as an independent institution. It was this institution that would gain the trust of the leading figures of the popular opposition, who would find support and refuge within the church throughout the 1980s and especially during the crucial year of 1989.

The Panorama at Bad Frankenhausen

Thomas Müntzer, the "people's reformer" who led the peasants to revolt in 1524 and 1525, had always been a popular image for the GDR within its pantheon of socialist heroes. The area around Halle had taken on an important role regarding how East Germans learned about the Peasants' War—many of the great peasant battles had been fought in the fields and surrounding valleys. Despite plans to convert the city of Mühlhausen's *Heimatmuseum* into a museum dedicated to the Peasants' War, Edith Brandt, the Secretary for Science, People's Education, and Culture for the District Council of Halle, used an article in *Neues Deutschland* on 9 July 1972 to call for yet another addition to the region's memory landscape. She made the case creating a "panorama" on the mountain above the town of Bad Frankenhausen that would be part of the 1975 commemoration of the 450th anniversary of the German Peasants' War.[77] The resulting project, which took over twelve years to complete, provides yet another example of how East Germany's memory culture entered a period of revision during the 1970s and 1980s. The panorama at Bad Frankenhausen, similar to the Luther commemoration, highlights how the evolving re-interpretation of Germany's past altered the official portrayal of Thomas Müntzer and depicts a clear example of how the SED's leadership was losing control even over its officially sanctioned memory-work projects.

Brandt's initial proposal was taken up by the SED *Politbüro,* which passed a resolution on 9 October 1973, calling for the panorama to be built at the top of the *Schlachtberg bei Frankenhausen,* the site of one of the largest battles during the Peasants' War of 1525, and to be dedicated to both the battle and to Thomas Müntzer's revolutionary achievements.[78] The Central Committee of the SED passed a similar resolution in March 1974 and the Presidium of the Council of Ministers of the GDR signed off on the project in April, which officially placed control over the project with the Ministry of Culture and the District Council of Halle.

The cultural department of the district council in Halle produced the first basic conception for the monument. The resulting document articulated three main goals: first, to portray how the revolutionaries of 1524 and 1525 fought selflessly and courageously toward the goal of changing society in the interests of the people; second, to develop and strengthen the socialist consciousness of the citizens of the GDR, especially the patriotic education of young people; and third, to communicate the ethical and moral values that exemplify a socialist personality in the GDR.[79] The description of the battle of Frankenhausen on 14 and 15 May 1525 followed the official Marxist historical interpretation of the Peasants' War as a class struggle and the first revolution on German soil: "This conflict had the character of an all-encompassing revolutionary war by the oppressed masses against feudalism."[80]

Part of the rationale for locating a national monument for the Peasants' War in Bad Frankenhausen related not only to the battlefield as an historic site of memory, but also its central location among several other battlefields in the area. The town of Bad Frankenhausen was in close proximity to other sites of memory that were more directly related to the history of the German working class, such as Halle, Leuna, Merseburg, and Leipzig. Tourism also played a role, since the town's spas and resorts already attracted many tourists. Moreover, the placement of the panorama within close proximity of the *Kyffhäuserdenkmal* (a monument built in the 1890s to honor Germany's unification) was intended draw a sharp contrast between the progressive traditions honored by the GDR and the memories commemorated by the reactionary elements in Germany's past.[81]

The conception drew inspiration from panorama monuments in the Soviet Union, in particular one to the battle of Borodino, as well as similar projects in Sevastopol and Volgograd. Like the portrayal of the battle of Borodino, the Bad Frankenhausen panorama was conceptualized as the portrayal of a single moment in the battle that would highlight the struggle between the masses, led by Thomas Müntzer, and the military forces of the feudal authorities during the battle on 14 and 15 May 1525: "The deciding factor here is to demonstrate how the masses fighting against the exploiting class for its own self interest releases great revolutionary energies and how under today's conditions the legacy of the revolutionaries will be fulfilled: 'the grandsons will fight even better.'"[82] Thus the ideological purpose of the monument was to evoke an emotional connection between the historic figures portrayed in the panorama and the contemporary visitor. It combined the transmission of historical knowledge about the specific historical event with a clear message regarding the duties of GDR citizens to continue the struggle against oppression in today's world. Moreover, the authors of the conception believed that the monument would become an integral part of ideological military training and would lead to greater socialist patriotism for the GDR state.

By the summer of 1975 the members of the academic working committee already agreed that the goals prescribed by the *Politbüro* and Central Committee could not be realized effectively if the subject material of the panorama monument was narrowly restricted to scenes from the two days of actual battle. In order to meet the ideological goals, the academic advisory committee, chaired by historians Manfred Bensing and Siegfried Hoyer, argued that the subject matter would need to be expanded. This recommendation to expand the subject matter marked the first departure from the original conception and also a departure from the examples in the Soviet Union, which portrayed a "moment in time" snapshot of an historic event. Although the expansion meant that the artistic rendering could deal with a much greater range of ideological elements, it broke the link between the events being portrayed in the monument and the site of memory where it was being constructed. Previous plans called for the contextual material to come in the form of a museum exhibit about the Peasants' War that the visitors would view in a separate room prior to their entry into the room housing the panorama itself. Now, the emphasis was placed on the ideological effectiveness of the panorama itself instead of on the overall impact of the museum and panorama.

The academic committee saw no contradiction between its new conception and the original intention of the *Politbüro*. The committee argued: "at the very least, Thomas Müntzer understood himself as representative of the revolutionary movement within a local or regionally defined area. He and the movement were certainly influenced by *general trends* of the German Peasants' War, which are in need of artistic interpretation regardless of whether the events in Frankenhausen were directly influenced by them."[83] The committee identified six general trends that needed to be addressed in the artistic rendering in order for the panorama to have the desired ideological and educational effect. The first priority was to establish the existing power relationship at the time, followed by a clear identification of how the leading figures of the revolution came from an emerging middle class, which was beginning to take power, but could not completely break away from the feudal structure.

The next two important elements revolved around the importance of alliances, both among classes and among regions, and the connection between the revolutionary ideology and its religious character. The last two elements dealt with the defensive position taken by the peasants following their initial victories and how they ultimately lost due to the strategy and tactics of the "counter-revolutionary" forces.[84] The authors of the report summarized their overall conception by reiterating the necessity and importance of portraying the Peasants' War as ending in defeat, which determined "that the basic ideas of the revolutionary powers could only be realized in the distant future."[85] The committee recognized the limitation of drawing a direct line of continuity between the Peasants' War to the revolutionary workers' movement and finally to the socialist society of the GDR while confining the monument to the time period of the Peasants' War. In a similar vein, the committee acknowledged that placing the war within the international context would be nearly impossible. Both elements, they suggested, could only be implied by the artist's rendering, whereas the specific links to the broader history of the workers' movement and to international revolutionary movements could be made in the exhibit of the museum section of the memorial.

From the beginning of the project, the planning committee hoped that Werner Tübke, professor of art at the Academy of Visual Arts in Leipzig and one of the GDR's leading artists, would accept the commission to produce the panorama. Tübke's previous works, such as the "Five Continents" (1958), the "German Workers' Movement" (1961), and the "National Committee Free Germany" (1969/1970) had made him the obvious choice for undertaking a painting on the scale the party desired. Indeed, functionaries within the Ministry of Culture had been in contact with Tübke beginning in 1974, even though he would not officially be offered the contract until 1 January 1976.[86] Throughout the process of negotiating the initial contract, Tübke demonstrated his desire to separate his work of art from the party-political aims of the SED. For Tübke, his participation was linked to his ability to maintain artistic authority, something that he would work hard to expand with each subsequent contract.

The next step in the conceptualization process was a trip to the Soviet Union in January 1976 by the leading figures associated with the panorama project.[87] Although the group had originally planned on visiting panorama monuments in Moscow, Sevastopol, and Volgograd, it was forced to confine its visit to Moscow and concentrate on its study of the Borodino monument.[88] According to the report filed by Richard Stephan, the concentration by the group on this one work of art caused a great deal of anxiety for Werner Tübke, who was beginning to think that he was being asked to produce a copy of the Borodino monument in Bad Frankenhausen. Tübke's rejection of the Borodino model was based primarily on its artistic merits, but his critique, according to Stephan, also contained some sharp political overtones: "With the Borodino panorama and other similar works, the Soviet people are being brainwashed and an entire generation is being raised without any aesthetic taste."[89] While Stephan did not share the extreme position taken by Tübke, he did acknowledge that the group understood his concerns and also thought that the Borodino panorama could not be replicated in Bad Frankenhausen. Stephan's reasoning for rejecting the Borodino model was similar to that of the academic committee's judgment that the battle at Frankenhausen would not have the intended ideological impact that a broader interpretation of the entire time period could have. Stephan extended this criticism of the Borodino model by adding that if one were to have the illusion of standing in the middle of the battle, as one has at Borodino, the portrayal of the battle as a class struggle would be lost.[90]

Upon returning to the GDR and consulting with the historians working on the project, Werner Tübke began creating study drawings of motifs, individuals, and scenes of work, battle, and even torture. This artistic preparation was spread out over three years until he finally produced a comprehensive artistic conception, which he submitted to the Ministry of Culture for approval in May 1979. Tübke envisioned the panorama painting as a departure from previous panorama works "in which a decisive moment of an historic event is portrayed within a temporal and localized level."[91] Instead, Tübke planned on portraying a composite picture of the Peasants' War through the use of symbols and allegories that would stress the dialectical historical process during the period of the "Early Bourgeois Revolution." Tübke wanted the panorama not only to tell a story about the Peasants' War, but also to depict the complexities of the intellectual process that occurred at this time. At the core of the concept was Tübke's use of what he called a "simultaneous picture" that incorporated many simultaneous storylines that one could trace throughout the panorama. Instead of producing a work divided into sections or distinct periods of time, Tübke used the flowing nature of the panorama to evoke a sense of continuity throughout the work. He hoped that the work would be so complex and intriguing that the visitor would become equally fascinated in the historical subject being portrayed and the visually rich depiction of his work.

While construction of the monument and museum building continued in Bad Frankenhausen, Werner Tübke, with the help of several assistants, continued to work on the conceptual rendering of the project. By May 1981, Tübke and his team had completed a 10:1 model of the painting in five connecting sections. The working model was critiqued in two separate reports, which were subsequently submitted to the Ministry of Culture. The first report was undertaken by the two lead historians working with the project, professors Manfred Bensing and Siegfried Hoyer, and concentrated primarily on the historical, political, and ideological aspects of Tübke's work.

Bensing and Hoyer offered words of praise for Tübke's portrayal of the Peasants' War as the climax of the first revolution on German soil, especially through his depiction of the Battle at Frankenhausen and the figure of Thomas Müntzer. They felt that Tübke had correctly captured the historical significance of the revolutionary struggle through conveying the failure of the bold ideas of the revolutionary wing, the aggressive stance of the masses and the leading role of Müntzer, as well as the meaning of the uprising for the advancement of progress.[92] However, in keeping with the new historical interpretation of Martin Luther, yet "not only in light of the Luther anniversary," Bensing and Hoyer objected to the low profile accorded to Luther and that when he did appear it was often in a negative or ambivalent manner, such as Luther with a Janus-head preaching one thing to the masses and another to the nobility. They also felt that the *Bergknappen* (early miners and from a Marxist perspective the forerunners of the modern working class) needed to play a more pronounced role. Overall, however, they were very pleased with his interpretation of historical events surrounding the Peasants' War.

The historians were especially impressed with Tübke's use of the four seasons in illustrating the four general developmental phases of the struggle. The winter scenes depict the oppression of the masses and the preparations for battle, the spring scenes show mounting resistance and the culmination of the struggle leading into the summer months. Autumn brings the cycle to an end with scenes of defeat, yet the onset of winter again signals that the struggle will be taken up once again.[93] In their minds, this never-ending cycle provided the ideal ideological message for the visitor without being overly explicit in its execution.[94]

The second evaluation came from the Leipzig art historian Karl-Max Kober, who prefaced his remarks by indicating that any work of art is open to critique and that he was certain that Tübke's work, given its magnitude, would not escape some very harsh criticism. Kober agreed, however, with his historian colleagues that Tübke had captured the essence of the period both through his detailed accuracy and period costuming: "Although it remains certain that we are dealing with a Tübke and with a contemporary

FIGURE 4.4. Werner Tübke (right) and Erich Honecker (second from right) reviewing the 1:10 rendering of Tübke's panorama "Early Bourgeois Revolution in Germany" on 2 October 1982 in Dresden. BArch Bild 183-1982-1002-014 / Klaus Franke.

painting, at the same time one feels to have been transported back into the world view (*Anschauungs- und Gestaltwelt*) of the sixteenth century as its has been handed down to us through the works of Grünewald, Dürer, Cranach, Altdorfer, Bruegels and others."[95] Yet Kober also acknowledged the problem that such extreme realism could degrade the work into functioning only as a colorful blackboard and ignore Tübke's artistic mastery. Indeed, Kober philosophized that future art historians would need to construct new categories for critiquing such a work, since it was so innovative and complex.

Following the Ministry of Culture's approval of the historical and artistic critiques, Werner Tübke began putting together a team of skilled artists who would eventually assist in painting the panorama. Tübke entered into a second contract with the Ministry of Culture in the summer of 1982 that guaranteed him artistic control over the final work of art as well as the right to decide which of the co-workers hired by the ministry would ultimately participate in the project. Of the initial fifteen candidates Tübke agreed to work only with five of the most talented. He began the painting phase of the project in August 1983 and was joined in January 1984 by the first of his assistants.

The issue of maintaining artistic control over the project had been a constant struggle for Werner Tübke. Signs of his apprehension were already present during the initial talks between himself and the Ministry of Culture. In a letter that he sent to the Minister of Culture Hoffmann on 21 July 1975, Tübke made his expectations clear: "Once the preparatory work is approved, I will be given a free hand for the completion, no one can talk me into anything. From the beginning, this project will be designed as a high quality painting, a personal painting by me with all the possibilities of excessiveness, etc.; it will not be conceptualized as a pedagogical illustration of history."[96] Tübke again reiterated his desire for artistic autonomy in the text of a contract extension in June 1982 that specified his complete control of all artistic matters as well as the training and supervision of any assistants working on the project.

Most striking, however, were Tübke's remarks made in a 1984 letter addressed to Heinz Wagner, the deputy minister of culture, particularly in his demands regarding the future use of the panorama site. In keeping with his emphasis that the panorama project was first and foremost a work of art, Tübke insisted that "a visit to the 'Panorama' is a *Museum visit* … a museum visit is not the participation in a battle. There must be a full stop to the housing development on top of the mountain [the *Schlachtberg*]. … A museum visit requires concentration. Do not allow the entire thing to degrade into an amusement park surrounded by culture! … It must be serious."[97] Tübke then began to list a series of specific aesthetic concerns that he had with the current plans for the site, including: "*Don't* build a fortress out of wagons! *No* rest or play area for children or youth. *No* parking lot nearby (pave over as little land as possible). No sea of flags around the panorama. Oaths don't have to take place up there."[98] It was clear that Tübke was frustrated with the nature of the commission. On the one hand, only an entity such as the state could finance such an enormous and involved work of public art, yet he clearly held those in the Ministry of Culture in contempt and feared being labeled a mere propagandist instead of an artist. Tübke even went so far as to call for a "correction of your own architectural tastelessness" concerning the exterior of the panorama building.[99]

Despite these internal conflicts and differences of opinion between Werner Tübke and the Ministry of Culture, the panorama painting was finally completed in October 1987. The formal ceremony of placing his signature to the work and handing the piece over to the Ministry of Culture was held on 16 October in the presence of *Politbüro* member and SED chief ideologue Kurt Hager. The panorama, which had most often been referred to as simply the Peasants' War Memorial, now received its official name: "Panorama Bad Frankenhausen. Peasants' War Painting by Werner Tübke 'Early Bourgeois Revolution in Germany 1525.'" Even the complexity of this official title demonstrates the transformation of this work, which had originally begun to honor the memory of Thomas Müntzer and the battle at Frankenhausen, grew to include images from the entire Peasants' War and extended its interpretation to the entire era of the so-called Early Bourgeois Revolution.

The final format for the panorama was 14.5 by 123 meters, or an area of roughly 1,800 square meters.[100] There were over five thousand different images of people, events, and symbolic characters such as Ikarus and several appearances by the devil. Karl Max Kober, who had been the artistic consultant for the Ministry of Culture throughout the project, prepared a guide for the exhibit aimed at both those who had already visited the panorama as well as those preparing for a visit. Although he acknowledged that each individual would read and interpret different messages from the painting, he did provide the reader with a virtual walk-through and offered a glimpse of how the SED intended the visitor to experience the panorama.

> The visitor enters the picture hall via steps from below. Once he has reached the highest step he will find himself fully surrounded by painting, which rises up 13 meters and spreads out into a grand rotunda. Naturally, there is no beginning or end so that the observation can begin anywhere. Yet, it must be reckoned, that most visitors usually begin with what is directly opposite of the entryway in order to gain a first impression. Werner Tübke knew that the

172 | *Tailoring Truth*

Figure 4.5. Werner Tübke signing his panorama "Early Bourgeois Revolution in Germany" in Bad Frankenhausen on 28 October 1987, marking the official completion of his painting. BArch Bild 183-1987-1028-401 / Friedrich Gahlbeck.

visitor's first glimpse would be directed straight forward and that this area of the work would thus receive a special meaning. Here is where we will begin our observation of the work. ... Approximately at the midpoint the figure of Thomas Müntzer, wrapped in black, juts out holding a sunken flag. The two banners on the right and left side of the rainbow mark on the one side the edge of this section of the painting and on the other leads us into the further events.[101]

When the panorama is viewed in this manner, the visitor's attention is directed first and foremost to the figure of Thomas Müntzer and the defeat of the Peasants during the Battle of Frankenhausen. Yet the panorama is indeed unique in that it is not an attempt to capture a moment in time. Instead, it walks the visitor through the historical progression of the Peasants' War, addressing issues of social and political structures, the role of the peasant in the economy, the role of the church and the Reformation, and culminates again with the battle that took place on the top of the very mountain where the memorial is located. It serves as a memorial site, and monument of an historic event, and as a piece of artistic expression and interpretation. The didactic and ideological elements contained within the painting and through the nature of reading the images and the overall story cannot be separated from the work. In the closing paragraphs of his book, Kober stated that if current observers took anything away from their visit it should be to understand that "a past generation made an attempt to control its own destiny" and although "the hopes of the time failed, as a utopia it still has an impact on the present so that the grandchildren can make it a reality and endows trust in life and in the future."[102] Thus, as was apparent from the original conception, the use of the panorama as a never-ending circle reinforced the aspirations of the SED to sustain a sense of continuing the traditions found in Germany's rich heritage.

In the end, the twelve-year-long project cost the GDR a total of 53.8 million Marks and included beyond the panorama portion of the building a separate area for a museum exhibit, a small gift shop, and a café. While Tübke completed his work in 1987, there remained a great deal of structural and technical work to be done. The official opening ceremonies were held on 14 September 1989 in conjunction with the 500th commemoration of Thomas Müntzer's birth (something Tübke had hoped to avoid).[103] Erich Honecker was scheduled to attend the opening himself and give the main address, but a sudden "cold" prevented him from attending.[104] Instead, *Politbüro* members Horst Sindermann, Hans-Joachim Böhme, and Kurt Hager attended the opening ceremony.[105]

Although the panorama rests atop the mountain that overlooks the town of Bad Frankenhausen, the commemoration festivities took place on the city's market square in order to accommodate the nearly ten thousand people attending. Kurt Hager held the opening speech in which he spoke of the great deeds of both Thomas Müntzer and Martin Luther, which together symbolized the great social transformation to which Werner Tübke's work was dedicated.[106] Hager also used the commemoration as a springboard to remind those present of the accomplishments of the GDR over the last forty years: "In forty years since the founding of the German Democratic Republic we can say with great satisfaction that Thomas Müntzer's vision for the future has come to fruition."[107] He attempted to use the occasion to address current political issues and downplay any speculations regarding the need for political change in the GDR. Invoking the image of the peasants fighting for their rights against their feudal lords in 1525, he described the unequal balance of power in West Germany and reiterated the SED's position that "a turn away from socialism and the establishment of a capitalist system will not happen in the GDR."[108]

Despite the social upheaval during summer and fall of 1989 in the GDR, the panorama emerged as a major tourist attraction. In his year-end report, the director Richard Stephan noted that during the period between its opening in mid-September and the end of the year, the panorama counted 61,352 visitors, which brought in over half a million Marks through admission fees and over 460,000 Marks through the sales of related publications and memorabilia.[109] Given the events of November 1989, it is not surprising that the daily visitor rate dropped between 35 percent and 50 percent during the months of November and December with many groups cancelling their reservations. His report also characterizes public reception of the work was "overwhelmingly positive" and that he found the most interest among those who were members of the GDR's Evangelical Church, indicating that the depiction of the Reformation and of Luther may have been of greater interest than the intended "Early Bourgeois Revolution." Nonetheless, Stephan characterized the first few months as an overall success, citing a higher than anticipated number of visitors, the "excitement" by some visitors upon seeing the work of art for the first time, and the fact that all of the foreign visitors who filled out an anonymous survey rated their experience as positive.[110] While Stephan's report, filed on 3 January 1990, no longer pressed the ideological aspects of the panorama and instead attempted to portray the painting and museum as simply a "cultural entity," the uncertainty of the GDR's political future comes through in how he now characterized the work at the panorama, while also hedging a bit when stating the museum had "fulfilled" its original charge.[111]

The history Tübke's panorama at Bad Frankenhausen during the 1970s and 1980s reflects how East Germany's memory politics were changing. Not only did Tübke alter the depiction of Thomas Müntzer to align him more closely with changes in GDR historical research, but throughout the construction process we can see the erosion of state's ability to control the monument's political message. With each revision of his contract, Tübke's artistic independence increased. The product he finally produced had little resemblance with the intent of the Politbüro's original resolution. Like other artists in the GDR, Tübke refused to simply create propagandistic art—he desired his work to be seen primarily as an original artistic expression. Tübke was not alone in such feelings toward state contracts, as can be seen with the work of Ludwig Engelhardt and his monument to Marx and Engels in the following chapter. From the time of the inception of the project through to the opening ceremony, the consistent emphasis of the panorama memorial project was to instill within the visitor a sense of connection to the unfulfilled vision of Thomas Müntzer and the peasants who rose up against their masters. Its public opening in September 1989 ironically marked another episode in German history when the people rose up against state power—this time, however, the people were successful.

Conclusion

The SED's rehabilitation of Prussia, Frederick the Great, Bismarck, and Luther as well as its move away from its primary focus on Thomas Müntzer as the primary instigator of the Peasants' War demonstrates how the state underwent a period of reassessment and an expansion of what were deemed acceptable elements of an East German historical consciousness. The alterations were intended to generate increased interest and popularity of historical figures and events that could in turn further support and sustain the SED's cultural legitimacy. Despite these intentions, the state's ability to exert tight control over the public presentation (and its reception by the populace) began to erode and ultimately crumbled.

The state may have had short-term goals in these rehabilitations as well. Most likely, it sought to fill its coffers with foreign currency through a swell in tourism. It might have wanted to demonstrate a closer working relationship with the East German churches in an attempt to stave off an emerging peace movement. It may have also been a concerted attempt by the SED to enhance its own international prestige. It could also have been an attempt to build in a means of letting off some pent up unrest, like a steam vent, so that the pressure did not lead to even larger popular protests. Despite these legitimate short-term concerns, the broader trends in state memory politics also played a significant role in the course that this development took during the 1980s.

The shift toward regional history, toward the deeds of "great men," and a departure from the very specific commemoration of the Peasants' War to a more general portrayal of the entire era of the Reformation were indeed an attempt by the party to broaden the state's historical legacy and inheritance into areas that earlier had been deemed off limits. Yet at the same time, this extension of what was acceptable actually may have weakened the regime's claim of legitimacy rather than strengthened it. The state's rehabilitation of Prussia was questionable given its earlier negative interpretations and may have awakened more interest in regional history among the general public than it created the historical links desired by the SED.

The state's commemoration of Luther aimed to elevate the GDR's international image and transfer some of the inherent legitimacy contained in the figure of Luther onto the state. Instead, the church sought to differentiate and distance itself from the state's interpretation and resisted attempts by the state to usurp the church's interpretation of Luther's legacy. While Werner Tübke could not have created his panorama without the state's massive financial investment, he was able to convince the regime to allow him greater freedom in his interpretation and not create a work that was simply a history book in pictures. Yet despite the changes in its conception, the panorama remained a work of cultural propaganda for the SED, one that may have come too late and at too great a cost for the crumbling regime. In each case we see examples of negotiation and compromise, increasingly favoring non-state actors and symbolizing the erosion of the state's ability to shape its own memory-work projects.

Notes

1. A. James McAdams argues that the West had de facto recognized East Germany by the 1980s, see A. James McAdams, *Germany Divided* (Princeton, NJ: Princeton University Press, 1994).
2. Timothy Garton Ash, *In Europe's Name: Germany and the Divided Continent* (New York: Vintage, 1993); William Griffith, *The Ostpolitik of the Federal Republic of Germany* (Cambridge, MA: MIT Press, 1978); and Angela Stent, *From Embargo to Ostpolitik: The Political Economy of West German-Soviet Relations* (Cambridge: Cambridge University Press, 1981).
3. Ronald Asmus, "The GDR and the German Nation: Sole Heir or Socialist Sibling?" *International Affairs (Royal Institute of International Affairs)*, Vol. 60, No. 3 (Summer 1984), pp. 403–18.
4. Beschluß des IX. Parteitages zum "Bericht des Zentralkomitees an den IX. Parteitag der SED," reprinted in: *Dokumente der Sozialistischen Einheitspartei Deutschland*, Vol. 16. (Berlin: Dietz, 1980) pp. 30–81, here p. 65.
5. Walter Schmidt, "Das Gewesene ist nie erledigt. Worauf muß sich eine Nationalgeschichte der DDR stützen?" in *Sonntag*, Vol. 35, No. 27 (1981), p. 9.

6. Horst Bartel, "Erbe und Tradition in Geschichtsbild und Geschichtsforschung in der DDR" *Zeitschrift für Geschichtswissenschaft*, Vol. 29 (1981), pp. 387–94.
7. Ibid., p. 389.
8. Martin Sabrow, "Der Sozialistische Umgang mit dem Erbe," lecture held in the series "Potsdam in Europe" on 4 December 2003, unpublished manuscript, p. 5.
9. SAPMO-BArch, DY 30/IV B2/9.06/87 Abteilung Kultur. Internal SED memo from Ursula Ragwitz to Kurt Hager dated 26 June 1980.
10. SAPMO-BArch, DY 30/IV B2/9.06/87 Abteilung Kultur. Response to questions by Kurt Hager to Ursula Ragwitz. Undated comments that accompanied a hand-corrected version of Ragwitz's original memo.
11. SAPMO-BArch, DY 30/IV B2/9.06/87 Abteilung Kultur. Internal SED memo from Ursula Ragwitz to Kurt Hager dated 26 June 1980. The book in question is Ingrid Mittenzweig, *Friedrich II. von Preußen: Eine Biographie* (Berlin: Deutscher Verlag der Wissenschaften, 1979).
12. Individual political parties, like the SPD, claimed to follow in the traditions of Karl Marx, Franz Mehring, and other leaders of the early Socialist movement in Germany, but such groups were not speaking for the West German state and were not considered an integral element of West Germany's national identity.
13. Mittenzwei, *Friedrich II*.
14. Asmus, "The GDR and the German Nation," pp. 411–13.
15. Mittenzwei, *Friedrich II*, p. 212.
16. Horst Bartel, Ingrid Mittenzwei, and Walter Schmidt, "Preußen und deutsche Geschichte," *Einheit*, No. 34 (1979), pp. 637–46, reprinted in Ingrid Mittenzwei and Karl-Heinz Noack, *Preußen in der deutschen Geschichte vor 1789* (Berlin: Akademie Verlag, 1983), pp. 53–66.
17. Maoz Azaryahu, *Von Wilhelmplatz zu Thälmannplatz: Politische Symbole im öffentlichen Leben der DDR* (Gerlingen: Bleicher, 1991), p. 142.
18. *Tagesspiegel*, 27 August 1980.
19. Alan L. Nothnagle, "From Buchenwald to Bismarck: Historical Myth-Building in the German Democratic Republic, 1945–1989," *Central European History*, Vol. 26, No. 1 (March 1993), pp. 91–114, here p. 107.
20. Bartel, Mittenzwei, and Schmidt, "Preußen und deutsche Geschichte," p. 54.
21. T.C.W. Blanning, "The Death and Transfiguration of Prussia," *The Historical Journal*, Vol. 29, No. 2 (June 1986), pp. 433–59, here p. 441. A five-volume set of books were produced in conjunction with the exhibit: a guide to the exhibit and four other volumes covering the political, social, cultural, and cinematic history of Prussia: Gottfried Korff, et al., *Preußen—Versuch einer Bilanz*, 5 vols. (Reinbeck bei Hamburg: Rowolt, 1981).
22. As quoted in Blanning, "The Death and Transfiguration of Prussia," p. 445.
23. Azaryahu, *Von Wilhelmplatz zu Thälmannplatz*, p. 146. On a personal visit by the author to the office of Federal Chancellor Helmut Kohl in 1997 it was clear that the legacy of Bismarck continued to play a strong role in the Federal Republic as a symbol of legitimacy and national continuity between the German Empire and the modern German state. Kohl had a row of portraits of all the Chancellors of the Federal Republic line the wall leading up to his own office, from Adenauer to Schmidt, with one addition to the collection—a large portrait of Chancellor Bismarck.
24. As quoted in Ronald Asmus, "The Portrait of Bismarck in the GDR," *Radio Free Europe, RAD Background Report*, 24 July 1984, p. 4, and originally appeared in *Junge Welt*, 10 February 1983.
25. *Neues Deutschland*, 16 December 1983.

26. As quoted in Asmus, "The Portrait of Bismarck in the GDR, p. 2, and originally published as part of an interview given by Walter Schmidt to the Free German Youth monthly *Junge Generation,* No. 6 (1984).
27. Ernst Engelberg, *Bismarck: Urpreuße und Reichsgründer* (Berlin: Siedler, 1985), pp. 759–60.
28. Ibid., p. 762.
29. The word "propaganda" as used by the SED and its functionaries most often refers to the process of ideological education or the popularization of the party's point of view. Within this context, the concept did not carry with it the connotation of deliberate manipulation that is has had in the west since World War II.
30. *Land* is the German designation for the federal states, most of which had been independent countries of their own right. GDR historians and politicians usually avoided the term in favor of either *Territorium* or *Region,* since these designators did not carry the inherent legitimacy that images of Saxony or Prussia did. At the same time, by highlighting the existence of multiple states within the broader cultural boundaries of "Germany," the state could argue that the existence of two (or three if one included Austria) states on German soil had a longer tradition than a unified German nation-state.
31. Manfred Unger, "Territorialgeschichte in der Geschichtspropaganda," in *Erfahrungen und Probleme einer wirksamen Geschichtspropaganda,* ed. Hartmut Meier and Hans-Jürgen Zippler (Berlin: Akademie für Geschichtswissenschaften beim ZK der SED, 1986), pp. 64–70, here p. 67.
32. Unger, "Territorialgeschichte in der Geschichtspropaganda," p. 69.
33. In fact, Saxon and Thuringian flags, not German or West German flags, were among the first flown during the popular protests in 1989.
34. An expanded version of this section on the 1983 commemoration of Martin Luther can be found in: Jon Berndt Olsen, "Recasting Luther's Image: The 1983 Commemoration of Martin Luther in the GDR" in *Divided But Not Disconnected: German Experiences of the Cold War,* ed. Tobias Hochscherf, Christoph Laucht, and Andrew Plowman (New York: Berghahn Books, 2010), pp. 63–76.
35. Alfred Meusel, *Thomas Müntzer und seine Zeit* (Berlin: Aufbau Verlag, 1952).
36. Leo Stern, *Martin Luther and Philipp Melanchthon* (Berlin: Rütten & Loening, 1953), see p. 73 for the quotation by Stern of Engels.
37. "Interview Erich Honeckers mit der BRD-Zeitschrift Lutherische Monatshefts: DDR-Lutherehrung. Manifestation der Humanität und Friedens," *Neues Deutschland,* 6 October 1983, p. 3.
38. "Interview Erich Honeckers," *Neues Deutschland,* 6 October 1983, p. 3.
39. Hans Süssmuth, "Luther 1983 in beiden deutschen Staaten: Kritische Rezeption oder ideologische Vereinnahmung?," in *Das Luther-Erbe in Deutschland: Vermittlung zwischen Wissenschaft und Öffentlichkeit,* ed. Hans Süssmuth (Düsseldorf: Droste, 1985), pp. 16–43, here p. 16.
40. Süssmuth, "Luther 1983," p. 38.
41. As quoted in Süssmuth, "Luther 1983," p. 39.
42. This designator as "one of the greatest sons" was most often heard in official circles as referring to Karl Marx or in literary circles referring to Wolfgang von Goethe, but this was one of the first occasions where Luther was referred to in such a manner.
43. Erich Honecker, "In der DDR wird die historische Leistung Martin Luthers bewahrt." Speech by Erich Honecker, delivered to the Martin Luther Committee of the German Democratic Republic on 13 June 1980. Reprinted in: *Zeitschrift für Geschichtswissenschaft,* Vol. 28, No. 10 (1980), pp. 927–31, here p. 927. Excerpts of his speech were also translated and published by the GDR Foreign Ministry in its *Foreign Affairs Bulletin,* 30 June 1980, pp. 145–46.

44. Honecker, "In der DDR," pp. 927–31.
45. "Notizen aus dem Wissenschaftlichen Leben," *Zeitschrift für Geschichtswissenschaft*, Vol. 28, No. 12 (1980), pp. 1177–78.
46. "Thesen über Martin Luther: Zum 500. Geburtstag," *Zeitschrift für Geschichtswissenschaft*, Vol. 29, No. 10 (1981), pp. 879–93, here p. 880.
47. Ibid., p. 886.
48. For a more detailed analysis of the theses see: Jan Herman Brinks, *Paradigms of Political Change: Luther, Frederick II, and Bismarck: The GDR on its Way to Unity*. (Milwaukee, WI: Marquette University Press, 2001), pp. 232–34.
49. Speech delivered by Bishop Leich at the founding session of the state Luther Committee, as cited in Ronald Asmus, "The GDR and Martin Luther," *Survey*, Vol. 28, No. 3 (Autumn 1984), pp. 124–56, here p. 134.
50. In 1967, the state also invited church officials to participate in the official state Luther Committee that was formed in conjunction with the 450th celebration of the Peasants' War. Most representatives of the Evangelical Church withdrew over political differences. See: Asmus, "The GDR and Martin Luther," p. 131.
51. Robert F. Goeckel, "The Luther Anniversary in East Germany," *World Politics*, Vol. 37, No. 1 (October 1984), pp. 112–33, here p. 117.
52. For a detailed list of suggested renovations see SAPMO-BArch 30/IV 2/2.036/48, letter from Gerald Götting to Erich Honecker dated 4 February 1981, pp. 28–36. See further, "Socialism Fulfills Humanist Legacy" from the report given by Gerald Goetting, Deputy Chairman of the Martin Luther Committee of the GDR, in *Foreign Affairs Bulletin*, No. 19 (November 1982), pp. 254–55.
53. "Anniversary Preparations Well Under Way," in *Foreign Affairs Bulletin*, No. 29/30 (29 October 1982), p. 239.
54. Ronald Asmus, "Opening of Luther Celebrations in the GDR," *Radio Free Europe, RAD Background Report*, No. 100 (German Democratic Republic) 9 May 1983.
55. "Mit Herrn Luther ist alles in Butter" *Der Spiegel*, Vol. 37, No. 10 (7 March 1983), p. 103.
56. KA-Merseburg, Archiv Nr. 9786, "Ordnung für die Koordinierung von Maßnahmen der kultur-politischen Propaganda, Agitation und Öffentlichkeitsarbeit anläßlich der Martin-Luther-Ehrung der Deutschen Demokratischen Republik 1983" distributed by the Organizationsbüro Martin-Luther-Ehrung 1983 der Deutschen Demokratischen Republik."
57. KA-Merseburg, Archiv Nr. 9786, p. 3.
58. Ibid., pp. 4–5.
59. "Thesen über Martin Luther," written by a working group of social scientists from the Academy of Sciences of the GDR and universities under the leadership of Horst Bartel, the director of the Central Institute for History at the Academy of Sciences of the GDR and reprinted in *Zeitschrift für Geschichtswissenschaft*, Vol. 29, No. 10 (1981), pp. 880–93. The reference here is to Thesis IV, p. 883. For comparison see: KA-Merseburg, Archiv Nr. 9786, p. 9.
60. KA-Merseburg, Archiv Nr. 9787, pp. 5–6. Bezirksrat Halle, "Maßnahmen zur Würdigung des 500. Geburtstages Martin Luthers im Jahre 1983 für den Bezirk Halle."
61. *Neues Deutschland*, 26 November 1982. Emphasis added.
62. SAPMO-BArch, DY 30/IV 2/2.036/48. "2. Beratung der Arbeitsgruppe beim ZK zur Koordinierung und Kontrolle der politischen Aktivitäten zur Martin-Luther-Ehrung" dated 4 March 1983, pp. 138–51, here p. 143.
63. Ibid., p. 147.
64. Peter Jochen Winters, "Hier Luther-Ecke, dort Marx-Ecke," *Frankfurter Allgemeine Zeitung*, 8 April 1983, p. 7.

65. SAPMO-BArch, DY 30/2570, "Toast des Generalsekretärs des ZK der SED und Vorsitzenden des Staatsrates der DDR, Erich Honecker, bei dem Essen anläßlich der Wiedereröffnung der Wartburg am 21. April 1983," pp. 14–22, here, p. 15.
66. Ibid., p. 16.
67. Asmus, "Opening of Luther Celebrations in the GDR," *Radio Free Europe, RAD Background Report*, 9 May 1983.
68. Goeckel, "The Luther Anniversary, pp. 118–20.
69. "Kirchentag in Erfurt findet bisher nicht gekannten Anklang" *Frankfurter Allgemeine Zeitung*, 16 May 1983, p. 5.
70. SAPMO-BArch, DY 30/IV 2/2.036/48, "Information über den Stand der politisch-ideologischen und organisatorischen Vorbereitung der Luther-Ehrung im Bezirk Dresden einschließlich des Kirchenkongresses und des Kirchentages" dated 1 July 1983, pp. 172–78, here p. 175.
71. SAPMO-BArch, DY 30/IV 2/2.036/48, "Information über Verlauf und Ergebnisse der Kirchentage der Evangelischen Kirchen anläßlich der Luther-Ehrung im Jahre 1983" dated 20 October 1983, pp. 198–208, here p. 202.
72. Detlef Urban, "Luther-Ausstellung in Ost-Berlin," *Deutschland Archiv*, Vol. 16, No. 8 (1983), pp. 790–93.
73. As quoted in: "Für sozialistische Grundsätze vereinnahmt," *Frankfurter Allgemeine Zeitung*, 11 November 1983, p. 6.
74. "Für sozialistische Grundsätze vereinnahmt," *Frankfurter Allgemeine Zeitung*, 11 November 1983, p. 6.
75. "Luthergedenken des deutschen Protestantismus in Eisleben," *Frankfurter Allgemeine Zeitung*, 11 November 1983, p. 1 and 6.
76. Peter-Jochen Winters, "Staatliche Lutherfeier ohne Bischof Forck," *Frankfurter Allgemeine Zeitung*, 11 November 1983, p. 6.
77. *Neues Deutschland*, 9 July 1972.
78. LHASA-Merseburg, Rat des Bezirkes Halle/4. Ablieferung/6696 (20423/4), Dr. Fritz Donner, "Chronologie des Monumentalgemälde 'Frühbürgerliche Revolution in Deutschland" von Werner Tübke im Bauernkriegs-Panorama Bad Frankenhausen" dated 10 December 1988, p. 360.
79. LHASA-Merseburg/Rat des Bezirkes Halle/4. Ablieferung/6693 (20423/1), Rat des Bezirkes Halle, "Konzeption für die Errichtung eines Panoramas auf dem Schlachtberg bei Bad Frankenhausen, Bezirk Halle, das dem deutschen Bauernkrieg und dem revolutionären Wirken Thomas Müntzers gewidmet ist," pp. 5–6. This document is undated, but can most likely be traced to February or March 1974, because the SED Secretariat of the Central Committee approved it on 6 March 1974.
80. LHASA-Merseburg/Rat des Bezirkes Halle/4. Ablieferung/6693 (20423/1), Rat des Bezirkes Halle, "Konzeption für die Errichtung eines Panoramas," p. 5.
81. Ibid., (RS).
82. Ibid., p. 6. The adage being quoted here is "Geschlagen ziehen wir nach Haus, die Enkel fechtens besser aus," which loosely translated within the context of the Peasants' War means that although the revolutionaries of the war failed to conquer their oppressor, the "grandsons" of today are prepared to take up the fight once again.
83. LHASA-Merseburg/Rat des Bezirkes Halle/4. Ablieferung/6694 (20423/2), Manfred Bensing and Siegfried Hoyer, "Wissenschaftliche Konzeption für die Gestaltung der Bauernkriegsgedenkstätte (Panorama) in Bad Frankenhausen," 8 December 1975, p. 283 (emphasis in the original).
84. Ibid., pp. 285–87.
85. Ibid., p. 287.

86. Harald Behrendt, *Werner Tübkes Panoramabild in Bad Frankenhausen: Zwischen staatlichen Prestigeprojekt und kunstlerischem Selbstauftrag*, (Kiel: Ludwig, 2006), pp. 19–20 and 99–100. See also: Gerd Lindner, "Zur Entwicklung der Konzeption des Panoramas zu Frankenhausen," a speech given at the Panorama Conference in Luzern, Switzerland in 1999 and reprinted at: http://panorama-museum.de/der-auftrag.html (accessed 1 October 2011).
87. The members of the "Panorama" group included: Werner Tübke, Gerhard Thiele (from the Institute of Monument preservation in Berlin), Wolfgang Thierse (from the Department of Fine Arts at the Ministry of Culture), Manfred Bensing (Chair of Contemporary History at the Karl-Marx-University in Leipzig), Richard Stephan (leader of the cultural section for the Leipzig District), and Horst Müller (Director of the construction firm Investbauleitung Bad Frankenhausen).
88. The group noted security concerns prevented them from visiting Sevastopol and a party conference in Volgograd meant that no one was able to receive them.
89. LHASA-Merseburg/Rate des Bezirkes Halle/4. Ablieferung/6625 (18222/2), R[ichard]. Stephan, "Gedanken zur Reise der Gruppe "Panorama" in die UdSSR vom 19. bis 24. 1. 76" dated 28 January 1976, p. 387. Stephan also mentions several times in his report how unpredictable Tübke's actions were and that he and Tübke had several arguments throughout the trip.
90. LHASA-Merseburg/Rate des Bezirkes Halle/4. Abteilung/6625 (18222/2), pp. 388–89.
91. LHASA-Merseburg/Rat des Bezirkes Halle/4. Abteilung/6694 (20423/2), "Konzeption zur künstlerischen Gestaltung (Nach Vorstellung von Gen. Prof. Werner Tübke, erarbeitet auf der Grundlage der wissenschaftlichen Konzeption und beraten durch den Arbeitsstab)," p. 63.
92. LHASA-Merseburg/Rat des Bezirkes Halle/4. Abteilung/6695 (20423/3), Manfred Bensing and Siegfried Hoyer, "Gutachten über den 1:10 Wandbildentwurf von Prof. Werner Tübke für die "Panorama—Gedenkstätte" in Bad Frankenhausen," p. 579.
93. Ibid.
94. The historians were also impressed with Tübke's use of the artistic style and symbols of the 1500s in order for observers to transport themselves back into the time of the Peasants' War and relive some of the scenes using the imagery that would have been commonplace at the time. In the end of their report they noted that observers would need help to understand the painting—not necessarily in the form of a guided tour through the panorama, but more along the lines of a cultural history of the early bourgeois revolution.
95. LHASA-Merseburg/Rat des Bezirkes/4. Abteilung/6695 (20423/3), Karl-Max Kober, "Gutachten über den 1:10 Wandbildentwurf von Prof. Werner Tübke für die "Panorama—Gedenkstätte" in Bad Frankenhausen," p. 565.
96. Letter from Werner Tübke to Minister of Culture Hans-Joachim Hoffmann, 21 July 1975, as quoted in *Werner Tübke, Bauernkrieg und Weltgericht: Das Frankenhauser Monumentalbild einer Wendezeit*, ed. Günther Meißner and Gerhard Murza (Leipzig: E.A. Seeman, 1995), p. 157.
97. Meißner and Murza, p. 160. The emphasis is that of Werner Tübke.
98. Ibid.
99. Ibid.
100. This equates approximately to a size of 47.57 x 403.54 feet or 19,375 square feet.
101. Karl Max Kober, *Werner Tübke: Monumentalbild Frankenhausen* (Dresden: VEB Verlag der Kunst, 1989), p. 10.
102. Ibid., p. 32.
103. Behrendt, *Werner Tübkes Panoramabild Bad Frankenhausen*, p. 99.

104. Given the intense challenges Erich Honecker faced back in Berlin, it is easy to understand why he decided to remain there and not attend the opening ceremony. However, it was also rumored at the time that Honecker had insisted on having the street leading up to the panorama paved as a condition for him attending the opening ceremony. Despite the fact that the GDR's political system and its infrastructure, most notably its streets, were literally crumbling at the time, the state's decision to follow through with Honecker's demands indicated the importance it placed on what would be the last grand commemoration event before the entire GDR fell apart only months later.
105. Sindermann was also the President of the People's Chamber and Deputy Chairman of the State Council; Böhme was also the First Secretary of the SED for the Halle District; Hager also held the position as Secretary of the Central Committee of the SED and was a member of the State Council.
106. "Frankenhausener Bauernkriegspanorama in die Hände des Volkes übergeben," *Neues Deutschland*, 15 September 1989, p. 1.
107. As quoted in: "In unserer Republik ist Müntzers Zukunftsvision in Erfüllung gegangen," *Neues Deutschland*, 15 September 1989, p. 6.
108. "In unserer Republik ist Müntzers Zukunftsvision in Erfüllung gegangen," *Neues Deutschland*, 15 September 1989, p. 6.
109. LHASA-Merseburg, Rat des Bezirkes Halle, 4. Abteilung, 6696 (20-42314), "Bericht des Bauernkriegs-Panorama Bad Frankenhausen über Arbeitsergebnisse, Erfahrungen und Probleme seit der Eröffnung am 19. September 1989," pp. 226–30, here p. 226.
110. Ibid., pp. 226–27.
111. Ibid., p. 229.

Chapter Five

THE COLLAPSE OF STATE-IMPOSED MEMORY CULTURE

Since the inception of the GDR in 1949, the SED had claimed a monopoly of power over society. It used a wide variety of tactics, ranging from the overt use of force by the secret police to more nuanced attempts to employ propaganda to maintain its hold over the citizens of East Germany. The various shifts in memory politics pursued by state and party functionaries that have been covered thus far ran primarily parallel to these tactics and complemented the party's overarching policies aimed at maintaining control. As we have seen, the party asserted such control by deciding how memorial projects were approved and funded, and by designating the events or people for whom commemoration events were organized. Shifts in state political priorities forced it to reassess its museum exhibits and teacher training programs and revise their content to stay in line with the party's needs. During the final stage in the development of East Germany's official memory culture the party leadership began to lose the ability to control the state's own memory politics, bringing to an end the process of erosion described in the previous chapter. East German sculptors and artists refused to produce the types of monuments desired by the party leadership. Participants in commemoration festivals attempted to reappropriate memories of historical figures that had previously been exalted by the state. By the mid-1980s it was clear that the party had lost control of its memory-work message and could no longer successfully negotiate compromise solutions for its legitimizing needs.

East German society was also beginning to feel the effects of the improved relationship with West Germany. The new openness vis-à-vis the West during the 1970s and 1980s led to dissolution in many segments of society because people became more aware of the economic, political, and cultural disparity between citizens in East and West Germany which in turn led to a growing disconnectedness between the East German government and its citizens.[1] A similar sense of disconnectedness can be seen within the realm of memory, an aspect that became the hallmark of East Germany's memory politics during this final stage. The upper levels of the SED leadership continued to hold strong beliefs about how the memories of Germany's leading socialist leaders should be represented to the public, while leading figures in the artistic community—such as Fritz Cremer, who shared both the political outlook of the *Politbüro* members and could count himself among those who fought in the "antifascist struggle"—disagreed with the party's dominant vision regarding monuments. In 1973, Cremer complained to Kurt Hager that the project director for the new parliamentary building did not take his opinions seriously. He lamented that he had been campaigning for years to move away from the "gigantomania" style of design.[2] Cremer was not alone in his disagreement with party leadership's vision of the past. Other artists, cultural figures, and activists also sought to differentiate their visions from those of the party and the level of disconnect began to rise significantly by the 1980s.

The slow downward turn and erosion of the party's ability to control the trajectory of its own memory politics began during the middle of the 1970s, as we have seen with Werner Tübke's ability to extract increasing artistic control through repeated renegotiations of his contract. While the SED under Erich Honecker broadened the historical roots of the East German state narrative, members of the party ranks and Soviet officials continued to complain that the party leadership had still neglected to constructed monuments to the leading figures of German communism in Berlin. The SED *Politbüro* decided on 19 February 1974 to prioritize several large-scale memorial projects. In Berlin, the SED proposed new monuments for Marx and Engels, Ernst Thälmann, Hermann Duncker, Wilhelm Pieck, Franz Mehring, Otto Grotewohl, Rosa Luxemburg, and Karl Liebknecht. Outside of Berlin, the party planned a memorial in Eisenach commemorating the Eisenach Party Congress, and two memorials in Leipzig honoring Georgi Dimitroff and August Bebel. Of the eleven projects the state only completed eight by 1990.[3] Of those eight, the Marx-Engels and the Ernst Thälmann monuments stood out as the party's priority. Not only were more resources allocated to these two projects than to the others, but SED General Secretary Erich Honecker played a direct role.

Although the party leadership had consistently referred to Marx and Engels in official speeches and writings as the "most important sons" of the German nation and that the East German state was the practical manifestation of their theories, the SED continued to be haunted by its inability to properly insert these figures into the memory landscape of the capital city. The party had also failed to construct a monument to honor Ernst

Thälmann, who had been a cult figure of both the party and state since its inception. Fellow party members pressured Honecker to move forward with these memory projects as did Soviet Ambassador Piotr Abrassimov, who questioned why the SED planned to return a statue of Frederick the Great, in his words the "symbol of Prussian militarism," to Berlin in October 1980 and was astonished that the GDR leadership was "not building a monument for Karl Marx or a monument for the leader of the German working class, the immortal Ernst Thälmann, next to the holy Memorial for the Victims of Fascism and Militarism, next to Bebelplatz, where resistance fighters held rallies against Nazism and the reactionary elements."[4] For Abrassimov, the SED had failed to capitalize on and instrumentalize the memory politics associated with Berlin's historic sites and figures that played an essential role to the legitimating narrative of the state. Such criticism and Honecker's own desire to see these monuments built provided the political impetus and financial resources to bring these projects finally to completion in 1986.

The resumption of both the Marx-Engels and Ernst Thälmann memorial projects, and the different course that each took, underscores the new obstacles that the state faced during the 1980s when negotiating the public depiction of these important historical figures. While these obstacles have most often been examined in relation to the work of Berlin's city planners, it is also important to look at these projects from the perspective of the SED's overall memory-work agenda.[5] The state ultimately, albeit reluctantly, conceded to the smaller-scale vision of Ludwig Engelhard's memorial for Marx and Engels. Meanwhile, Honecker's decision to bypass the East German artistic community and award the commission for the Thälmann monument to a Soviet sculptor sent a clear message that state would look elsewhere if East German sculptors would no longer follow its directives. These examples also highlight how despite signs that the general public, the academic historians, and East German artists were losing interest in the earlier labor-movement-centered state narrative, the aging SED leadership continued to cling to its own culture of remembrance and its own antifascist experience as the foundation for the state's raison d'etre.

While the state's experience constructing these two memorials proved frustrating, it had an even more difficult time maintaining control over in the memory-work category of commemorations. Throughout the history of the GDR, scattered individuals and groups resisted the regime, but these opposition groups began to gain a much stronger foothold in East German society during the 1980s. Given the attention and resources that the state devoted toward its memory-work, it is not surprising that one of the first public manifestations of this new wave of resistance came during the 1988 commemorative parade honoring the memories of Rosa

Luxemburg and Karl Liebknecht to voice its opposition. During this celebration, a small group of dissidents attempted to reappropriate Luxemburg's memory by invoking carefully chosen quotations from her works in a manner that clearly questioned, and threatened to undermine, SED policies. The dissidents turned a core element of the regime's identity against itself, and thus exposed the hollowness of its claims to cultural legitimacy. By uncovering the SED's suppression of alternate memories, the dissidents sought to highlight the contradiction between the regime's proclaimed heritage and the reality of its own anti-democratic policies. In the end, the failure of the party to control the variety of popular memories evoked by Rosa Luxemburg reveal the reality that the state's memory culture had indeed eroded.

Together, these three examples illustrate the final erosive stage of the state-centered memory culture that the regime had worked so diligently to control for more than forty years. The nature of the erosion process demonstrates that the collapse of the SED's monopoly over official memory politics was not sudden, but rather part of a longer process of the state's cultural legitimacy eroding from within. This type of erosion ran parallel to other forms of collapse and protest that faced the SED during final years of its reign. Ultimately, the protesters who took to the streets in the fall of 1989 were responsible for the overthrow of the SED, but the process of eroding cultural legitimacy provided the necessary intellectual freedom to depart from state's antifascist narrative and seek out new lines of tradition and legitimacy of their own.

The Return of Marx and Engels

Negotiation between the party and the sculptors who carried out its memory-work had always been a key component of state's public representation of the past. The mutually dependent nature of the relationship between the party and the sculptors insured that a compromise could be reached and the projects completed. Within the unique context of East German society, the state (and its state-funded institutions) remained the only entity with sufficient resources to fund large-scale memorial projects. There were no private foundations or wealthy patrons who could independently fund the work of East Germany's monumental sculptors. At the same time, if the state wanted to have its national monuments designed and built by its own citizens (a point of prestige for most nations), then it too needed to negotiate and compromise with the sculptors. The rift between the sculptors and the party centered less on the message or content of a given piece of art than on its size. Leading sculptors, such as Fritz

Cremer, consistently voiced their opinion against creating Soviet-inspired overly exaggerated monumental sculptures.[6]

The state's relationship with sculptors must also be seen within the larger context of the state's often-contested relationship with East Germany's cultural elite as a whole. Relations between the SED leadership and the artistic elite declined steadily since the late 1960s, punctuated dramatically by the expulsion of songwriter Wolf Biermann in 1976. It had only slightly recovered during the early 1980s under Honecker's more tolerant cultural policies and his efforts to identify the regime with artistic and cultural opposition to the NATO double-track missile decisions. This political and cultural atmosphere provides an interesting background to view the different approaches employed by the state when pursuing both the Marx-Engels and Ernst Thälmann monument projects.

The return of Marx and Engels as subjects of a public memorial in Berlin reappeared in party and public discourse during the early 1970s with the construction of East Germany's new parliament building, the *Palast der Republik* (Palace of the Republic). City planners returned to previous conceptions of the site that called for constructing a monument to Marx and Engels on the western side of the new parliament building on top of a large platform (the only portion of the former plan from the early 1950s that had been built and was now used as a reviewing stand for military parades). Similar to the earlier plans, the working idea in the 1970s saw a large statue of Marx and Engels looking to the East (symbolically with their backs to the West) and gazing upon the new house of parliament.

The *Politbüro* charged the Ministry of Culture with overseeing the construction of the Marx-Engels monument. On the recommendation of Fritz Cremer, who was the artistic director for the new parliament building, the ministry awarded the contract for the monument to Ludwig Engelhardt. According to Friedrich Nostitz, who served as the project director, Erich Honecker had hoped Cremer would take on the commission himself, but that "Cremer had respect for that which others can do better."[7] Engelhardt was a different kind of artist than Cremer—he was not seen as a *Staatskunstler* (a state artist). Instead, Engelhardt held no political affiliation and came across as very "middle class" in his appearance—someone serious and upright who wore dark jackets and polished shoes.[8] Yet, Cremer saw Engelhardt as a talented sculptor who had already completed several important commissions, including the Heinrich Heine monument in Berlin, a concentration camp memorial in Neubrandenburg, and several others. Once Engelhardt received the commission, he wasted no time and already had a working model by the end of 1973.[9]

Engelhardt's Marx-Engels sculpture formed the core element of a larger *Gesamtkunstwerk* from a variety of artists working in collaboration. The original design included a grouping of several pieces employing a variety of artistic media that together would impart a sense of triumph of communism over the horrors of capitalism. Using the geographic symbolism of capitalist West Berlin's border just blocks directly to the west, the monument configuration began with a marble relief by sculptor Werner Stötzer depicting a scene of writhing human bodies suffering from the harsh realities of capitalism. Behind it, now facing east, was a set of bronze reliefs by sculptor Margaret Middell, illustrating utopian life under communism. To the east were positioned a group of tall stelae by Arno Voigt and Peter Fischer, who used a newly developed chemical process to transfer photographs onto the steel siding. The photographs chosen were intended to highlight the "success" of communism throughout the world, including recent "victories" in the Third World.[10]

Completing the monument grouping and forming the focal point of the ensemble was Engelhardt's statue of Marx and Engels. Marx was seated and Engels was standing just behind him and to his left. The figures of Marx and Engels were purposely depicted in a stoic and seemingly unheroic fashion in order to bring the figures closer to the observer, both physically and symbolically. As the architectural historian Bruno Flierl has noted: "The value of the monument ensemble as a whole is based on its relatively large size in relation to the city's overall size, whereas the individual sculptures, and the Marx-Engels group in particular, are of an optimal size for observation by the viewer and must remain therefore relatively small."[11] Even some within the party elite praised the proportionality of Engelhardt's work. Heinrich Gemkow, Deputy Director of the Institute for Marxism-Leninism, reported to Kurt Hager that he was pleased to see Marx and Engels were not presented as *"übermenschlich"* monumental figures, but rather "depicted quite human-like in their size, position, and gestures" allowing the viewer to see them as role-models.[12] In this respect, the sculptural ensemble followed the trends of other leading GDR sculptors, such as Fritz Cremer, who believed that socialist monuments needed to be as realistic in size as possible, while still maintaining a sense of importance.[13]

In positioning the Marx-Engels monument to the west of the planned parliament building, the state originally intended to illustrate the triumph of Marx over the vestiges of Germany's imperial past and occupy the same place as the "National Monument" that Emperor Wilhelm II had built in 1897 in commemoration of what would have been his grandfather's 100th birthday.[14] For Engelhardt, the positioning of the new Marx-Engels monument on top of what remained of the old monument's foundation signified a negation of memories associated with the German Empire. The Marx-Engels ensemble was to be a "national monument of a new kind."[15]

Despite the purported link between the new monument and a national monument, the connection was tenuous at best. The linkage of Marx and Engels to the founding of the GDR functioned only on a theoretical level, whereas the former National Monument to Kaiser Wilhelm I commemorated Germany's first emperor. In many respects, Cremer's monument at Buchenwald functioned more akin to a national monument than the planed Marx-Engels project.

Once the artistic conception was finalized, the Engelhardt group presented it to the SED *Politbüro* for approval, which it secured on 28 June 1977, followed shortly by similar resolutions passed by the GDR Council of Ministers and the Berlin city magistrate.[16] During the week prior to the official approval by the *Politbüro*, however, the SED's leading ideologue at the time, Albert Norden, wrote in a letter to Erich Honecker that he felt Engelhardt's current work displayed too much formal stiffness compared to the sense of liveliness and movement inspired by the Lenin monument. Indeed, Norden did not hold back in his criticism of the statue—"Why does Engels stand while Marx sits? What is supposed to be communicated by that? What is Marx sitting on? Is that the typical stance for an intellectual giant? Does one not need to fear that he is going to fall from that ultra-narrow chair at any given moment?"[17] Other party and state officials voiced similar criticism of Engelhardt's portrayal of Marx and Engels as he continued to refine the statue at his studio in Gummlin. According to a report filed after a visit in April 1978 by leading state and party functionaries, the visitors complimented Engelhardt's emphasis on the historical importance of the two figures, but noted that his model still lacked dynamism and energy—especially in the composition of Marx.[18]

Over the years a pattern emerged. Various delegations traveled to Gummlin, visited with Engelhardt, and voiced both praise and critique of the project. Each time, Engelhardt altered his sculpture slightly, but never really strayed from the original design he submitted to the *Politbüro* in 1977. Despite the ongoing difference of opinion between Engelhardt and the party, Erich Honecker spoke proudly of the new project in 1981 during the Tenth Party Congress, when he announced: "The construction of a Marx-Engels monument in Berlin, in front of the Palace of the Republic on the Marx-Engels-Platz, will be of extraordinary importance. It will signify the triumph of the ideas of the founders of scientific communism on German soil."[19]

The timeline for completion of the Marx-Engels monument grew as the party asked for additional changes and as plans for completing the construction surrounding the new parliament building were finalized. Construction of the parliament building itself finished in 1976. Unfortunately for Engelhardt and his team, parliamentarians, party officials, and the gen-

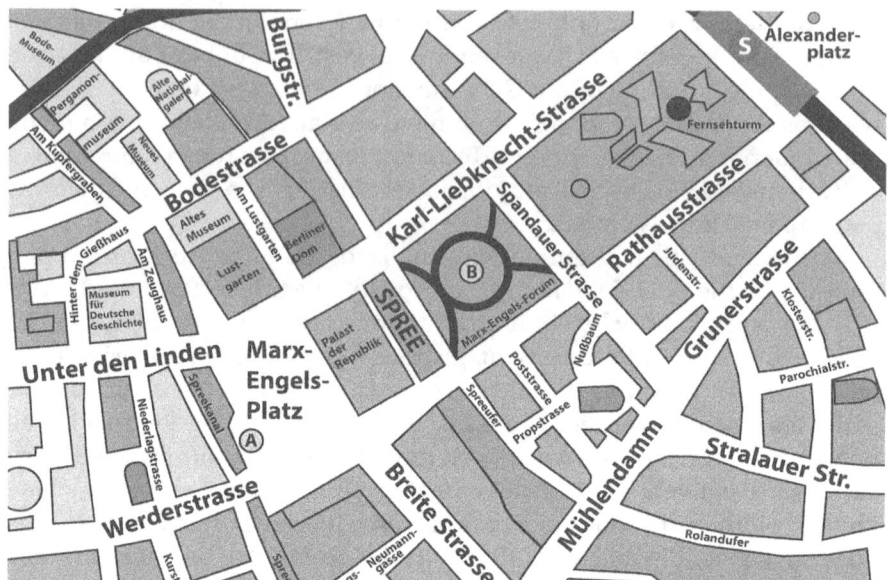

FIGURE 5.1. Map of Berlin showing the original position for the Marx-Engels monument (A) next to the Spree Canal on the Marx-Engels-Platz and its final position (B) in the middle of the Marx-Engels-Forum. The television tower is just to the east followed by Alexander Platz. Illustration by the author.

eral public had become accustomed to parking their cars on the adjacent (and still vacant) Marx-Engels-Platz since the building's opening. Playing to the popular sentiment of the Berlin citizenry, Konrad Nauman, the SED First Secretary of the Berlin District, and East Berlin's Mayor Erhard Kraack began a lobbying effort to prevent the completion of the Marx-Engels monument if it meant losing what they viewed as an essential city parking lot. Suggestions for the construction of an underground parking garage beneath the Marx-Engels-Platz were abandoned after assessing how costly such an alternative would be (especially if the roof would need to be fortified to support the weight of tanks and other armored vehicles that typically drove across the square during military parades).[20]

The monument project ran into additional obstacles as the final cost estimates were tallied. In order to place the statue at the edge of the Spree Canal, which forms the southern branch of the Spree River around Berlin's Museum and Fisher Islands, the city would need to shore up the banks and build a new structure to connect the Marx-Engels-Platz to the Palace of the Republic grounds. Both of these measures would increase the overall cost of the project significantly. Added to these practical and economic difficulties came an ideological problem—the party had hoped to unveil the new monument during a special symposium hosted at the Palace of the Republic marking the 100th anniversary of Marx's death on 14 March 1983.[21] These mounting complications, combined with the added pressure of a hard deadline, meant that the party needed to make a final decision as to whether or not it would proceed with the current plan or alter it completely.

Wolfgang Junker, Minister of Construction, and Erhardt Gißke, General Director of the Construction Office of Berlin, proposed a solution in a letter to Günter Mittag, the SED Secretary for Economics. They called for relocating the monument ensemble to the east side of the parliament building on the grounds of the *Park an der Spree*. The monument's new location, they argued, would cost considerably less and would still guarantee a worthy place for Marx and Engels to be honored.[22] The issue was handed over to the SED's Secretary for Culture, Kurt Hager, who seconded this opinion in a letter addressed to Erich Honecker on 2 December 1982 and added the suggestion that the park be renamed the "Marx-Engels-Forum," to which Erich Honecker agreed.[23] Kurt Hager was now confronted with the difficult task of convincing Ludwig Engelhardt that moving the monument was the best solution to the current obstacles. While Engelhardt pressed his case to preserve the original design and placement of the monument ensemble, he also began to fear that he might be stripped of control over the artistic side of the project. In a letter dated 5 January 1983, Engelhardt asked Hager to place in writing that he would preserve artistic control and to share his views with Honecker.[24]

The process of finding a new home for the monument came to an end when the SED *Politbüro* formally adopted the revised plan in January 1983, much to Engelhart's disappointment. The artist had prided himself on constructing the perfect visual interpretation that led the visitor away from capitalism in the West, through the struggles of communism, and allowed Marx and Engels to gaze upon the Palace of the Republic and communist Eastern Europe with symbolic pride. Relegated now to the eastern side of the parliament building, the ensemble lost much of its aesthetic symbolism as well as its ability to create a counter-memory to that of the German Empire. The new constellation left Marx and Engels with their backs to the Palace of the Republic. They gazed instead at the crown jewel of East Germany's technological achievements, the Berlin television tower. In his letter to Hager conceding that the monument ensemble could be moved, Engelhardt noted that he had consulted with his collaborators and while they all felt the original placement on the Marx-Engels-Platz remained the best option, they would respect the SED's decision to relocate it to the park.

The next step in the planning process involved placing the plans and sketches of the Marx-Engels monument ensemble on public display in Berlin during the month of April 1983 in conjunction with the Karl Marx symposium—the same one that previously had been planned to coincide with the monument's unveiling. For the first time, delegates to the conference as well as the general public could now view what the party planned.[25] Public reaction to the SED's plans was not overwhelmingly positive. Men and women complained both in the visitors' comment book at the exhibit and in letters to the party newspaper *Neues Deutschland*. Most of the public's discontent focused on the new positioning of the monument behind the Palace of the Republic and what was perceived to be a denigration of Berlin's central square, the Marx-Engels-Platz, "*the* square of the capital. It is the red heart of our land. And now? A parking lot. A monument to the greatest revolutionaries, thinkers and human beings now is being set apart from the center of life."[26] Such negative views are also found in an internal interim report sent to Kurt Hager's office at the SED. The report pointed out that most of the comments focused on the images depicting Engelhardt's sculpture. While some voiced their support for the realistic portrait-style depiction of Marx and Engels, many more criticized the lack of emotion displayed by the figures and that the two seemed to "stare off into nowhere with too little relationship to one another."[27]

The party responded to the public feedback by publishing a critique by the art historian Helmut Netzker in *Neues Deutschland* on 29 April 1983. Netzker emphasized to the readers that one must look at the monument ensemble as a whole and not concentrate solely on Engelhardt's sculpture. He also noted that the sculpture differed from traditional monuments in that it was designed to be three dimensional and portrayed more than just the head or the bust of a person, which had been much more common in monument design. Most importantly, and disarmingly, Netzker pointed to the individualized experience that each person has when they look at a sculpture, especially one of such famous figures as Marx and Engels: "In this case, it is especially difficult, since millions of potential viewers in our country have developed over time, in similar ways, formed their own visual conception of Karl Marx and Friedrich Engels, which instinctively arise when confronted with the photographs of this yet unfinished monument."[28] Ultimately, Netzker's article was an attempt to deflect criticism of the project by explaining that everyone would interpret the sculpture differently and that in the end, the artist would succeed in producing a worthy memorial for Marx and Engels.

Despite these attempts to gather public feedback and comment, Engelhardt's final casting of the Marx-Engels monument underwent few alterations from its initial design. When Honecker spoke during the monument's dedication ceremony on 4 April 1986, he tended to avoid talking about the monument he was unveiling and instead trumpeted Marx and Engel's impact on world history. Honecker's lack of attention to Engelhardt's monument during the dedication ceremony stood in stark contrast to the lavish praise he would heap on Lev Kerbel's sculpture of Ernst Thälmann just eleven days later. Indeed, despite Engelhardt's 3.85-meter (approximately 12.5-foot) depiction of Marx and Engels at a proportion of about twice life-size, critics continued to disparage the statue as too small in relation to its importance for the East German state.[29] Even the East German satirical magazine *Eulenspiegel* mocked the monument on the front cover of an April 1986 issue.[30]

The dedication ceremony for the Marx-Engels-Forum took place on 4 April 1986, a few weeks prior to the opening of the Eleventh Party Congress. In his speech, Honecker focused on the recurrent theme that the GDR represented the culmination of the work begun by Marx and Engels: "The ideas of Marx and Engels were further developed and enriched by Vladimir Lenin. Russian workers and peasants under the leadership of Lenin realized these goals for the first time in history during the Great Socialist October Revolution. Following the victory over fascism by the Soviet Union and those allied with her in the anti-Hitler coalition, these ideas found a foothold in other parts of Europe, Asia, and Latin America."[31] Honecker went on to draw more specific connections between Marx and Engels and the SED's role as the vanguard party of the proletariat,

FIGURE 5.2. View of the Marx-Engels-Forum with Ludwig Engelhardt's sculpture forming the focal point in the middle of the park. For a close-up view of the monument, see figure 6.2. BArch Bild 183-1987-0527-010 / Hubert Link.

proclaiming that the GDR "continues the work of the party of Ernst Thälmann and fulfills the legacy of the antifascist resistance fighters."[32] As with so many other instances in the past, Honecker linked the fate of the current regime with the unwavering memory of the state's founding antifascist myth and its legacy rooted in the works of Marx and Engels. It is difficult to imagine that Honecker's words found much resonance outside of the party faithful in 1986. Popular opposition in East Germany was on the rise and only three years later East Germans would take to the streets proclaiming their desire for a "better Germany"—one without the SED.

The immediate impact and general popularity of the Marx-Engels monument was minimal. There were no grand reviews published in the scholarly or popular press aside from a full-page article on the day of its dedication, which highlighted Honecker's speech and the continued meaning of Marx and Engels for the GDR. The text of the article, however, did provide an explanation of how East Germans were meant to read and interpret the new monument: "Dominant in both portraits is their intense and forward-looking gaze. It is the expression of the visionary energy that will remain emphatically in the memory of every visitor."[33] Yet, the lack of political and popular interest in the memorial kept any further coverage of it out of the popular and scholarly press, something that came as a personal blow to Ludwig Engelhardt, who resented the deafening silence.[34] In a letter to Kurt Hager, Engelhardt expressed his disappointment in the lack of attention directed toward his monument:

> I must admit that this year was difficult for me. The silence surrounding our work is almost total. I never thought about what the reaction to the existence of the monument would be like (you know that I always dreamed of approval during the years of work—without that it would have been impossible to continue). But I never imagined that the reaction would be like it has been. ... If not celebration and roses, at least there is now quietness. I would not have been in the position to hand out explanations or justifications after the past few months.[35]

Ten years later, Kurt Hager noted in his memoir that he was actually quite pleased with Engelhardt's portrayal of Marx "as a scientist (and not as a fiery hero) and Engels as the 'second fiddle,' somewhat in the background, and unmistakably the strategist and organizer."[36]

One might have thought that building a monument to Marx and Engels would have been a top priority for a state that based its own legitimacy on the works of these two philosophers. Yet, despite repeated efforts, the party struggled to find a way to harness control away from the artists, city planners, and others who held a stake in the construction of this monument. On the one hand, the SED leadership was unable or unwilling to force its will onto the GDR's artistic community and demand that East German artists conform to the party's vision. On the other hand, the SED's persistence in pursuing this monument despite the pushback it was feeling underscores how the party continued to narrowly define the parameters of East Germany's official memory culture. In the end, it seems that the compromise solution pleased no one completely. The party's lack of public praise signaled its disappointment while Engelhardt had to come to terms with the new placement of his monument and the resulting alteration of its symbolic meaning. However, Engelhardt did manage to find something positive from the way he saw people interact with his sculpture when he noted: "They do something that they would not have done in this place without these objects: they allow themselves to be affected by the reality of our world from a very specific viewpoint— our viewpoint."[37]

A Monument for Ernst "Teddy" Thälmann

Although the dedication ceremony for a new monument and park honoring the memory of Ernst Thälmann came only weeks after the dedication ceremony for the Marx-Engels-Forum, it represented a very different type of memorial project. The Thälmann project marked one of the SED's final attempts to manipulate, steer, and sustain a legitimizing memory culture in the GDR. The impetus for the new Thälmann monument was similar to the party's renewed interest in Marx and Engels—How could East Germany continue to claim it had inherited the traditions of Marx, Engels, and Thälmann without a major monument in its capital city dedicated to any of these historical figures? In both cases, the lack of a monument did not reflect the party's disinterest in constructing one but rather its inability to harness the resources (both financial and artistic) to turn its desire into reality.

East German sculptors, art critics, and cultural functionaries continually opposed the Ruthild Hahne's efforts during the 1950s and 1960s and hindered the party's ability to simply build her vision of Thälmann. Once Otto Grotewohl and Walter Ulbricht passed away, she lost the high level support needed for her to continue working on her monumental portrayal of Thälmann leading a group of workers on a march through the streets of Berlin.[38] Although interest in creating a suitable monument for Thälmann in the capital never went away, there was a lull during the first part of the 1970s as Erich Honecker took the reins of power. The party's interest reawakened, however, as plans to complete the governmental district neared completion.

The Leipzig sculptor Klaus Schwabe received a commission to construct a new monument of Ernst Thälmann, which he completed in 1979. Schwabe had already completed several other major works in Leipzig, but the Thälmann monument was meant to be his first major work of national importance. Originally, Schwabe's sculpture was intended to sit on the square in front of the SED Central Committee's building, which was next to the plot of land designated for the new Palace of the Republic. Since the overarching concept of the parliament building included the work on the Marx-Engels monument, the two projects quickly ran into trouble with one another. City planners and architects complained that Schwabe's sculpture would create an aesthetic problem for both the parliament building and the Marx-Engels monument.[39] As a result high-level party support for Schwabe's project quickly faded away.

Nonetheless, by looking at Schwabe's original design, which was ultimately rejected by the party leadership, we can trace the emergence of some of the SED's major problems regarding its memory-work during the waning years of its rule. Schwabe conceptualized a monument that was both a memorial and a place of personal experience. The ensemble had two main parts with a path leading between the two. On the left was a group of victims of Nazi oppression. On the right was a mirror-laden wall in the shape of a quarter-circle. The idea was that the visitor would place himself in the middle of the quarter-circle and look into the mirror. The reflected image would incorporate the visitor into the scene depicted behind him. Thus, the visitor would no longer be a static observer of art, but could imagine being a part of the sculpture itself. Continuing down the path, Schwabe planned off to the left an incline made of broken crystal, which people were attempting to ascend. Here Schwabe departed from earlier GDR iconography of a triumphant march into the future. Instead, he depicted the road to the future as full of difficulties, albeit passable.[40]

Originally, Schwabe did not offer any direct reference to Thälmann himself, but did eventually add it to the ensemble after considerable pressure by party functionaries. In the end, however, the party abandoned Schwabe's memorial. The rejection was not only due to the aesthetic problems encountered in juxtaposition with the Marx-Engels monument, but also (and quite possibly more importantly) because Schwabe's depiction ran counter to the SED leadership's conception of how Ernst Thälmann should be remembered. Schwabe's constellation of figures and especially the individualization of the experience did not match the party's insistence on a clear and straightforward propaganda message. In a 1988 interview, Schwabe reiterated his conception of socialist memorials by stating, "Socialist memorial art is not the completion of an imaginary 'gallery of ancestors', but rather the meaningful concretization of our revolutionary values and ideals in everyday life."[41] Clearly Schwabe was not without strong socialist convictions, but without the support from either the SED leadership or the collective working on the new Palace of the Republic, his plans quickly faded into irrelevancy.[42]

A competing idea for a Thälmann monument called for the reconstruction of Mies van der Rohe's 1926 monument to Karl Liebknecht and Rosa Luxemburg in front of the SED Party headquarters. In addition to the reconstructed monument, a smaller bronze sculpture of Ernst Thälmann would be placed in front of it and thus link Thälmann's memory with those associated with Liebknecht and Luxemburg. Together, these two monuments were intended to commemorate the scene from 13 June 1926, when Thälmann spoke at the monument's dedication ceremony.[43] Yet, like Schwabe's initial proposal, this one too soon faded into the background without any public explanation for why it was abandoned.

On 10 July 1979, the *Politbüro* ordered the closure of the aging gas works facility in the Prenzlauer Berg district of East Berlin, a traditionally working class neighborhood to the north of the government district, and the creation of an Ernst-Thälmann-Park in its place. This idea, apparently, found its greatest support from Erich Honecker himself, who along with most of the other *Politbüro* members, passed by this stretch of land during his daily commute from the gated neighborhood of Wandlitz. The new venue for the Thälmann memorial had a much larger footprint, which in turn would allow for a much larger monument as well as the incorporation of decorative landscaping and Honecker's pet project—a new housing development.[44]

The plan for the park was to preserve three of the partially destroyed natural gas storage facilities and convert them into new facilities in the near future. The city had already slated one of the three to be converted into a planetarium and a restaurant. The plans also included the construction of a new city hall for Prenzlauer Berg and a multiuse building for public events and exhibits. The architect working on the multiuse building drew inspiration from Mies van der Rohe's New National Gallery and again raised the idea of reconstructing van der Rohe's Liebknecht-Luxemburg memorial so that the two new structures would form a link of architectural continuity.[45]

Hoping to bypass the difficulties that the party had encountered with Ruthild Hahne and Klaus Schwabe's earlier Thälmann projects, Erich Honecker decided to give the commission to the Soviet sculptor Lev Kerbel, who had created the massive sculpture of Karl Marx's head for the city of Karl-Marx-Stadt (Chemnitz) in 1971.[46] Moreover, by awarding the commission to a Soviet sculptor, the SED was able to bypass its own artistic community's resistance to producing what many considered to be a distinctly Soviet form of "propaganda art." Honecker first met with Kerbel during a reception at the GDR embassy in Moscow during the Twenty-Sixth Party Congress of the CPSU in 1981, where he inquired if Kerbel would be interested in the new project. In doing so, Honecker personally nullified the standing agreement that the GDR had with the *Verband Bildender Künstler* (the Association of Fine Artists), which held the commission since the 1974 *Politbüro* resolution. By turning the project over to Lev Kerbel, Honecker sought to distance himself from the GDR artists' association and guarantee that the new monument would be of a size and scope that would in his opinion "correctly" symbolize Ernst Thälmann's importance to the East German state. The grand scale of this project also reflected how Honecker and others of the founding cohort wanted themselves to be perceived by history. Since many of the SED elite had fought alongside Thälmann, they hoped to enhance their own grandeur through their association with him.

Kerbel's proposal included a 13-meter (42.7-foot) statue showing a bust of a brave and powerful looking Ernst Thälmann with a raised, clenched fist and a flag waving in the background. This image of Thälmann marching through the streets in protest of the Nazis had been ingrained in the consciousness of the East German public since the immediate postwar years and continued to have deep political and sentimental value among the GDR's aging elite. While several colossal monuments were constructed in East Germany, including the Soviet memorial in Treptow, the Lenin monument in Berlin, the Karl Marx statue in Karl-Marx-Stadt, and the Lenin monument in Dresden, it is significant that East Germans designed none of them. Most East German artists drew a distinction between "monumental art" and "monumental propaganda." Following the trend begun by Fritz Cremer in the 1960s, East German artists felt that the former was acceptable as long as the work maintained its artistic value, whereas the latter did not follow German artistic tradition—hence the continuous frustration between the party leadership and the artist community.[47]

Kerbel's proposal drew staunch criticism from the GDR artistic community.[48] On 3 March 1982, *Neues Deutschland* published pictures of the model, both of the housing and park projects as well as of Kerbel's Thälmann sculpture. The reactions by the artistic community centered on two main problems—the style of the monument was outdated; and no East German artists were able to compete for the commission. The SED Party Secretary at the College of Fine Arts in Dresden noted:

> The project is welcomed heartily, but there is deep regret and astonishment that: 1. no public competition, even with international participation, took place and thereby prevented not only the best artistic-conceptual solution from being

selected, but also denied the possibility for a GDR-artist to articulate his relationship to Thälmann and the KPD. The best proposal, regardless of the nationality of the artist, would have been realized. 2. The Association of Fine Artists was not consulted in either the choice of theme or the final decision. The dismay among the colleagues in [the department] of sculpture is enormous ... the discussion within the association has already taken shape—at the next meeting of the association leadership in Berlin they will demand information. The level of anxiety is as high as before the 6th Plenary in 1972. The party leadership should also be aware that there is also a concern that anti-Sovietism (i.e. nationalism) will be visible in this critical assessment of the selection process.[49]

The distancing of the party leadership away from the cultural base within the GDR demonstrates not only the apparent disconnect, but also the inability of the artistic community to negotiate a compromise solution with the party as it had done in so many other instances. The mutually dependent nature between the state and the GDR artistic community had been broken.

Despite some local resistance to the removal of the natural gas containers, Lev Kerbel, with Honecker's help, was able to push through architectural plans that provided a backdrop of new apartment buildings behind the statue. Ironically, the removal of the gas works, which symbolized the working-class heritage of the district, broke the historical linkage between the figure of Ernst Thälmann and neighborhood. The new image was one of looking into the future, rather than commemorating the past. Thälmann was no longer depicted as a hero leading the working class, but as a figure declaring victory over his oppressors. Reality, however, did not match this idealized perception of the situation in the GDR. When the gas containers were finally destroyed in July 1984, the party clearly signaled that they were not interested in respecting the wishes of those who lived in the area. This only served to strengthen the growing awareness that the current GDR regime had nothing in common with aspirations imbedded in the image of Ernst Thälmann.

The official celebration of Ernst Thälmann's 100th birthday in 1986 served as the backdrop for the unveiling ceremony of the new monument and the official opening of the Ernst-Thälmann-Park. It attracted additional attention because it fell on the eve of the Eleventh Party Congress of the SED, which would turn out to be its last. Most of the party delegates had arrived early for the celebration and many foreign guests also attended. Following the playing of the GDR's national anthem,[50] Erich Honecker spoke to the crowd and attempted to merge the memories of Thälmann as a fighter with the continuous struggle by the people of the GDR to create a better life for the workers: "Nothing reminds us anymore of what was once here, nothing of the stench, of people's poor working

FIGURE 5.3. Dedication ceremony of Lew Kerbel's sculpture of Ernst Thälmann in Berlin, 15 April 1986. BArch Bild 183-1986-0415-052 / Bernd Settnik.

and living conditions, nothing more of the almost daily attacks by the *Schupo* and *SA* gangs, who claimed the lives of many proletariats. Today the proletariat is now the lord of this city, the city of freedom, the capital of the GDR, Berlin."[51] Honecker's overarching message was that the GDR had accomplished all that for which Thälmann had fought. The reality was that three years prior to the collapse of the GDR, many of the "accomplishments" claimed by Honecker were only cosmetic improvements designed to mask the decaying nature of the state's infrastructure and the regime's political power.

After decades of trying to work with East German artists to create the kind of monument that the SED leadership desired, the regime's decision to look beyond its borders to find someone who would reflects a fundamental change had taken place regarding the relationship between the state and the GDR artists. The Thälmann monument was the last of the large-scale political memory projects in Berlin prior to the collapse of the GDR and illustrates the desperate attempt by the regime to cling to its founding myth as an antifascist state. Those who attended the dedication ceremonies represented primarily the party faithful, not the general public from Berlin or even the Prenzlauer Berg neighborhood. Instead of working together with the residents of Prenzlauer Berg and in cooperation with East German artists, the SED regime made one last effort to impose its vision of the past into the East German memory landscape. The party's chronic inability to relate to the general public's perception of the past was key to the erosion of the regime's cultural legitimacy.

Wresting the Memory of Rosa Luxemburg from State Control

The final act that solidified the collapse of the SED's control over East Germany's memory culture came on 17 January 1988, when a group of human rights activists were arrested in Berlin during the annual memorial march in honor of Karl Liebknecht and Rosa Luxemburg. The state cracked down on the group's use of unauthorized banners and slogans, which the East German secret police, the *Stasi,* viewed as a threat against one of the most sacred of state rituals. Each year, thousands of Berliners marched down the streets from central Berlin to the Socialists' Cemetery in Friedrichsfelde. The state ritual drew on earlier traditions of Berlin's working class; the party elite regarded it as an annual affirmation of the state's identity and its antifascist raison d`être since its resumption in 1946. According to ritual, the crowds would pass by the assembled *Politbüro* members and each factory or place of work would lay a wreath next to the gravesites of Luxemburg and Liebknecht. The party utilized the march for propaganda purposes each year to reinforce the socialist identity of the state.[52]

However, in 1988 this particular day of remembrance turned into an act of open protest through the active reappropriation of Rosa Luxemburg's words and legacy by members of the popular opposition in a manner that struck the core of the SED's own memory politics. The resulting wave of arrests led to an outpouring of solidarity with those in prison and marked the beginning of a popular protest movement that eventually led to the massive demonstrations in the fall of 1989. The intellectuals and artistic elite who spearheaded this action of dissent were by no means the first to be forced into the West in order to silence them or the first to use the words of Rosa Luxemburg against the SED. Both songwriter Wolf Biermann, probably the most famous person in the GDR to be stripped of his citizenship, and the Evangelical Pastor Heino Falke had previously come under fire when they invoked certain excerpts from Rosa Luxemburg writings, including the famous slogan "Freedom is always the freedom of those who think differently," as a means of protesting against SED control. Yet, the unique circumstances that led to these particular expulsions in 1988 go to the root of the eroding antifascist myth that the SED leadership could no longer contain. Moreover, the necessity to deport these intellectuals was a clear sign that the GDR had no concept of how to deal with internal dissent other than suppressing and exiling those who thought differently.[53]

The events outlined above did not arise in a vacuum, but were a part of a longer disintegration of SED power and the rise of popular opposition movements throughout Eastern Europe. The ideas of Poland's Solidarity, Gorbachev's reform efforts in the Soviet Union, and the popular opposition movements that were gaining strength within the Soviet Bloc all contributed to an atmosphere of mounting dissent in the GDR. While the East German regime under Honecker did not signal any desire to follow others down the road of reform, the new spirit of openness in the other socialist states created ripple effects in the GDR and gave nascent dissidents the courage to stand up.[54]

Singer-songwriter Stephan Krawczyk and his wife, Freya Klier, a well-known theater director, came up with the idea to use Rosa Luxemburg's memory as a means of attacking the state during the fall of 1987. Krawczyk was a popular performer who had taken up the mantle of Wolf Biermann, a fellow songwriter who had been stripped of his citizenship in 1976. As was the case with Biermann, the *Stasi* targeted Krawczyk for observation for propagating anti-government sentiment in his lyrics. As the date for the demonstration drew near, Krawczyk and Klier began planning their counter-demonstration together with the recently founded working group Citizenship Rights in the GDR (*Staatsbürgeschaftsrecht der DDR*), one of several organizations aimed at preparing and aiding those wishing to emigrate. The *Stasi* had been closely monitoring the group ever since it sent its "declaration" to Minister of the Interior Friedrich Dickel on 12 December 1997.[55]

The participants in the counter-demonstration planned to meet at 9 A.M. at the square in front of the House of Sport and Recreation near the *Frankfurter Tor*. From there, the group planned to go to the Prenzlauer Berg assembly point for those participating in the official march. Once they had integrated into the larger group, the counter-demonstrators planned on participating in the march and then to unveil their own slogans when the right moment came. The slogans that the group decided to concentrate on were: "Freedom is always the freedom of those who think differently"; "He who doesn't move doesn't feel the chains"; and "The only way to rebirth is the widest democracy," all of which were taken from Rosa Luxemburg's writings.[56] The purpose of choosing these particular phrases, according to one participant, was "to make the public aware that the Liebknecht-Luxemburg commemoration has been misused by the SED-state for its own purposes for years and to act upon the human right to demonstrate guaranteed by the GDR Constitution."[57] To what extent those planning to participate really thought they could march the entire length of the demonstration without drawing any attention from the *Stasi* is difficult to ascertain. On 13 January the Deputy Minister of State Security Rudi Mittig called for increased surveillance of opposition groups. In an internal memo to all *Stasi* heads of departments, Mittig announced that the Citizenship Rights group was planning to "misuse" the Liebknecht-Luxemburg parade "for its own hostile objectives."[58] During the following days, the *Stasi* interviewed 118 people and warned them not to disrupt the upcoming commemoration and demanded that they sign a declaration that they would not break East German laws. In an attempt to head off some of the most vocal protesters nineteen people were granted an exit visa and seventeen of those had left the GDR prior to the commemoration on 17 January.[59]

In her 16 January 1988 diary entry, Freya Klier recounts the preparations on the night before the protest. Her comments provide additional insight into her motivations for using the ritualistic act of the Liebknecht-Luxemburg demonstration and suggest how she thought Luxemburg's memory could help their cause:

> We prepared for the meeting in May, and reached an agreement about the Luxemburg-Demo for tomorrow morning. The "Solidarity Church" won't participate, since it is mainly an initiative of the emigration self-help group. The initiative overlaps with Stephan's [Krawczyk] and my plan from this fall to protest the ban preventing us from working. With our participation we want to draw attention to our interpretation of Rosa's legacy—the banner has long been ready, a quotation from her. ... The walk out to the memorial in Friedrichsfelde

FIGURE 5.4. Dissidents preparing their banners on the eve of the Liebknecht-Luxemburg parade in January 1988. Robert-Havemann-Gesellschaft / Berhard Freutel.

has special symbolic importance for him [Stephan]. He is not just a follower of Luxemburg's ideas, just one Luxemburg quotation read out loud during a concert was the reason for him having to suffer under a work ban.[60]

The slogan that was the most controversial and so potentially disruptive to the state ritual was Rosa Luxemburg's phrase: "Freedom is always the freedom of those who think differently."[61] As Hermann Weber, a West German historian of the GDR, noted at the time, both Rosa Luxemburg and her writings had long been a thorn in the side of the Stalinist wing of the German Communist Party. The full quotation, Weber observed, reads: "Freedom only for the followers of the government, only for the members of a party—even if its numbers be so plentiful—is no freedom. Freedom is always the freedom of those who think differently. Not because of the fanaticism of 'justice,' but rather because all that is instructive, healthy, and cleansing about political freedom depends on this essence and is denied its effectiveness when 'freedom' is made into a privilege."[62] The SED, and the KPD before it, had repeatedly and openly tried to suppress the democratic values that were also a part of Rosa Luxemburg's legacy and memory. Instead, the SED wanted to sustain a constant image of Luxemburg as a revolutionary and as a martyr in the struggle against fascism. Her disagreements with Lenin, her desire for democratic rule, and all other aspects of her legacy that did not speak to the legitimizing needs of the party were suppressed.[63]

Despite the intricate planning and preparation by those involved in the counter-demonstration, thirty-five protesters did not make it much farther than just outside of their own apartments on the morning of 17 January before being arrested by the *Stasi*, who had been well informed. Stephan Krawczyk, who had helped the others come up with the appropriate Luxemburg quotations, decided at the last minute to change the slogan he planned to display. Under his jacket, Krawczyk concealed a bed sheet with the words "Against the Work Ban in the GDR." Krawczyk was arrested just outside of his apartment. Others, such as Till Böttger, Andreas Kalk and Bert Schlegel, all members of the "Environmental Library" opposition group, were arrested on their way to the demonstration.[64] For those who did make it to the meeting place in front of the House of Sport and Recreation, three hundred *Stasi* agents were waiting, with another eighty held in reserve. Before being ushered away, both of the main West German television channels captured some of the commotion from the first wave of arrests.[65] Others were arrested further along the parade route as they attempted to pull out their banners.[66]

Although there was no mention of the demonstration the next day in the GDR's official newspapers, it had been the lead story in West Germany during both the evening news and throughout the day on Monday.[67] Official East German coverage of the event spoke only of 200,000 Berliners who marched in honor of the memory of "Karl and Rosa" and in "demonstration of the unity of party and people."[68] Unreported went the arrests of 105 demonstrators, most all of them connected in one way or another to the organized counter-demonstration.[69] Despite Klier's decision not to participate on the day of the demonstration, her apartment was searched, as were those of several others suspected of planning the demonstration.

The following day, men and women throughout the GDR began to demonstrate in solidarity with those arrested. Demonstrations during the week that followed were the greatest wave of protest since the 1953 uprising. All around Berlin and throughout the GDR opposition groups gathered to plot out a response and collectively called for the release of those arrested. Vigils took place in over forty cities in the GDR, most resulting in the founding of solidarity committees and the drafting of protest resolutions.[70] Four youths were arrested when they began a hunger strike in solidarity with those arrested. Despite the momentary upswing in protest action, Klier was upset with the slow pace of the new demonstrations and produced a short video on 21 January, which aimed to solicit solidarity and sympathy among the West German artists. When the video aired on West German television a few days later, it did manage to attract some attention in the West, but did not have the overwhelming effect she had desired.[71]

On 25 January, the Stasi undertook another wave of arrests, this time taking Freya Klier, Bärbel Bohley, and other leading figures of the still relatively small Initiative Freedom and Human Rights (*Initiative Frieden und Menschenrechte* or IFM) opposition group.[72] Some of those who had been arrested in their apartments during the initial arrest wave were released, but the majority were given a fast-track trial and sentenced to either six months of detention or deportation to the West. For many who participated in the demonstration, this had been their ultimate goal—those who saw emigration as a fundamental human right. For others, however, being stripped of their citizenship and deported to the West was one of the harshest punishments that the state could hand down.

In a clear attempt to tarnish the reputation of the leaders of the counter-demonstration, *Neues Deutschland* published an article on 26 January alerting the public that the leaders of the counter-demonstration were under arrest and charged with high treason (*Landesverrat*). The article spelled out the situation plainly:

> On January 25, 1988, several people were arrested by GDR authorities under suspicion of maintaining treasonous relations and against whom preliminary proceedings have begun. Among those arrested are: Wolfgang Templin, Ralf Hirsch, Bärbel Bohley and Freya Klier.

The investigation into the criminal activities of Stephan Krawczyk has in the mean time been expanded to include charges of maintaining treasonous relations, based on the discovery of links with groups controlled by secret service agencies in West Berlin.[73]

Publicly, the regime depicted those involved in the demonstrations as acting on behalf of Western security agencies, such as the West German *Bundesnachrichtendienst* (BND). But within senior party and government circles, leaders were alarmed that the protesters had turned the regime's own instruments of cultural legitimacy on the regime itself—in their mind, a dangerous and even treasonous act. Looking back on these events, former *Politbüro* member Günter Schabowski discussed the threat that this act of dissent posed for the SED: "Following the Liebknecht-Luxemburg-Demonstration in January 1988, during the well-known actions of the opposition forces, representatives of opposition groups demanded the freedom to dissent in reference to Rosa Luxemburg and hit the nerve of the SED leadership, who had claimed Rosa as a revolutionary champion for themselves, the Ministry for State Security called for creating measures to prevent similar incidents at major political events in the future."[74] Clearly, this particular act of protest frightened the party leadership and threatened its ability to control the public image of Luxemburg and other socialist heroes on whom it had built its cultural legitimacy.

Adding fuel to the fire, the president of the East German PEN writer's union, Dr. Heinz Kamnitzer, wrote an inflammatory article in *Neues Deutschland* on 28 January. In his article, Kamnitzer bemoaned the actions of the counter-demonstrators as disrespectful of the "Martyrs of the Communist Party" because their aim was to draw attention to themselves instead of paying tribute to Luxemburg and Liebknecht. Kamnitzer wasted no time getting to the root of his argument, stating: "What happened there was as reprehensible as blasphemy. No church could accept it if someone were to degrade a memorial procession for a Catholic cardinal or an Evangelical bishop. In the same respect, no one can expect us to accept it, when someone purposefully disrupts and dishonors the remembrance of Rosa Luxemburg and Karl Liebknecht."[75] Kamnitzer went on to argue that the quotation from Rosa Luxemburg had been taken out of context and that Luxemburg had distanced herself from this earlier position. Indeed, the fact that this quotation came from an unpublished manuscript, Kamnitzer argued, proved that she never intended for it to be published and that by November 1918 she actually agreed with the tactics of the Bolsheviks. Thus, Kamnitzer's response to the January counter-demonstrations was based on an attempt to play on people's ethical and moral feelings regarding the proper manner to honor the dead, but also on an argument that the historical truth had been misused. Together these two arguments were supposed to stave off further solidarity protests and conceal the fact that the party had indeed lost its ability to control the public memory and legacy of Rosa Luxemburg.

A cloud of misinformation and rumors surrounded the fates of those still under arrest and many were surprised to hear that both Klier and Krawczyk had agreed "voluntarily" to leave the GDR (although Klier later stated that they were forced to leave).[76] The misinformation campaign spread by the *Stasi*, the press, and other party-loyal entities was part of a final effort to put the January demonstration to rest and discredit the leaders of the movement as traitors to the GDR. In reality, Stephan Krawczyk, Freya Klier, and Ralph Hirsch were stripped of their citizenship. Bärbel Bohley and Werner Fischer retained their GDR passports and were granted a two-year travel visa. The state also issued five-year visas to Wolfgang and Regina Templin. However, one of the stipulations was that they were not allowed back into the GDR for the duration of their visas.[77]

The departure of these leading opposition figures virtually silenced the open opposition in the GDR for almost a year and the level of public protest never again reached the same level again until May 1989. However, the reappropriation of Rosa Luxemburg's legacy as a symbol for democracy by the emerging dissident movement in East Germany signals that the SED had truly lost the ability to control and direct its own memory-work message. Most importantly, it could not control those elements of the past that were most central to the cultural legitimacy of the GDR. Luxemburg's words pointed to the weakest link in the chain of historical figures and events that the GDR had professed for years as the basis for its existence. Moreover, this counter-demonstration further exposed and demonstrated the discrepancy between the SED's progressive rhetoric and its repressive actions. The state found it increasingly difficult to rationalize the distinctions it drew between its suppression of its own dissidents and the repression of communist dissidents by reactionary elements during the 1920s and 1930s. Its own party legacy had now come full circle. The party itself was now providing the moral ammunition that would slowly prompt hundreds of thousands to take to the streets in 1989 and ultimately bring about the collapse of SED rule.

Conclusion

The considerable financial and political resources that the SED leadership devoted to the construction of its last two sites of memory during the mid-1980s signaled the party's final attempt to saturate the public sphere with its official iconic interpretation of the past. The party's inability to fully control the process of creating the Marx-Engels monument and its need to find a non-East German sculptor to complete the Thälmann memorial were both signs that the relatively stable and well-developed state memory culture in the GDR was in the process of eroding.

Erich Honecker could no longer rely on his own artistic community to support the memory projects of the party and the state, but his decision to commission a Soviet sculptor only increased the level of resentment within the GDR cultural elite and galvanized its resistance to further manipulation. This distancing of the party from the artistic community was representative of the larger separation that had been developing for some time between the party elite and the rest of the GDR society, between an illusion of stability and reality of structural decay (both literally and figuratively). As more and more citizens of the GDR began to recognize this disconnect between the party and people, more and more people began to question the very essence of the historical narrative that the party had so painstakingly developed and nurtured over the past forty years.

The severe reaction by the state to the actions of the East German dissidents who used the words of Rosa Luxemburg to fight for human rights and democracy demonstrates both the importance that the party placed on its ability to control East Germany's memory culture and its fear that such counter-memories could bring about its downfall. The slow erosion of the state's memory culture during the 1980s, combined with the reemergence of popular historical figures such as Martin Luther and Bismarck in the public sphere, created a new atmosphere of freedom, which opposition groups would ultimately claim for themselves and use to bring about the collapse of the SED regime during the fall of 1989.

Notes

1. Charles Maier, *Dissolution: The Crisis of Communism and the End of East Germany* (Princeton, NJ: Princeton University Press, 1997).
2. SAPMO-BArch, DY 30/27378. Letter from Fritz Cremer to Kurt Hager dated 14 June 1973.
3. Hubertus Adam, "Erinnerungsrituale—Erinnerungsdiskurse—Erinnerungstabus: Politische Denkmäler der DDR zwischen Verhinderung, Veränderung und Realisierung" *Kritische Berichte*, Vol. 20, No. 3 (1992), pp. 10–35, here p. 28.
4. As cited in: Thomas Flierl, "'Thälmann und Thälmann vor allem:' Ein Nationaldenkmal für die Hauptstadt der DDR, Berlin" in *Kunstdokumentation 1945–1990: Aufsätze, Berichte, Materialien*, ed. Günter Feist, Eckhart Gillen, and Beatrice Vierneigel (Cologne: DuMont Buchverlag, 1996), pp. 358–85, p. 381.
5. Thomas Flierl, "'Thälmann und Thälmann vor allem'; Bruno Flierl, *Gebaute DDR: Über*

Stadtplaner, Architekten und die Macht (Berlin: Verlag für Bauwesen, 1998), pp. 121–71; Brian Ladd, "East Berlin Political Monuments in the Late German Democratic Republic: Finding a Place for Marx and Engels," *Journal of Contemporary History*, Vol. 37, No. 1 (2002), pp. 91–104; Brian Ladd, *The Ghosts of Berlin: Confronting German History in Urban Landscape* (Chicago: University of Chicago Press, 1997).

6. Fritz Cremer in "Bildende Kunst und Architektur: Marteralien der Plenartagung vom 31. Mai 1968," Deutsche Akademie der Künste zu Berlin, *Arbeitshefte*, No. 2 (1969), p. 19.
7. Friedrich Nostritz, "Es kam die Frage auf, warum Marx sitzt und Engels steht," *Berliner Zeitung*, 11 September 2010.
8. Ibid.
9. Ladd, "East Berlin Political Monuments," p. 98.
10. For a more detailed description of the early conceptual plan see: Ladd, "East Berlin Political Monuments," p. 98. See also: Eva-Marie Klother, *Denkmalplastik nach 1945 bis 1989 in Ost- und West-Berlin* (Münster: Lit, 1996), pp. 146–49.
11. Bruno Flierl, *Gebaute DDR*, p. 158.
12. SAPMO-BArch, DY 30/27378. Letter from Heinrich Gemkow to Kurt Hager with attachment dated 6 July 1976.
13. This aspect of the project is not surprising, since Fritz Cremer was involved as an advisor to the "Engelhardt Group" during the conceptual phase of the project until 1974. The project follows in the tradition of other East German sculptures in the "Socialist-Realist" style that dominated East German artistic interpretation. Yet, the East German interpretation attempted to remain true to the deeply rooted German concept of artistic creativity and resisted adapting its art to the grandiosity often found in Soviet works of public art.
14. Adam, "Erinnerungsrituale," p. 29.
15. Bruno Flierl, *Gebaute DDR*, p. 159.
16. SAPMO-BArch, DY 30/J IV 2/2/1680. Protocol of the *Politbüro* meeting on 28 June 1977, Protokoll 26/77.
17. SAPMO-BArch, DY 30/27378. Letter from Albert Norden to Erich Honecker dated 18 June 1977.
18. SAPMO-BArch, DY 30/27378. Protocol of the visit to Engelhardt's studio in Gummlin dated 15 April 1978. The high-ranking delegation sent out to consult with Engelhardt included, among others, Heinz-Joachim Hoffman (Minister of Culture), Ursula Ragwitz (Director of the Department of Culture at the SED), and Wilfried Maaß (Deputy Minister of Culture).
19. Erich Honecker, "Die Erfordernisse der weiteren geistig-kulturellen Entwicklung im Sozialismus" (Aus dem Bericht des Zentralkomitees an den X. Partietag der Sozialistischen Einheitspartei Deutschlands, 11. bis 16. 1981) in *Die Kulturpolitik unserer Partei wird erfolgreich verwirklicht*, Erich Honecker (Berlin: Dietz, 1982), p. 301.
20. SAPMO-BArch, DH/1/33091. Letter from Wolfgang Junker to Günter Mittag dated 6 October 1982 (Anlage). According to Junker the Marx-Engels-Platz could accommodate 800 parking spaces, but this would be reduced to around 200 if the monument were to be built as planned. See also: Bruno Flierl, *Gebaute DDR*, p. 160, and Ladd, "East Berlin Political Monuments," pp. 99–100.
21. Bruno Flierl cites the planned date for the symposium as 14 March 1984, but this must be an error, since Karl Marx died in 1883.
22. SAPMO-BArch, DH/1/33091. Letter from Wolfgang Junker to Günter Mittag dated 6 October 1982 (Anlage).
23. SAPMO-BArch, DY 30/27378. Letter from Kurt Hager to Erich Honecker dated 2 December 1982. See also Ladd, "East Berlin Political Monuments," p. 100. Ladd argues that

the parking lot issue also played a major role in winning over Hager's support for the shift and that monetary issues were possibly secondary.
24. SAPMO-BArch, DY 30/27378. Letter from Ludwig Engelhardt to Kurt Hager dated 5 January 1983.
25. "Ein 'Marx-Engels-Forum' in Ost-Berlin," *Frankfurter Allgemeine Zeitung*, 11 April 1983, p. 4.
26. Letter from Gerd Lüdersdorf, as quoted in Ladd, "East Berlin Political Monuments," p. 101. Original found in: SAPMO-BArch, DR 1/1759A, pp. 34–35.
27. SAPMO-BArch DY/30/27378. Interim Report about the Exhibit "Marx-Engels-Denkmal—Ein Arbeitsbericht."
28. Helmut Netzker, "Gedanken zur Ausstellung über das Marx-Engels-Forum," *Neues Deutschalnd*, 29 April 1983, p. 4.
29. Michael Simmons, "Mega status for Marx: Soviet Leader Gorbachev pays tribute to socialist pioneers on East German visit," *The Guardian*, 21 April 1986.
30. *Eulenspiegel*, No. 15 (1986). The caption accompanying the sketch of the monument read: "Why is Engels standing?" "Because he wants to see how the housing problem is being solved." "And Marx?" "He is astonished by the low rents."
31. SAPMO-BArch, DY 30/2570. SED ZK Büro Erich Honecker: "Rede des Generalsekretärs des Zentralkomitees der SED und Vorsitzenden des Staatsrates der DDR, Erich Honecker, zur Einweihung des Marx-Engels-Forums am 4. April 1986 in Berlin," pp. 3–4 (Bl. 38–39).
32. Ibid., pp. 4–5 (Bl. 39–40).
33. Wolfgang Spickermann and Dietmar Eisold, "Marx-Engels-Forum in Berlin eingeweiht," *Neues Deutschland*, 5/6 April 1986, p. 4.
34. Ladd, "East Berlin Political Monuments," p. 103.
35. SAPMO-BArch, DY/30/27378. Letter from Ludwig Engelhardt to Kurt Hager dated 15 September 1986.
36. Kurt Hager, *Erinnerungen* (Leipzig: Faber & Faber, 1996), p. 288.
37. SAPMO-BArch, DY/30/27378. Letter from Ludwig Engelhardt to Kurt Hager dated 15 September 1986.
38. See chapter 2 for an analysis of Ruthild Hahne's failed Thälmann project.
39. SAPMO-BArch, DY/30/IV B 2/9.06/73. Letter from Ursula Ragwitz to Kurt Hager dated 14 June 1977. Ragwitz comments on the incompatibility of the two monuments early on in the process.
40. Adam, "Erinnerungsrituale," p. 29; "Kunstlerisch gestaltet: Ideen Thälmanns für diese Zeit. Blick in die Werkstatt des Leipziger Bildhauers Klaus Schwabe," *Leipziger Volkszeitung*, 28 March 1980.
41. "Vor dem X. Kongreß des Verbandes Bildener Künstler: Denkmalkunst, die von unseren revolutionären Idealen Kunde gibt. Gespräch mit dem Bildhauer Prof. Klaus Schwabe," *Neues Deutschland*, 14 November 1988.
42. Hubertus Adam notes that the model of Schwabe's Thälmann memorial project was deliberately destroyed during its transport back from an exhibition. Although Adam does not say who destroyed the model, one can infer that he is referring to the party's cultural functionaries who were adamantly opposed to Schwabe's project. See: Adam, "Erinnerungsrituale" p. 29.
43. Peter Monteath, "Ein Denkmal für Thälmann" in *Ernst Thälmann; Mensch und Mythos*, Peter Monteath (Amsterdam: Rodopi, 2000), pp. 179–201, here p. 189.
44. In this manner, the Thälmann project was very similar to the Lenin Monument and housing complex completed in 1970.
45. Thomas Flierl, "'Thälmann und Thälmann vor allen,'" p. 378.

46. Honecker also gave the dedication speech for this monument, which was full of overwhelming praise for the sculptor. See: Erich Honecker, "Marx, Engels, Lenin weisen uns den sicheren Weg," Rede bei der Enthüllung des Karl-Marx-denkmals in Karl-Marx-Stadt, 9 October 1971, in Honecker, *Die Kulturpolitik*, pp. 37–42.
47. Thomas Flierl, "'Thälmann und Thälmann vor allen,'" p. 381. Here Flierl cites an internal memo produced by Ursula Ragwitz, the head of the Department of Fine Arts at the Central Committee of the SED. Of special note is that Ragwitz underlines the sentiment within the artistic community that "monumental propaganda" is uniquely Soviet and did not evolve naturally in Germany and thus found no following.
48. Ladd, "East Berlin Political Monuments," p. 97.
49. SAPMO-BArch, DY 30/Vorl. SED 32725: Bestand Abt. Kultur des ZK der SED, as reproduced in: Thomas Flierl, "'Thälmann und Thälmann vor allen,'" pp. 380–81.
50. In practice, the GDR national anthem was never sung during the last decade of the GDR, since it still referred to a unified Germany. Instead, only the music was played at state events.
51. SAPMO-BArch, DY 30/2335, Büro Erich Honecker. "Rede des Generalsekretärs des Zentralkomitees der SED und Vorsitzended des Staatsrates der DDR, Erich Honecker, auf der Manifestation zur Einweihung des Ernst-Thälmann-Parks Berlin am 15. April 1986."
52. See chapter 1.
53. Writing in the summer of 1989, Daniel Hamilton argued that Erich Honecker had indeed developed an approach using forced expulsions as a spigot with which to channel dissent. However, internal and external developments prevented Honecker's approach from succeeding. See: Daniel Hamilton, "Dateline East Germany," *Foreign Policy*, No. 76 (Fall 1989), pp. 176–97; Steven Pfaff, *Exit-Voice Dynamics and the Collapse of East Germany: The Crisis of Leninism and the Revolution of 1989* (Durham, NC: Duke University Press, 2006); Dirk Philipsen, *We Were the People: Voices from East Germany's Revolutionary Autumn of 1989* (Durham, NC: Duke University Press, 1992).
54. Timothy Garton Ash, *In Europe's Name: Germany and the Divided Continent* (New York: Random House, 1993). Garton Ash offers an insightful look at the interconnectedness of the popular opposition movements in Eastern Europe during the 1980s.
55. BStU, MfS HA XX/9 1652, "Erklärung anlässlich des Tages der Menschenreche" dated 10 December 1987, pp. 277–80.
56. Stefan Wolle, *Die heile Welt der Diktatur: Alltag und Herrschaft in der DDR 1971–1989* (Berlin: Ch. Links Verlag, 1998), p. 298. See also: BStU, MfS HA IX 10302, "Information über die Unterbindung von unter Missbrauch der Kampfdemonstration der Berliner Werktätigen am 17. Januar 1988 geplanten provokatorisch-demonstrativen antisozialistischen Aktivitäten" dated 18 January 1988, pp. 10–15, here p. 13.
57. Günter Jeschonnek, "Der 17. Januar 1988—und kein Ende?" *Deuschland Archiv*, Vol. 21, No. 8 (1988), pp. 849–54, here p. 850.
58. BStU, MfS BdL/Dok. 008399, pp. 1–4, p. 1. Memo from the Deputy Minister of State Security Mittig to the heads of department dated 13 January 1988.
59. BStU, MfS HA IX 10302, pp. 10–15, p. 11.
60. Freya Klier, *Abreiskalender: Ein deutsch-deusches Tagebuch* (Munich: Knaur, 1989), p. 260.
61. Rosa Luxemburg originally wrote this phrase in the 1920s in regards to the Russian Revolution. This quotation could alternately be translated as: "Freedom is always the freedom of those who dissent."
62. Hermann Weber, "Stichwort: Die SED und Rosa Luxemburg," *Deutschland Archiv*, Vol. 21, No. 3 (March 1988), p. 244.
63. For an excellent assessment of the GDR's use of Rosa Luxemburg's legacy, see: Eric Weitz, "'Rosa Luxemburg Belongs to Us!' German Communism and the Luxemburg

Legacy," *Central European History*, Vol. 27, No. 1 (1994), pp. 27–64; Martin Sabrow, "Rosa durfte nicht luxemburgisch sein—Überlegungen zu einem paradoxen historischen Symbol in der Gedenkkultur der DDR," *Berliner Zeitung*, 14 January 2000, p. 11; Gilbert Badia, "Rosa Luxemburg," in *Deutsche Erinnerungsorte*, ed. Etienne François and Hagen Schulze (Munich: C.H. Beck, 2001), vol. 2, pp. 105–21. For an understanding of the GDR's official view of Rosa Luxemburg, see: Annelies Laschitza and Günter Radczun, *Rosa Luxemburg: Ihr Wirken in der deutschen Arbeiterbewegung* (Berlin: Dietz, 1971).
64. Ehrhardt Neubert, *Geschichte der Opposition in der DDR 1949–1989* (Berlin: Ch. Links Verlag, 1997), p. 696.
65. Wolle, *Die heile Welt der Diktatur*, pp. 298–99.
66. According to Stefan Wolle, one ingenious ARD radio reporter from West Germany managed to hide his microphone under a hat and record up to 30 minutes of conversations while the demonstrators were being loaded into vans for transport to prison.
67. Wolle, *Die heile Welt der Diktatur*, p. 300. Except for a small portion of the GDR in the area of Dresden, everyone in East Germany could receive West German radio and television.
68. "Aufmarsch von über 200 000 Berliner an der Gräbern von Karl und Rosa," *Neues Deutschland*, 18 January 1988, p. 1.
69. BStU, MfS HA IX 10302, p. 11.
70. Christian Joppke, *East German Dissidents in the Revolution of 1989* (New York: New York University Press, 1995), p. 131.
71. Neubert, *Geschichte der Opposition*, p. 697.
72. BStU, MfS BdL/Dok. 008482, pp. 1–3. Memo from Minister of State Security Erich Mielke to department heads dated 25 January 1988.
73. "Ermittlungsverfahren wegen landesverräterischen Beziehungen," *Neues Deutschland*, 26 January 1988, p. 2. The news release for this article also appears in Mielke's internal memo to *Stasi* department heads on January 25. BStU, MfS BdL/Dok. 008482, pp. 1–3, here p. 3.
74. Günter Schabowski, *Der Absturz* (Berlin: Rohwolt, 1991), p. 166.
75. Heinz Kamnitzer, "Die Toten mahnen," *Neues Deutschland*, 26 January 1988, p. 2.
76. Klier, *Abreiskalender*, p. 297–301. See also: Neubert, *Geschichte der Opposition*, p. 698.
77. BStU, MfS BdL/Dok. 008484, pp. 1–4. Memo from Minister of State Security Erich Mielke to department heads dated 8 February 1988.

Conclusion

On 3 October 1989—a few days before East Germany's fortieth anniversary celebrations—SED General Secretary Erich Honecker hosted a gala event dedicated to the heroes of antifascism. Among the 400 invited guests were members of the wartime antifascist resistance movement, party members from the SED's founding generation, and all of the current top-ranking SED leadership and government officials.[1] Guests attending the gala event were treated to a lunch and a cultural program that included singing, musical, and dance performances that contained a mixture of classical and folk songs and ended with the singing of the *"Internationale."* Erich Honecker offered a toast to those assembled in which he stated: "The foundation for this new, socialist Germany had to be prepared. Many of us fought in the "Third Reich" for the collapse of the Hitler-dictatorship. It was people from every strata of our society, who as German patriots, humanists and internationalists saw it as their duty to participate in this way, despite differences of world view or religion. ... They fought with the Red Army, in the French Resistance, in countries such as Yugoslavia, Greece, and Demark. Everywhere, German antifascists, of whom many are present today, proved that there were two Germanys."[2]

Despite the mounting pressure against the state throughout the summer and into the fall, Honecker continued to cling to the antifascist myth of a better Germany, based on different historical traditions and memories than its neighbor to the West. The irony of the commemoration is, however, only seen when viewed within the broader context of that day's other historic events. It was also on this day, 3 October, that the East German government suspended all visa-free travel to Czechoslovakia, which had been the last country to which East German citizens could travel without first obtaining a visa. Meanwhile, eighteen East Germans burst into the U.S. Embassy in East Berlin demanding asylum. The East German military cordoned off Alexanderplatz in the heart of Berlin, a popular gathering place for East Berlin youth, ostensibly to drill in preparation for the marches planned for 7 October. Yet this show of force also sent a message

---

Notes for this chapter begin on page 234.

to potential protesters that the military was ready for them. Elsewhere in East Germany, others tried to board the moving trains that were transporting East German refugees from Prague to West Germany, but were forcefully turned away by armed guards.[3]

Notwithstanding these and other protest actions that were beginning to threaten the very existence of the regime, the SED leadership continued to cling to its rituals of commemoration. Two days later, on 5 October, Honecker and the other members of the *Politbüro* began their day with a ceremony at the Socialists' Cemetery in Berlin-Friedrichsfelde in conjunction with the state's fortieth anniversary. A ritual wreath-laying ceremony at the monument dedicated to the heroes of socialism and victims of fascism aimed to once again reinforce the GDR's founding narrative as an antifascist state. The aging leadership of the GDR continued to clutch on to its own belief that its myth of a "better Germany" would provide the wind necessary to navigate these rough waters. Party officials held similar wreath-laying ceremonies at the Monument for the Victims of Fascism and Militarism on Unter den Linden Street, at the memorial for Soviet soldiers in Berlin-Treptow, and at the monument for Polish soldiers and German victims of fascism in the People's Park in Berlin-Friedrichshain. Despite the reality of mounting open protest on the streets across East Germany, the SED leadership clung to a belief that it could shore up its legitimacy through remembering the victims of fascism one more time.[4]

When the official day of commemoration finally arrived on 7 October, the state celebrated its fortieth anniversary with all the pomp and circumstance it could muster. Yet, as former *Politbüro* member Gunter Schabowski recorded in his memoir: "The din of the anniversary in 1989 was a grand production, but did not produce the desired effect on people's thoughts and emotions. It was sucked away as if in a sound-absorbing chamber."[5] The people on the street were no longer willing to accept the state's commemorative rituals and demanded tangible changes. On the same day in the city of Schwante, forty-three members of the opposition founded the first democratic political party in the GDR, the SDP, around opposition leaders Markus Meckel, Martin Gutzeit, and Ibrahim Böhme. In the evening, a group of just over one thousand protesters took to the streets in the East Berlin neighborhood of Prenzlauer Berg and was met with stiff opposition from state security forces.

It was only a matter of time before the entire state apparatus began to fall. By 9 November, when East Germans freely crossed the border into West Berlin for the first time since the construction of the Berlin Wall in 1961, the regime was on its way out. The erosion of the state's control over its own official projection of memory was one part of this process, but it was the people on the street who—released from their fears of Soviet reprisal—ultimately brought down the government and marshaled the changes needed for democracy and ultimately unification with West Germany a year later.[6] As opposition leaders, cultural figures, and others resisted the SED's attempts to continue its efforts to impose a strict rendering of the past onto the state's memory landscape, others became more and more willing to join forces in opposition.

From the moment the German Communist Party reconstituted itself in 1945 to the SED's loss of power more than four decades later, East German socialists sought to instrumentalize memory and history to legitimize their rule. The SED's memory policies and vision of the "correct" German past was not, however, stagnant. Instead, its memory policies progressed through several developmental stages before solidifying in the late 1970s. Once firmly rooted in a very specific interpretation of antifascism and the history of German labor movement, the SED, professional historians, museum workers, sculptors and others began to expand the topical scope of East Germany's memory landscape, ultimately taxing the party's ability to steer and control its message. This loss of control created a public space for other non-dominant counter-memories to be voiced during the 1980s, a trend that emerged during the course of the Martin Luther celebrations in 1983 and culminated in the wresting away of control over Rosa Luxemburg's legacy in 1988.

Martin Sabrow and others have characterized the academic writing of East German historians as having progressed through three broad developmental stages. The first is the immediate postwar period, based on the desire to create a clean break from the past. The second period, which stretched from the early 1950s to the 1970s, is characterized by the regime's need to locate the GDR within a longer narrative of German history. This so-called dual-track of historical development linked the GDR with Germany's progressive working class, while simultaneously separating itself from the reactionary and fascist elements, which were attributed instead to the traditions of West Germany. Finally, the expansion of historical research into topics previously deemed off limits, such as Prussia, Luther, and other leaders of what usually had been referred to as the historical roots of West Germany were now also incorporated by East German historians into the GDR's state narrative.[7]

The first two of these stages correspond roughly to the first two developmental stages of East Germany's official state memory politics. However, there was an important, and somewhat different, third stage in the development of an official East German memory culture—a phase in which the regime sought to establish deeper emotional bonds between the citizens and the state. Sabrow's final stage also corresponds to a "fourth phase" of East German memory culture—a time when the regime sought to incorporate previously taboo topics of German history into East Germany's historical "narrative." But difficulties with this effort led to a fifth and final phase in East German memory politics, when elements of the regime sought either to reverse course or to return to their original pattern of emphasizing the SED's heritage—a rather hesitant, too-little, too-late effort that failed to garner even strong support within the party. Instead, these efforts provided small openings for sporadic dissidents to turn the party's own instruments of memory culture against it. The attempts by opposition groups in 1988 to reclaim the legacy of Rosa Luxemburg were perhaps the most dramatic and visible of such efforts.

Although aspects of East Germany's memory politics were closely related to the development of East German historical research, some elements were peculiar to cultivation and implementation of an official East German "memory culture" per se. The developmental stages of the state's memory politics diverged in part from the course of East German historical scholarship in part because of the different ways each attempt to link the past and the present. Whereas historians deal primarily with facts and interpretation, those working in the field of memory politics attempt to portray the past in a manner that can create an emotional link between specific interpretations of the past and contemporary society. In the case of East Germany, the SED's strategy led it to rely heavily on tailoring historical narratives through popularizing a strict canon of iconic figures and events.

Monuments, museums, and commemoration festivals were the primary elements of the SED's memory-work for propagating these official interpretations of the past. Monuments served to saturate public spaces with icons of remembrance that related directly to the history of communism in the GDR. Museums served to narrate the state's interpretation of the past in a manner that would endow the GDR with a strong aura of continuity and legitimacy. Commemorations provided the opportunity for rituals to reinforce specific memories of historical figures and events. Together, the SED intended this constellation of memory-work to provide a solid legitimizing foundation for both the GDR and its own claim to govern. While these efforts may have provided some degree of non-materialist legitimation for the regime among some segments of society, the efforts and resources committed to this task ultimately failed to mask the contradictions between the regime's rhetoric and the realities of its own un-democratic policies of suppression.

During the initial stage in the development of a uniquely East German memory culture, the SED sought to salvage those elements of the immediate past that would help to legitimize its efforts to wield influence over the future of the German state. Such early efforts included the reconstruction of the Socialists' Cemetery in Friedrichsfelde that had been destroyed by the Nazis and the resumption of the traditional working class parades commemorating the lives of Rosa Luxemburg and Karl Liebknecht. The first museum exhibit to deal with the Nazi period, "The Other Germany," reinforced the SED's new vision of the past by presenting a history of antifascist resistance that singled out the communists and socialists as the only true defenders of the Germans against the Nazis. Additionally, the commemoration activities celebrating the 100th anniversary of the 1848 revolution attempted to develop a sense of historical continuity between the ideals of the revolutionaries and the politics of the SED. Together, these aspects formed the basis for the SED's claims to be working toward a morally better German state.

Building upon its earlier initiatives within the realm of memory politics, the second stage in the development of East Germany's official memory culture centered on the SED's attempt to graft memories of the party and the working class onto the new East German state. This process necessitated the creation of state heroes and the commemoration of historical events that could root the GDR in both the traditions of the KPD/SED and the broader history of the German working class. Buchenwald concentration camp provided the state with an ideal location to fuse together these memories. Like Ravensbrück and Sachsenhausen, Buchenwald primarily housed communist, socialist, and other political prisoners. By elevating the national importance of these victims and survivors over all others, the regime established a founding myth for the state that was rooted in an antifascist struggle and communist victimhood. Building upon this interpretation, the Museum for German History attempted to locate the place of the GDR within the larger context of Germany's historical development and the history of German social development. The museum developed an historical narrative based on a Marxist interpretation of the past that emphasized the experience of the German working class. This narrative allowed the state to position itself as the culmination of hundreds of years of social evolution and political revolution. The last element in this second stage of state memory projects involved the attempted construction of massive monuments to heroes of the German working class. The state pursued plans for building monuments dedicated to Marx and Engels as well as a separate monument dedicated to Ernst Thälmann. The state failed to complete either of these two memorial projects due to competing visions of how these figures should be portrayed as well as practical financial constraints during the postwar period of reconstruction. This failure thwarted the state's ability to capitalize early and dominate the public sphere with its new pantheon of heroes. Ultimately, it would need to wait until the 1980s to finally see each of these project completed.

With its official narrative now established, the state turned its attention during the third phase of memory politics toward cultivating new emotional bonds through expanding its memory landscape outside of Berlin and intensifying its pedagogical work related to museums and historical sites. In some respects, these issues differed from the work of East Germany's academic historians, who continued to highlight the history of the German working class throughout the 1960s and into the 1970s. Although the city of Berlin was the focal point of East German political power, the SED realized that it needed its state narrative also to be anchored in the local histories of towns throughout its territory. One mechanism that the state employed was the restoration and modernization of the local *Heimat*museums that were scattered throughout the GDR. Here, the East German narrative found in the Museum for German History was adapted to take into account the history of the local working class. "National" events were presented as an integral part of a city or region's historical development and thus connected the outlying municipalities to the East Germany's broader state narrative. In addition to the geographic extension of the state narrative, the state sought to bolster its ability to control how young members of society experienced visits to its museums and historical sites. The approach taken by the state was to work more closely with teachers and to link the past more concretely to current events. The inability of the state's memory-workers to succeed with these stepped up efforts is evident by the fact that these educators repeatedly felt the need to reassess and retool their pedagogical offerings in an on-going effort to connect with the East German youth.

East Germany's altered relationship vis-à-vis West Germany due to Brandt's policy of de facto recognition of "two states, one nation" during the 1970s allowed the SED to feel more confident. At the same time, Brandt's policies brought new challenges for the East German state to differentiate itself and respond to the notion that a common German identity still existed. This prompted the East German state to enter into a new stage in its memory politics that sought to cultivate the notion of a separate East German nation and thus link historic figures with roots within its own borders to the historical lineage that led to the "triumph" of the SED. The party's new goal, having won some recognition of its borders and its role as an actor in international affairs, was to secure ultimate recognition of its full sovereignty, especially following the Helsinki Final Act of 1975. The state's memory politics was once again aligned with the trends of East German academic historians. The state now celebrated historic figures such as Frederick the Great, Bismarck, and Luther who had previously been excluded from such praise. However, if East Germany was now going to lay claim to all of German history that had roots on its territory, it needed to find a way to incorporate such figures alongside the antifascists and workers it had always favored. With this expansion in the topical breadth of East Germany's memory-work came the first signs that the state was losing its ability to control how these figures were commemorated in public venues. The party faithful questioned why "reactionary" figures like Frederick the Great could return to the streets of Berlin. The Evangelical Church attempted to counter the state's attempt to appropriate the figure of Luther with its own celebrations and Werner Tübke's panorama painting offered an interpretation of the Reformation and the Peasants' War that departed from earlier state-sanctioned representations.

The final stage in the development, erosion, and ultimate collapse of the state's memory policies in the GDR, one which did not have a true comparison within the area of East German academic scholarship, came during the 1980s as the state attempted to reassert earlier forms of public remembrance. Having failed to construct monuments in honor of Marx, Engels, and Thälmann, the GDR set out once again to rectify this situation. The Marx-Engels-Forum became a thorn in the side of the SED leadership, which ultimately had to accept a statue that was not as monumental as Honecker and others had hoped. In an effort to avoid a similar situation with the Thälmann project, Honecker bypassed the East German artistic community entirely by awarding the commission to a Soviet sculptor. The SED's inability to find an East German sculptor willing to produce the type of monument desired by the SED leadership highlights the deepening separation between East Germany's cultural elite and the regime. Ultimately, this rupture became a chasm when dissidents like Bärbel Bohley, Freya Klier, and Stefan Krawczyk used the legacy of Rosa Luxemburg to strike at the heart of the SED's legitimizing memory culture. By wresting away control over Luxemburg's memory and turning her legacy against the state, the dissidents helped exposed the inconsistencies between the stated traditions of the GDR and its political reality. The harsh crackdown by the state against those involved in the protest action highlighted just how vulnerable the state was to this tactic and solidified the erosion process of the state's culture of memory.

The recognition by these opposition leaders of the hollowness of the state's memory culture combined with the fresh winds of reform coming from the East produced a moment of spiritual liberation. Many now saw the antifascist memory culture of the GDR, based on the moral concept of creating and sustaining an "other" and "better" Germany, as being just as confining and repressive as fascism itself. The moral duty to antifascism that set the parameters for acceptable public commemorations allowed the state to be just as controlling and one-sided as the image of fascism it was officially opposing. The elevation of this counter-memory of experience during the Nazi period to the level of a state narrative for the GDR allowed this "proud antifascist legacy" to "legitimize a new kind of unfreedom."[8] Yet, by reclaiming this antifascist legacy, the democratic opposition was able to break out of the moral paradigm that had governed public discourse about the past and insert its own vision of a "better" or "other" Germany instead.

These five stages represent not only how the SED approached memory-work between 1945 and 1990, but also how it evolved over time. With each new challenge to its claim to power—either from within or without—the party sought to adapt its memory policies as part of a response effort. The SED hoped that by controlling the public representations of the past, what Maurice Halbwachs termed the "frameworks of memory," it could influence how collective memories were constructed. The party hoped that it could call upon these memories to legitimize its rule and rationalize its hold on power. Real difficulties emerged, however, when it attempted to transfer the memories and experiences of the wartime generation to the youth who came of age in the postwar era. The competing historical claims of West Germany proved to be another decisive challenge that prompted the GDR to move beyond the relatively safer ground of antifascism and compete with the Federal Republic for ownership over many other aspects of its shared historical legacy. With each new expansion of acceptable historical figures and events, those who oversaw the party's memory-work found it increasingly difficult to dictate the public portrayal of the past. The party leadership hoped it could regain some control by returning to the theme of antifascism and the history of the working class by constructing monuments in Berlin to Marx, Engels, and Thälmann. Even here, it became increasingly clear to the leadership that it was losing its ability to sufficiently influence the East German artistic community, which had been an important partner in establishing the cultural legitimacy of the state. Finally, when dissidents attacked regime's stance on the legacy of Rosa Luxemburg they struck at the heart of the SED's self-legitimating narrative and were able to cause a great deal of damage to the stability of the dictatorship.

The process of understanding and living with the memories of life in East Germany remains an on-going process. The SED is no longer present to impose its vision of the past on the memory landscape and new voices are being heard, sometimes for the first time in public. This process of coming to terms with East Germany's legacy may take several generations before we see the emergence of a common German national identity that no longer contains sub-sets for *Wessis* (former West Germans) and *Ossis* (former East Germans).[9] As the post-1990 debates discussed below demonstrate, the legacy of the SED's memory-work has shaped how Germans have attempted to deal with some of these lingering questions since reunification. The process of merging the memory cultures of West and East Germany is already well underway, but it will remain a task for future generations as well.

Afterword: Retailoring Truth

Memories of the GDR remain an active component in German political and cultural life. The debate that surrounded the 1990 publication of Christa Wolf's novella *What Remains?* symbolizes the difficulty Germany faces in integrating the experiences of East Germans within the broader narrative of the German nation.[10] Dennis Tate has argued that cultural memory of the GDR has been dominated by two main strains—one that focused on remembering the GDR as a type of *"Stasiland"* and another that highlighted positive aspects of everyday life—*"Ostalgie."*[11] While the *Stasiland* label seems to have been more of a fascination by West German and international scholars, *Ostalgie* can be seen as both an attempt by East Germans to reclaim memories of their own experience or as a construction driven by consumerism and popular culture. One need only look at the market success of old East German brands, such as *Spreewald Gurken, Rotkäppchen Sekt,* or *Mocca Fix Gold* following their prominent role in the successful film *Good Bye, Lenin!*[12] The film is full of retailored truths about life in the GDR and even the historical events that led to German unification. One scene in particular, that of the statue of Lenin flying through the air, is closer to reflecting elements of a truly East German memory culture than references to the consumer goods. In reality, however, the statue of Lenin did not fly through the air, but was chopped up into 129 smaller pieces and buried on the outskirts of Berlin. Although Berlin's former Cultural Senator Thomas Flierl (PDS) raised the idea of giving Lenin a new home somewhere in Berlin, the idea never found broad support.[13]

In theory, all of the memorials in the former East became part of the GDR's historical legacy and continued to play a significant role in public memory debates following the fall of the Berlin Wall. In his qualitative and quantitative study of historical consciousness during the years 1989 and 1990, Feliz Lutz concluded that although the SED's historical understanding diverged from the historical consciousness of its citizens, the East German state had left a lasting impression on the minds of those who lived in the GDR. Above all, Lutz found that these lasting effects could be seen in ideologically tinted patterns of historical interpretation and understanding.[14] This politicized understanding of the past was seen as a significant hurdle for politicians and cultural institutions that desired to successfully unify East and West German societies. Some leading cultural figures like Christoph Stölzl, the former director of the German Historical Museum (DHM), held very strong opinions regarding what should happen with the East German memory projects that remained. In 1991, Stölzl said that just as the Allied forces forbade the display of Nazi symbols in 1945, and both governments in East and West Germany did the same, so too should Germany now have the right to remove monuments that were dedicated to honoring people like Lenin—likening it to preserving a statue to Göring.[15]

Many of the monuments, museums and commemoration events covered in this work became the subject of great scrutiny following the collapse of the SED regime. The Panorama Monument in Bad Frankenhausen was probably among the few that saw very little change since 1990. The main reason for this is probably that Werner Tübke had been so successful in negotiating artistic autonomy that he was able to create a piece of art that could be separated from other overtly propagandistic pieces of state-sponsored art.[16] The only real change made by the museum after unification was the removal of the exhibit in the foyer that depicted the Marxist interpretation of the Peasants' War meant to condition visitors before they were brought into the panorama. As a replacement, the museum has hosted several temporary exhibits, ranging from artwork from the period of the Reformation to a celebratory exhibition of Tübke's other work.[17] The museum and its panorama proved to be a viable tourist attraction in reunified Germany. In 1997, the panorama museum welcomed its one-millionth guest and continued to welcome over 100,000 visitors each year.[18] In 2004, the year of Werner Tübke's death, the museum reached a high point of just over 115,000 visitors.[19]

The process of retailoring truth at the Buchenwald concentration camp was much more controversial than the cosmetic changes made in the Panorama Museum. Following unification, a special commission of historians assessed the Buchenwald site and recommended how best to recast the memorial in a way that better suited the altered political situation. The greatest hurdle for the retailoring of Buchenwald was its dual history as a camp used by both the Nazis and the Soviets. The most controversial aspect was whether to include those who were interned there by the Soviets and whether this would detract from honoring the memory of those who suffered under Nazi rule. The commission recommended handling each history of the camp separately in order to give each one its own space.[20]

In 1995 the Buchenwald museum opened a new permanent exhibit, one that expanded the number of victim groups honored (no longer only or primarily the communists) and included sections that discussed the political prisoners, the Jewish, Roma, and Sinti prisoners, as well as the relationship between the camp and the city of Weimar. Especially controversial was the inclusion of "Red Kappos" (the communist collaborators) and marked a substantial departure from the "official" interpretation during the GDR. Of the 56,000 victims of fascism who perished at Buchenwald, the museum now states that only seventy-six were actually communists.[21] Instead of attacking the role of the underground communist organization at the camp, the exhibit attempts to relativize the importance of the communists by asserting that there was a wide range of acts of resistance found at Buchenwald.

In 1997, Buchenwald opened its second major exhibit honoring the victims of the Soviet internment camp, *Speziallager Nr. 2*. Here, some 28,500 inmates were held by the Soviets following the German capitulation between 1945 and 1950. Of those, some 7,000 are estimated to have perished at the camp from hunger and exhaustion. More controversial than the retailoring of the other permanent exhibit, this exhibit prompted attacks from both the Left and the Right aimed at the director of the museum Volkhard Knigge.[22] The Left was concerned that the state was financing a memorial for collaborators and Nazi criminals who had justly been apprehended by the Soviet forces following the end of the war. From the Right, Knigge was attacked (and accused of *Volksverhetzung* [sedition]) because he would not keep the Nazi past of individual prisoners secret. For quite some time during the late 1990s, Knigge continued to be a primary target for right-wing extremists.[23]

The final element of retailoring Buchenwald as a site of memory fit for unified Germany concerned the memorial complex dedicated to the victims of fascism, which included stone stelae depicting the history of the camp, gravesites, columns dedicated to the nations represented in the camp population, and finally the group sculpture of the liberation by Fritz Cremer and the memorial tower that sat atop the Ettersberg mountain. Instead of altering or demolishing this particular monument, the museum's leadership decided to erect new monuments to honor the other victims in the camp and to construct a special exhibit that examined the instrumentalization of the camp as a place of memory by the GDR. In 1993, a monument was built to honor the Jewish victims. Another monument was dedicated in 1995 to honor the Roma and Sinti victims (the first such monument on German soil to do so). Another monument was created in 1995 to commemorate all of the victims of the concentration camp as well. Finally, in October 1999, the memorial site opened its third permanent exhibit, which examines the creation and function of the Buchenwald national memorial site by the GDR. This exhibit, like the monument for the Sinti and Roma, was the first of its kind in Germany—a museum dedicated to the intrumentalization of the past by the East German regime. Together these new exhibits and the multiple monuments reflect the difficulties of the dual (or triple) historical burden that the Buchenwald site must portray within the context of unified Germany. The retailoring process took some time and was not without controversy, yet Buchenwald remains an important site of memory for the Federal Republic and continues to draw a significant number of visitors each year—more than 400,000 annually (and even an official visit by U.S. President Barack Obama in 2009).

Similar to the need to strip the Buchenwald site of its ideological message, the MfDG also underwent a comprehensive retailoring after unification and was subsumed into the already planned DHM. Originally announced by Chancellor Helmut Kohl in his government declaration in 1985, the DHM was intended to serve as an answer to the MfDG in East Berlin. Officially presented to the public in 1987 as a gift from West Germany to the people of West Berlin, the founding of the museum was part of the 750th commemoration festivities honoring the city of Berlin. Plans to erect a new museum near the Reichstag in Berlin were scrapped once it was clear that the two Germanys were going to unite. Instead of constructing a new building, the DHM simply took over the MfDG on the Day of German Unification—3 October 1990.[24] The decision to close the MfDG found little resistance, except from those who worked at the museum themselves (they suffered the same phenomenon known as *Abwicklung* as many other East German academics during the immediate period following unification).[25]

Yet, the DHM had its fair share of controversies to weather before opening its doors. The most difficult task for the museum leadership, headed by Christoph Stölzl, was to find a new identity for the museum, since it was no longer serving as a foil to the East German museum. Instead, Stölzl and his team decided to concentrate on what he termed the fortunate and unfortunate interdependencies of German and European history.[26] Early on Stölzl decided that a complete renovation and expansion of the building was necessary in order to ensure that the DHM provided a clear break from the MfDG. During the early years of the DHM, the museum concentrated on putting together a series of temporary exhibits that ranged in topic from the early GDR to the West German Economic Miracle and the 1848 revolution to the consequences of the student revolts of the 1960s. Stölzl convinced Chancellor Kohl to bypass federal regulations governing contracting prestige projects and invited the world-renowned architect I.M. Pei to build a new extension. When the new wing opened in 2003 it hosted a special exhibit on the "Idea of Europe" that highlighted the pre-history of European integration and foreshadowed one of the main themes that would be part of the new permanent exhibit scheduled to open three years later. Stölzl and his successor Hans Ottomeyer wanted to imbed the history of Germany in the history of Europe. Critics, who once thought the DHM was too national, now wondered if the museum was not national enough.[27]

The new permanent exhibit opened to the public in June 2006 with a ceremony attended by both Chancellor Angela Merkel and former Chancellor Helmut Kohl. The new director, Hans Ottomeyer, remarked at the opening that the exhibit portrayed German history with all its contradictory developments—both the good and the evil. Quoting Lessing, he said: "History should not burden our minds, but enlighten our understanding."[28] Highlights from the permanent exhibit demonstrate the Janus-head of history that the DHM has tried to portray—Martin Luther's bible from 1535, the globe from Hitler's office with a bullet hole in place of Berlin (shot by a Soviet soldier), a portrait of Frederick the Great by Albrecht Dürer, the Constitution written by the 1848 Paulskirche Parliament, the Communist Manifesto, and the personal desks of both Adolf Hitler and Erich Honecker.[29] By portraying German history and the history of the Germans within a broader European context, the curators bypassed many more controversial topics that plagued other sites of memory during this period of transition.

In many respects, dealing with the legacy of East Germany's monuments proved to be more difficult than with the museums and historic sites discussed above—especially in the new capital city of Berlin. The removal of the Lenin monument in 1991 sparked a great deal of debate in Berlin and elsewhere in the former East over how society should decide which sites of memory constructed in the GDR should be preserved and which should be removed. Just three days after the Lenin statue was trucked off to its resting place, the city established a new Commission for Dealing with Political Monuments of the Postwar Period in Former East-Berlin. The commission, comprised of six Berliners (two from the West and four from the East), was charged with documenting and evaluating the monuments in Eastern Berlin constructed between 1945 and 1990. Its initial report, presented in 1993, called for a rather conservative approach toward preserving the East German past. With only a few exceptions, the commission asked that most of the monuments be preserved, albeit with minor alterations or additional signage.[30]

The criteria used by the commission reflect the delicate balancing act that politicians and scholars had to (and still have to) follow. Those monuments that were slated for removal followed the logic that any monument, whose primary purpose was to strengthen the political legitimacy of a dictatorial regime, had lost its *raison d'être* and thus should be torn down. Yet, many less controversial monuments were saved by the rationale that neighborhoods in the eastern portion of Berlin had the same right to preserve their past, as did the neighborhoods in the West.[31] In general, the commission was less aggressive when monuments were well integrated into green areas and parks than those that were placed in more urban settings. Other monuments were less successful in being preserved—the monument in honor of the border police, the relief on the *Marstall* commemorating the November Revolution, and the *Spartakus* monument were all slated for removal.

Another monument that made the commission's list for removal was the Thälmann monument in the Prenzlauer Berg neighborhood. The rationale for the removal of this particular monument was both political and aesthetic. Unlike other monuments to Thälmann throughout the former GDR, the Thälmann monument in Berlin (by the Soviet sculptor Lev Kerbel) was a colossal depiction of Thälmann's bust holding a raised fist and a waving flag with the hammer and sickle behind him. The Thälmann monument did not share any stylistic common ground with any other monument created in the GDR other than possibly the Soviet memorial in Berlin-Treptow or Kerbel's other major sculpture in East Germany—the Karl Marx head in Chemnitz. Thus, the Berlin commission objected to the monument primarily on aesthetic grounds that it was simply too large and did not belong in an urban setting.[32] Moreover, the commission argued that the Thälmann monument portrayed a "heroizing, uncritical depiction of his person in the form of a monumental sculpture that is not in tune with his real historical importance."[33] The commission balanced such criticism with the observation that the removal of this particular monument of Thälmann should not prevent a different one from finding a home elsewhere in the city in the future.[34]

News of the Thälmann monument's removal provoked a great deal of outrage by citizens who lived in the area surrounding the monument and by the Berlin chapter of the PDS party (the successor party to the communist SED, now called *die Linke*). The residents of the Ernst-Thälmann-Park felt that they were losing a part of their own personal history. The PDS charged that the recommendation to remove the monument was politically motivated. Prenzlauer Berg District Mayor Manfred Dennert (SPD) responded, however, that the "monstrosity beautifies neither the district nor Thälmann."[35] The district council continued to move forward with planning on how best to use the space that would be vacated by the removal of the monument, but a lack of funds in the mid-1990s prevented its removal. A Bavarian millionaire, Josef Kurz, made an offer to pay for the removal if he could have it for his personal collection of monuments (an *Asylpark* or asylum park for monuments from the former GDR), but he died before this could be arranged. The DHM also showed some interest, but ultimately decided not to pursue the idea any further.[36]

The lack of movement to remove the monument prompted some local politicians, such as Karl Hennig of the CDU-Prenzlauer Berg, to attempt to change the name of the Ernst-Thälmann-Park that surrounds the monument to *Kulturpark* saying: "We are not concerned with Thälmann the person, but the park and the monument represent an alienated culture."[37] Local residents turned out in strength at the district council meeting when the CDU made the proposal to voice their opposition. Several admitted that it was difficult to keep the park and the monument clean from graffiti and vandalism, but that the residents around the park had always played a role in keeping it clean. Others went so far as to say that changing the name to *Kulturpark* would only send a signal of vindication to the extreme Right. Shortly a year after the initial suggestion for the name change, the district council dropped the idea after relegating it to a subcommittee and polling local residents.

Beyond these public attempts to remove the monument and change the name of the park, the most prominent attacks against the monument came in the form of vandalism. The monument has been the site of a great deal of graffiti—most of it harmless in nature, but also including some Nazi symbols and slogans. In May 2000, a group of local residents decided to form the Action Alliance Thälmann Monument. Its goal was to keep Thälmann "shiny" and clean. Initially, the group of some twenty activists raised approximately 6,500 DM, which was then matched by the local

FIGURE 6.1. Lev Kerbel's sculpture of Ernst Thälmann covered in graffiti in November 2011. Photographed by the author.

Berlin government, to pay for a professional cleaning of the monument. The volunteers worked for a week straight alongside the professionals to remove the coats of graffiti and apply a protective layer so that future attempts at vandalism could be more easily removed. By the end of the week, the monument looked like new. Unfortunately, the graffiti was back within just two days.[38] Members of the Action Alliance were not, however, deterred in their endeavor. The group continued to organize volunteer efforts to maintain the monument and expanded its membership. It also grew beyond its original restoration work and organized annual rallies at the foot of the monument to demonstrate a continued connection between Ernst Thälmann and the people of Berlin.

The number of people who attend such rallies, however, has been quite low—in the hundreds not the thousands or even tens of thousands that could have been seen at similar rallies during GDR times. Nonetheless, by 2003 it seemed that the window of opportunity for the removal of the monument had been shut for good. Berlin's Cultural Senator Thomas Flierl (PDS) stated that the "time of the storming of the monuments is over. We need these witnesses of history in order to demonstrate what sort of distance we have to that time for which it stands." Even members of the SPD and CDU had by this time conceded defeat, citing that even if they wanted to still remove the monument it would now cost millions to do so and that there were other pressing priorities.

That window of opportunity may not have been as closed as it seemed. In April 2012 CDU politician and citizens' rights activist Angelika Barbe reopened the debate when she stated: "a Thälmann monument is the false symbol for the remembrance of communism and its crimes. I wish for the word freedom to be built like a skyscraper on this site."[39] Although the Berlin-Pankow CDU party spokesman, Johannes Kraft, added that despite adding better lighting and increasing the police presence in the area, the monument continued to be the target of graffiti and vandalism. Kraft said that he would welcome a discussion about the monument's future. The local SPD and Green politicians voiced their mixed support—not entirely embracing the idea of removing the monument, but not opposing the idea outright.[40] Only the Left Party issued a press statement demonstrating its unequivocal opposition to Barbe's suggestion.[41] Despite the responses that Barbe's statement evoked among the professional politicians, it seems not to have had the same effect on everyday Berliners. Instead, the general desire to move on is summed up by a letter to the editor printed in the *Berliner Kurier* from an author who self-identified himself as no fan of the SED's cult of personality: "I am getting sick of the constant discussion about tearing down GDR era monuments in the eastern part of the city. ... You are going about it just like the GDR leadership. Monuments, like the statue of "Old Fritz" on Unter den Linden, disappeared under the cover of night. Or they blew up palaces and churches just because they didn't fit into the SED leadership's worldview. Should the same thing now happen to the GDR-era monuments?"⁴²

While the debates like this one about the future of the Thälmann monument illustrate a persistent desire by some to revisit the possibility of replacing the GDR-built memory landscape with something new, these debates also are starting to demonstrate a more sophisticated level of remembrance. While earlier debates focused around a desire to remove power symbols of the SED, more recent debates indicate a longer perspective of memory—reflecting a desire to still alter the memory landscape, but not to erase it entirely. Moreover, we see in this particular example a

FIGURE 6.2. Ludwig Engelhardt's sculpture of Karl Marx and Friedrich Engels in Berlin, 22 July 1991. The graffiti along the bottom of the statue reads: "We are not guilty" with the word "not" covered over. BArch B 145 Bild-F088849-0006 / Joachim F. Thurn.

citizens group that formed in defense of not only the memory represented by the monument, but also their own memories of life in the GDR and a desire to preserve some of the built environment that reflects those memories.

Although the story of the Marx-Engels monument shares some commonalities with that of the Thälmann monument, the post-1990 debates have followed a different trajectory. Based on the recommendations of the 1993 Berlin memorials commission, the statue of Marx and Engels on the Marx-Engels-Forum in Berlin-Mitte was spared removal—it was judged to be appropriate in its portrayal of two German historical figures whose societal impact was larger than that which was celebrated by the GDR in its propaganda. Since its unveiling, the monument, commonly referred to by Berliners as "*Sacco und Jacketti*" or "*Nahverkehrsdenkmal*" (because one person is always standing), has been a popular tourist stop.[43] It was famously painted with the graffiti stating, "*Wir sind unschuldig*" ("We are not guilty") and people have hung signs on Marx that say "*Das nächste Mal machen wir's besser!*" ("Next time we'll do it better").[44] The photographs by Sibylle Bergemann, who documented Engelhardt's work between 1975 and 1986, have been displayed at several highly successful post-1990 exhibitions. Yet the monument has never been able to shake off its opponents and instead provoked a fair amount of debate regarding its future since 1990. On the one side are those who advocated a restoration of "historic" Berlin, which would incorporate the park into a new Humboldt-Forum, where the Marx-Engels statue may (or may not) remain a part of the larger concept. Others (typically on the political Left) have advocated retaining the Marx-Engels monument and park as an integrated work of art (*Gesamtkunstwerk*) and as a three-dimensional document of the recent German past. Despite the occasional burst of public debate about its future, however, no major changes were made for the first twenty years following unification.

In 2010, however, the Berlin Senate decided to relocate the monument away from of its original place at the center of the Marx-Engels-Forum and place it some eighty meters away on the northwest corner of the park. The statue was not only moved, but also turned around—facing west. Friedrich Nostitz (the technical-artistic director of the original Engelhardt group and designer of the accompanying stelae) and the architect Peter Flierl consulted on the new positioning of the statue and stelae. Writing in the *Berliner Zeitung*, Nostitz commented that he was pleased that Marx and Engels now looked west toward Manchester instead of Eastern Europe and thought that the late Ludwig Engelhardt would approve of such a change.[45]

The move was not done for political or aesthetic reasons as earlier public debates may have suggested, but out of pure practicality. The city had decided to build the U5 subway line and the ideal place for mounting the necessary underground tunneling was through the center of the park—utilizing the Spree Canal as a low-impact way to supply the construction project with all the necessary materials. The Berlin transportation authority (BVG) promised the Berlin Senate that it would return the Marx-Engels-Forum to its original state once construction was completed in 2018.[46] What will ultimately happen to the Forum once construction is complete has not yet been completely decided. Berlin's governing mayor Klaus Wowereit stated at the time that he hoped Berlin could use this opportunity to have a public debate about the future of the Marx-Engels statue within the context of the larger vision of what should be done with the historical government district.[47]

The controversy over Marx and Engels once again came to a head in February 2012, when the Federal Minister of Construction, Peter Ramsauer (CSU) called for the complete removal of the Marx-Engels monument from central Berlin and instead proposed that it be deposited in the Socialists Cemetery in Berlin-Friedrichsfelde, stating, *"Das ist ja so eine Art sozialistisches Reste-Zentrum"* ("That is already a kind of Socialist dump").[48] This brought about a sharp reaction from leaders of the SPD, the Greens, and the Left party—all of whom saw the minister's remarks as an attempt to erase a part of Berlin (and GDR) history. Berlin Senator Michael Müller (SPD) responded, "The suggestion that the Marx-Engels monument be transported to Friedrichsfelde is just as astonishing as it is forgetful of history (*geschichtsvergessen*): Berlin has a checkered history and is a tolerant metropolis—the palace and the monument can coexist here."[49] Berlin's cultural secretary, André Schmitz, added that the idea of removing the monument to Friedrichsfelde to make some sort of "socialist zoo" (*sozialistische Streichelzoo*) was not the correct answer to the question of what to do with Marx and Engels.[50]

The professional politicians were not alone in their quick response to Ramsauer's suggestion. The public quickly flooded the Facebook page of the local Berlin television news show *Abendschau* following their coverage of the minister's remarks. Although the comments ranged from accusations that a Bavarian had no right making suggestions about what could or could not be done in the city of Berlin to ideological attacks against Ramsauer's conservative politics, others were quite insightful. One respondent noted:

> The monument belongs on the palace square! Many, if not most, visitors to Berlin complain that they can hardly make out the path of the Wall. The Wannsee Villa, the Stasi Headquarters, [and] the Wannsee train station all belong to Berlin, not just the pleasant places. Let's not fake or destroy history like the Egyptians, who allowed the images of their ancestors to be chiseled away, the Spanish, who eradicated a people in South America, the Taliban, who blew

up sculptures, etc. ... the list is endless! Even when we destroy, the memory remains! Regardless if the past is good or destructive. And, how should we explain history to our children, if we are simultaneously (and unsuccessfully) trying to erase it?[51]

Similarly, in letters to the editor, Berliners joined in the general debate. The *Tagesspiegel* printed a reader letter that made the following suggestion: "The monument of Marx and Engels should be positioned along the Spree Canal with a view to the West and a cardboard sign should say 'Great, at least they rebuilt the palace.'"[52] Another Berliner wrote to the *Berliner Zeitung* stating, "The monument of Marx and Engels must remain in its place in Berlin-Mitte. It is a part of the East German cultural heritage (*Kulturgut*). I am disgusted how insensible Mr. Raumsauer treats history."[53] The Berlin tabloid newspaper *B.Z.* ran a section in its "Dafür & dagegen" ("For and Against") section, printing arguments from both sides of the debate: "The history of the divided city is fortunately history. Our past cannot be forgotten. Placing the monument on the outskirts of town would be the beginning of forgetting." Representing the opposing view, the *B.Z.* wrote: "Today in the capital there is already a Karl-Marx-Allee in the east and a Karl-Marx-Strasse in the west. That is sufficient to honor the philosopher Marx."[54]

Minister Ramsauer's idea, however, also found some support—albeit a bit more tempered than his original remarks. The director of the Stasi Memorial Hohenschönhausen, Hubertus Knabe, agreed that the time was rife for the monument to be moved, "I can only agree with Mr. Ramsauer. When one knows, how many people in the name of Marx and Engels were killed, then such monuments are automatically forbidden."[55] Former conservative Berlin Mayor Eberhardt Diepgen (CDU) wrote an extended opinion-editorial in the *Tagesspiegel* newspaper in which he argued for a complete rethinking of the historic section of Berlin. He argued that since the primary purpose of the monument constellation (the statue placed at the center of the square along with the accompanying stelae and reliefs) was to symbolize the inevitable and unstoppable triumph of socialism, its placement at the center of Berlin demonstrates a claim to power that is no longer valid in today's pluralistic and democratic society. Diepgen concluded: "Thus it is not the figures, but the desired dominance of the ensemble that is a relic from a vanquished epoch and the wrong symbol for the capital."[56]

The fate of Marx and Engels remains up in the air. The monument's future has been folded into the wider discussion regarding plans for the Humboldt-Forum and other large-scale building projects in the historic government district. However, the debate around whether to keep Marx and Engels as a central monument group in the capital highlights how the remnants of East Germany's memory projects remain a lively part of contemporary political discussions. While no one is advocating a return to the communist system that created such sites of memory, many remain concerned with how its legacy is preserved.

These retailored memories of the post-unification era are only part of a larger story about memory politics after the fall of the Berlin Wall. The federal state, local governments, and private foundations have all contributed to a growing number of new museums and memorials dedicated to memory-work projects neglected or suppressed during the GDR period. The new memorial and museum dedicated to the history of the Berlin Wall at Bernauer Strasse or the *Tränenpalast* border crossing station next to the Friedrichstrasse train station. The DDR Museum in Berlin claims to offer visitors a "hands-on" view of everyday life in the GDR, while the Memorial at Berlin-Hohenschönhausen utilizes the Stasi's main prison to offer a critical look at the repressive nature of East German regime.[57]

Outside of Berlin, dozens of other new museums and monuments have been built that address additional aspects of life in the GDR. In Marienborn, on the border between Saxon-Anhalt and Lower Saxony, the Memorial for Divided Germany uses the former border station as a springboard to explore the history of divided Germany as well as life in the border region. New museums dedicated to everyday life in the GDR have opened in Eisenhüttenstadt (*Dokumentationszentrum Alltagskultur der DDR*) and Lutherstadt Wittenberg (*Haus der Geschichte*).[58] While the museum in Eisenhüttenstadt focuses on collecting objects of everyday life, the museum in Lutherstadt Wittenberg houses its collection *in situ* inside a converted apartment building with different apartments depicting home life during different decades. Dozens more have opened in smaller cities and towns such as the DDR-Museums in Burg im Spreewald, Malchow, Pirna, and Tutow or the *Zeitreise* (Time Travel) in Radebeul to name just a few.[59] The *Zeitgeschichtliches Forum* in Leipzig, like the *Tränenpalast* in Berlin, was a project of Bonn's *Haus der Geschichte*. This federally funded museum focuses on the dual-track story of repression and opposition in the GDR with rotating temporary exhibits that are often co-produced with the Bonn institution and not always solely focused on East German history. Finally, we also find evidence where rebuilding has been an act of memory alteration or re-creation. In Dresden, for example, the bombed out ruins of the Frauenkirche, which the GDR had purposely left as ruble and a memorial to the Dresden bombings, the so-called Anglo-American Terror Attacks, reopened in 2005 after an extensive fundraising campaign by a local citizens action group and a network of international partners.

Alterations to the memory landscape in the former GDR is not settled. Alterations, additions, and demolitions are surely still to be expected. New monuments, like the Monuments for Freedom and Unity planned for Berlin and Leipzig, will continue to find both proponents and opponents as popular memories of the GDR continue to be formed and contested in the public sphere. At the same time, we might also see a loosening up of how these sites of memory are treated. In June 2007, a one-off advertising campaign dressed the figures of Marx and Engels in furry bunny costumes. Passersby were not "shocked" or "disturbed" by such actions—instead they mainly stopped and posed for pictures with the two.[60] Possibly, this sort of humorous use of such sites of memories indicates a more sophisticated and distanced approach toward these sites of memory than what we saw in the period immediately following unification in the concepts of *Stasiland* and *Ostalgie*. Yet, no one could argue with the point that the current memory debates are very different than those during the GDR period. The debates during the second and third decade after unification appear to demonstrate the emergence of a mature memory culture—one that is no longer focused on coming to terms with the immediate past, but rather one that is an integral part of political discourse in which diverse memories equally find a home.

Notes

1. "Treffen des Politbüros mit Widerstandskämpfern und Aktivisten der ersten Stunde" *Neues Deutschland*, 4 October 1989, p. 1.
2. SAPMO-BArch, DY 30/2335, "Toast des Generalsekretärs des Zentralkomitees der SED und Vorsitzenden des Staatsrates der DDR, Erich Honecker, beim Treffen des Politbüros des ZK der SED mit Antifaschisten der ersten Stunde" dated 3 October 1989, pp. 196–97.
3. Anthony Wilson-Smith, "The Great Escape: Thousands Flee East Germany on the Eve of its 40th Anniversary," *Maclean's*, Vol. 102, No. 42 (16 October 1989), pp. 32–36.
4. "Kämpfer gegen den Faschismus, für Sozialismus und Frieden geehrt," *Neues Deutschland*, 6 October 1989, p. 1.
5. Günter Schabowski, *Der Absturz* (Berlin: Rowohlt, 1991), p. 180.
6. On the collapse of the East German regime and the process of German unification see, Konrad H. Jarausch and Martin Sabrow, eds., *Weg in den Untergang: Der innere Zerfall der DDR* (Göttingen: Vandenhoeck & Ruprecht, 1999), Konrad H. Jarausch, *Rush to German Unity* (Oxford: Oxford University Press, 1994), and Charles S. Maier, *Dissolution: The Crisis of Communism and the End of East Germany* (Princeton, NJ: Princeton University Press, 1997).
7. See in particular: Martin Sabrow, "Der Sozialistische Umgang mit dem Erbe," lecture held in the series "Potsdam in Europe" on 4 December 2003, unpublished manuscript, and Martin Sabrow, "Dealing with the GDR Past Among German Historians," *Transitions*, Vol. 44, No. 2 (2003), pp. 79–92. For similar interpretations see also: Ulrich Neuhäuser-Wespy, "Von der Urgesellschaft bis zur SED: Anmerkungen zur 'National-

geschichte der DDR,'" *Deutschland Archiv*, Vol. 16, No. 2 (1983), pp. 145–52; Jan Herman Brinks, *Paradigms of Political Change: Luther, Frederick II, and Bismarck: The GDR on its Way to Unity* (Milwaukee, WI: Marquette University Press, 2001); and Alexander Fischer and Günther Heydemann, eds., *Geschichtswissenschaft in der DDR* (Berlin: Duncker & Humblot, 1988), volumes 1 and 2 for historiographical essays on each particular era of historical research in the GDR.

8. Konrad H. Jarausch, "The Failure of East German Antifascism: Some Ironies of History as Politics," *German Studies Review*, Vol. 14, No. 1 (February 1991), pp. 85–102, here p. 85.
9. Eric Langenbacher, "Changing Memory Regimes in Contemporary Germany?" *German Politics and Society*, Vol. 21, No. 2 (Summer 2003), pp. 46–69.
10. Christa Wolf, *Was bleibt: Erzählungen* (Frankfurt am Main: Luchterhand, 1990). For an analysis of the controversy see: Gail Finney, "The Christa Wolf Controversy: Wolf's *Sommerstück* as Chekhovian Commentary," *The Germanic Review*, Vol. 67, No. 3 (Summer 1992), pp. 106–10. Also see: Peter Bender, *Unsere Erbschaft: Was war die DDR, was bleibt von ihr?* (Hamburg: Luchterhand, 1992).
11. Dennis Tate, "Introduction: The Importance and Diversity of Cultural Memory in the GDR Context" in *Twenty Years On: Competing Memories of the GDR in Postunification German Culture*, Renate Rechtien and Dennis Tate (Rochester, NY: Camden House, 2011), p. 7.
12. See also Paul Betts, "The Twilight of the Idols: East German Memory and Material Culture," *Journal of Modern History*, Vol. 72, No. 3 (September 2002), pp. 731–65.
13. Konrad Adam, "Politische Denkmalpflege: Wie die rote Berliner Stadtregierung eine kolossalstatue Lenins retten will," *Die Welt*, 3 August 2005, p. 1. See also Uwe Aulich, "Lenin wird wieder ausgebuddelt: Monumental Kopf soll auf die Zitadelle Spandau," *Berliner Zeitung*, 7 July 2009, p. 23. Part of the Lenin monument is scheduled to be moved to the Spandau Zitadelle, joining dozens of other monuments from Berlin's past that were deemed politically unacceptable in an exhibit called "Enthüllt: Berlin und seine Denkmäler" scheduled to open in 2014 (http://www.enthuellt-berlin.de).
14. Felix Philipp Lutz, *Das Geschichtsbewußtsein der Deutschen: Grundlagen der politischen Kultur in Ost und West* (Cologne: Böhlau, 2000), pp. 349–50.
15. Karl E. Meyer, "Editorial Notebook: Berlin's Denkmal War," *The New York Times*, 17 November 1991.
16. Harald Eggebrecht, "In Professor Tübkes Riesentrommel: Das Bauernschlachtpanorama in Frankenhausen," *Süddeutsche Zeitung*, 14 May 1994. See also: Eduard Beaucamp, "Sprengung des Elfenbeinturms," *Frankfurter Allgemeine Zeitung*, 28 October 2000, *Bilder und Zeiten*, p. 1.
17. Eduard Beaucamp, "Zeremonien des Abschieds," *Frankfurter Allgemeine Zeitung*, 24 July 1999.
18. "Tübke-Panorama," *Frankfurter Allgemeine Zeitung*, 10 September 1997, p. 43.
19. Sebastian Preuss, "Fanclub für Tübke: Das Baurnkriegspanorama in Bad Frankenhausen soll privatisiert werden," *Berliner Zeitung*, 1 April 2005, p. 24.
20. Peter Jochen Winters, "Gedekstätten sind Lernorte," *Frankfurter Allgemeine Zeitung*, 18 March 1994, p. 14.
21. Siegfried Stadler, "Korrekturen an den rotten Legenden," *Frankfurter Allgemeine Zeitung*, 10 April 1995, p. 33.
22. "Gedenkstätten: Dubiose Vergangenheit," *Der Spiegel*, 51/1995, 18 December 1995, p. 20.
23. Jens Schneider, "Volkhard Knigge Lieter der Gedenkstätte Buchenwald: Im Profil," *Süddeutsche Zeitung*, 28 May 1997. See also: "Auf Leichen gebaut" *Der Spiegel*, 21/1997, 19 May 1997, pp. 126–27.

24. Alexander Schuller, "Das Historische Museum—ein deutsches Nichts?" *Die Welt am Sonntag*, 2 November 1997.
25. "Erste Adresse," *Der Spiegel*, 38/1990, 17 September 1990, pp. 101–104. *Abwicklung* is a difficult term to translate, but in the context of post-1990 Germany, *Abwicklung* was used to describe the laying off of workers who were judged to have gained their positions due to political connections.
26. Ilona Lehnart, "Zäsuren ausstellen," *Frankfurter Allgemeine Zeitung*, 28 October 2002, p. 45.
27. Peter Richter, "Sein und Stein: Wie die Deutschen lernten, ihre Geschichte zu lieben: Ein Blick hinter die Mauer," *Frankfurter Allgemeine Zeitung*, 25 May 2003, p. 21.
28. Barbara Müller, "Aus 2000 Jahren—die Spur der Deutschen," *Hamburger Abendblatt*, 2 June 2006, p. 3.
29. Ibid. See also: Stefan Seewald, "Ein Ort für die kollektive Erinnerung," *Berliner Morgenpost*, 3 June 2006, p. 6.
30. *Bericht der Kommission zum Umgang mit den politischen Denkmälern der Nachkriegszeit im ehemaligen Ost-Berlin* (Berlin: Abegeordnetenhaus, 1993).
31. Stephan Speicher, "Marx und Engels Bleiben," *Frankfurter Allgemeine Zeitung*, 17 February 1993, p. 37.
32. J.B., "Zur Geschichte des deutschen Denkmals," *Süddeutsche Zeitung*, 16 February 1993, p. 4.
33. *Bericht der Kommission*, p. 34.
34. Ibid., p. 35; M.H., "Thälmann-Denkmal," *Süddeutsche Zeitung*, 17 February 1993, p. 2.
35. As quoted in Peter Jochen Winters, "Auf der Müllhalde der Geschichte," *Frankfurter Allgemeine Zeitung*, 18 February 1993, p. 29.
36. "Marx und Lenin für den Freizeitpark," *Der Spiegel*, 43/1993, 25 October 1993, pp. 106–111; "Kein Geld für rote Fossilen," *Focus*, 5 April 1993, p. 60. See also, Russel Lemmons, "Imprisoned, Murdered, Besmirched," in *Memory Traces: 1989 and the Question of German Cultural Identity*, ed. Silke Arnold-de Simine (Bern: Peter Lang, 2005), pp. 309–34.
37. As quoted in "Prenzlberger CDU will Teddy ans Fell," *TAZ*, 25 October 1996, p. 28.
38. Kirsten Küppers, "Thälmann soll wieder glänzen," *TAZ*, 17 October 2001, p. 24.
39. As quoted in Ronald Gorny, "Das Thälman-Denkmal muss abgerissen werden," *Berliner Kurier*, 1 April 2012, p. 6.
40. Ronald Gorny, "Das Thälman-Denkmal muss abgerissen werden," *Berliner Kurier*, 1 April 2012, p. 6. See also: Thomas Trappe, "Niemand hat die Absicht, Thälmann abzureissen," Prenzlauer Berg Nachrichten, http://www.prenzlauerberg-nachrichten.de/alltag/_/niemand-hat-die-absicht-das-thalmann-denkmal—17735.html (accessed on 26 September 2012).
41. To view the press release, see: http://www.linksfraktion.de/pressemitteilungen/abgeordnete/thaelmann-denkmal-teil-deutscher-geschichte/ (accessed 26 September 2012).
42. Norbert Koch-Klaucke, "Lass endlich die Bildstürmerei!" *Berliner Kurier*, 2 April 2012, p. 2.
43. "*Sacco und Jacketti*" translates as "sport coat and jacket," while "*Nahverkehrsdenkmal*" means a monument to the local transportation system.
44. Leserbrief "Sacco und Jacketti," *Der Tagesspiegel*, 29 January 2012, p. 16.
45. Friedrich Nostitz, "Es kam die Frage auf, warum Marx sitzt und Engels steht," *Berliner Zeitung*, Magazin No. 212, 11 September 2010.
46. Thomas Fülling, "Minister: Marx und Engels sollen weg" *Berliner Morgenpost*, 21 January 2012, p. 2.
47. Markus Falkner, "Marx und Engels blicken sieben Jahre lang nach Westen," *Berliner Morgenpost*, 15 April 2010.

48. As quoted in Thomas Fülling, "Minister: Marx und Engels sollen weg."
49. Ibid.
50. Katrin Betinna Müller, "Immer schön vergessen," *Die Tageszeitung,* 20 February 2012, p. 16.
51. From the *Abendschau* Facebook page (http://www.facebook.com/abendschau.rbb) comments section of the 21 January 2012 post (accessed on 26 September 2012).
52. "Sakko und Jacketti" *Berliner Tagesspiegel,* 29 January 2012, p. 16.
53. "Leserbriefe," *Berliner Zeitung,* 21 January 2012, p. 9.
54. "Soll das Denkmal von Marx und Engels aus Mitte verschwinden?" *B.Z.,* 20 January 2012, p. 8.
55. As quoted in Esteban Engel, "Streit in Berlin: Marx und Engels sollen weg," *Aachener Zeitung,* 20 January 2012, p. 4.
56. Eberhardt Diepgen, "Marx und Engels—Wohin im Stadtbild?" *Der Tagesspiegel,* 22 January 2012, p. 10.
57. Sara Jones, "At Home with the Stasi: *Gedenkstätte Hohenschönhausen* as Historic House," in *Remembering the German Democratic Republic: Divided Memory in a United Germany,* ed. David Clarke and Ute Wölfel (London: Palgrave Macmillan, 2011), pp. 211–22.
58. Although the museum is called *Haus der Geschichte,* there is no association between this museum and the federal museum *Haus der Geschichte* in Bonn.
59. Andreas Ludwig, "Representations of the Everyday and the Making of Memory: GDR History and Museums, in Clarke and Wölfel, *Remembering the German Democratic Republic,* pp. 37–53.
60. "Marx und Engels als Osterhasen," *Berliner Kurier,* 28 June 2007, p. 5.

BIBLIOGRAPHY

Archival Collections

Berliner Landesarchiv, Berlin
Stadtverornetenversammelung und Magistrat der Hauptstadt der DDR, Berlin

Buchenwald Archiv, Weimar (BwA)
    BwA 06 2/13
    BwA 06 2/28
    BwA 06 2/14
    BwA 06 2/24
    BwA VA/45
    BvA VA/48
    BwA VA/54
    BwA VA/80
    BwA VA/109

Bundesbeauftragte für die Unterlagen des Staatssicherheitsdienstes der ehemaligen Deutschen Demokratischen Republic, Berlin (BStU)
MfS BdL (Büro der Leitung)
MfS HA IX (Strafrechtliche Ermittlungen, Untersuchungsorgan, 1953–1989/90)
MfS HA XX (Abwehr im Staatsapparat, in Parteien, Kultureinrichtungen und Kirchen, Bekämpfung des Untergrunds, 1964–1989/90)

Deutsches Historisches Museum, Berlin (DHM)
    Hausarchiv: MfDG/40
    Hausarchiv: MfDG/79
    Hausarchiv: MfDG/87
    Hausarchiv: MfDG/103
    Hausarchiv: MfDG/120
    Hausarchiv: MfDG/139
    Hausarchiv/MfDG/161
    Hausarchiv/MfDG/1043
    Hausarchiv/MfDG/1174
    Hausarchiv/MfDG/1200
    Hausarchiv: MfDG/Päd. Abteilung/ Besucherstatistik.

Friedrich Ebert Stiftung, Archiv der sozialen Demokratie, Bonn (FES/AdsD)
  SPD/PV/Ostbüro/0285

Kreisverwaltung Merseburg-Querfurt, Kreisarchiv, Merseburg (KA-Merseburg)
  Archiv Nr. 10489
  Archiv Nr. 9786
  Archiv Nr. 9787

Kulturhistorisches Museum, Merseburg
  Hausarchiv, Non-inventoried items

Landeshauptarchiv Sachsen-Anhalt, Merseburg (LHASA-Merseburg)
  Bezirksleitung der SED Halle, IV/A2/9.02/40
  Rat des Bezirkes Halle/4. Ablieferungung/6624 (18222/1) [Abteilung Kultur]
  Rat des Bezirkes Halle/4. Ablieferungung/6625 (18222/2) [Abteilung Kultur]
  Rat des Bezirkes Halle/4. Ablieferungung/6693 (20423/1) [Abteilung Kultur]
  Rat des Bezirkes Halle/4. Ablieferungung/6694 (20423/2) [Abteilung Kultur]
  Rat des Bezirkes Halle/4. Ablieferungung/6695 (20423/3) [Abteilung Kultur]
  Rat des Bezirkes Halle/4. Ablieferungung/6696 (20423/4) [Abteilung Kultur]

Robert-Havemann-Gesellschaft, Berlin
  Photo Archive

Stadtarchiv Weimar (STA-Weimar)
  HfA nach 1945

Stiftung Archiv Partei und Massen Organizationen der DDR im Bundesarchiv, Berlin (SAPMO-BArch). Note: some archive signatures have changed.
  DR 1 (Ministerium für Kultur)
  DR 3 (Ministerium f. Hoch- und Fachhochschulwesen)
  DY 6 (Nationalrat der Nationalen Front)
  DY 27 (Kulturbund der DDR)
  DY 30 (Sozialistische Einheitspartei Deutschlands)
  DY 32 (Gesellschaft für Deutsch-Sowjetische Freundschaft)
  DY 55 (Vereinigung der Verfolgten des Naziregimes)
  DY 57 (Komitee der Antifaschistischen Widerstandskämpfer der DDR)
  NY 4036 (Nachlass Wilhelm Pieck)
  NY 4090 (Nachlass Otto Grotewohl)
  NY 4182 (Nachlass Walter Ulbricht and Lotte Ulbricht)
  NY 4286 (Nachlass Kurt Hager)

Periodicals and Newspapers

Aachener Zeitung
American Historical Review

Arbeitshefte (Deutsche Akademie der Künste zu Berlin)
Aus Politik und Zeitgeschichte
Berliner Kurier
Berliner Morgenpost
Berliner Tagesspiegel
Berliner Zeitung
B.Z.
Buchenwald-Information
Central European History
Der Spiegel
Deutsche Architektur
Deutschland Archiv
Die Tageszeitung
Die Welt
Die Welt am Sonntag
Einheit
Eulenspiegel
Foreign Affairs Bulletin
Frankfurter Allgemeine Zeitung
Frankfurter Rundschau
German Politics and Society
German Studies Review
Hamburger Abendblatt
Heimatgeschichte
International Affairs (Royal Institute of International Affair)
Journal of Contemporary History
Journal of Modern History
Kritische Berichte
Maclean's
Neue Museumskunde
Neues Deutschland
New German Critique
New Yorker
Newsweek International (Atlantic Edition)
Radio Free Europe, RAD Background Report
Representations
Social Research
Sonntag
Spiegel Online
Survey
Tägliche Rundschau
TAZ
The German Review
The Globe and Mail
The Guardian
The Historical Journal

The Public Historian
World Politics
Zeitschrift für Geschichtswissenschaft

Memoirs and other Primary Sources

Hager, Kurt. *Erinnerungen*. Leipzig: Faber & Faber, 1996.
Honecker, Erich. *Die Kulturpolitik unserer Partei wird erfolgreich verwirklicht*. Berlin: Dietz, 1982.
Klier, Freya. *Abreiskalender: Ein deutsch-deusches Tagebuch*. Munich: Knaur, 1989.
Schabowski, Günter. *Der Absturz*. Berlin: Rohwolt, 1991.
Sozialistische Einheitspartei Deutschland. *Dokumente der Sozialistischen Einheitspartei Deutschland*. Vol 16. Berlin: Dietz, 1980.
Sozialistische Einheitspartei Deutschland. *Dokumente der Sozialistischen Einheitspartei Deutschlands*. Vol. 4, Berlin: Dietz, 1954.

Secondary Sources

Abusch, Alexander. *Der Irrweg einer Nation: Ein Beitrag zum Verständnis deutscher Geschichte*. Berlin: Aufbau Verlag, 1946.
Adam, Hubertus. "Erinnerungsrituale—Erinnerungsdiskurse—Erinnerungstabus: Politische Denkmäler der DDR zwischen Verhinderung, Veränderung und Realisierung." *Kritische Berichte*, Vol. 20, No. 3 (1992), pp. 10–35.
Allan, Sean and John Sandford. *DEFA: East German Cinema, 1946–1992*. New York: Berghahn Books, 1999.
Allinson, Mark. *Politics and Popular Opinion in East Germany, 1945–1968*. Manchester: Manchester University Press, 2000.
Applegate, Celia. *A Nation of Provincials: The German Idea of Heimat*. Berkeley: University of California Press, 1990.
Arnold-de Simine, Silke, ed. *Memory Traces: 1989 and the Question of German Cultural Identity*. Bern: Peter Lang, 2005.
Asmus, Ronald. "The GDR and Martin Luther." *Survey*, Vol. 28, No. 3 (Autumn 1984), pp. 124–56.
———. "The GDR and the German Nation: Sole Heir or Socialist Sibling?" *International Affairs (Royal Institute of International Affairs)*. Vol. 60, No. 3 (Summer 1984), pp. 403–18.
Assmann, Aleida. *Erinnerungsräume: Formen und Wandlungen des kulturellen Gedächtnisses*. Munich: C.H. Beck, 1999.
———. "Transformations Between History and Memory." *Social Research*, Vol. 75, No. 1 (Spring 2008), pp. 49–72.
Assmann, Jan. *Das kulturelle Gedächtnis: Schrift, Erinnerung und politische Identität in frühen Hochkulturen*. Munich: C.H. Beck, 1997.
Azaryahu, Maoz. *Von Wilhelmplatz zu Thälmannplatz: Politische Symbole im öffentlichen Leben der DDR*. Gerlingen: Bleicher, 1991.

Badia, Gilbert. "Rosa Luxemburg." In François and Schulze, eds., *Deutsche Erinnerungsorte*, pp. 105–21.
Bartel, Horst. "Erbe und Tradition in Geschichtsbild und Geschichtsforschung in der DDR." *Zeitschrift für Geschichtswissenschaft*, Vol. 29 (1981), pp. 387–94.
Bathrick, David. *The Powers of Speech: The Politics of Culture in the GDR*. Lincoln: University of Nebraska Press, 1995.
Bauernkämper, Arnd. *Das umstrittene Gedächtnis: Die Erinnerung an Nationalsozialismus, Faschismus und Krieg in Europa seit 1945*. Paderborn: Ferdinand Schöningh, 2012.
———. *Die Sozialgeschichte der DDR*. Munich: Oldenbourg, 2005.
Beckert, Werner A. *Die Wahrheit über das Konzentrationslager Buchenwald*. Weimar: 1945.
Behrendt, Harald. *Werner Tübkes Panoramabild in Bad Frankenhausen: Zwischen staatlichen Prestigeprojekt und kunstlerischem Selbstauftrag*. Kiel: Ludwig, 2006.
Behrens, Heidi, and Andreas Wagner, eds. *Deutsche Teilung, Repression und Alltagsleben: Erinnerungsorte der DDR-Geschichte*. Leipzig: Forum Verlag Leipzig, 2004.
Bender, Peter. *Unsere Erbschaft: Was war die DDR, was bleibt von ihr?* Hamburg: Luchterhand, 1992.
Berger, Stefan, and Bill Niven, eds. *Writing the History of Memory*. London: Hodder Arnold, 2013.
Bericht der Kommission zum Umgang mit den politischen Denkmälern der Nachkriegszeit im ehemaligen Ost-Berlin. Berlin: Abgeordnetenhaus, 1993.
Betts, Paul. "The Twilight of the Idols: East German Memory and Material Culture." *Journal of Modern History*, Vol. 72, No. 3 (September 2002), pp. 731–65.
von Beyme, Klaus, Werner Durth, Niels Gutschow, Winfried Nerdinger, and Thomas Topfstedt, eds. *Neue Städte aus Ruinen: Deutscher Städebau der Nachkriegszeit*. Munich: Prestel, 1992.
"Bildende Kunst und Architektur: Marteralien der Plenartagung vom 31. Mai 1968," Deutsche Akademie der Künste zu Berlin, *Arbeitshefte*, No. 2 (1969).
Blanning, T.C.W. "The Death and Transfiguration of Prussia." *The Historical Journal*, Vol. 29, No. 2 (June 1986), pp. 433–59.
Blessing, Benita. *The Antifascist Classroom: Denazification in Soviet-Occupied Germany, 1945–1949*. New York: Palgrave Macmillan, 2010.
den Boer, Pim, and Willem Frijhoff, eds. *Lieux de mémoires et identities nationals*. Amsterdam: Amsterdam University Press, 1993.
Bonnell, Victoria. *Iconography of Power: Soviet Political Posters under Lenin and Stalin*. Berkeley: University of California Press, 1997.
Bourdieu, Pierre. *Distinction: A Social Critique of the Judgment of Taste*. Cambridge, MA: Harvard University Press, 1984.
Brinks, Jan Herman. *Paradigms of Political Change: Luther, Frederick II, and Bismarck: The GDR on its Way to Unity*. Milwaukee, WI: Marquette University Press, 2001.
Bruce, Gary. *The Firm: The Inside Story of the Stasi*. Oxford: Oxford University Press, 2010.
Buruma, Ian. *Wages of Guilt: Memories of War in Germany and Japan*. New York: Farrar Straus Giroux, 1994.

Cameron, Catherine M., and John B. Gatewood. "Excursions into the Un-Remembered Past: What People Want from Visits to Historical Sites." *The Public Historian*, Vol. 22, No. 3 (Summer 2000), pp. 107–27.
Chauliac, Marina. "Die Jugendweihe." In Sabrow, ed., *Erinnerungsorte der DDR*, pp. 161–68.
Clarke, David, and Ute Wölfel, eds. *Remembering the German Democratic Republic: Divided Memory in a United Germany*. London: Palgrave Macmillan, 2011.
Confino, Alon. "Collective Memory and Cultural History: Problems of Method." *American Historical Review*, Vol. 102, No. 5 (December 1997), pp. 1386–403.
———. *Germany as a Culture of Remembrance: Promises and Limits of Writing History*. Chapel Hill: University of North Carolina Press, 2006.
Cornelißen, Chistoph. "Der wiederentstandene Historismus. Nationalgeschichte in der Bundesrepublik der fünfziger Jahre." In Jarausch and Sabrow, eds., *Die historische Meistererzählung*, pp. 78–108.
Crew, David, ed. *Consuming Germany in the Cold War*. Oxford: Berg, 2003.
Czok, Karl. "Die Gründungstagung der Arbeitsgemeinschaft Heimat- und Landesgeschichte der Deutschen Historiker-Gesellschaft in Görlitz." *Zeitschrift für Geschichtswissenschaft*, Vol. 9, No. 8 (1961), pp. 1876–881.
Danyel, Jürgen. "Unwirtliche Gegenden und abgelegene Orte? Der Nationalsozialismus und die deutsche Teilung als Herausforderungen einer Geschichte der deutschen 'Erinnerungsorte.'" *Geschichte und Gesellschaft*, Vol. 24 (1998), pp. 436–75.
Darnton, Robert. *Berlin Journal, 1989–90*. New York: Norton, 1991.
Deutsche Akademie der Künste (DDR). *Das Buchenwald Denkmal*. Dresden: Verlag der Kunst, 1960.
Deyda, Ewald. "Zur Zusammenarbeit der Nationalen Mahn- und Gedenkstätte Buchenwald mit Studenten und Schülern." *Zeitschrift für Geschichtswissenschaft*, Vol. 27, No. 6 (1979), pp. 529–34.
Dietrich, Gerd, ed. *Um die Erneuerung der deutschen Kultur: Dokumente zur Kulturpolitik 1945–1949*. Berlin: Dietz, 1983.
Diner, Dan. "On the Ideology of Antifascism." *New German Critique*, No. 67 (Winter 1996), pp. 123–32.
Dorpalen, Andreas. *German History in Marxist Perspective: The East German Approach*. Detroit, MI: Wayne State University Press, 1985.
Eckert, Rainer, Iklo-Sascha Kowalczuk, and Isolde Stark, eds. *Hure oder Muse? Klio in der DDR: Dokumente und Materialien des Unabhängigen Historiker-Verbandes*. Berlin: Berliner Debate, 1994.
Eley, Geoff, and Ronald Suny, eds. *Becoming National: A Reader*. Oxford: Oxford University Press, 1996.
Eley, Geoff, and Jan Palmowski, eds. *Citizenship and National Identity in the GDR*. Stanford: Stanford University Press, 2008.
Engelberg, Ernst. *Bismarck: Urpreuße und Reichsgründer*. Berlin: Siedler, 1985.
Epstein, Catherine. *The Last Revolutionaries: German Communists and their Century*. Cambridge, MA: Harvard University Press, 2003.
Feist, Gunter, Eckhart Gillen, and Beatrice Vierneisel, eds. *Kunstdokumentation 1945–1990: Aufsätze-Berichte-Materialien*. Cologne: DuMont Buchverlag, 1996.

Fenemore, Mark. *Sex, Thugs and Rock 'n' Roll: Teenage Rebels in Cold-War East Germany.* New York: Berghahn Books, 2008.
Finney, Gail. "The Christa Wolf Controversy: Wolf's *Sommerstück* as Chekhovian Commentary." *The German Review,* Vol. 67, No. 3 (Summer 1992), pp. 106–10.
Fischer, Alexander. "Der Weg zur Gleichschaltung der Geschichtswissenschaft in der SBZ 1945–1949." In Fischer and Heydemann, eds., *Geschichtswissenschaft in der DDR,* pp. 45–75.
Fischer, Alexander, and Günther Heydemann, eds. *Geschichtswissenschaft in der DDR.* Berlin: Duncker & Humblot, 1988.
Flacke, Monika, ed. *Auftrag Kunst.* Berlin: Deutsches Historisches Museum, 1995.
Flierl, Bruno. *Gebaute DDR: Über Stadtplanner, Architekten und die Macht.* Berlin: Verlag für Bauwesen, 1998.
Flierl, Thomas. "'Thälmann und Thälmann vor allem:' Ein Nationaldenkmal für die Hauptstadt der DDR, Berlin." In Feist, Gillen, and Vierneigel, eds., *Kunstdokumentation 1945–1990,* pp. 358–85.
Fox, Thomas. *Stated Memory: East Germany and the Holocaust.* Rochester, NY: Camden House, 1999.
François, Etienne, and Hagen Schulze. *Deutsche Erinnerungsorte.* 3 Volumes. Munich: C.H. Beck, 2001.
Frei, Norbert. *Adenauer's Germany and the Nazi Past: The Politics of Amnesty and Integration.* New York: Columbia University Press, 2002.
Frevert, Ute. *A Nation in Barracks: Military Conscription and Civil Society.* Oxford: Berg, 2001.
Fuchs, Anne. *After the Dresden Bombing: Pathways of Memory, 1945 to the Present.* London: Palgrave Macmillan, 2011.
Fulbrook, Mary. *Anatomy of a Dictatorship: Inside the GDR, 1949–1989.* Oxford: Oxford University Press, 1995.
———. *Dissonant Lives: Generations and Violence through the German Dictatorships.* Oxford: Oxford University Press, 2011.
———. *German National Identity after the Holocaust.* Cambridge: Polity Press, 1999.
———. *The People's State: East German Society from Hitler to Honecker.* New Haven, CT: Yale University Press, 2005.
———, ed. *Power and Society in the GDR, 1961-79.* New York: Berghahn Books, 2013.
Garton Ash, Timothy. *In Europe's Name: Germany and the Divided Continent.* New York: Vintage Books, 1993.
Geertz, Clifford. *The Interpretation of Cultures.* New York: Basic Books, 1973.
Gillis, John, ed. *Commemorations.* Princeton, NJ: Princeton University Press, 1994.
Glaessner, Gert-Joachim, ed. *Die DDR in der Ära Honecker: Politik, Kultur, Gesellschaft.* Opladen: Westdeutscher Verlag, 1988.
Glore Crimmens, Cortney. "Reinterpreting the Soviet War Memorial in Berlin's Treptower Park after 1990." In Clarke and Wölfel, eds., *Remembering the German Democratic Republic,* pp. 54–64.
Goeckel, Robert F. "The Luther Anniversary in East Germany." *World Politics,* Vol. 37, No. 1 (October 1984), pp. 112–33.

Gray, William Glenn. *Germany's Cold War: The Global Campaign to Isolate East Germany, 1949–1969*. Chapel Hill: University of North Carolina Press, 2003.
Grieder, Peter. *The East German Leadership, 1946–73: Conflict and Crisis*. Manchester: Manchester University Press, 1999.
Griffith, William. *The Ostpolitik of the Federal Republic of Germany*. Cambridge, MA: MIT Press, 1978.
Hain, Simone. "Berlin Ost: 'Im Westen wird man sich wundern.'" In von Beyme, Durth, Gutschow, Nerdinger, and Topfstedt, eds., *Neue Städte aus Ruinen*, pp. 32–37.
Halbwachs, Maurice. *On Collective Memory*. Translated and edited by Lewis A. Coser. Chicago: University of Chicago Press, 1992.
Hamilton, Daniel. "Dateline East Germany." *Foreign Policy*, No. 76 (Fall 1989), pp. 176–97.
Harsch, Donna. *Revenge of the Domestic: Women, the Family, and Communism in the German Democratic Republic*. Princeton, NJ: Princeton University Press, 2008.
Heimann, Thomas. *Bilder von Buchenwald: die Visualisierung des Antifaschismus der DDR, 1945–1990*. Cologne: Böhlau, 2005.
Heinz, Helmut. "Die Konzeption der ersten Ausstellung im Museum für Deutsche Geschichte 1952." *Zeitschrift für Geschichtswissenschaft*, Vol. 28, No. 4 (1980), pp. 340–56.
Herbert, Ulrich, and Olaf Groehler. *Zweierlei Bewältigung: Vier Beiträge über den Umgang mit der NS-Vergangenheit in den beiden deutschen Staaten*. Hamburg: Ergebnisse, 1992.
Herf, Jeffery. *Divided Memory: The Nazi Past in the Two Germanys*. Cambridge, MA: Harvard University Press, 1997.
Hertle, Hans-Hermann, and Stefan Wolle. *Damals in der DDR: Der Alltag im Arbeiter und Bauernstaat*. Munich: Goldmann, 2006.
Hochscherf, Tobias, Christoph Laucht, and Andrew Plowman, eds. *Divided But Not Disconnected: German Experiences of the Cold War*. New York: Berghahn Books, 2010.
Honecker, Erich. *Die Kulturpolitik unserer Partei wird erfolgreich verwirklicht*. Berlin: Dietz, 1982.
Isnenghi, Mario. *I luoghi della memoria*. 3 Volumes. Rome: Laterza, 1997.
Jarausch, Konrad H. *After Hitler: Recivilizing the Germans, 1945–1995*. Oxford: Oxford University Press, 2006.
———. "Care and Coercion: The GDR as Welfare Dictatorship." In Jarausch, ed., *Dictatorship as Experience*, pp. 47–69.
———. "The Failure of East German Antifascism: Some Ironies of History as Politics." *German Studies Review*, Vol. 14, No. 1 (February 1991), pp. 85–102.
———. *Rush to German Unity*. New York: Oxford University Press, 1994.
———. "Zeitgeschichte und Erinnerung. Deutungskonkurrenz oder Interdependenz?" In Jarausch and Sabrow, eds., *Verletzes Gedächnis*, pp. 9–37.
Jarausch, Konrad H., ed. *Dictatorship as Experience: Towards a Socio-Cultural History of the GDR*. New York: Berghahn Books, 1999.

Jarausch, Konrad H., and Martin Sabrow. *Die historische Meistererzählung: Deutungslinien der deutschen Nationalgeschichte nach 1945.* Göttingen: Vandenhoeck & Ruprecht, 2002.

———. *Verletztes Gedächtnis: Erinnerungskultur und Zeitgeschichte im Konflikt.* Berlin: Campus, 2002.

———. *Weg in den Untergang: Der innere Zerfall der DDR.* Göttingen: Vandenhoeck & Ruprecht, 1999.

Jarausch, Konrad H., and Michael Geyer. *Shattered Past: Reconstructing German Histories.* Princeton, NJ: Princeton University Press, 2002.

Jeschonnek, Günter. "Der 17. Januar 1988—und kein Ende?" *Deutschland Archiv,* Vol. 21, No. 8 (1988), pp. 849–54.

Johnson, Molly Wilkinson. *Training Socialist Citizens: Sports and the State in East Germany.* Boston: Brill, 2008.

Jones, Sara. "At Home with the Stasi: *Gedenkstätte Hohenschönhausen* as Historic House." In Clarke and Wölfel, eds., *Remembering the German Democratic Republic,* pp. 211–22.

Joppke, Christian. *East German Dissidents in the Revolution of 1989.* New York: New York University Press, 1995.

Kaelbe, Hartmut, Jürgen Kocka, and Hartmut Zwar, eds. *Sozialgeschichte der DDR.* Stuttgart: Klett Cotta, 1994.

Kammen, Michael. *Mystic Chords of Memory: The Transformation of Tradition in American Culture.* New York: Knopf, 1991.

Kattago, Siobhan. *Ambiguous Memory: The Nazi Past and German National Identity.* Westport, CT: Praeger, 2001.

Kiau, Rolf. "Zur Entwicklung der Museen der DDR." *Neue Museumskunde,* Vol. 12, No. 4 (1969), pp. 415–59.

Kirschenbaum, Lisa. *The Legacy of the Siege of Leningrad, 1941–1995.* Cambridge: Cambridge University Press, 2009.

Kleßmann, Christoph. *Arbeiter im 'Arbeiterstaat' DDR: Deutsche Traditionen, sowjetisches Modell, westdeutsches Magnetfeld, 1945–1971.* Bonn: Dietz, 2007.

———. *Die doppelte Staatsgründung: Deutsche Geschichte 1945–55.* Bonn: Bundeszentrale für politische Bildung, 1991.

———. *Zwei Staaten, eine Nation: Deutsche Geschichte 1955–1970.* Bonn: Bundeszentrale für politische Bildung, 1997.

Klother, Eva-Maria. *Denkmalplastik nach 1945 bis 1989 in Ost- und West-Berlin.* Münster: Lit, 1996.

Klueting, Edeltraud, ed. *Antimodernismus und Reform: Beiträge zur Geschichte der deutschen Heimatbewegung.* Darmstadt: Wissenschaftliche Buchgesellschaft, 1991.

Knigge, Volkhard. *Versteinertes Gedenken: das Buchenwalder Mahnmal von 1958.* Spröda: Edition Schwarz Weiss, 1997.

Kober, Karl Max. *Werner Tübke: Monumentalbild Frankenhausen.* Dresden: VEB Verlag der Kunst, 1989.

Kocka, Jürgen. "Eine durchherrschte Gesellschaft." In Kaelbe, Kocka, and Zwar, eds., *Sozialgeschichte der DDR,* pp. 547–54.

Kocka, Jürgen, and Martin Sabrow, eds. *Die DDR als Geschichte: Fragen, Hypothesen, Perspektiven.* Berlin: Akademie Verlag, 1994.

Koonz, Claudia. "Between Memory and Oblivion." In Gillis, ed., *Commemorations*, pp. 258–80.
Kopstein, Jeffrey. *The Politics of Economic Decline in East Germany, 1945–1989*. Chapel Hill: University of North Carolina Press, 1997.
Korff, Gottfried, et al. *Preußen–Versuch einer Bilanz*, 5 vols. Reinbeck bei Hamburg: Rowolt, 1981.
Kosel, Gerhard. "Aufbau des Zentrums der Hauptstadt des demokratischen Deutschlands Berlin." *Deutsche Architektur*, No. 4 (1958), pp. 177–83.
Koshar, Rudy. *From Monuments to Traces: Artifacts of German Memory, 1870–1990*. Berkeley: University of California Press, 2000.
———. *Germany's Transient Pasts: Preservation and National Identity in the Twentieth Century*. Chapel Hill: University of North Carolina Press, 1998.
Kowalczuk, Ilko-Sascha. *Legitimation eines neuen Staates: Parteiarbeiter an der historischen Front. Geschichtswissenschaft in der SBZ/DDR, 1945–1961*. Berlin: Links Verlag, 1997.
Kowalczuk, Ilko-Sascha, and Stefan Wolle. *Roter Stern über Deutschland*. Berlin: Ch. Links, 2001.
Kramer, Jane. *The Politics of Memory: Looking for Germany in the New Germany*. New York: Random House, 1996.
Lacquer, Thomas. "Memory and Naming in the Great War." In Gillis, ed., *Commemorations*, pp. 150–67.
Ladd, Brian. "East Berlin Political Monuments in the Late German Democratic Republic: Finding a Place for Marx and Engels." *Journal of Contemporary History*, Vol. 37, No. 1 (2002), pp. 91–104.
———. *The Ghosts of Berlin: Confronting the German Past in the Urban Landscape*. Chicago: University of Chicago Press, 1997.
Landsman, Mark. *Dictatorship and Demand: The Politics of Consumerism in East Germany*. Cambridge, MA: Harvard University Press, 2005.
Langenbacher, Eric. "Changing Memory Regimes in Contemporary Germany?" *German Politics and Society*, Vol. 21, No. 2 (Summer 2003), pp. 46–69.
Lansing, Charles B. *From Nazism to Communism: German Schoolteachers under Two Dictatoriships*. Cambridge, MA: Harvard University Press, 2010.
Laschitza, Annelies and Günter Radczun. *Rosa Luxemburg: Ihr Wirken in der deutschen Arbeiterbewegung*. Berlin: Dietz, 1971.
Lemke, Christian. *Persönlichkeit und Gesellschaft. Zur Theorie der Persönlichkeit in der DDR*. Köln: Opladen, 1980.
Lemmons, Russel. "Imprisoned, Murdered, Besmirched." In Arnold-de Simine, ed., *Memory Traces*, pp. 309–34.
Leo, Annette. "Nicht Vereint: Studien zum Geschichtsbewusstsein Ost- und Westdeutscher." In Behrens and Wagner, eds., *Deutsche Teilung*, pp. 58–68.
Leuchtenburg, William E., ed. *American Places: Encounters with History*. Oxford: Oxford University Press, 2000.
Lindenberger, Thomas, ed. *Herrschaft und Eigen-Sinn in der Diktatur: Studien zur Gesellschaftsgeschichte der DDR*. Cologne: Böhlau, 1999.
Lüdtke, Alf. *Eigen-Sinn: Fabrikalltag, Arbeitererfahrungen und Politik vom Kaiserreich bis in den Faschismus*. Hamburg: Ergebnisse Verlag, 1993.

Lüdtke, Alf, and Peter Becker, eds. *Akten, Eingaben, Schaufenster: Die DDR und ihre Texte*. Berlin: Akademie Verlag, 1997.
Ludwig, Andreas. "Representations of the Everyday and the Making of Memory: GDR History and Museums." In Clarke and Wölfel, eds., *Remembering the German Democratic Republic*, pp. 37–53.
Lutz, Felix Philipp. *Das Geschichtsbewußtsein der Deutschen: Grundlagen der politischen Kultur in Ost und West*. Cologne: Böhlau, 2000.
Lutz, Peter. *Die Parteielite im Wandel: Funktionsaufbau, Sozialstruktur und Ideologie der SED-Führung*. Cologne: Opladen, 1970.
Maier, Charles. *Dissolution: The Crisis of Communism and the End of East Germany*. Princeton, NJ: Princeton University Press, 1997.
———. *The Unmasterable Past: History, Holocaust, and German National Identity*. Cambridge, MA: Harvard University Press, 1988.
Maines, Rachel, and James Glynn. "Numinous Objects." *The Public Historian*, Vol. 15, No. 1 (Winter 1993), pp. 9–25.
Major, Patrick. *Behind the Berlin Wall: East Germany and the Frontiers of Power*. Oxford: Oxford University Press, 2010.
Major, Patrick, and John Osmond, eds. *The Workers' and Peasants' State: Communism and Society in East Germany under Ulbricht, 1945–1971*. Manchester: Manchester University Press, 2002.
Marcuse, Harold. *Legacies of Dachau: The Uses and Abuses of a Concentration Camp, 1933–2001*. Cambridge: Cambridge University Press, 2001.
Matern, Hermann. "Ergebnis der Untersuchung Walter Bartel: 24.5.1953." In Niethammer, ed., *Der gesäuberte Antifaschismus*, pp. 403–13.
Maur, Hans. "Heimatgeschichtliche Forschungen ehöhen Bildungsniveau musealer Gedenkstätte der Arbeiterbewegung." *Heimatgeschichte*, No. 15 (1983), p. 20.
McAdams, A. James. *Germany Divided*. Princeton, NJ: Princeton University Press, 1994.
McCauley, Martin. *Marxism-Leninism and the German Democratic Republic: The Socialist Unity Party (SED)*. London: Macmillan, 1979.
McDougall, Alan. *Youth Politics in East Germany: The Free German Youth Movement, 1946–1968*. Oxford: Clarendon Press, 2004.
McLellan, Josie. *Antifascism and Memory in East Germany: Remembering the International Brigades, 1945–1989*. Oxford: Oxford University Press, 2004.
Meier, Hartmut, and Hans-Jürgen Zippler, eds. *Erfahrungen und Probleme einer wirksamen Geschichtspropaganda*. Berlin: Akademie für Geschichtswissenschaften beim ZK der SED, 1986.
Meier, Helmut, and Walter Schmidt, eds. *Erbe und Tradition in der DDR: Die Diskussion der Historiker*. Cologne: Pahl-Rugenstein, 1989.
Meißner, Günther, and Gerhard Murza, eds. *Werner Tübke, Bauernkrieg und Weltgericht: Das Frankenhauser Monumentalbild einer Wendezeit*. Leipzig: E.A. Seeman, 1995.
Meng, Michael. *Shattered Spaces: Encountering Jewish Ruins in Germany and Poland*. Cambridge, MA: Harvard University Press, 2011.

Merkel, Peter H. *German Unification in the European Context.* University Park, PA: Penn State University Press, 1993.
Merridale, Catherine. *Night of Stone: Death and Memory in Twentieth-Century Russia.* New York: Viking, 2000.
Meuschel, Sigrid. *Legitimation und Parteiherrschaft in der DDR: Zur Paradox von Stabilität und Revolution in der DDR 1945–1989.* Frankfurt: Suhrkamp, 1992.
Meusel, Alfred. *Thomas Müntzer und seine Zeit.* Berlin: Aufbau Verlag, 1952.
Mittenzwei, Ingrid. *Friedrich II. von Preußen: Eine Biographie.* Berlin: Deutscher Verlag der Wissenschaften, 1979.
Mittenzwei, Ingrid, and Karl-Heinz Noack. *Preußen in der deutschen Geschichte vor 1789.* Berlin: Akademie Verlag, 1983.
Mitter, Armin, and Stefan Wolle. *Untergang auf Raten: Unbekannte Kapitel der DDR-Geschichte.* Munich: Bertelsmann, 1993.
Moeller, Robert G. *War Stories: The Search for a Usable Past in the Federal Republic of Germany.* Berkeley: University of California Press, 2003.
Monteath, Peter. "Ein Denkmal für Thälmann." In Monteath, ed., *Ernst Thälmann; Mensch und Mythos,* pp. 179–201.
———. *Ernst Thälmann; Mensch und Mythos.* Amsterdam: Rodopi, 2000.
Mosse, George. *Fallen Soldiers: Reshaping the Memory of the World Wars.* Oxford: Oxford University Press, 1990.
Müller-Enbergs, Helmut, Jan Wielgohs, and Dieter Hoffman, eds. *Wer war wer in der DDR? Ein biographisches Lexikon.* Bonn: Bundeszentrale für politische Bildung, 2001.
Naimark, Norman. *The Russians in Germany: A History of the Soviet Zone of Occupation, 1945–1949.* Cambridge, MA: Harvard University Press, 1995.
Netzker, Helmut. *Formen-werten-wirken: Zum bildhauerischen Schaffen in der DDR 1965 bis 1982.* Berlin: Dietz, 1985.
Neubert, Ehrhardt. *Geschichte der Opposition in der DDR 1949–1989.* Berlin: Ch. Links Verlag, 1997.
Neuhäusser-Wespy, Ulrich. *Die SED und die Historie: die Etablierung der marxistisch-leninistischen Geschichtswissenschaft in der DDR in der fünfziger und sechziger Jahren.* Bonn: Bouvier, 1996.
———. "Von der Urgesellschaft bis zur SED: Anmerkungen zur 'Nationalgeschichte der DDR." *Deutschland Archiv,* Vol. 16, No. 2 (1983), pp. 145–52.
Niekisch, Ernst. *Deutsche Daseinsverfehlung.* Berlin: Aufbau Verlag, 1946.
Niemann, Heinz. *Hinterm Zaun: Politische Kultur und Meinungsforschung in der DDR: Die geheime Berichte an das Politbüro der SED.* Berlin: Edition Ost, 1995.
Niethammer, Lutz, ed. *Der gesäuberte Antifaschismus.* Berlin: Akademie Verlag, 1994.
Niethammer, Lutz, Alexander von Plato, and Dorothe Wierling, eds. *Die Volkseigene Erfahrung: Eine Archäologie des Lebens in der Industrieprovinz der DDR.* Berlin: Rowohlt, 1991.
Nora, Pierre. "Between Memory and History: Les Lieux de Mémoire." *Representations* (Spring 1989), pp. 7–25.

———. *Realms of Memory: Rethinking the French Past.* New York: Columbia University Press, 1996.
Nothnagle, Alan. *Building the East German Myth: Historical Mythology and Youth Propaganda in the German Democratic Republic, 1945–1989.* Ann Arbor: University of Michigan Press, 1999.
———. "From Buchenwald to Bismarck: Historical Myth-Building in the German Democratic Republic, 1945–1989." *Central European History,* Vol. 26, No. 1 (March 1993), pp. 91–114.
"Notizen aus dem Wissenschaftlichen Leben." *Zeitschrift für Geschichtswissenschaft,* Vol. 28, No. 12 (1980), pp. 1177–178.
Olsen, Jon Berndt. "Recasting Luther's Image: The 1983 Commemoration of Martin Luther in the GDR." In Hochscherf, Laucht, and Plowman, eds., *Divided But Not Disconnected,* pp. 63–76.
Otto, Rudolf. *The Idea of the Holy.* London: Oxford University Press, 1958.
Overesch, Manfred. *Buchenwald und die DDR, oder Die Suche nach Selbstlegitimation.* Göttingen: Vandenhoeck & Ruprecht, 1995.
Palmowski, Jan. "Building an East German Nation: The Construction of a Socialist Heimat, 1945–61." *Central European History,* Vol. 41, No. 3 (2006), pp. 503–26.
———. "Citizenship, identity and community in the GDR, 1949–90." In Eley and Palmowski, eds., *Citizenship and National Identity in the GDR,* pp. 73–91.
———. *Inventing a Socialist Nation: Heimat and the Politics of Everyday Life in the GDR, 1945–1990.* Cambridge: Cambridge University Press, 2009.
Pence, Katherine. "Schaufenster des sozialistischen Konsums: Texte der ostdeutschen 'consumer culture.'" In Lüdtke and Becker, eds., *Akten, Eingaben, Schaufenster,* pp. 91–118.
———. "Women on the Verge: Consumers between Private Desires and Public Crisis." In Pence and Betts, eds., *Socialist Modern,* pp. 287–322.
Pence, Katherine, and Paul Betts, eds. *Socialist Modern: East German Everyday Culture and Politics.* Ann Arbor: University of Michigan Press, 2008.
Penny, H. Glen, III. "The Museum für Deutsche Geschichte and German National Identity." *Central European History,* Vol. 28, No. 3 (September 1995), pp. 343–72.
Pfaff, Steven. *Exit-Voice Dynamics and the Collapse of East Germany: The Crisis of Leninism and the Revolution of 1989.* Durham, NC: Duke University Press, 2006.
Pfundt, Karen. "Die Gründung des Museums für Deutsche Geschichte in der DDR." *Aus Politik und Zeitgeschichte,* No. 23 (1994), pp. 23–30.
Philipsen, Dirk. *We Were the People: Voices from East Germany's Revolutionary Autumn of 1989.* Durham, NC: Duke University Press, 1992.
Poiger, Uta. *Jazz, Rock and Rebels: Cold War Politics and American Culture in a Divided Germany.* Berkeley: University of California Press, 2000.
Port, Andrew. *Conflict and Stability in the German Democratic Republic.* Cambridge: Cambridge University Press, 2007.
Portelli, Alessandro. *The Order Has Been Carried Out: History, Memory, and the Meaning of a Nazi Massacre in Rome.* New York: Palgrave Macmillan, 2003.
Rechtien, Renate, and Dennis Tate. *Twenty Years On: Competing Memories of the GDR in Postunification German Culture.* Rochester, NY: Camden House, 2011.

Reichel, Peter. *Politik mit der Erinnerung*. Munich: Hanser, 1995.
———. *Vergangenheitsbewältigung in Deutschland: Die Auseinandersetzung mit der NS-Diktatur von 1945 bis heute*. Munich: C.H. Beck, 2001.
Reuter, Elke, and Detlef Hansel. *Das kurze Leben der VVN von 1947 bis 1953: die Geschichte der Vereinigung der Verfolgten des Naziregimes in der sowjetischen Besatzungszone und in der DDR*. Berlin: Edition Ost, 1997.
von Richthofen, Esther. *Bringing Culture to the Masses: Control, Compromise and Participation in the GDR*. New York: Berghahn Books, 2008.
Ries, Nancy. *Russian Talk: Culture and Conversation during Perestroika*. Ithaca, NY: Cornell University Press, 1997.
Riesenberger, Dieter. "Entwicklung und Bedeutung der Geschichtsmuseen in der DDR." In Fischer and Heydemann, eds., *Geschichtswissenschaft in der DDR*, pp. 479–510.
———. "Heimatgedanke und Heimatgeschichte in der DDR." In Klueting, ed., *Antimodernismus und Reform*, pp. 320–43.
Ross, Corey. *The East German Dictatorship: Problems and Perspectives in the Interpretation of the GDR*. London: Arnold, 2002.
Rudnick, Carola S. *Die andere Hälfte der Erinnerung: Die DDR in der deutschen Geschichtspolitik nach 1989*. Bielefeld: Transcript, 2011.
Sabrow, Martin. "Auf der Suche nach dem materialistischen Meisterton. Bauformen einer nationalen Gegenerzählung in der DDR." In Jarausch and Sabrow, eds., *Die historische Meistererzählung*, pp. 33–77.
———. *Das Diktat des Konsenses: Geschichtswissenschaft in der DDR 1949–1969*. Munich: Oldenbourg, 2001.
———. "Dealing with the GDR Past Among German Historians." *Transitions*, Vol. 44, No. 2 (2003), pp. 79–92.
———. *Erinnerungsorte der DDR*. Munich: C.H. Beck, 2009.
———, ed. *Verwaltete Vergangenheit: Geschichtskultur und Herrschaftslegitimation in der DDR*. Berlin: Akademische Verlagsanstalt, 1997.
Sabrow, Martin, and Peter Th. Walther, eds. *Historische Forschung und sozialistische Diktatur: Beiträge zur Geschichtswissenschaft in der DDR*. Leipzig: Leipziger Universitätsverlag, 1995.
Sabrow, Martin, Rainer Eckert, Monika Flacke, Klaus-Dieter Henke, and Roland Jahn, eds. *Wohin treibt die Erinnerung? Dokumentation einer Debatte*. Göttingen: Vandenhoeck & Ruprecht, 2007.
Sabrow, Martin, Ralph Jessen, and Klaus Große Kracht, eds. *Zeitgeschichte als Streitgeschichte: Grosse Kontroversen seit 1945*. Munich: C.H. Beck, 2003.
Schmidt, Walter. "Das Gewesene ist nie erledigt. Worauf muß sich eine Nationalgeschichte der DDR stützen?" *Sonntag*, Vol. 35. No. 27 (1981), p. 9.
Schroeder, Klaus. *Der SED-Staat: Partie, Staat und Gesellschaft, 1949–1990*. Munich: Hanser, 1998.
Simpson, Simone. *Zwischen Kulturauftrag und künstlerischer Autonomie: Dresdner Plastik der 1950er und 1960er Jahre*. Cologne: Böhlau, 2008.
Spilker, Dirk. *The East German Leadership and the Division of Germany: Patriotism and Propaganda, 1945–53*. Oxford: Oxford University Press, 2006.
Staritz, Dietrich. *Geschichte der DDR, 1949–1985*. Frankfurt: Suhrkamp, 1985.

Steege, Paul. *Black Market, Cold War: Everyday Life in Berlin, 1946–1949.* Cambridge: Cambridge University Press, 2008.
Steege, Paul, Andrew Bergerson, Maureen Healy, and Pamela E. Swett. "The History of Everyday Life: A Second Chapter." *Journal of Modern History,* Vol. 80, No. 2 (2008), pp. 358–78.
Steiner, André. *Von Plan zu Plan: Eine Wirtschaftsgeschichte der DDR.* Berlin: Aufbau Verlag, 2007.
Steinlauf, Michael. *Bondage to the Dead: Poland and the Memory of the Holocaust.* Syracuse, NY: Syracuse University Press, 1996.
Stent, Angela. *From Embargo to Ostpolitik: The Political Economy of West German–Soviet Relations.* Cambridge: Cambridge University Press, 1981.
Stern, Leo. *Martin Luther and Philipp Melanchthon.* East Berlin, Rütten & Loening, 1953.
Süssmuth, Hans, ed. *Das Luther-Erbe in Deutschland: Vermittlung zwischen Wissenschaft und Öffentlichkeit.* Düsseldorf: Droste, 1985.
———. "Luther 1983 in beiden deutschen Staaten: Kritische Rezeption oder ideologische Vereinnahmung?" In Süssmuth, ed., *Das Luther-Erbe in Deutschland,* pp. 16–43.
Tate, Dennis. "Introduction: The Importance and Diversity of Cultural Memory in the GDR Context." In Rechtien and Tate, eds., *Twenty Years On,* pp. 1–19.
"Thesen über Martin Luther: Zum 500. Geburtstag." *Zeitschrift für Geschichtswissenschaft,* Vol. 29, No. 10 (1981), pp. 879–93.
Tompkins, David G. *Composing the Party Line: Music and Politics in Early Cold War Poland and East Germany.* West Lafayette, IN: Purdue University Press, 2013.
Trostorff, Klaus. "Die Nationale Mahn- und Gedenkstätte Buchenwald." *Neue Museumskunde,* Vol. 18, No. 2 (1975), pp. 85–92.
Tumarkin, Nina. *Lenin Lives! The Lenin Cult in Soviet Russia.* Cambridge, MA: Harvard University Press, 1983.
———. *The Living and the Dead: The Rise and Fall of the Cult of World War II in Russia.* New York: Basic Books, 1994.
Turner, Henry Ashby, Jr. *Germany from Partition to Reunification.* New Haven, CT: Yale University Press, 1992.
Unger, Manfred. "Territorialgeschichte in der Geschichtspropaganda." In Meier and Zippler, eds., *Erfahrungen und Probleme einer wirksamen Geschichtspropaganda,* p. 64–70.
Urban, Detlef. "Luther-Ausstellung in Ost-Berlin." *Deutschland Archiv,* Vol. 16, No. 8 (1983), pp. 790–93.
Voigt, Dieter, ed. *Die Gesellschaft der DDR: Untersuchungen zu ausgewählten Berichten.* Berlin: Duncker & Humblot, 1984.
Voßke, Heinz. *Geschichte der Gedenkstätte der Sozialisten in Berlin-Friedrichsfelde.* Berlin: Dietz, 1982.
Watson, Rubie, ed. *Memory, History, and Opposition under State Socialism.* Santa Fe, NM: School of American Research, 1994.
Weber, Hermann. *Geschichte der DDR.* Munich: Deutsche Taschenbuch Verlag, 1995.

———. "Stichwort: Die SED und Rosa Luxemburg." *Deutschland Archiv*, Vol. 21, No. 3 (March 1988), p. 244.
Weber, Petra. *Justiz und Diktatur: Justizverwaltung und politische Strafjustiz in Thüringen, 1945–1961*. Munich: Oldenbourg, 2000.
Weitz, Eric. "'Rosa Luxemburg Belongs to Us!' German Communism and the Luxemburg Legacy." *Central European History*, Vol. 27, No. 1 (1994), pp. 27–64.
Wierling, Dorothee. "Youth as Internal Enemy: Conflicts in the Education Dictatorship." In Pence and Betts, eds., *The Socialist Modern*, pp. 157–82.
Wierskalla, Sven. *Vereinigung der Verfolgten des Naziregimes (VVN) in der Sowjetischen Zone und in Berlin, 1945–1948*. Norderstedt: Grin Verlag, 1994.
Wilson-Smith, Anthony. "The Great Escape: Thousands Flee East Germany on the Eve of its 40th Anniversary." *McClean's*, Vol. 102, No. 42 (16 October 1989), pp. 32–36.
Wolf, Christa. *Was bleibt: Erzählungen*. Frankfurt: Luchterhand, 1990.
Wolle, Stefan. *Die heile Welt der Kiktatur: Alltag und Herrschaft in der DDR 1971–1989*. Berlin: Ch. Links Verlag, 1998.
Young, James. *Textures of Memory: Holocaust Memorials and Meaning*. New Haven, CT: Yale University Press, 1997.
Zatlin, Jonathan. *The Currency of Socialism: Money and Political Culture in East Germany*. Cambridge: Cambridge University Press, 2007.
Zimmer, Hasko. *Der Buchenwald-Konflikt: Zum Streit um Geschichte und Erinnerung im Kontext der deutschen Vereinigung*. Münster: Agenda Verlag, 1999.
Zimmering, Raina. *Mythen in der Politik der DDR: Ein Beitrag zur Erforschung politischer Mythen*. Opladen: Leske + Burich, 2000.

INDEX

A
Abrassimov, Piotr, 185
Abusch, Alexander, 20
Academy of Arts, 83, 89, 93
Academy of Visual Arts (Leipzig), 167
Ackermann, Anton, 23
Action Alliance Thälmann Monument, 227–28
Aljoschin, Sergei, 84
Allinson, Mark, 102
antifascism, 11, 21, 45, 94, 122, 148, 213, 215, 219–20
Arnold, Walter, 85, 91
Assmann, Aleida, 8, 18
Association of Fine Artists (*Verband Bildender Künstler*), 198–99
Association of Nazi Persecutees (VVN), 24, 39–46, 58–62; monument and, 58–62; museum exhibit and, 39–46
Auer, Ignaz, 25
August "the Strong" (King of Saxony), 148
Augustinian Monastery, 154

B
Bach, Johann Sebastian, 138–39
Bad Frankenhausen, 142, 164–75
Bad Frankenhausen Panorama. *See* Bad Frankenhausen
Barbe, Angelika, 228
Bartel, Horst, 139, 152
Bartel, Walter, 59–62, 122–23
Bathrick, David, 24
Battle of Frankenhausen. *See* Bad Frankenhausen
Bebel, August, 21, 23, 106, 108, 184–85
Becher, Johannes, 85
Becker, Werner A., 55, 57
Beethoven, Ludwig van, 141
Bensing, Manfred, 165, 168
Bergemann, Sibylle, 230
Bergner, Edwin, 121, 123
Berlin, 1, 3, 11, 19, 80–81, 93, 103, 105, 144–45, 184, 190, 200–201, 205, 214, 224–26, 229–34; Berlin Wall, 2–3, 6, 76, 79, 92, 102–4, 214, 221, 233; City Palace, 3, 93; city planning, 22, 80–82, 85, 87, 89, 93, 95, 185, 187, 194, 196; Commission for Dealing with Political Monuments of the Postwar Period in Former East-Berlin, 225–26, 230; Hohenschönhausen, 3, 232–33; Magistrate, 22, 25–28, 71, 80–82, 189; Revolution of 1848 and, 34–45; School of Fine Arts, 34; Soviet Occupation Sector, 28, 36
Biermann, Wolf, 187, 201–2
Bismarck, Otto von, 13, 20–21, 59, 143, 145–48, 175, 208, 218
Bizonia, 35
Blücher, Gebhard Leberecht von, 145

Board of Trustees of the National Memorials in Buchenwald, Sachsenhausen, and Ravensbrück, 54, 64–66
Bohley, Bärbel, 205, 207, 219
Böhme, Hans-Joachim, 173
Böhme, Ibrahim, 214
Borodino, 165, 167
Böttger, Till, 204
Brandt, Edith, 164
Brandt, Willy, 137, 151, 162, 218
Brecht, Bertolt, 61
Breitscheid, Rudolf, 28
Buchenwald concentration camp, 1, 3–4, 11–12, 42–43, 52–53, 94–95, 104, 120, 130–33, 189, 217, 222; board of trustees, 54, 64–66; Buchenwald Committee, 59, 62; criticism of, 121; dedication ceremony, 54, 67–68; early commemoration events, 55–58; fundraising and, 64–67; as the GDR's founding myth, 54, 69; resolution by Council of Ministers, 60; teacher seminars, 121–24; volunteers, 64; VVN and, 58–62; youth and, 119–20
Bundesnachrichtendienst (BND), 206
Busse, Ernst, 57

C
Cameron, Catherine, 105
Carstens, Karl, 151, 161
CDU. *See* Christian Democratic Union
Chemnitz, 85–86, 197–98, 226
Christian Democratic Union (CDU), 36–37, 227–28, 232; in East Germany, 153, 159
Citizenship Rights in the GDR (*Staatsbürgerschaftsrecht der DDR*), 202–3
City Museums of Merseburg (*Städtische Museen Merseburg*), 112
Clausewitz, Carl von, 140–41
Collegium Augustinum, 154
Collein, Edmund, 84–85
Committee of Antifascist Resistance Fighters, 62

Communist Party of Germany (KPD), 1, 11–12, 18–22, 24–28, 39, 45, 55, 57, 60, 88, 105, 107, 109, 115–16, 122, 199, 204, 206, 215, 217. *See also* Party of Democratic Socialism; Socialist Unity Party of Germany
Communist Party of the Soviet Union (CPSU), 84, 109, 198
Confino, Alon, 4
counter-memory, 21, 188, 191, 219
CPSU. *See* Communist Party of the Soviet Union
Cremer, Fritz, 61–63, 69, 83–85, 89, 91, 184, 186–89, 198
Czok, Karl, 110

D
Dahlem, Franz, 39, 60
Dähn, Fritz, 84, 92
Davidov, Fyodor, 91
DDR Museum (Berlin), 233
Dennert, Manfred, 226
Dickel, Friedrich, 202
Diehl, Ernst, 74
Diepgen, Eberhardt, 232
Dieters, Heinrich, 37
Dieters, Lidwig, 61
Dimitroff, Georgi, 184
Dohm, Bernhard, 72
Dokumentationszentrum Alltagskultur der DDR (Eisenhüttenstadt), 233
Dorpalen, Andreas, 10
Duncker, Hermann, 184

E
Early Bourgeois Revolution. *See* Peasants' War
Ebert, Friedrich, 28, 81, 84, 85
Eggerath, Werner, 59
Eichhorn, Toni, 27
Eisenach, 124, 154, 157–59, 184
Eisenach Party Congress, 184
Eisleben. *See* Lutherstadt Eisleben
Engel, Rudolf, 83
Engelberg, Ernst, 146
Engelberger, Otto, 61

Engelhardt, Ludwig, 175, 185, 187–195, 229–30
Engels, Friedrich, 1, 12–13, 52–54, 77, 80–87, 94–95, 107, 140, 150, 175, 184–95, 217, 219–20, 229–34. *See also* Marx-Engels monument
Environmental Library, 204
Erbe. See heritage and tradition
Erfurt, 110, 154, 159
Ernst-Thälmann-Park, 197, 199, 226–27
Evangelical Church in Germany (West), 150
Evangelical Church of the GDR, 142, 149, 153–54, 157, 159, 161–63, 174, 219

F
Falke, Heino, 201
FDJ. *See* Free German Youth
Federal Republic of Germany (FRG), 1, 3–4, 7, 10, 53, 68, 73, 78, 80, 92, 94, 102–3, 105–6, 127, 137–38, 140–45, 149–51, 161–63, 174, 183, 204, 206, 214–15, 218, 220, 222, 224
FIAPP, 80
Fischer, Alexander, 19–20
Fischer, Peter, 188
Fischer, Werner, 207
Flierl, Bruno, 188
Flierl, Peter, 230
Flierl, Thomas, 221, 228
Fox, Thomas, 4
François, Etienne, 7
Frankenhausen. *See* Bad Frankenhausen
Frankfurt Parliament, 33, 38
Frauenkirche (Dresden), 11, 233
Frederick II, King of Prussia. *See* Frederick the Great
Frederick the Great, 13, 20, 23, 139, 141, 143–46, 148, 175, 185, 218–19, 225; monument of, 83, 144, 229
Frederick William, 83
Free German Youth (FDJ—*Freie Deutsche Jugend*), 29, 65–66, 68, 121, 124–25, 146
FRG. *See* Federal Republic of Germany

Friedrichsfelde Cemetery. *See* Socialists' Cemetery in Berlin-Friedrichsfelde

G
Garton Ash, Timothy, 6
Gatewood, John, 105
GDR Academy of Sciences, 143, 152
Gedenkstätte der Sozialisten. See Socialists' Cemetery in Berlin-Friedrichsfelde
Gemkow, Heinrich, 188
German Administration for People's Education, 34
German Historical Museum (DHM), 222, 224–26
German Labor Movement, 12, 25–28, 46, 52, 109, 115, 146; portrayal in history, 12, 21, 24, 30, 140–41, 185, 215
German People's Congress, 36–38
German road to socialism, 32
Geschke, Ottomar, 40
Gißke, Erhardt, 191
Gneisenau, August Graf Neidhardt von, 145
Goethe, Johann Wolfgang von, 24, 57–58, 83, 85, 138–39, 141
Gorbachev, Mikhail, 6, 202
Göring, Hermann, 222
Götsche, Peter, 61
Götting, Gerald, 153, 159, 161
Graetz, René, 89–91
Gropius, Walter, 58
Grotewohl, Hans, 61
Grotewohl, Otto, 28, 54, 58–59, 73, 184; Buchenwald monument and, 64–68; Ernst Thälmann monument and, 88, 90–91, 195; Marx-Engels monument and, 81, 84–85
Gruson, Otto, 92
Grzimek, Waldemar, 85
Gutzeit, Martin, 214

H
Hager, Kurt, 140–41, 146; Marx-Engels monument and, 184, 188, 191–92, 194; Museum for German

History and, 71–72; Panorama Bad Frankenhausen and, 171, 173–74
Hahne, Ruthild, 84, 89–93, 95, 195, 197
Halbwachs, Maurice, 24, 220
Händel, Georg Friedrich, 139
Harig, Gerhard, 72–73
Haus der Geschichte (Lutherstadt Wittenberg), 233
Heimat, 11, 104, 110–13, 118–19, 147, 156, 158, 164, 218
Heine, Heinrich, 187
Heinrichs, Waldemar, 89
Hennig, Karl, 227
Henselmann, Hermann, 55, 57–58
Herf, Jeffrey, 4, 9
heritage and tradition, 138–42
Heymann, Stefan, 57
Hirsch, Ralf, 205, 207
historical consciousness, 3, 9–10, 21, 45, 51, 73, 105–6, 119–20, 122, 125, 127, 130–32, 139, 147, 156, 163, 175, 221; emotional response and, 102–4, 109, 218; Revolution of 1848 and, 31–34; youth and, 119–38
historical sites, 3, 11–12, 71, 91, 93, 103, 105, 131, 143, 153–55, 157, 165, 185, 218, 225
Hoffmann, Hans-Joachim, 170
Holzhauer, Helmut, 84
Honecker, Erich, 68, 87, 93, 118–19, 144–45, 184, 202, 208, 213–14, 219, 225; Ernst Thälmann monument and, 197–200; Martin Luther Year and, 150–53, 157–58, 160–61; Marx-Engels monument and, 187, 189, 191–95; Panorama Bad Frankenhausen and, 169, 173
Horn, Richard, 89
Howard, Walter, 83–86
Hoyer, Siegfried, 165, 168
Humboldt-Forum, 230, 232

I
Independent Social Democratic Party of Germany (USPD), 109, 115
Initiative Freedom and Human Rights (IFM—*Initiative Freiden und Menschenrechte*), 205

International Federation of Former Political Prisoners (FIAPP), 80

J
Jakob, Otto, 123
January fighters, 25–26
Jarausch, Konrad, 5, 8
John, Alfred, 112
Jugendweihe, 120, 122, 125
Junker, Wolfgang, 191

K
Kaiser, Jakob, 35–36
Kalk, Andreas, 204
Kamnitzer, Heinz, 206
Kapp Putsch, 26, 109
Karl-Marx-Stadt. *See* Chemnitz
Kattago, Siobhan, 4
Kerbel, Lew, 93, 193, 197–201, 226–27
Kies, Hans, 91
Kleinbauer, Dieter, 117
Klier, Freya, 202–3, 205, 207, 219
Knabe, Herbertus, 232
Knigge, Volkhard, 223
Kober, Karl-Max, 169–71, 173
Koch, Petra, 117–19
Koelle, Fritz, 85
Koerth, Alfred, 118
Kohl, Helmut, 137, 151, 224–25
Kopstein, Jeffrey, 5
Kosel, Gerhard, 85
Kowalczuk, Ilko-Sasha, 19
Kraack, Erhard, 190
Kraft, Johannes, 228
Krawczyk, Stephan, 201–4, 206–7, 219
Kuczynski, Jürgen, 72
Kulturhistorisches Museum (Merseburg), 112. *See also* Merseburg County Museum
Külz, Wilhelm, 37
Kunstgewerbemuseum (Berlin), 145
Künzler, Franz, 28
Kurz, Josef, 226
Kyffhäuserdenkmal, 165

L
Lammert, Will, 85
Landsman, Mark, 5

Lassalle, Ferdinand, 108
Leich, Werner, 153, 158
Lenin, Vladimir, 2, 23, 70, 77, 92, 105, 122, 107, 140, 157, 189, 193, 198, 204, 221–22, 225
Leo, Annette, 4
Liebknecht-Luxemburg parade, 11, 19, 26, 28, 46, 197, 201–7
Liebknecht, Karl, 1, 21, 23, 25–30, 38–39, 105, 184, 186, 197, 201, 206, 217. *See also* Liebknecht-Luxemburg parade
Liebknecht, Kurt, 82–85, 89
Liebknecht, Wilhelm, 25, 108
Lingner, Reinhold, 28, 61, 88
local history, 12, 104, 110–19, 131–32
Loch, Hans, 59
Luther, Martin, 11, 13, 21, 139–42, 148–64, 175, 208, 215, 218–19, 225; Panorama Bad Frankenhausen and, 168, 174–76. *See also* Martin Luther Year
Lutherstadt Eisleben, 154, 156–57, 161–62
Lutherstadt Wittenberg, 154, 156–57, 233
Lutz, Feliz, 221
Luxemburg, Rosa, 1, 11, 13, 21, 23, 25–30, 38, 184, 186, 197, 201–2, 204, 206–8, 215–17, 219–20. *See also* Liebknecht-Luxemburg parade

M

Maier, Charles, 6
Marenko artists collective, 61–62
Maron, Karl, 26
Martin Luther Year (1983), 152, 156; church commemoration and, 159–62; church resistance and, 160; committee, 151–53, 159, 161; competition with the Karl Marx Year, 156; exhibit at the Museum for German History and, 160; in East Germany, 151–63; in West Germany, 150–51, 163; local activities in Halle district and, 156; restoration projects and, 153–54; theses, 152, 155; tourism and, 154, 159

Marx, Eleanor, 107
Marx, Jenny, 106–109, 131
Marx, Karl, 1, 12–13, 21, 23, 52, 77, 80–87, 103, 105–6, 109, 146, 156, 185, 192, 197–98, 226, 229. *See also* Marx-Engels monument
Marx-Engels-Forum (Berlin), 85, 190–91, 193, 195, 219, 230–31
Marx-Engels monument, 2, 80–89, 93–94, 175, 184–96, 208, 217, 219–20, 229–232; committee, 81–82; critique of, 84, 192; dedication ceremony, 193; Goethe-Schiller monument as model for, 83, 85; reception of, 194
Marx-Engels-Platz (Berlin), 80–84, 189–92
Marx-Engels Square. *See* Marx-Engels Platz (Berlin)
Matern, Hermann, 80
Matthes, Hubert, 61
McDougall, Alan, 5
Meckel, Markus, 214
Mehring, Franz, 27–28, 38, 184
Melanchthon, Philipp, 154
memorials, 1–5, 11–12, 52, 57–58, 105, 109, 184, 196, 221, 230, 233; Berlin-Hohenschönhausen, 3, 232–33; Clara Zetkin, 103, 106–9, 131; Ernst Thälmann (Ziegenhals), 105; Gotha Conference, 108–9, 131; Jenny Marx, 106–9, 131; Marienborn, 3, 233; removal of, 22–24, 80, 144, 225–26, 228, 230–31; Soviet Soldiers in Berlin-Treptow, 198, 214, 226. *See also* Buchenwald concentration camp; Ernst-Thälmann monument; Marx-Engels monument; Socialists' Cemetery in Berlin-Friedrichsfelde
memory culture. *See* state memory culture
Merkel, Angela, 225
Merseburg, 11, 104, 110–19, 165
Merseburg County Museum, 110–19
Meuschel, Sigrid, 5
Meusel, Alfred, 72–73, 75–77, 149
MfDG. *See* Museum for German History

Middell, Margaret, 188
Ministry of Culture, 90, 92–93, 110–11, 113, 121, 123, 164, 167–68, 170–71, 187
Ministry of Higher Education, 71
Ministry of People's Education (*Volksbildungsministerium*), 90
Mirtschin, Heinz, 160
"misery" theory, 20
Mittag, Günter, 191
Mittenzwei, Ingrid, 141, 143, 146
Mitter, Armin, 6
Mittig, Rudi, 203
monument to the *Märzgefallenen* (Weimar), 58
Moscow, 70, 80–81, 92, 167, 198
Müller, Michael, 231
Müntzer, Thomas, 139, 142, 149–52; depiction in Panorama Bad Frankenhausen, 164–66, 168, 171, 173–75
Museum for German History (MfDG—*Museum für Deutsche Geschichte*), 11–12, 39, 52–53, 61, 70–80, 94–95, 104, 106, 119–20, 124–33, 149–50, 160, 217–18, 224; Buchenwald Memorial and, 61; concept for, 71–73; coordination of historical sites and, 106–9; critique of, 77–78; as a designed academic museum, 79; exhibit renovations and, 128–30; grand opening of, 74–75; special exhibits and, 78–79, 160–61; visitor responses and, 75–76; visitor's council and, 128; youth and, 119, 124–30, 218

N
National People's Army (NVA), 117, 124
Nauman, Konrad, 190
Netzker, Kurt, 192
Neuhäußer-Wespy, Ulrich, 103
Neumann, Franz, 35
Niekisch, Ernst, 19–20
Nimtz, Walter, 127
Nomokel, Karl, 65
Nora, Pierre, 7

Norden, Albert, 189
Nostitz, Friedrich, 187, 230
Nothnagle, Alan, 5
November Revolution. *See* Revolution of 1918
Nuschke, Otto, 37
NVA. *See* National People's Army

O
Obama, Barack, 224
Oelßner, Fred, 70, 76, 82, 84
Oelzner, Rudolf, 85
Opfern des Faschismus (OdF). *See* Victims of Fascism
Orlow, Sergei, 84
Ostalgie, 221, 234
Ostpolitik, 137, 162; cultural delimitation with West Germany, 139, 149, 163
"Other Germany" exhibit, 12, 19, 24, 39–46, 70, 217; conception for, 39–40; content of, 40–42; political nature of, 44; visitor feedback and, 42–43
Otto, Rudolph, 105
Ottomeyer, Hans, 224–25

P
Palace of the Republic (*Palast der Republik*), 3, 187, 189–92, 196–97
Panorama Bad Frankenhausen ("Early Bourgeois Revolution in Germany"), 142, 164–76, 219, 222, 224
Park an der Spree, 191
Party of Democratic Socialism (PDS), 221, 226, 228. *See also* Communist Party of Germany; Socialist Unity Party of Germany
Paulick, Richard, 61
Peasants' War, 39, 41, 77, 114, 126–27, 142, 150–52, 160, 163–64, 166, 219, 222; depiction in the Panorama Bad Frankenhausen and, 164–75
Pei, Ieoh Ming (I. M.), 224
Pieck, Wilhelm, 25–30, 37–38, 77, 81, 83–84, 88, 90, 122, 184; construction

of the Socialists' monument and, 25–29; Ernst Thälmann monument and, 88, 90; Marx-Engels monument and, 81, 83–84
Port, Andrew, 6
Pretzien, Gustav, 112
Prussia, 13, 70, 78, 142–48, 175–76, 185, 215
Prussian Renaissance, 139, 143, 148

R
Ragwitz, Ursula, 140–41
Ramsauer, Peter, 2–3, 231–32
Rau, Heinrich, 59
Rau, Johannes, 150
Rauch, Christian Daniel, 83, 144
Ravensbrück concentration camp, 3, 52, 64, 66, 69, 91, 105, 217
regional history, 12, 110, 116, 142–48, 175–76
Reihl, Robert, 61
Reitschel, Ernst, 83
Revolution of 1848, 10, 12, 19, 21, 24–26, 31–39, 115, 126–27, 146, 217, 224–25; commemoration (1948) in East Germany and, 31–38, 217; commemoration (1948) in West Berlin and, 36–37; recovering counter-memories and, 33
Revolution of 1918, 21, 41, 115, 126–27, 226
Revolutionary Cemetery Berlin-Friedrichshain, 25–27, 38
Richthofen, Ester von, 5
Rohe, Mies van der, 25, 28, 197

S
Sabrow, Martin, 3, 5, 10, 20, 103, 139, 215
Sachsenhausen concentration camp, 3, 52, 64, 66, 69, 105, 122, 217
Saemerow, Ernst, 64
SBZ. *See* Soviet Occupation Zone
Schabowski, Günter, 206, 214
Scharnhorst, Gerhard von, 145
Schehr, Johnny, 28
Scheibe, Richard, 34
Schiller, Friedrich, 24, 57, 83, 85, 138–39, 141
Schinkel, Karl Friedrich, 23
Schlageter monument (Berlin), 22
Schlegel, Bert, 204
Schlüter, Andreas, 83
Schmidt, Helmut, 137
Schmidt, Walter, 139, 146
Schmitz, André, 231
Schönherr, Karl, 92
Schroeder, Klaus, 5
Schulze, Hagen, 7
Schütz, Heinrich, 139
Schwennicke, Carl-Hubert, 35
SED. *See* Socialist Unity Party of Germany
Seitz, Gustav, 27, 61, 83–85, 88
Selbmann, Fritz, 65
Sevastopol, 165, 167
Sindermann, Horst, 159, 173
Singer, Paul, 25
SMAD. *See* Soviet Military Administration in Germany
Social Democratic Party of Germany (SPD), 27, 35–36, 70, 107–9, 115–16, 226, 228, 231
Social Democratic Party of the GDR (SDP), 214
Socialists Cemetery in Berlin-Friedrichsfelde, 1, 3, 12, 19, 24–30, 201, 214, 217, 231
Socialist Unity Party of Germany (SED), 2–13, 18–24, 27–39, 42–46, 51–53, 55, 59–62, 68–73, 79–82, 84–85, 87–89, 91–96, 102–6, 108–13, 118, 120–21, 128, 130–33, 138–43, 145, 148–49, 152, 154, 156–57, 161, 164, 167, 171, 173, 174–76, 183–87, 189–202, 204, 206–8, 213–22, 226, 228–29; cultural section of, 120, 140, 164; Eleventh Party Congress, 193, 199; first cultural conference, 23; Ninth Party Congress, 138; *Politbüro*, 60, 81–82, 84, 88, 91–93, 140, 156, 164–66, 171, 173, 175, 184, 187, 189, 191, 197–98, 201, 206, 214; Seventh Party Congress, 118;

Sixth Party Congress, 198; Tenth Party Congress, 189; Third Party Congress, 70. *See also* Communist Party of Germany; Party of Democratic Socialism
Soviet internment camp (*Speziallager*), 4, 55, 59, 223
Soviet Military Administration in Germany (SMAD), 1, 19, 57–59
Soviet Occupation Sector. *See under* Berlin
Soviet Occupation Zone (SBZ), 1, 11, 18–22, 24, 27, 30–31, 35–37, 40, 43–44, 58–59, 66, 78, 94
Soviet Union (USSR), 10–11, 18, 31–33, 51, 53, 70, 83–84, 88, 91–93, 95, 108, 137, 165–67, 185, 193, 197–98, 202, 208, 219, 226
Sozialistische Einheitspartei Deutschlands. *See* Socialist Unity Party of Germany
Spartacist uprising. *See* January fighters
SPD. *See* Social Democratic Party of Germany
Speziallager. *See* Soviet interment camp
Spielmann, Georg, 67
Stasi (Staatssicherheitsdienst), 157, 201–6, 207, 214, 231–33
Stasiland, 221, 234
state memory culture, 2–4, 9, 11–13, 18–20, 24, 26–27, 51, 94, 131–32, 142, 195, 201, 208, 215–17, 219, 221, 234; collapse of, 183–86, 207–8; emotional bonds and, 102–119; erosion of, 137–42, 175–76, 208; establishing a narrative for, 51–96; generational transfer and, 119–130; as Marxist counternarrative, 10, 12, 20, 53, 103–4, 107, 139, 141, 147, 149, 155, 164, 169, 217, 222 (*see also* German Labor Movement); Marxist museum narrative and, 39–46, 70–80, 113–14, 124–30. *See also* counter-memory; historical consciousness
State Security Service. *See* Stasi
Steege, Paul, 31

Steinmetz, Max, 152
Stephan, Richard, 167, 174
Stern, Leo, 149
Stölzl, Christoph, 222, 224
Stötzer, Werner, 188
Swolinzky, Curt, 35
Sylt, Wilhelm, 28

T
Tausendschön, Kurt, 61
Templin, Regina, 207
Templin, Wolfgang, 205, 207
Thälmann, Ernst, 1–2, 11–13, 23, 28, 52–54, 60–61, 67–68, 80, 87–95, 103, 105, 123, 184–85, 187, 193–201, 208, 217, 219–20, 226–30; as central memory figure, 88, 91, 185. *See also* Thälmann monument
Thälmann monument (Berlin), 2, 87–95, 184–85, 187, 195–201, 208, 217, 219–20, 226–30; dedication ceremony, 200; graffiti, 228; Klaus Schwabe phase, 196–97; Lew Kerbel phase, 193–201; Ruthild Hahne phase, 89–93
Thälmann monument (Weimar), 61, 68
Thälmann monument (Ziegenhals), 105
Thälmannplatz, 88, 91–92
Tiergarten Park (Berlin), 23
Tränenpalast museum, 233
Trostorff, Klaus, 124
Tschorn, Hans, 59
Tübke, Werner, 167–76, 184, 219, 222; contracts between the Ministry of Culture and, 167, 170, 175, 184

U
Ulbricht, Walter, 28, 59–60, 81, 84, 88–89, 91–92, 195; Ernst Thälmann monument and, 88–89, 195; Marx-Engels monument and, 81
Ullmann, Eduard, 70–71, 73, 79
Unger, Manfred, 147–48
Union of Soviet Socialist Republics (USSR). *See* Soviet Union

V

Verband Bildender Künstler. See Association of Fine Artists
Vereinigung der Verfolgten des Naziregimes (VVN). *See* Association of Nazi Persecutees
Verner, Paul, 156–57, 160
Victims of Fascism (OdF), 39, 52, 57–59, 61–62, 68–69, 81, 185, 214
Victory Alley (Berlin), 23
Voigt, Arno, 188
Volgograd, 165, 167
Volksbildungsministerium. See Ministry of People's Education
VVN. *See* Association of Nazi Persecutees

W

Wagner, Heinz, 170
Wandel, Paul, 72, 88
Warnke, Herbert, 84
Wartburg Castle, 149, 154–55, 157–60
Weber, Hermann, 204
West Germany. *See* Federal Republic of Germany
Wilhelm I, Emperor of Germany, 188–89
Wilhelm II, Emperor of Germany, 78, 188–89
Wilhelmplatz. *See* Thälmannplatz
Wittenberg. *See* Lutherstadt Wittenberg
Wolf, Christa, 221
Wolle, Stefan, 6, 19
Wolter, Heinz, 146
Wowereit, Klaus, 231

Y

Yorck von Wartenburg, Ludwig, 145
Young, James, 4, 69

Z

Zantoff, Heinz, 39
Zeitgeschichtliches Forum (Leipzig), 3, 233
Zetkin, Clara, 103, 106–9, 131
Zeughaus, 70–71, 85
Zimmering, Raina, 53
Zwarg, Walter, 112

Studies in Contemporary European History

Volume 1
Between Utopia and Disillusionment: A Narrative of the Political Transformation in Eastern Europe
Henri Vogt

Volume 2
The Inverted Mirror: Mythologizing the Enemy in France and Germany, 1898–1914
Michael E. Nolan

Volume 3
Conflicted Memories: Europeanizing Contemporary Histories
Edited by Konrad H. Jarausch and Thomas Lindenberger with the Collaboration of Annelie Ramsbrock

Volume 4
Playing Politics with History: The Bundestag Inquiries into East Germany
Andrew H. Beattie

Volume 5
Alsace to the Alsatians? Visions and Divisions of Alsatian Regionalism, 1870–1939
Christopher J. Fischer

Volume 6
A European Memory? Contested Histories and Politics of Remembrance
Edited by Małgorzata Pakier and Bo Stråth

Volume 7
Experience and Memory: The Second World War in Europe
Edited by Jörg Echternkamp and Stefan Martens

Volume 8
Children, Families, and States: Time Policies of Childcare, Preschool, and Primary Education in Europe
Edited by Karen Hagemann, Konrad H. Jarausch, and Cristina Allemann-Ghionda

Volume 9
Social Policy in the Smaller European Union States
Edited by Gary B. Cohen, Ben W. Ansell, Robert Henry Cox, and Jane Gingrich

Volume 10
A State of Peace in Europe: West Germany and the CSCE, 1966–1975
Petri Hakkarainen

Volume 11
Visions of the End of the Cold War
Edited by Frederic Bozo, Marie-Pierre Rey, N. Piers Ludlow, and Bernd Rother

Volume 12
Investigating Srebrenica: Institutions, Facts, Responsibilities
Edited by Isabelle Delpla, Xavier Bougarel, and Jean-Louis Fournel

Volume 13
Samizdat, Tamizdat, and Beyond: Transnational Media During and After Socialism
Edited by Friederike Kind-Kovács and Jessie Labov

Volume 14
Shaping the Transnational Sphere: Experts, Networks, and Issues from the 1840s to the 1930s
Edited by Davide Rodogno, Bernhard Struck, and Jakob Vogel

Volume 15
Tailoring Truth: Politicizing the Past and Negotiating Memory in East Germany, 1945–1990
Jon Berndt Olsen

Volume 16
Memory and Change in Europe: Eastern Perspectives
Edited by Małgorzata Pakier and Joanna Wawrzyniak

Volume 17
The Long Aftermath: Cultural Legacies of Europe at War, 1936-2016
Edited by Manuel Bragança and Peter Tame

Volume 18
Whose Memory? Which Future?: Remembering Ethnic Cleansing and Lost Cultural Diversity in Eastern, Central and Southeastern Europe
Edited by Barbara Törnquist-Plewa

Volume 19
Wartime Captivity in the 20th Century: Archives, Stories, Memories
Edited by Anne-Marie Pathé and Fabien Théofilakis

Volume 20
Ambassadors of Realpolitik: Sweden, the
CSCE, and the Cold War
  Aryo Makko

Volume 21
Migration, Memory, and Diversity:
Germany from 1945 to the Present
  Edited by Cornelia Wilhelm

Volume 22
From Eastern Bloc to European Union:
Comparative Processes of Transformation
since 1990
  *Edited by Günther Heydemann and Karel
  Vodicka*

www.ingramcontent.com/pod-product-compliance
Lightning Source LLC
Chambersburg PA
CBHW072147100526
44589CB00015B/2131